SLOW VIOLENCE 2019 JOANIE LEMERCIER

MATT

MATT

DESIGNING WITH THE WORLD

FOREWORD

MIREIA ESCOBAR*

The Museu del Disseny-DHub reiterates its commitment to the public and the future of the planet through the long-term exhibition *Matter Matters. Designing with the world*. This project highlights the way in which our collections can serve as essential tools for reflecting on the great challenges of our time and imagining a design that is more respectful of the world.

The exhibition encourages visitors to seriously reflect on the role of design considering the challenges we face today. With matter as a common thread, the exhibition questions design practices that often have ignored the limitation of resources and the impact of a growth model based on fossil fuels. In this way, it poses a central question: is it possible to design based on interdependence with the world instead of perpetuating an extractivist logic?

With this exhibition and the corresponding catalogue, the DHub, as a focal point for the city's creative industries, asks us to think critically about the objects and materials we consume, to adopt more environmentally friendly practices, and to work together for a more conscientious and sustainable world.

Featuring more than 600 objects from the Museu del Disseny-DHub's collections and other national and international contributions, the exhibition is organised around different types of material and interconnected narratives that reveal the material and contextual relationships of these objects. This approach challenges the apparent autonomy of objects and encourages sustainable design practices that respect the environment and promote regeneration.

To this end, the DHub, committed to the conservation and dissemination of its abundantly rich collections, offers a wide range of services and activities, including exhibitions, educational programmes, workshops, guided tours and opportunities for dialogue. This approach not only facilitates access to cultural heritage, but also encourages a critical and transformational understanding of the role of design in our everyday lives and in the future of the planet.

We wish to express our deep gratitude to the donors, lenders, institutions and entities whose generosity was crucial in bringing the exhibition to fruition. This project was also made possible thanks to the collaborative work of experts across a variety of disciplines – design, architecture, philosophy, anthropology, physics and biology – whose contributions were essential in enriching the content of the exhibition and the catalogue. This collaborative network is an inspiring example of how teamwork can give rise to new ways of thinking, creating and acting in the face of today's challenges.

* Mireia Escobar is director of Indústries Creatives and the Disseny Hub.

30 BILLION METRIC TONS OF THINGS

JOSE LUIS DE VICENTE*

As leading institutions that preserve, organize and disseminate the material culture of humanity, design museums cannot help but question their role in a world where the anthropogenic mass already surpasses all biomass. The Museu de Dissney's collections, exhibitions and lines of research must contribute to broadening our relationship with the objects that surround us, which inevitably leads to exploring the ecological, colonial, technological and political aspects that shape them.

1. The amount that changes everything

At the end of 2020, a crucial milestone went practically unnoticed by most people: anthropogenic mass, or the number of things produced by human beings, surpassed for the first time all biomass, that is, the weight of all living things on the planet. According to a study published in *Nature*,[1] this anthropogenic mass has already reached '30 billion metric tons,' an amount difficult to imagine. To put it into perspective, this weight is equal to nearly 50 million Eiffel Towers spread around the world. More specifically, we are surrounded by mountains of concrete, plastic, glass, metal and all kinds of materials which humans have created and deposited in their environment.

This material overflow is not only a physical problem, but also a conceptual one. As cities continue to grow and infrastructures expand, the world is filled with 'things' that, at one time, were necessary, useful or desired, but now very often have lost their original purpose. Thus, anthropogenic mass is more than an indicator of human's impact on the Earth; it also represents our material culture. Every object is a footprint of our society's needs, desires and values.

2. What do we mean by 'things'? From artifacts to hyperobjects

The word 'things' might seem simple, yet it embodies a fascinating complexity. Things surround us, and still rarely do we think of them as anything more that inert objects. What does a thing really mean? Timothy Morton, in his theory of hyperobjects,[2] encourages us to see things differently. A hyperobject is an entity so vast and dispersed over space and time that it is beyond our ability to fully comprehend. A clear example is climate change or the global accumulation of plastic waste.

Hyperobjects, like the concept of anthropogenic mass itself, demands that we confront the magnitude of our actions. Although we cannot see the whole, every fragment, every piece of plastic or cement structure that we observe forms part of this planetary hyperobject. Therefore, the notion of 'artifact' – an object made by humans for a purpose – takes on a new meaning. Artifacts are not only functional things; they are also representations of a global process of production and disposal.

3. Museums: storehouses of things, objects and artifacts

In a world filled with things, museums are privileged places for observing and reflecting on material culture. Traditionally, museums have been repositories for objects with historical, aesthetic or functional value. However, today, many museums are embracing new interpretations of what it means to conserve and exhibit objects.

Nowadays, museums are 'hinges' between a world that is disappearing and one that is emerging. This transition not only entails looking at the past, but also projecting into the future, and for this we need to reconsider which things are worthy of being kept. Today's museum is not simply a warehouse of pretty or functional objects; it is a space where 'things' are recontextualized. From the most mundane chair to electronic waste, every object is a gateway to understanding the complexity of our impact on the planet.

In this sense, contemporary museums are ceasing to be mere custodians of the past and becoming laboratories of new ideas about how we live with things. The city, for example, is one of the most complex 'objects' that exists. Urban design, furniture and even rubbish, are part of this immense network of things which co-exist with us, and which require a new way of thinking to be understood and managed.

4. From 'thinking' to 'thinging': A necessary change

To address the ecological crisis and our relationship with the anthropogenic mass, anthropologist Tim Ingold proposes a change in perspective: to stop thinking in terms of 'thinking' and start practicing what he calls 'thinging'.[3]

1 https://www.nature.com/articles/s41586-020-3010-5.

2 https://www.revistadelauniversidad.mx/articles/4598b A892-bf9d-4c57-bdb0-002031bb75fa/hiperobjetos.

3 https://eprints.ncrm.ac.uk/id/.

Instead of seeing objects as static entities, Ingold wants us to view them as processes. Things do not simply exist; they are formed, transformed, and ultimately disappear or become something else. This change in focus is essential if we want to better understand and manage the impact of our actions.

The notion of 'thinging' encourages us to rethink our relationship with things. Rather than viewing them as isolated objects, we should understand things as parts of an interconnected system. This includes not only the physical objects that we create, but also the ecosystems and social networks into which they are inserted. To be truly ecological, we need to understand that our actions in relation to things not only affect their immediate existence, but also their life cycle and their impact on the world.

In this context, museums play a crucial role. They are spaces where things can be seen, studied and reinterpreted, not only as fragments of the past but active elements of a present and future in constant transformation. The design museum of today is a place for rethinking material culture from a new perspective, leading to new conceptions of the role of things in our daily lives.

The '30 billion metric tons of things' that we have created not only testifies to our production capacity, but also reflects our need to rethink how we coexist with the material world. From artifacts to hyperobjects, from museums to cities, the challenge that we face is to learn to see things not as static elements but as parts of a global process of change.

We need to rethink the value of material culture and use museums as spaces for exploring new ways of understanding things. At the same time, we must advance toward a more dynamic vision of objects, where engaging in 'thinging' allows us to act more conscientiously and ecologically. Only in this way will we be able to begin to manage things – and the planet – responsibly and sustainably.

Within this framework, the exhibition *Matter Matters* at the Museu del Disseny de Barcelona-DHub becomes a space for, in addition to questioning our relationship with materials and their shared memory, helping us to imagine new ways of designing with the world.

* Jose Luis de Vicente is director of the Museu del Disseny de Barcelona (DHub).

Michel Lamoller / *Anthropogenic Mass 11 (Shanghai)* / 2022

MATTER IN EMERGENCY AND EMERGENCE

OLGA SUBIRÓS*

Scene 1. Slow Violence

The Hambach open-pit mine is visible from the International Space Station, stretching for more than 46 square kilometres and reaching 300 metres deep. Where a 12,000-year-old forest once stood, less than 40 kilometres from Cologne, the largest vehicle ever built operates: the Bagger 293 excavator.[1] There are six in all, each capable of moving up to 240,000 m^3 of earth a day to extract coal to produce electricity in several thermal power plants in the region, accounting for the largest amount of CO_2 emissions in Europe today.

The audiovisual installation by Joanie Lemercier, *Slow Violence*[2] (2019, on-going), co-directed by Juliette Bibasse, which documents the occupation of the Hambach mine by environmental activists, serves as a symbol of the global climate disaster, transformed into a battlefield for the preservation of life. The title of the work refers to the concept developed by Rob Nixon, a scholar and writer who specializes in environmental and post-colonial studies, which states that 'Slow Violence is a violence that occurs gradually and out of sight, a violence of delayed destruction that is dispersed across time and space, an attritional violence that is typically not viewed as violence at all.'[3]

Scene 2. Strata Incognita

A microscope reveals that a teaspoon of soil contains more life than there are humans on earth. Below our feet, millions of creatures interact, struggling, reproducing, transforming death into life. These processes purify water, make the air breathable and cultivate 95% of the food we eat. And yet, every year nearly 24 billion tons of fertile soil is lost due to erosion, desertification, contamination and other factors related to unsustainable land use. This has led to a decrease in the amount of carbon in the soil and an increase in the amount of carbon dioxide in the atmosphere.[4]

Strata Incognita[5] is an audiovisual installation created by the collectives Grandeza Studio and Locument that functions as a counterpart to *Slow Violence*. While the first scene shows the extraction of raw materials as the predominant means by which the world is built, Strata Incognita turns its attention to the ground, the great unknown to be cared for, exploring its importance poetically, scientifically and philosophically while urging us to question why we continue designing and producing what cannot be returned to the earth as a nutrient.

Scene 3. Still Life

Two hundred ceramic pieces, arranged chronologically from the 13th to the 21st century along a twelve-metre wall, are organized iconographically around the themes of water, land and air. The installation is situated in front of a balcony viewpoint facing the city, showing in real time an urban environment undergoing a climate emergency. The juxtaposition between representation and presentation of reality inside the museum questions our understanding of what nature means to us today and if there really is a difference between culture and nature.

Still Life, the name of the installation, refers to Timothy Morton's critique of the anthropocentric notion of 'nature' as an entity separate from humans, arguing that this idea perpetuates an artificial division between what is human and produced by humans and what is non-human, which has enabled nature's destruction. According to Morton, to address the climate crisis, we must overcome this idea of 'nature' and think in ecological terms that include humans and other life forms, with the understanding that they exist in a symbiotic, interconnected, fragile and unstable relationship.

Designing with or without the world?

The evolution of global commerce, especially since the 15th century, along with industrial development during the 19th and 20th centuries, was characterized by an intensive use of natural resources, based on an ideology of unlimited growth and global extractivism.[7] The extraction of fossil fuels and minerals radically transformed territories and ways of life, inaugurating an era of mass consumption, particularly since the 1950s, furthering what is known as the Great Acceleration[8] of human activity and its impact on the planet.

1 BWE Bucket Wheel Excavators https://www.takraf.com/product/bucket-wheel-excavators/.

2 https://joanielemercier.com/slowviolence/.

3 Rob Nixon: *Slow violence and the environmentalism of the poor*, Cambridge, Massachusetts, Harvard University Press, 2011.

4 Deteriorating soil health: 'A teaspoon of soil contains more life than there are humans on earth' (2022) https://doi.org/10.56367/OAG-036-10403.

5 https://www.grandeza.studio and https://www.thelocument.com/.

6 Timothy Morton: *Ecology Without Nature: Rethinking Environmental Aesthetics*, Cambridge, Harvard University Press, 2009.

7 Extractivism: https://www.tandfonline.com/doi/full/10.1080/03066150.2022.2069015#abstract.

8 https://www.hup.harvard.edu/books/9780674545038.

Humanity has become a dominant force in shaping the Earth's surface. Today, anthropogenic mass is greater than all living biomass. At the current pace, fifteen planets would be needed to sustain human's ecological footprint, for which not everyone bears the same responsibility, since the global North generates an ecological footprint five times larger than that of the countries of the global South.[9] Faced with the impact of human activity in the form of climate emergencies, species extinction, depletion of raw materials and the public health crisis, among other systemic upheavals, this system is being reassessed.

The exhibition *Matter Matters* at the Museu del Disseny-DHub in Barcelona is the result of the desire to contribute to this reassessment. The presentation encourages in-depth reflection in which matter is the common thread so that we ask ourselves: can we continue designing 'without' the world, ignoring its finiteness and the impact of unlimited growth based on fossil fuels? What caused this detachment from the world? Which practices have designed and design 'with' the world? Do we need a new cosmology that redefines our place in the world, in which the human species is not understood as the owner of the world but as an inseparable part of it?

The current hegemonic cosmology still sees a world where nature is isolated from humans in a hierarchical relationship of power. This rationalist, anthropocentric perspective, the legacy of the Enlightenment, interprets and organizes the world in a binary system that divides 'culture' and 'nature,' 'subject' and 'object,' 'thinking' and 'doing,' 'natural' and 'artificial,' 'organic' and 'inorganic,' 'living' and 'non-living,' 'masculine' and 'feminine,' 'human' and 'animal,' 'civilized' and 'uncivilized." This framework of thought is what has enabled, and enables the colonization and extraction of raw materials, territories and lives without considering the consequences.

A paradigm change would involve not only decarbonizing and decolonizing the planet, but also decolonizing our minds and bodies to think, feel and imagine a world in which life is possible. In this regard, Karen Barad, a physicist, philosopher and contemporary feminist, provides us with the tools for a new mental framework. Barad describes a world where all the material realities with which we coexist are interconnected in physical/chemical, ecological, geopolitical, economic, historical, cultural and social relationships. We are, and we are made up of, these interconnections in a constant state of becoming. For this reason, the exhibition borrows as its title Karen Barad's catchphrase 'Matter Matters': 'Matter matters, it counts, it has meaning. Matter is a matter of responsibility,'[10] and the subtitle of the exhibition, 'Designing "with" the world,' appeals to this responsibility.

In addition to the installations *Slow Violence*, *Strata Incognita* and *Still Life*, the exhibition contains a selection of more than six hundred objects from the Museu del Disseny-DHub's collections, as well as new work and local and international loans. The objects are not displayed individually, but are collectively arranged in intertwined material and narrative relationships, questioning their interpretation as autonomous objects.

9 Human Made Mass https://www.nature.com/articles/s41586-020-3010-5

10 Karen Barad has given us permission to title the exhibition using her catchphrase 'Matter Matters'. She has also contributed an article to its publication.

Both the exhibition and the catalogue follow the same object and narrative presentation structure in the following sequence: intra-connected matter, petrochemical matter, plant matter, animal matter, microbiological matter, mineral matter, digital matter, intangible matter and affectional-fictional matter. Authors from different disciplines, including philosophy, design, architecture, urbanism, chemistry, physics, geology, anthropology, sociology, social psychology, economics, and art and design history contribute to each matter-topic. In this way, the exhibition and the catalogue interweave voices which normally have been regarded as belonging to different disciplinary discourses. They are essential contributions for a new understanding of the world and helping to replace current toxic paradigms.

The materiality of the objects in the Museu del Disseny's collections serves a starting point for this reflection, in order to understand how and of what these objects are made and what was required to make them. It shows design practices 'without' the world of objects with materialities resulting from extractive practices and other objects that have worked and work 'with' the world. The latter include both traditional preindustrial practices, still relevant due to their minimal environmental impact, and contemporary designers who explore new materials as alternatives to petrochemical-based resources. These designers have adopted innovative practices in symbiosis with microbiological intelligences as approaches which promote communities of affection with what exists, to produce a durable and regenerative design which at the end of its life becomes compost, returning to the earth and becoming food for new life.

Matter Matters makes the Museu del Disseny-DHub an active agent that reconsiders its patrimony and encourages a dialogue with contemporary thought and design to build more aware and just societies. The exhibition reminds us that matter is not an unlimited resource, but a network of relationships of which we form a part. It is time to leave behind obsolete practices that perpetuate unbridled extractivism and consumption, and instead embrace a regenerative design that not only minimizes harm but also repairs the planet and returns to the ground as a nourisher of life. Design, as a key practice in the shaping of the world, has an unavoidable responsibility vis-à-vis the climate crisis. The present moment demands radical change: designing symbiotically with the world and rethinking materials, processes and our relationship with what surrounds us. As designers, creators and inhabitants of the planet, we have the responsibility to choose: continue designing 'without' the world or opt for a design future 'with' the world. Change is no longer an option – it is an urgent individual and collective necessity.

* Olga Subirós is architect, curator and researcher. PhD candidate in Architecture and Design at RMIT University.

Still Life
Ceramics from the Museu del Disseny-DHub Barcelona Collection
Part of the installation by Isabel Fernández del Moral and Olga Subirós, 2024
Image by Olga Subirós Studio

SITUATED MATTER: MATERIAL PAST, PRESENT AND FUTURE

VALÉRIE BERGERON / ROBERT THOMPSON CASAS / IVÁN RODRÍGUEZ
MATERFAD. CENTRO DE MATERIALES DE BARCELONA*

The importance of materials in our culture is much greater than we often think. Housing, transportation, food, clothing, communication and practically all aspects of our daily lives are characterized by the materials we use. When we take a critical and conscious view of the objects that surround us from the perspective of their materiality, questions and considerations arise regarding the different materials that make them up. What is the origin of these materials? Are they connected to extractivist or colonizing practices? How do we relate to these objects? Do we care about the materials they are made of? These questions invite us to reflect on the relevance and impact of these materials in our lives.

Situated Matter, an installation co-curated by MATERFAD that welcomes visitors to the *Matter Matters* exhibition, includes a tour of twenty everyday objects that a young person living in an urban setting in the global North typically uses: a t-shirt, sunglasses, a cell-phone, Tupperware... The exhibit asks us to reflect on the materiality of these objects, focusing on the choices we constantly make as both consumers and users.

Each object in *Situated Matter* is displayed in a specific manifestation, one of the thousands of choices the market offers consumers to satisfy a need. Keeping in mind that this range of options is practically infinite, the exhibit describes two versions of each product that offer opposing models, visions and impacts. The 'yesterday' choice is immediate and impulsive, ignoring environmental, social and cultural costs, and not taking responsibility for the consequences. Ultimately, it represents a behaviour we must drop. The 'today' choice, on the other hand, is made considering a critical, informed and conscious assessment of the characteristics of the product, the materials used to make it, and the impact it generates at all levels. A third option, that of 'tomorrow,' invites us to imagine future solutions based on new materialities and scientific and technical developments, but also on dematerializations and ancestral practices.

This approach allows us to see everyday objects with new eyes and reminds us of the importance of our material decisions in a broader context. When we think about the impact of mass manufacturing of products and the materials that go into them, we often focus on the environmental implications of the life-cycle, which certainly are of vital importance in the context of a climate emergency. Still, developing a multifaceted critical perspective on consumption and materials demands we pay attention to other factors that often go unnoticed.

The choice of materials for manufacturing objects affects the entire supply chain, from the extraction of raw materials to how we manage waste. In many regions, extraction is carried out under precarious working conditions, with risks to the health and safety of workers and child labour practices. This affects whole communities. Take Kolwezi, Democratic Republic of the Congo (DRC), where Amnesty International has reported forced evictions due to the expansion of copper and cobalt extraction projects in a context of serious human rights violations. The DRC produces 70% of the world's cobalt, an essential mineral used to make batteries and needed in key sectors of the green transition such as electric mobility and renewable energies encouraged mainly in the global North. This instance of 'green colonialism' is just one example of more than 4,000 environmental conflicts documented by the Environmental Justice Atlas,[1] which collects disputes regarding land access, extraction of minerals and fossil fuels, water management and preservation of biodiversity, among others.

1 http://ejatlas.org/.

Food containers
Moulded polyethylene and polypropylene
André Ricard Sala, 1994
Manufactured by Plásticos Ta-Tay SA, Montornès del Vallès
Donation, 2001 MADB 136.708

Paying attention to all life cycle and supply chain related impact of products is crucial for responsible industry and consumption. The search for multi-sector solutions to global problems is an even greater challenge which adds complexity to the design and development process.

For example, bioplastics obtained from plant-based resources are an alternative to plastics of fossil origin, because their carbon footprint is smaller and many are biodegradable in controlled environments. Still, generalized production and use of this kind of material pose important challenges: from the need to improve the efficiency of the production process, to the problems created by the introduction of these materials in current waste management systems. In addition, we cannot overlook the ethical concerns associated with their production, since bioplastics are mostly manufactured using agricultural crops such as corn or sugar cane, thus vying directly with the use of farmland for food production.

In this scenario, it is obvious that our material decisions have profound and multifaceted consequences. An exhaustive analysis of the matter that makes up our surroundings must include all possible points of view and assess the global implications of the use of each material in every context. In the face of this reality, it is essential to recognize the complexity of the situation and come up with solutions using all the tools within our reach.

Artificial Intelligence (AI) platforms promise to revolutionize the science of materials in the short term by combining the computational power of large language models (LLM) with human intuition and creativity, to explore new materials based on what we consider today waste.

First, this collaboration will help identify new opportunities in waste streams, thereby revealing the hidden potential of discarded resources and promoting technological and environmental development. Second, a simplification of current complex recycling logistics is expected thanks to the integration of predictive models and real-time materia traceability. This will optimize recycling processes and ensure that materials are recovered efficiently. At the same time, it will also reduce waste and the energy needed to retrieve it.

Finally, AI-driven predictive modelling will enable the properties of materials to be adapted compositionally so that they can be programmable. This customized approach will allow for taking maximum advantage of the potential of recycled material, thus promoting circularity and reducing environmental impact.

In short, there is more and more evidence of the prospects of integrating AI with human talent to revolutionize the science of materials, paving the way for an era of unprecedented rediscovery where waste is incorporated into perpetual value systems.

In addition, this documented regulation will allow for more prudent consumption of available resources thanks to the adoption of a simple and moderate lifestyle that could play a critical role in protecting the environment and future sustainability. This involves reducing consumption and waste, natural resource preservation, using durable and repairable products, and decreasing food waste.

By adopting frugal practices, individuals and communities can positively affect social behaviour regarding consumption, encouraging commercial policies and practices that are environmentally friendly and respectful of living things.

* Materfad is the FAD Materials Centre.
Iván Rodríguez: Current Executive Director.
Valerie Bergeron: Director until March 2024.
Robert Thompson: Current Scientific Director.

Sakyo 272 ballpoint pen
Moulded ABS resin
Inoxcrom design team, 1988
Manufactured by Inoxcrom SA, Barcelona
Donation, Inoxcrom SA, 1998 MADB 136.247

Cutlery set
Silver
Luis M. Feduchi, 1953
Manufactured by Platerías Meneses, Madrid
Donation, Luz Feduchi Benlliure, 1995 MADB 135.740-0

CALCULATING EMPIRES
A GENEALOGY OF POWER AND TECHNOLOGY SINCE 1500

KATE CRAWFORD / VLADAN JOLER*

How can we understand the operations of technology and power in our era? Our technological systems are increasingly complex, interconnected, automated and opaque. Social institutions, from schools to prisons, are becoming data industries, incorporating pervasive forms of capture and analysis. Even places that were once off-limits to capital, from our emotional expressions to outer space, are now subject to computational control and extraction. Meanwhile, the industrial transformations in AI are concentrating power into even fewer hands, while accelerating polarization and alienation. If we are to address the urgent challenges of the contemporary time – including technocratic fascism, climate catastrophe, colonial wars, and wealth inequality – we need to contend with the interwoven nature of their histories. In order to have a future, we must first confront our past.

Calculating Empires[1] is a large-scale research visualization exploring how technical and social structures co-evolved over five centuries. The aim is to view the contemporary period in a longer trajectory of ideas, devices, infrastructures, and systems of power. It traces technological patterns of colonialism, militarization, automation, and enclosure since 1500 to show how these forces still subjugate and how they might be unwound. By tracking these imperial pathways, *Calculating Empires* offers a means of seeing our technological present in a deeper historical context. And by investigating how past empires have calculated, we can see how they created the conditions of empire today.

1 https://calculatingempires.net/.

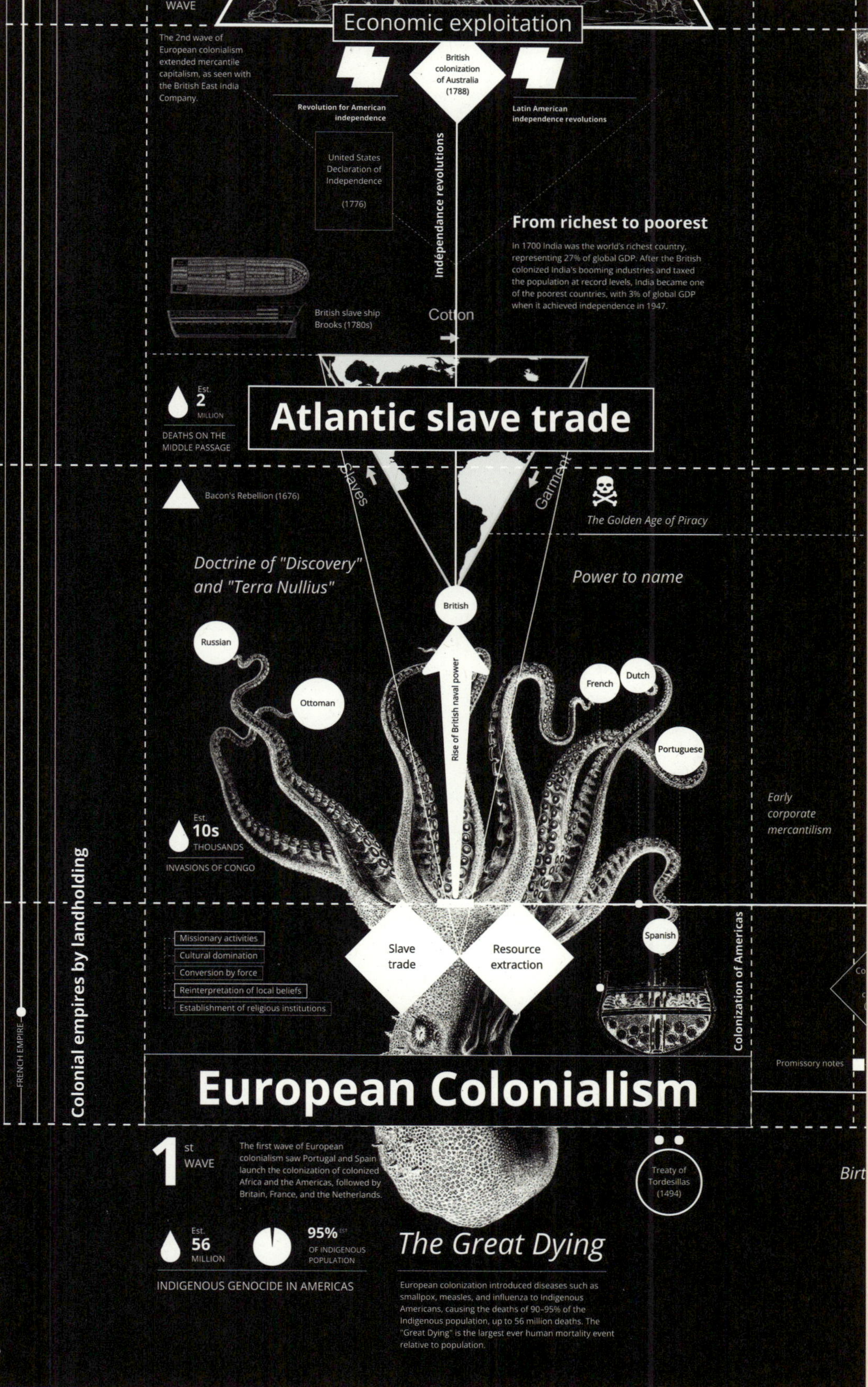

Kate Crawford / Vladan Joler
Calculating Empires
2023

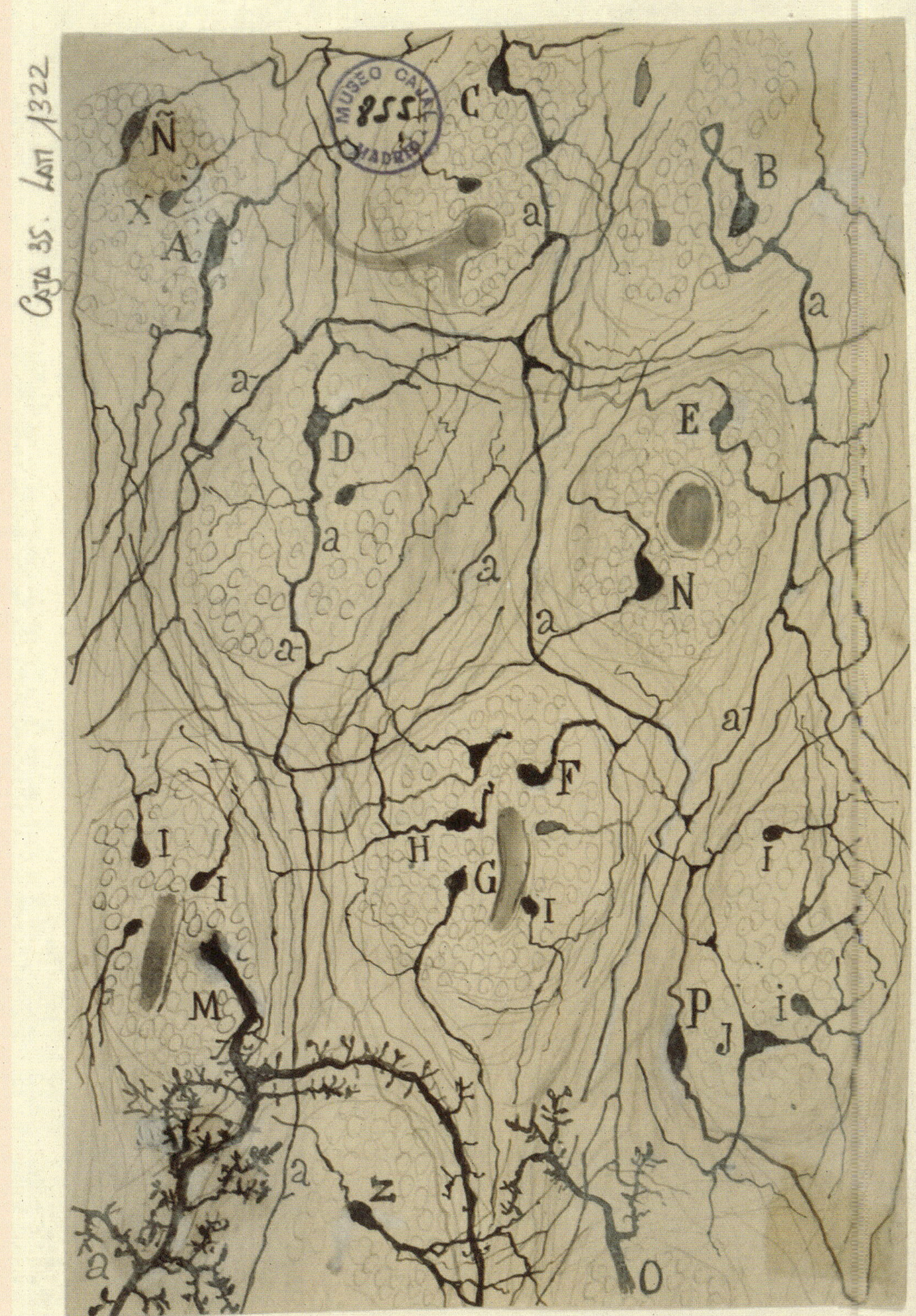

Santiago Ramón y Cajal
Scientific drawing, area of voluminous neural cords and otic ganglion
c. 1917
Paper, black India ink, graphite, stearin and gouache
[Madrid] Bequest of Cajal-CSIC. Inventory number LC03967

Calculating Empires centers on four themes: *communication*, *computation*, *classification* and *control*. Across the centuries, the work illustrates the shifts in communication devices, infrastructures, and computational architectures, and how they are entwined with the histories of social control and classification. The vertical axis represents time, beginning with the 16th century at the base. The horizontal axis features a collection of systems: from algorithms to architecture, bodies to borders. Navigation is flexible: you can follow a theme, a time period, or set of ideas.

If we read from left to right, the work begins with the history of communication devices and the interfaces needed to access them. Next we see programming languages and the communication infrastructures that operate in the background: from submarine telegraph cables, to satellites, to the electromagnetic spectrum.

As we follow the data flows from those communications systems, they are collected and organized by museums, film and TV archives, data brokers, and AI training datasets. That data is then used to train algorithms and models that have their own histories, shaped by the labor of programmers and crowdworkers. It is all powered by energy-intensive computational hardware that is expanding exponentially in multiple directions, from hyperscale data centers, to biological computing, to quantum.

The work then moves to the themes of classification and control. It begins with time as a concept that orders human actions and labor, and then education as another social structuring process that shapes and organizes social norms, values, and hierarchies. Next we turn to the history of ideas about emotions and intelligence, as well as the shaping of the human body itself.

We see practices of classification and control in biometrics and medical data, in the disciplinary systems of prisons and policing, and in the way borders and bureaucracy regulate the movements of people and information.

This brings us to the heart of *Calculating Empires*: colonialism and the paths of empires over history, with their accompanying political and economic ideologies that inform industrial production and energy extraction.

The final section of the work contends with the strata of planetary classification: from the mineral layer of the lithosphere, all the way up to the astrosphere. Then we consider the concept of space in other ways, how mapping and architecture are themselves systems of control. Finally, we see multiple layers of militarized power, from surveillance technologies, to authoritarian doctrines, to entire military systems.

The contemporary tendency toward simplification and solutionism has weakened the ability to handle dense information, while our technical and environmental realities only become more complex and interdependent. By visualizing these interlaced histories of empire in intricate detail, we hope to better understand our current predicament. In the words of French historian Fernand Braudel, "if one wants to understand the world, one has to determine the hierarchy of forces, currents, and individual movements, and then put them together to form an overall constellation." *Calculating Empires* invites the visitor inside this constellation.

Calculating Empires begins with a key moment when global networks – both cultural and mercantile – began to take shape in the 1500s. New trade routes meant the expansion of European empire. Advances in shipping and navigational instruments enabled the annexation of lands and genocide of Indigenous populations while introducing new viruses, drugs, and weapons. The Gutenberg press reorganized information power and laid the groundwork for a political and cultural transformation. New scientific instruments and calculation systems were developed. The meticulous cataloging and privatization of land, animals, plants, and space commenced a layered agenda of colonization that continued to expand for centuries. These practices of past empires are now echoed in the highly concentrated technology and military industries of the 21st century.

Every reading of this work is different, and you're invited to draw your own connections. Hundreds of individual drawings and texts span centuries of conflict, enclosure, and control. We suggest taking your time and reading slowly – a radical act in an era of speed and simplification. A close examination of these patterns over several centuries reveals the ascendance of particular ideas and technologies, the concentration of power and wealth, and the colonization of land, infrastructure, and human lifeworlds.

The history of science and technology is also a story of visualizations. From the Venn diagram to the neural network, visual illustrations have shaped the conceptual horizons of the scientific imaginary. We use the same method to show how technology is political, not separate from it. Even diagrammatic representations – from the Gantt chart to the logic gate – are forms of organizing information which embed a political structure.

Calculating Empires takes Donna Haraway's provocation literally that we need to map the "informatics of domination." The technologies of today are the latest manifestations of a long line of entangled systems of knowledge and control. This is the purpose of our visual genealogy: to show the complex interplay of systems of power, information, and circumstance across terrain and time, in order to imagine how things could be otherwise.
This work can never be complete: it is necessarily partial, subjective, and drawn from our own positionality. But that openness is part of the project. You are invited to read, reflect, and consider your own history in the recurring stories of calculation and empire. As the overwhelming now continues to unfold, *Calculating Empires* offers the possibility of looking back, in order to consider how different futures could be envisioned and realized.

* Kate Crawford is senior researcher at Microsoft Research. Co-founder and former Director of Research at the AI Now Institute at New York University. Visiting Professor at the MIT Center for Civic Media.
Vladan Joler is artist and activist. Director of the Share Foundation and professor at the University of Novi Sad, Serbia.

Coltan Tantalite Columbite (Fe)

Consortium of the Museu de Ciències Naturals de Barcelona. Photograph by Joan Rosell Riba

OBJECTS, EXTRACTIVISM AND COLONIALISM IN THE MUSEUM

MARÍA ÍÑIGO CLAVO*

In recent decades, museums have begun to be identified as more than simply a place for representation and are now seen as one of the main modern technologies used to legitimize colonization and exploitation. This has led to a crisis regarding how history should be presented that remains unresolved. First, it was made clear how postmodern strategies mask power relations with their pastiche of superimposed referents. Museum pieces used to explain history were no longer just venerated as heritage objects, but began to be understood as circumscribed entities incapable of containing and communicating the complex power relations implicit in any historical process. Some museums found a temporary solution in working with documents and handling works of art and objects in the same way as archival items; others expanded their exhibit labels and panels to make these complexities more visible in discourse. Faced with this "display uncertainty"[1] debates about repatriation have gained more prominence, though other museums have decided to also address reparation measures internally. Two already established aspects have opened new possibilities over the last couple decades: a post-decolonial perspective and its penetrating dialogue through institutional critical work that contemporary art has engaged in since the 1970s.

But this process has not been without its contradictions. One the one hand, both contemporary art since the 1980s and a post-decolonial perspective have stressed the urgency of contextualizing all the objects suspended in time in museum display cabinets, in short, by introducing colonial history and examining the museum's role in it. As such, one could understand the complicity of science, technology and progress in a history of suffering; and one could also recognize the acquisition of these objects by museums as a symptom of a culture of spoliation and extermination. At the same time, however, as Ariella Azoulay observed, every historical process is an exercise in imperialism.[2] How can history be reconstructed in museums to produce a counter-imperialist history? How can empires be analysed with a tool which is inherently imperialist? What new role can objects play in this context, keeping in mind that the weight of all the objects human beings have produced already exceeds the total biomass of our planet? Should objects have the same heritage status as they did in the last century, when their accumulation is compromising the planet's regenerative capacity? How should this challenge the idea of a design museum and the disciplinary field itself?

If most artistic projects critical of the erosion and exhaustion of the planet agree on anything, it is the silent nature of this process. Specifically, many of the critical tools that political art provides involve the mapping and visualization of this hidden, invisible and silent power in our everyday lives. The map *Calculating Empires* by Kate Crawford and Vladan Joler offers a genealogy of technological progress from 1500 to the present, how it is linked to a history of plunder of natural and human resources, and how it is the history of an elite group. The map is a response to the technological euphoria of progress and its historical amnesia, revealing a genealogical dimension of the creation of devices for communication, classification, calculation and control. The work is always exhibited with objects that make up the local collection with which the piece is displayed, along with a selection of minerals from the Scientific Department of Mineralogy of the Natural Museum of Natural Sciences.

1 Olga Fernández López: "The Uncertainty of Display. Exhibitions In-Between Ethnography and Modernism", in Iain Chambers, Giulia Grechi and Mark Nash (eds), *The Ruined Archive*, Milan, Politecnico di Milano, 2014.

2 Ariella Aïsha Azoulay: *Potential History: Unlearning Imperialism*, New York, Verso, 2019.

First representation of a cabinet of curiosities in Ferrante Imperato, *Dell'historia Naturale* 1601
Image digitised by Smithsonian Libraries

Allegory of Charles III Plate
Earthenware decorated with oxides
1788–1789
Manufactured by Real Fábrica de Loza y Porcelana de Alcora
Old collection MCB 20.135

Plate
Earthenware decorated with oxides
Barcelona, 1675–1724
Purchase, 1932 MCB 5.134

Plate
Earthenware decorated with oxides
Barcelona, 1600–1699
Purchase, 1932 MCB 4.842

Plate
Earthenware decorated with oxides
Francesc Quer, 1918
Manufactured by Fábrica Hijo de Jaime Pujol y Bausis, Esplugues de Llobregat
Purchase, 1918 MCB 1.587

This involves intense dialogue and collaboration between the artists and the exhibition's curatorial research team, responsible for selecting and proposing the objects. In this case, the function of the selected objects is to make clear the connections between our modernity and the values and wealth it generated through extractivism and slavery, to make it visible and unavoidable. It ensures that we cannot talk about modernity without reckoning with its dark side.

For Barcelona, in the context of the exhibition *Matter Matters* at the Museu del Disseny-DHub, a series of ceramic pieces were selected according to the following criteria: first, they were made between Catalonia and Valencia and second, they contain references to Spanish colonization. Four of the pieces were created at the Real Fábrica de Loza Fina y Porcelana de l'Alcora (Royal Factory of Fine Earthenware and Porcelain of Alcora), in the province of Castellón, founded in 1727 by noble landowners of the region.[3] The strategic location of the factory was related to the clay soils that could be extracted and the area's rich pottery tradition. However, like any "high culture" 18th century endeavour, it distanced itself from popular knowledge and local ceramic traditions because they were deemed to be too primitive. A great deal of effort was invested in mimicking the exquisite French style, first Baroque and later Rococo, and European experts were brought in to try to find the most refined porcelain formula possible that approximated European models.

3 Ceramic Museum of Alcora. https://lalcora.es/museu-de-ceramica/.

The pieces included in *Calculating Empires* reflect the bourgeois values of the period. The two sculptural series from 1765 by Johann Christian Knipffer (1762-1785) are an allegory of an enlightened Europe, civilized, noble and militarily strong, in contrast to an allegory of America that contained myths of cannibalism and indigenous lack of culture. In fact, the idea of civilization that took root in Europe was impossible to conceive of without the elaboration of an idea of primitivism and savagery. The notion of savages in a state of nature was the perfect foundation for believing that, like nature, they were not entitled to any rights. These inventions of the "other" were nothing more than a way of perpetuating the dehumanization of Latin American communities to justify colonization.

Along with the ceramic pieces appears the *Allegory of Charles III* (1788-1789) by Manuel Salvador Carmona (1734-1820), made of earthenware, a material known for imitating porcelain and thus significantly lowering costs. The image is also an imitation, based on the painting *Allegory of a Reign* by the Baroque artist Francesco Solimena (1657-1747), but the ceramicist substituted the image on the medallion in the painting for that of King Charles III. The choice of this ceramic piece is a nod to the monarch who authorized the Port of Barcelona to engage in business directly with the Antilles in 1765, resulting in the enrichment of Catalan merchants through the cotton and slave trade. The series also contains two candelabras created ten years earlier by Julián López (*c.* 1711-1792), known for their remarkable rococo style, with two torches held by two black servants as testimony to the silencing of slavery in our lands. Three plates with the image of a boat with its sails unfurled allude to the triumphalist imagery of "discovery" and the Spanish imperial age. These icons from different centuries reveal the latent nature of these values over time.

Allegory of America, sculpture
Earthenware
1775–1779
Manufactured by Real Fábrica de Loza y Porcelana de Alcora
Purchase, 1965 MCB 100.076

Allegory of Europe, sculpture
Earthenware
1775–1779
Manufactured by Real Fábrica de Loza y Porcelana de Alcora
Purchase, 1965 MCB 100.072

Lastly, alongside these images, so common in everyday Spanish life, is a sculptural arrangement that shows an indigenous woman holding up the Santa María ship as an allegory of the Spanish conquest. The piece is made of elements plundered from the colonies: silver, gold and semi-precious stones. Made by Theodor Heiden (1853-1928), one of the most well-known goldsmiths in Munich, the sculpture was awarded first prize at the Exhibition of Fine Arts and Artistic Industries in Barcelona, in 1896, and was acquired by the Barcelona City Council one year after the Spanish disaster, that is, the traumatic loss of the last Spanish colony. While this historical event signalled the beginning of an unprecedented national identity crisis, triumphalist representations like this homage to colonization, made with gold and precious stones that now contrasted with the poverty in Spain, endured. This was simply a desperate attempt to preserve some kind of cultural leadership, like the notion of Spanishness popularized a decade later. What is striking about this piece is that the Maritime Museum of Barcelona continued to use it as part of a narrative that celebrates Catalan colonial history and entrepreneurism.

Applying the principles of transhistorical conservation and supervision of artistic or cultural property, the dialogue between this selection of objects and the artists' work supports the genealogical proposal that connects histories of progress and their technological development to a history of local power and its accumulation of wealth. The critical gesture of exhibiting these objects with a minerals collection makes this clear, showing how a culture of "wellbeing" is impossible to understand without the mining which, in addition to the former colonies, also affects European rural areas. It is impossible to think of mining without the deforestation and water and air pollution that harm local communities left with an adulterated landscape and whose traditional, agricultural and tourist activities are adversely affected.

Today, the ceramic industry is still essential to the construction and decoration economy: kaolinite (France, England, Saxony, Bohemia and the Southern United States), magnesite (China, Turkey, Russia, Australia, North Korea and several European countries and on Mars), feldspar (Extremadura, Galicia, Segovia, Avila), diatomite, talc, gypsum, silica, and calcium oxide. Current demands by ecologist groups revolve around updating the Spanish Law of Mines passed in 1973 during the Franco era and clearly designed to benefit exploitation.[4] The current proposal seeks to promote a circular economy aligned with environmental measures to combat climate change and the rehabilitation of affected spaces to restore biodiversity and prevent the generation of waste, while working with local communities to make decisions that deeply impact their way of life.

This museological display re-conceptualizes bourgeois values that still exist today in their celebration of colonization and exploitation of nature and human beings, resituating them in the form of institutional criticism. A dialogue is established between Spanish imperialist history (and the extraction of gold, silver and precious stones) and the history of rural mining. These minerals, arranged, classified, archived and organized in display cabinets, question the complicity of modern sciences and modern science museums in this long history of power, technological monopoly, extractivism and colonialism.

4 Carlos Ramírez Sánchez-Maroto: "Environmental notes of the Mining Law of 21 July 1973, on its fiftieth anniversary, and the need and necessity of updating it.", *Actualidad Jurídica Ambiental*, 28 November 2023.

* María Iñigo Clavo is researcher, curator and artist. PhD in Fine Arts from the Complutense University of Madrid. Currently professor at the UOC.

Centrepiece. *Santa Maria caravel held up by an indigenous woman*
Silver, marble, gemstones and gold
Theodor Heiden, Munich, c. 1896
Purchase, 1897 MADB 6.883

0 INTER CONNEC MAT

A-
TED
TER

HOW MATTER MATTERS

KAREN BARAD*

Where did we ever get the strange idea that nature – as opposed to culture – is ahistorical and timeless? We are far too impressed by our own cleverness and self-consciousness.... We need to stop telling ourselves the same old anthropocentric bedtime stories.

—Steven Shaviro, *Doom Patrols*

Scholars in feminist studies, science studies, cultural studies, and critical social theory are among those who struggle with the difficulty of coming to terms with the 'weightiness' of the world. On the one hand, there is an expressed desire to recognize and reclaim matter and its kindred spirits (e.g., the body) exiled from (or swallowed up by) the familiar and comforting domains of culture, mind, and history, not simply to altruistically advocate on behalf of the subaltern but in the hopes of finding a way to account for our own finitude. Can we identify the limits and constraints, if not the grounds, of discourse-knowledge in its productivity? But despite its substance, in the end, according to many contemporary attempts at its salvation, it is not matter that reels in the unruliness of infinite possibilities; rather, it is the very existence of finitude that gets defined as matter. Caught once again looking at mirrors, it is either the face of transcendence or our own image. It is as if there are no alternative ways to conceptualize matter: the only options seem to be the naiveté of empiricism or the same old narcissistic bedtime stories.

I propose a posthumanist account of performativity that challenges the positioning of materiality as either a given or a mere effect of human agency. In an agential realist account, materiality is an active factor in processes of materialization. Nature is neither a passive surface awaiting the mark of culture nor the end product of cultural performances. The belief that nature is mute and immutable and that all prospects for significance and change reside in culture merely reinscribes the nature-culture dualism that feminists have actively contested. Nor, similarly, can a human-nonhuman distinction be hard-wired into any theory that claims to take account of matter in the fullness of its historiality. To presume a given distinction between humans and nonhumans is to cement and recirculate the natureculture dualism into the foundations of feminist theory, foreclosing a genealogy of how nature and culture, human and nonhuman, are formed. Hence any performative account worth its salt would be ill advised to incorporate such anthropocentric values in its foundations.

A crucial part of the performative account that I propose is a rethinking of the notions of discursive practices and material phenomena and the relationship between them. In an agential realist account, discursive practices are not human-based activities but specific material (re) configurings of the world through which boundaries, properties, and meanings are differentially enacted. And matter is not a fixed essence; rather, matter is substance in its intra-active becoming – not a thing but a doing, a congealing of agency. Apparatuses are material (re)configurings or discursive practices that produce (and are part of) material phenomena in their becoming. Discursive practices and material phenomena do not stand in a relationship of externality to each other; the material and the discursive are mutually implicated in the dynamics of intra-activity. In an agential realist account, performativity is understood not as iterative citationality (Butler) but as iterative intra-activity. Intra-actions are agentive, and changes in the apparatuses of bodily production matter for ontological as well as epistemological and ethical reasons: different material-discursive practices produce different material configurings of the world, different difference/diffraction patterns; they do not merely produce different descriptions. Objectivity and agency are bound up with issues of responsibility and accountability. Accountability must be thought of in terms of what matters and what is excluded from mattering.

In an agential realist account of technoscientific practices, the knower does not stand in a relation of absolute externality to the natural world – there is no such exterior observational point.[1] The condition of possibility for objectivity is therefore not absolute exteriority but agential separability-exteriority within phenomena. We are not outside observers of the world. Neither are we simply located at particular places in the world; rather, we are part of the world in its ongoing intra-activity. This is a point Niels Bohr tried to get at in his insistence that our epistemology must take account of the fact that we are a part of that nature we seek to understand. Unfortunately, however, Bohr cut short important posthumanist implications of this insight in his ultimately humanist understanding of the 'we.'

1 Donna Haraway, 'Situated Knowledges: The Science Question in Feminism and the Privilege of Partial Perspective', *Feminist Studies*, vol. 14, no. 3, 1988; Vicki Kirby, *Telling Flesh. The Substance of Corporeal*, London, Routledge, 1997; Joseph Rouse, *How Scientific Practices Matter: Reclaiming Philosophical Naturalism*, Chicago, University of Chicago Press, 2002; and Niels Bohr, 'The Unity of Human Knowledge', in *Essays 1958-1962 on atomic physics and human knowledge*, Woodbridge, Conn.: Ox Bow Press, 1963.

Vicki Kirby eloquently articulates this important posthumanist point: "I'm trying to complicate the locatability of human identity as a here and now, an enclosed and finished product, a causal force upon Nature. Or even ... as something within Nature. I don't want the human to be in Nature as if Nature is a container. Identity is inherently unstable, differentiated, dispersed, and yet strangely coherent. If I say 'this is Nature itself,' an expression that usually denotes a prescriptive essentialism and that's why we avoid it, I've actually animated this 'itself' and even suggested that 'thinking' isn't the other of nature. Nature performs itself differently."[2]

The particular configuration that an apparatus takes is not an arbitrary construction of our choosing; nor is it the result of causally deterministic power structures. Humans do not simply assemble different apparatuses for satisfying particular knowledge projects but are themselves specific parts of the world's ongoing reconfiguring. To the degree that laboratory manipulations, observational interventions, concepts, and other human practices have a role to play, it is as part of the material configuration of the world in its intra-active becoming. Humans are part of the world-body space in its dynamic structuration.

There is an important sense in which practices of knowing cannot fully be claimed as human practices, not simply because we use nonhuman elements in our practices but because knowing is a matter of part of the world making itself intelligible to another part.

Alexander von Humboldt
Geographie der Pflanzen in den Tropen-Ländern
1807
Leibniz-Institut für Länderkunde, Leipzig

Vermicomposting
Noslenlou, 2012

2 Vicki Kirby, *Telling Flesh. The Substance of Corporeal*, London, Routledge, 1997.

Sunset image over the Indian Ocean taken by astronauts aboard the International Space Station (ISS)
NASA Earth Observatory, 2010
Public domain

Practices of knowing and being are not isolable; they are mutually implicated. We don't obtain knowledge by standing outside the world; we know because we are of the world. We are part of the world in its differential becoming. The separation of epistemology from ontology is a reverberation of a metaphysics that assumes an inherent difference between human and nonhuman, subject and object, mind and body, matter and discourse. Onto-epistemology - the study of practices of knowing in being - is probably a better way to think about the kind of understandings that we need to come to terms with how specific intraactions matter. Or, for that matter, what we need is something like an ethicoonto-epistemology - an appreciation of the intertwining of ethics, knowing, and being - since each intra-action matters, since the possibilities for what the world may become call out in the pause that precedes each breath before a moment comes into being and the world is remade again, because the becoming of the world is a deeply ethical matter.

* Karen Barad is PhD in Theoretical Physics. Professor of Feminist Studies, Philosophy and History of Consciousness at the University of California, Santa Cruz.

VIBRANT MATTER. THE FORCE OF THINGS STEPS TOWARD AN ECOLOGY OF MATTER*

JANE BENNETT*

The force of the ordinary ... can be obscured, reduced, or eliminated ... by a lack of appreciation of the richness of its connections to the larger world it composes.

—Thomas Dumm[1]

Ecology can be defined as the study or story (*logos*) of the place where we live (*oikos*), or better, the place that we live. For a thing-power materialist, that place is a dynamic flow of matter-energy that tends to settle into various bodies, bodies that often join forces, make connections, form alliances. The Earth, then, is *natura naturans*, a swarm of productive activity, or, as Deleuze and Guattari describe it, "an immense Abstract Machine" whose "pieces are the various assemblages and individuals, each of which groups together an infinity of particles entering into an infinity of more or less interconnected relations." In this ecological tale, "a fiber stretches from a human to an animal, from a human or an animal to molecules, from molecules to particles, and so on to the imperceptible."[2] For a thing-power materialist, humans are always in composition with nonhumanity, never outside of a sticky web of connections or an *ecology*.

Thing-power is the lively energy and/or resistant pressure that issues from one material assemblage and is received by others. Thing-power, in other words, is immanent in collectives that include humans, the beings best able to recount the experience of the force of things. Thing-power materialism emphasizes the closeness, the intimacy, of humans and nonhumans.[3] And it is here, in a heightened sense of that mutual implication, that thing-power materialism can contribute to an ecological ethos. To call something ecological is to draw attention to its necessary implication in a network of relations, to mark its persistent tendency to enter into a working system.[4] That system, however, can be more or less mobile, more or less transient, more or less conflictual: thing-power materialism does not endorse the view, absorbed from the nineteenth-century roots of the science of ecology by deep ecologists, that "ecological" means "harmonious" or tending toward equilibrium. To be ecological is to participate in a collectivity, but not all collectives operate as *organic* wholes.

I am not sure just how an increase in recognition of the force of things would play out in terms of consumption practices. My hope is that it would increase the deliberateness or intentionality involved – less thoughtless waste, and so perhaps less waste overall. I do think that a renewed emphasis on our entanglement with things, an entanglement that renders us susceptible to an array of dangers and diseases as well as joys and inspirations, is compatible with a "wise use" orientation to consumption. Tread lightly upon the earth, both because things are alive and have value as such *and* because we should be cautious around things that have the power to do us harm.[5]

Thing-power materialism is also compatible with what James Nash described as the ecological virtue of frugality. Distinguishable from austerity, frugality is a disciplined form of consumption, an "earth-affirming norm," a "sparing" in production and consumption – literally sparing of the resources necessary for human communities and sparing of the other species that are both values in themselves and instrumental values for human needs. Frugality minimizes harm to humans and other lifeforms, enabling thereby a greater thriving of all life. At its best, therefore, frugality can be described paradoxically as hedonistic self-denial, since it is a sensuous concern, or, as Alan Durning notes, 'a true materialism that does not just care *about* things, but cares *for* them.'[6]

My primary goal has been to give expression to thing-power. This is not the same as questing for the thing-in-itself. I don't seek the thing as it stands alone, but rather the not-fully-humanized dimension of a thing as it manifests itself amidst other entities and forces. My contention is that this peculiar dimension persists even inside the ubiquitous framing of human thought and perception.

1 Thomas L. Dumm, *Politics of the Ordinary*, 7.

2 Gilles Deleuze and Félix Guattari, *Thousand Plateaus*, University of Minnesota Press, 254-56, 250.

3 I've tried to avoid conceiving of that relationship in terms of "subjects" and "objects," though I have come to see that such a formulation is not entirely dispensable.

4 The modern use of the term "ecology" "came from Darwin through Ernst Haeckel, who ... spoke of 'nature's Economy'(1866) with reference to interrelationships and interactions among competing organisms in a community." Joseph M. Petulla, *American Environmentalism*, College Station, TX: Texas A&M University Press, 1980, 31-32. Arnold Berleant argues that in recent years the scope of the ecological has enlarged: "The notion of an ecosystem has expanded the organism-environment interaction to encompass an entire community of bacteria, plants, and animals, joined with the physical, chemical, and geographical conditions under which they live ... We are slowly beginning to realize that no domain of our planet can any longer be regarded as an independent and sovereign realm. Indeed, the concept of environment as outside, external to the human organism, is a comforting notion now utterly discarded both by ecological studies and post-Cartesian philosophy." Arnold Berleant, *The Aesthetics of Environment*, Philadelphia: Temple University Press, 1992, 4-5.

5 I am grateful to Stephen White and John O'Dougherty for helping me to think about the implications of thing-power for an environmental ethics.

6 James A. Nash, "On the Subversive Virtue: Frugality," in *Ethics of Consumption,* edited by David A. Cricker and Toby Linden, Lanham, MD: Rowman and Littlefield, 1998, 427.

Charles Eisen
Allegorical engraving of the Vitruvian primitive hut. Frontispiece of the work by Marc-Antoine Laugier: *Essai sur l'architecture*, 2nd ed.
1755

La Borda
Lacol SCCL, 2018

I have also suggested that a playful, naive stance toward nonhuman things is a way for us to render more manifest a fugitive dimension of experience. In the moment of naivete, it becomes possible to discern a resemblance between one's interior thinghood (e.g., bones) and the object-entities exterior to one's body. In the sympathetic link so formed, which also constitutes a line of flight from the anthropocentrism of everyday experience, thing-power comes to presence.

In developing the idea of thing-power, my aim was to enliven the debate over materiality – what it is and does. It is important that "materiality" be a contested term in political theory, especially as it replaces "reality" as the name for the stuff to which theory must be tied if it is to make a difference. My friend's assumption – that there is really only one way to theorize the relevance of materiality to politics – relegates other materialisms to the apolitical ether of idealism or aestheticism. But thing materialism is, I think, a viable competitor alongside the historical materialism of Marx and the body materialism of cultural studies. I present it as a contestable figuration of materiality among others, each of which emphasizes a different set of powers and does different political work. Historical materialism has tended to emphasize the structured quality of materiality – its ability to congeal into economic classes, stratified patterns of work, and dominant practices of exchange. Its political strength lies in its ability to expose hidden injuries of class, global economic inequities, and other unjust effects of capital flows and sedimentations. Body materialism has tended to focus on the *human* body and its collective practices (or arts of the self). It highlights the susceptibility of nature and biology to culture, and it exposes the extent to which cultural notions and ideals are themselves embodied entities and thus materialities that could be reshaped through politics. Thing-power materialism, for its part, focuses on *energetic forces* that course through humans and cultures without being exhausted by them. It pursues the quixotic task of a materialism that is not also an anthropology. Its political potential resides in its ability to induce a greater sense of interconnectedness between humanity and nonhumanity. A significant shift here might mobilize the will to move consumption practices in a more ecologically sustainable direction.

Jan Collaert I, after Stradanus
New inventions of Modern Times [*Nova Reperta*].
The production of silk, plate 8
c. 1600

Repairing a hole with a darning mushroom
Wuerzele, 2014

* Article featured in *Political Theory*, Vol. 32, No. 3 (June 2004), pp. 347-372. Published by: Sage Publications, Inc.

‡ Jane Bennett is political theorist and philosopher. Professor in the Department of Political Science at Johns Hopkins University.

AN ECOLOGY OF MATERIALS

TIM INGOLD*

What is a material? How can we say what a material is? That's a very difficult question to answer. It is easy to say, "That's wood, that's metal, that's pewter, that's tin." But what are we talking about? What is wood, what is tin, what is copper? What do we mean when we speak of materials? The scientific chemist, of course, will think of matter in terms of its invariant atomic or molecular constitution: water is two hydrogen atoms and an oxygen atom, salt is a sodium atom linked to a chlorine atom: wherever you have water, or wherever you have salt, you have these atomic combinations. Water is an interesting case in point, however. The molecular structure could not be simpler, and yet the properties of water – what water *does* under different conditions – are still so complex as to defy full understanding. For example, nobody yet knows why ice is slippery. There's a lot we don't understand about chemically the simplest materials. They remain beyond our comprehension in terms of what they actually do. So the maker is less like a scientific chemist than an alchemist.

I have noticed, both in my own work and in the work of many colleagues, that as we become more interested in materials themselves and in what they do, we are also beginning to think more like alchemists, and to have greater respect for what the alchemists achieved. They were not so interested in what a material *is*. They wanted to know what it *does*, what happens to a material when you mix it with other materials, or heat it up, or cool it, or treat it in particular ways. This is also what a cook wants to know. A cook, experimenting in the kitchen, puts different ingredients together and looks to see what happens to them if you heat them or boil them, freeze them or cool them down. So the maker, working with materials, is like an alchemist: he's interested not in what the materials are but what they do. In short, *materials are what they do*. So to define or specify a material is, in a way, to tell a story, about what happens to it when it is treated in particular ways.

For example, gold is an element in the periodic table, and the chemist or the scientist would define it as such. But if you were an alchemist you might say that gold yellows and gleams, that it shines ever more brightly under running water, and can be hammered into thin leaf.

In the 1960s the craftsman and furniture designer David Pye proposed a distinction *between* what he called the *properties* and the *qualities* of materials.[1] He argued that the properties of materials are given in what they are: they have a particular density, weight or tensile strength, which can be established through careful scientific testing or experiment. The *qualities* of materials, by contrast, are ideas in people's heads: we ascribe certain qualities to things, but these are merely products of our imagination. But this only reproduces the division between mind and matter, which we want to try and get away from. I think it is better, if we are concerned with the properties of materials, to think of these properties as belonging to the knowledge of practitioners that comes from a lifetime of experience of working with them. And this means that when we talk about the properties of materials, they are really stories of what happens to them.

In a sense, we could say that materials don't really exist; rather they carry on, or *perdure*, through time. Every material, in a way, is a becoming – it's not an object in itself but a potential to become something. So to describe a material, I think, is to pose a riddle: it is a riddle that gives the material its voice, and then the answer is discovered by observation and engagement with what is there. Medieval texts are full of riddles of this kind. I could make one up for you, and it would go like this: "I yellow and gleam; I shine ever more brightly under running water. Hammer me, and I will get thin. What am I?" The answer can be found simply by observing – by looking around in the world and finding what answers to that description. We call it 'gold.' But we don't need to have that word at all. We know what we are talking about through observation, through engagement in the world.

So the artisan, the craftsman, the maker, is someone who has to be ever-observant of the movements of stuff around him, and has to bring the movement of his or her own conscious awareness into line with the movements of the surrounding materials. Thus making something is a mode of questioning and response, in which the maker puts a question to the material, and the material answers to it; the maker puts another question, the material answers again, and so on. Each answers to the other. I use the term *correspondence* to capture this mutual responsiveness. In making, the maker follows the material and that process of following the material is a correspondence between the flow of the material and the movement and flow of the maker's consciousness. One could draw the flow of material as one wavy line, and the flow of consciousness as another, running roughly parallel. Correspondence, then, is a matter of bringing these two lines into agreement. To adopt a musical analogy, it is like two lines of melody responding to one another in counterpoint.

1 David Pye: *The Nature and Art of Workmanship*, Cambridge: Cambridge University Press, 1968, p. 47.

What I am *against* is the 'freezing' of the flow of materials in the form of an object, and the freezing of the flow of consciousness in the form of an image, leading to the idea that making is an interaction between image and object. For me, making is not about images and objects at all, but about the coupling of awareness, and of movements and gestures, with the forces and flows of materials that bring any work to fruition. The important thing to recognise about these flows is that they don't connect things up. To adopt a helpful metaphor from Deleuze and Guattari, imagine a river flowing between its banks. You can imagine one place A on one side of the river, and another place B on the other side. And you could build a bridge and cross from A to B. The flowing water of the river, however, does not go from anywhere to anywhere else. It just keeps flowing along, between its banks, at 90 degrees to the line between A and B. It goes along, not across.

It is to these flows that we need to attend if we are to understand making. Whereas the lines we might draw between objects, or between objects and persons, are lines that connect – like the line across the bridge from A to B – the flow-lines of materials and awareness do not connect but entangle. They comprise not a *network* but a *meshwork*. And to shift from talking about objects and their relations to materials and their entanglements is equivalent to a shift from a network view to a meshwork view. I think this meshwork view corresponds very closely to the ecologists' idea of the web of life. And it means that we have to distinguish not only between objects and materials but also between objects and things.

This word 'object' is very problematic: it's a word that many of us would like to be able to put to one side. It's a problem firstly because you think: "where there are objects there must be subjects," and the subject/object dichotomy has raised a host of difficult issues, not least that of the Cartesian split between mind and body. Most philosophers are agreed that the dichotomy has to go. But there are many rival philosophical camps, and each camp, while claiming to have solved the problem of how to get rid of the dichotomy, accuses its rivals of merely reproducing it in its discourse. For the onlooker to these arcane debates, it is all very tiresome. To my mind, however, the problem with the object, as indeed with the subject, lies not with the *ob-* or the *sub-* but with the *-ject*. It implies an entity that is already thrown, already cast, in a fixed and final form. It confronts us, face-to-face, as a *fait accompli*. When we talk about materials, on the other hand, they are always becoming. Everything is something, but being something is always on the way to becoming something else. Materials, if you will, are substances in becoming.

Thus the move from a focus on objects to a focus on materials is equivalent to a shift from a philosophy of being to a philosophy of becoming. Gatherings of materials in movement are what we call *things*. The distinction between objects and things goes back to the philosophy of Martin Heidegger. For Heidegger, the object is 'out there,' a *fait accompli*: you are 'over against' it.[2] The thing, by contrast, is to be understood as a gathering of materials in movement. So to touch or observe a thing is to bring the movements of our own being (or rather, becoming) into correspondence with the movements of the materials.

2 Martin Heidegger, "The Thing," in his *Poetry, Language, Thought* (trans. Albert Hofstadter), New York: Harper & Row, pp. 165-182.

The final point I want to make is that if we think of things in that way – as gatherings of materials in movement – then *we are things too*. People – we – are living organisms, and as organisms, we too are gatherings of materials in movement. In fact, we are entire ecosystems. I believe that according to the latest studies, 90 per cent of the cells in the human body belong to various kinds of bacteria – but that's another story. As gatherings of materials, people are a bit like compost heaps. If you were to take the lid off a human being you would see a writhing mass of activity going on beneath, like the writhing worms in a healthy heap of compost. And the thing about living bodies, human or non-human, is that they are sustained because they are continually taking in materials from their surroundings and discharging into them, in the processes of respiration and metabolism. Quite simply, to live we have to breathe; we also have to eat, and to defecate.

The organism can only keep on going because of this continual interchange of substance across its outer membrane or skin. Quite generally, things perdure – that is they can carry on – because they leak, because of the interchange of materials across the ever-emergent surfaces by which they differentiate themselves from the surrounding medium. The bodies of organisms and indeed of other things leak continually; in fact their lives depend on it. And in my view this shift of perspective, from *stopped-up objects* to *leaky things*, is what ultimately distinguishes what I want to call an ecology of materials from mainstream studies of material culture.

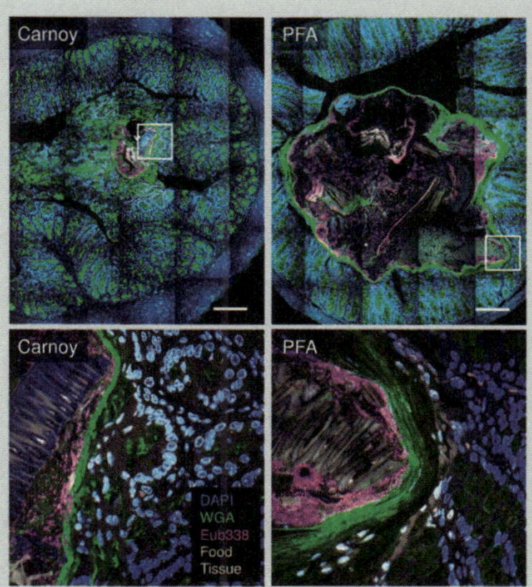

Hasegawa, Mark Welch, Rossetti, Boris, and GG
Spatial structure of gut microbiome
2017

The pottery lesson
Dmitry Makeev, 2006

* Tim Ingold is professor of Social Anthropology at the University of Aberdeen.

HYPEROBJECTS AND CREATIVITY

TIMOTHY MORTON*

Hyperobject is a name I invented for something that is so vastly distributed in time and space, relative to the observer, that we might not think it's even an object at all. It's good to have a word for things that are now only too thinkable, if not totally visible – global warming, radiation, the biosphere... Words enable you to think. Stabilizing all kinds of intense and novel feelings and sensations in a word allows for a release of (creative) energy, because you don't have to keep on figuring the basic coordinates out – you have a word, which means things are capable of being figured out, seen... This doesn't make everything all right, of course, but it does mean that the way you undergo the gigantic things that structure your life, from hurricanes to the mass mobilization algorithms we call social media (a phrase that begins to sound like "military intelligence"), doesn't take up all your spare psychic processing power.

If you think about Björk's amazing song, "Hyperballad," you'll find that it's a sort of exploded version of a love song.[1] Björk never directly says, "I love you," or another indicative sentence like that. She shows you the wiring under the board of the emotion, what the philosopher Julia Kristeva would call the *genotext*.[2] In so doing, Björk shows you how that wiring is connected to all kinds of beings that aren't Björk: car parts, bottles, cutlery, the objects the narrator throws off the cliff in the first verse. I was inspired by that song to create the term *hyperobject*, because it seemed that Björk was evoking something that included her, but that was bigger than her, but that wasn't *more* than her, if you see what I mean: something physically bigger, but *ontologically* smaller. Ontology means *the logic of how things exist*. Things exist in strange piles of other things that don't add up to a whole that is greater than the sum of its parts. Things can slip out, fall off cliffs, find themselves in a beautiful strange love song. Björk imagines pitching *herself* off the cliff, and seeing herself among the rocks and the bits and pieces she's already chucked over. Car parts are symptoms of her feelings – she is throwing them over to allow herself to cope with her lover, the song says; but they are also parts of cars; and they are also things that lie next to rocks and human bodies in a song called "Hyperballad."

In the same way, this little piece of trinite is sitting on my shrine at home. Trinite is a mineral created in the first atom bomb test, in New Mexico. One side is strangely sparkly green – a mixture of all the elements that got churned up in the blast. The other side is plain, clay-like – the side that was facing away from the blast. Trinite is part of a nuclear explosion, and it's part of the desert sand, and it's part of a Buddhist shrine. Hyperobjects can intersect with one another, and with other beings, other bodies; and they can be broken down into little bits and redistributed. My first example of a hyperobject was Styrofoam. Imagine all the Styrofoam in the world, ever. But mealworms can eat Styrofoam successfully, in other words, they can digest this thing that might last for hundreds of years. Wholes don't exhaust their parts, otherwise mealworms couldn't bite bits of Styrofoam and digest them.

That means, when you think it through, that all kinds of creativity and novelty are possible in the world. The world is bursting with revolutionary potential. They are like titans, not gods. They are huge, but they can be defeated and dismantled. Hyperobjects are very good to think with.

Here are three questions we might ask about these strange gigantic beasts, the hyperobjects:

> 1. We have suddenly become aware of the Anthropocene, the geological period brought about by human carbon emissions. But how does the Anthropocene affect human society, thought and art?
>
> 2. How can humans think and plan for the scales sufficient to take global warming and radiation into account: scales that are measured in tens of thousands of years?
>
> 3. We often think and act towards the environment as if a horrifying cataclysm is about to take place. But what if the problem were precisely that the cataclysm has already occurred?

And here's another thing to think about: the trouble with events such as global warming and mass extinction is not that we can't picture them at all. That's not what the hyperobject concept is about at all.

The trouble with events such as this is that we can picture them. We can picture them, all too readily. The trouble is that in picturing them, our own capacity to visualize gets activated, and for all kinds of reasons, this capacity is disturbing to us, despite the fact that it's one thing that makes us quite special as human beings. Perhaps, and this is purely speculative, it's because the capacity to visualize depends on the capacity to hallucinate, which depends on what some ethnobotanists now call human-plant coevolution.

1 Björk, "Hyperballad," *Post* (One Little Indian, 1995).

2 Julia Kristeva, *Revolution in Poetic Language*, New York, Columbia University Press, 1984.

The writers we collected in this volume all have something to say about hyperobjects, because they are all capable of visualizing them in writing. They know that hyperobjects don't exist "over yonder" or up above us or below us, like gigantic space ships. They are in us. They are us. Consider the fact that as a member of the human species, you are a part of a massively distributed entity that is now acting like the asteroid that hurtled towards Earth sixty-five million years ago, wiping out the dinosaurs and many other species. That's what global warming really means: mass extinction.

Hyperobjects stick to you, inside and out: the radiation in my body, the mercury in my blood... they are "viscous" that way, and not just in a physical sense. Think about how some humans now think it would be best to colonize Mars, to avoid global warming (and other issues).

The trouble is, on Mars you have to create a biosphere from scratch. You have the same problem as the one down here on Earth. So in a strong sense, not to do with spatial extension (distance in time and space), you are still "on Earth." You are, to use the technical lingo, phenomenologically glued to Earth wherever else you think you are. When you think about it this way, is the extractive and fossil fuel burning processes involved in making space ships to colonize Mars that great a way of avoiding global warming? Or is it in fact part of the problem, not just physically (all those resources wasted and worse), but in terms of psychology and philosophy? The attitudes that seduce us into abandoning Earth have been baked into post- Neolithic social space for thousands of years.

Which doesn't mean they can't be undone. "Civilization" in the Mesopotamian, agricultural sense is simply a very long lasting hyperobject in itself. It's huge. But it's not infinite. We can change it. And when you have a word for something, you have some kind of power over it.

Trinity test, the first nuclear explosion in history
16 July 1945
Photograph by Jack W. Aeby

Small piece of trinitite, detail showing the lateral structure
Shaddack, 2009
CC-BY-3.0

And the bigger news is that this power to change what is in fact a historical (not an eternal) situation has deep roots in ontology, which is the study not of what exists, but of *how things exist*. Hyperobjects force us to realize that collections of things are also things – a football team is just as real as a football player, global warming is just as real as these raindrops on my porch. And this means that they are in fact ontologically *weak*. They may be physically huge: the physical systems involved in neoliberal capitalism, for instance, now cover most of Earth's surface. But this should not frighten or intimidate us into the kind of cynical reason that proves that it's correct by blocking off all the exits to social change, in a competition as to whose picture of human paralysis is more intense, and therefore more correct. Since when did caring about poor suffering workers mean talking in such a disempowering way?

No. Hyperobjects are physically huge but they are ontologically tiny. There's one thing called global warming but there are thousands of things called rainstorm, gentle sunlight on a spring day, snow encouraging me to ski down this mountain. These things aren't exhausted by being caused by global warming. That's not all that they're about, just like being a citizen in a far-right regime doesn't mean that you yourself subscribe to far-right views. And because Hyperobects are collections of other things, vast heaps of things in fact, they can overlap. You can be part of several hyperobjects. You're not absorbed into a hyperobject forever and ever like a droplet of water in an ocean.

That's the message. Science can now understand how things exist in dimensions and on scales far in excess of normal human functioning. But that means that they're not to be taken lying down, like fate or destiny or contingency or nature. I sometimes think that terms like that stand for entities that operate on scales that are at present too vast or too tiny for humans to do much more right now than report and observe them. We have to undergo them. But we can figure out how to work with them and transform society in order to accommodate their reality in ways that are beneficial to humans and nonhumans alike.

* Timothy Morton is member of the object-oriented philosophy movement. Professor and holder of the Rita Shea Guffey Chair at Rice University.

MATTER AS KIN. A NON-BINARY (NATURE-CULTURE) MATTER FUTURE

INSTITUTE FOR POSTNATURAL STUDIES*

Imagine yourself, picture your body from the tip of your head to the end of your toes, all your parts and limbs, surrounded by infinite microparticles, immersed in minuscule spheres floating around you, creating a subtle but constant pressure on your skin. Feel your limits, molecules, and atoms of matter that move everywhere around. Think about the very tiny space that separates you from this thick air. You are being touched, you are being shaped. As strange as it might sound, your body is immersed, submerged, and diving into a substance full of matter. You are constantly intra-acting.

Karen Barad's concept of intra-action provides a transformative lens for understanding the world. Challenging traditional notions of discrete entities and interaction, they offer a view of existence that is dynamically produced through relational processes instead. Think again of your body and its matter, your particles and the environment merging, intertwined, entangled. Being is fundamentally relational. Existence is not a static state but a process of becoming, and of mutual relations.

Unlike traditional views that see matter as passive and inert, Barad argues that matter is an active participant in the world's becoming.[1] Their approach to "intra-action" posits that entities do not preexist their interactions. Instead, they emerge; relationships and entities involved in them are mutually constituted. If knowing and being are entangled, then our knowledge practices are inherently ethical. How we engage with the world affects what can come into being. And how we imagine and consider it: thinking of the other shaping you can help to blur many limits too and dissolve the binary oppositions such as subject/object, human/non-human, and nature/culture, to move beyond these dualisms and to understand the world in more interconnected and relational terms.

That matter matters is undoubtedly a euphony resonating at the center of the contemporary ecological debate. Matter is, to put it again in Barad's terms, our onto-epistemology, reminding us of the inseparability of ontology (the nature of being) and epistemology (the nature of knowing). It is our reality, both of thoughts and bodies, of ideas and atoms and minerals and organic beings, all interconnected as dynamic processes. Emphasizing the agency of matter, but also the entanglement of knowing and being, and the ethical dimensions of our practices, opens up new ways of understanding and engaging with the world.

In recent years, the rigid boundaries that have long separated nature and culture are being increasingly challenged. As we grapple with the consequences of climate change, biodiversity loss, and environmental degradation, it becomes evident that the dichotomy between nature and culture is not only artificial but also detrimental to our understanding and interaction with the many worlds that shape reality. To think of matter as Kin offers a transformative perspective that envisions a non-binary future where matter is recognized as entanglement, dissolving the traditional notion of a world divided into opposites.

The separation of nature and culture has its roots in Western philosophy, where the natural world has often been viewed as a passive backdrop to human activity, a mere resource to be exploited. This anthropocentric worldview has led to a hierarchical relationship. Within the lower stratum where nature is positioned, matter continued to be conditioned by the vertical understandings that categories and taxonomies of Western science has imposed on them Living and non-living, sentient and non-sentient, matter has also been captured within its moral and political systems.

However, this perspective fails to acknowledge the intricate interconnections and interdependencies that bind all forms of life and matter. Recognizing that matter is not inert or devoid of agency but rather a dynamic participant in the web of life is the only way out of such structures. Matter is relational, it shapes our present both as a physical and also as a temporal condition. It is our past and our potential, too; it is the world's relational agency and therefore, its ultimate future. Matter melts time, matter "matters" forms and beings. Matter matters the world around and within us all.

In her book *Parallel Minds*,[2] Laura Tripaldi explores the relationship between the spider and its web as a profound metaphor for understanding materiality and matter, complex systems, self-organization, and the interconnectedness of entities within a network. The web is a product of the spider's actions and interactions with its environment. It emerges from the spider's repeated, local actions, which are influenced by external factors like gravity, wind, and the surrounding architecture. The spider and the web are in a constant state of intra-action. The web is the material continuation of the body that produces it, and it is not just a static structure but a dynamic system that can be modified, repaired, and adapted by the spider based on the feedback it receives. This dynamic relationship highlights the importance of feedback loops in complex systems. The spider and the web together form a network where each influences the other, akin to nodes and connections in a broader network. Materials themselves have a form of intelligence. The spider uses its body and silk to create a web, demonstrating an intrinsic knowledge of material properties and how to manipulate them.

1 Karen Barad. *Meeting the Universe Halfway: Quantum Physics and the Entanglement of Matter and Meaning*, Duke University Press, 2007.

2 Laura Tripaldi. *Parallel Minds: Discovering the Intelligence of Materials*. Urbanomic, 2022.

This perspective aligns with new materialist theories, which argue that matter is vibrant and possesses its vitality. By viewing matter as kin, we acknowledge that everything, rocks, rivers, plants, and animals, but also plastics, microchips, apples, and electrons are not mere objects but active and complex agents with whom we share a relational existence. A non-hierarchical and non-binary matter future envisions a world where the boundaries between the natural and cultural realms are fluid and permeable. In this context, from a postnatural ecological perspective, kinship might become a dynamic and interconnected network that extends beyond human relationships to include more-than-human entities, ecosystems, and the environment. A broader view of kinship emphasizes the interdependence of all living and non-living components of the world, recognizing that humans are part of a larger system.

One of the key implications of viewing matter as kin is that we might be more likely to adopt practices that are inclusive and equitable. This approach challenges the exploitation and marginalization of both vulnerable communities but also natural resources. New materialisms stand from the interconnectedness of social and ecological issues, advocating for approaches that address both simultaneously. Furthermore, a non-binary matter future encourages us to embrace diversity in all its forms. Just as biodiversity is crucial for the resilience of ecosystems, cultural diversity enriches our collective knowledge and fosters care. In that sense, matter as kin offers a profound shift in our understanding of the relationship between nature and culture, guiding us toward a more harmonious and resilient future.

To fully embrace the possibilities that new materialism theories bring to non-binary futures, reshaping matter, agency, and human-nature relationships, means a new understanding of ecological processes, emphasizing the interconnectedness and co-constitution of all entities in an ecosystem, putting all matter on the same level and looking at it beyond anthropocentric views. Whether we like it or not, this will also have to include the new materialities derived from our actions. In this new space of thought, plastiglomerates, radioactivity, and the viscous and delocalized materials of the Anthropocene, will need a place for our kinship, together with the beautiful flowers, its vegetal cells, or the dust of the butterfly's wings.

In 2014, in the middle of the ocean, a large cod swallowed a plastic dildo. The fish might have mistaken the artifact for one of the multicolored octopi that are its usual food source. In the great essay "Toxic Progeny",[3] Heather Davis opens her text with such an impactful and improbable metabolic encounter. A cod swallowing a silicone object, entering its guts, and arriving in its stomach is, ironically, an image hard to digest. But this event serves her to unfold a truly interesting theory: there is an explicit enmeshment and a strange congruence of oceanic plastic as it ties into nonreproductive sex and queer futurity.

The essay brings together the worlds of plastic and queer theory under the conditions of non-reproduction and extinction, a world where our progeny may not even be human much less our biological offspring. Plastic will be there forever, as its main problem is its non-decomposability. A non-filial human progeny, as she calls it, that will most certainly outlive us.

3 Heather Davis. *Toxic Progeny: The Plastisphere and Other Queer Futures*, A Journal of Continental Feminism, Volume 5.2. 2015.

Following Barthes's lucid words from his essay on plastic,[4] where he points to the negative reality of this material, she argues that neither hard nor deep, it must be content with a substantial attribute that is neutral despite its utilitarian advantages. For Davis the trick of plastic, and here we could include many of the other matters we will have to coexist with, is that, through its seductive surface, its alchemical qualities and mutability, they are treated as if they are ephemeral, somehow vanishing into the ether after they have been discarded. But neither the plastic that fills the cracks of a polluted rock, nor the cobalt that forms your phone's chip, nor the tonnes of waste that surround our endless dumps can escape that matter is relational, that matter is kin.

Now, again, imagine yourself surrounded by infinite microparticles, your pores breathing in and out as you intra-act with the infinite microorganisms that you inhale. Imagine the spider webbing a world around it, and the cod swimming and swallowing the synthetic matters floating in the troubled waters of eternity. Embrace this transcorporeality, embrace the interconnectedness of all things around you. That is, precisely, where a new kin non-binary-matter-future begins.

4 Roland Barthes, *Mythologies*, Les Lettres nouvelles. 1957.

* Institute for Postnatural Studies is a Centre for artistic experimentation that explores and questions post-nature as a framework for contemporary creation. Founded in 2020 in Madrid.

1

PET
CHE
MATTER

RO—
MICAL

NUNCA MÁIS [NEVER AGAIN]

Never Again emerged as a social movement with one objective: to determine the environmental, legal, and political responsibilities behind the disaster caused by the Prestige oil tanker off the coast of Galicia in 2002, which ended up sinking in the Atlantic after a heavy storm leading to the worst environmental catastrophe in the history of Spain. More than 63,000 tonnes of crude oil were spilled, and polluted over 2,000 km of the Galician coast, affecting France as well. Twenty years later, stains of the oil can still be found.

A vase of flowers designed by Curro Claret made of *xapapote* (tar resulting from the decomposition of the crude oil in the sea) from the Galician beaches denounces the pollution and advocates recycling, while Rosa María Costas uses ink derived from oil as her means of expression in a poster that is also a protest against the spill.

Poster *Nunca Máis* (Never Again)
Ink on paper
Rosa María Costas Rodríguez, Barcelona, 2002
Donation, Fundació Comunicació Gràfica, 2019 MDB 8.723

>
Chapapote Vase
Recycled petroleum residue
Curro Claret, Barcelona, 2011
Donation, Curro Claret, 2024

PLASTICS: FROM SOLUTION TO PROBLEM

ISABEL CAMPI*

Harshly criticized for its environmental footprint, the world of plastic is complex and contradictory. On the one hand, its defenders praise the beauty, usefulness and economy of the objects made from it, while on the other, its detractors claim that plastics are the main cause of pollution on the planet. These hard to refute truths lead to conclude that a world without plastic today is as utopian as defenders were 150 years ago.[1]

From a technical perspective, plastics are polymeric organic materials of high molecular mass. They are substances made up of organic macromolecules called polymers, which are large groups of molecules joined through a chemical process called polymerization. Plastics possess a series of properties impossible to find in other materials: they are cheap, light, waterproof, insulators against electricity and heat (although they do not always resist it), are resistant to the effects of many chemical products, weather resistant, easy to work with and capable of combining all the functions of an object in a single piece, and often in thin sheets. Their biggest downside is they are not biodegradable and at times, burning them can be highly contaminating.

Plastics have a weak identity. Throughout their history, wood, stone, marble, silk, cotton and wool have been associated and endowed with a strong personality. Subjected to certain forces, they always react in the same way. Craftsmen and manufacturers could refer to a material as something capable of precise and consistent behaviour.[2] Social recognition of its meaning reflected the fact that few materials were available, that these were clearly differentiated, and it was known that over time they preserved the same properties. But the acceleration of progress and the introduction of new materials have impeded identity creation mechanisms, making them ineffective.

Plastic is a mutant material insofar as it can be moulded into any shape or image: it can be opaque, semi-transparent, transparent, hard, stiff, soft, flexible, etc.[3]

Plastics emerged as imitation materials, yet after World War II, following the bold action taken by some designers, they entered the cultural sphere. Its distinctive features were simple sculptural forms, rounded edges, primary colours, bright textures and products made from a single piece.

Plastic challenges the principle of sincerity of the material proposed by Modernism. As such, its unbridled development has outpaced the tension between authentic and imitation materials. In other words, plastics are genuine in their falsehood.

Natural plastics

Natural plastics, some already known in ancient times, are materials found in nature such as horn, bitumen, tortoiseshell, amber and shellac. They are materials that, once heated, soften so that they can be shaped. Traditionally, they were used to make small objects like snuff boxes, cigarette holders, jewellery, and cameos. Since raw materials were scarce, the resulting objects were expensive and, in a way, valuable.[4]

Semisynthetic plastics

In the mid-19th century, chemists began to test formulas to replace natural plastics and developed semisynthetic ones, characterized by their part natural and part artificial components.

The first semisynthetic cellulosic plastics were a combination of natural materials like cellulose (cotton based) made to react with nitric acid and later mixed with different plasticizers such as vegetable oil, camphor and alcohol. The transformation systems were the same as for natural plastics: moulding, calendering, extrusion, blow moulding and casting.

Hard rubber, also called "vulcanite" or "ebonite," was rubber hardened with sulphur, a process which came to be called vulcanization. It was a deep black material that was a good imitation of ebony and, cut and polished, looked like jet. It was used to make black or mourning jewellery.

However, without a doubt, the most well-known semisynthetic plastic was celluloid, the commercial name for the cellulose nitrate which successfully replaced marble. Invented in the mid-19th century by British chemist Alexander Parkes, it was introduced to much acclaim at several universal expositions. While Parkes did not enjoy commercial success with "Parkesine," in the United States, the Hyatt brothers, in the 1870s, did, giving it the name Celluloid. The Hyatts found many practical applications for this new material such as billiard balls, shirt collars, whale corsets, combs, cutlery and stylographic handles, prosthetic teeth and myriad small objects. Because of its transparency and flexibility, celluloid was the most common film base for motion pictures until the 1950s. The problem with celluloid, however, is its flammability and instability, the source of more than a few problems in its preservation.

1 Luis F. Martínez Montreal: "Baquelitas. Creando el futuro." In Luis Caballero García, Rafael Ortiz Domínguez and Luis F. Martinez Montreal, *Baquelitas. Creando futuro*, Madrid, Museo Nacional de Artes Decorativas/Ministerio de Educación, Cultura y Deporte, 2015, pp. 9-21.

2 Ezio Manzini: *La matière de l'invention*. París, Editions du Centre Pompidou, 1989.

3 Paola Antonelli: *Mutant Materials in Contemporary Design*. New York, The Museum of Modern Art, 1995.

4 Susan Mossman: *Early Plastics. Perspectives 1850-1950*. London, Leicester University Press/The Science Museum, 1997.

Other cellulose-based plastics are cellophane, cellulose acetate, viscose rayon, and casein. The latter, also called "galelith" – which is sometimes confused with celluloid –, can be cast in infinite shades to make buttons, buckles and trimmings for clothes.

Synthetic plastics

The first fully synthetic plastic was Bakelite. Its creator, Belgium-born chemist Leo Baekeland, spent ten years methodically researching a way out of the technological framework of celluloid chemists, to focus on the condensation reaction of phenol with formaldehyde. In 1907, he presented his initial findings to the New York Chemist Club, but it would take him a few more years to turn his product into a profitable company.[5] Through compression moulding and temperature, he produced a material that he named Bakelite, aimed at the new electricity, radio and automobile markets. Throughout the 1930s, Bakelite, manufactured in a vast range of colours, was used to make billiard balls, telephones, ashtrays, sockets, tableware, canteens, car parts, and, especially, radio receivers. It was the preferred plastic of Art Deco designers and the Streamline Moderne style they fervently adopted during the Great Depression, because it was cheap, modern, pleasant to the touch, colourful, durable, heat resistant, and has electrical insulation properties.[6] According to these designers, Bakelite was the first plastic that neither lied nor needed to be ashamed of its appearance.

Throughout the 1930s, the petrochemical industry had a significant interest in the development of synthetic plastic because it required a large demand for petroleum-based products. During the Second World War, production of industrial plastic increased dramatically as it proved to be an excellent replacement material.

Nylon, discovered in 1935 by Wallace Hume Carothers, leader of chemical labs at Dupont, was a light, abrasion-

Comb
Openwork ivory
Emili Ferrer, 1920
Manufactured by Casa J. Cardús, Barcelona
Donation Montserrat Badia Cardús, 2021 MDB 13.836

Parasol
Rayon taffeta, knitted embroidery, mercerized cotton. Cane handle, Bakelite top
Barcelona, 1930
Donation, Carme Roselló Izquierdo, 2016 MDB 210

Telephone *Model N. 5523-A*
Moulded Bakelite and metal
Manufactured by Standard Eléctrica SA, Spain, c. 1956
Donation, Marta Montmany Madurell, 2009 MADB 138.657

resistant plastic, insoluble in gasoline, with a low friction coefficient that quickly regained its shape, and had good resistance to fungi and insects. During the war, it was used to make parachute cords and fabric in place of silk. After the war, its main success was in hosiery and knitted fabrics.

Polyethylene is a flexible plastic fabric that can be transparent. Discovered in 1933 in the laboratories of Imperial Chemical Industries (ICI) (Works, Winnington), it was often used during the war as insulation for telecommunication cables. During peacetime, in the 1940s, it became the ubiquitous grocery bag in the United States. To take advantage of surplus polyethylene production, Earl Tupper came up with the idea to manufacture lunch pails and market them through an ingenious system of gatherings of housewives that came to be known as Tupperware parties. The famous Tupperware is an example of practical and functional design that never prided itself on awards and flashy creators.

5 Wiebe E. Bijker: *Of Bycicles, Bakelites and Bulbs. Towards a Theory of Sociological Change*. Massachussetts, Massachusetts Institute of Technology, 1995.

6 Jeffrey Meikle: "New Materials and New Technologies." In Tim Benton, Ghislaine Wood and Charlotte Bentons: *Art Deco 1910-1929*, London, Victoria & Albert Museum, 2003, pp. 348-369.

The formula for methacrylate, or plexiglass, was discovered in 1877, but it was not until 1928, that Röhm and Haas manufactured it commercially. While initially used as lining, it enjoyed widespread success in the mid-1930s when it was made in thin transparent sheets. During the war, it was used for Spitfire airplane cockpits instead of glass. In sheets or as a transparent block, coloured or not, when subjected to heat plexiglass bends easily and can be cut with simple workshop tools. Since it did not require large investments in moulds, local designers experimented with it frequently. Transparent methacrylate furniture gave the impression of floating in the air – a fitting fantasy for the Space Age.[7]

Polyester is a very hard and relatively fragile plastic reinforced by layers of glass fibre, resulting in a composite. During the war, it was used to make radar screens and, after the conflict ended, for coachwork, sports boat hulls and pools. In the 1970s, Spanish designers saw great possibilities in this material, which they used to make chairs, stools and small tables.

Acrylonitrile, butadiene and styrene (ABS), invented in 1948, are the names of the three monomers that grant this polymer its stiffness, hardness, durability, stability at high temperatures, tenacity and mechanical resistance. In addition to these qualities, the possibility of a bright finish, vivid colours and rounded shapes that connected outstandingly with the pop aesthetic made ABS the go-to plastic of the seventies.[8] In Catalonia, the ABS furniture by the Italian company Kartell, which leased its moulds to companies in El Vallès for injection, enjoyed enormous success. While less familiar, Plásticos Trilla was far more popular because it manufactured the well-known stackable drink crates.

Polyvinyl chloride, or PVC, has a long history dating back to 1835, though it was not mass produced until the Second World War, when it was used to make pipes, gutters and windows. Manufactured in thin sheets, PVC is the famous vinyl that experienced so much success in the 1970s with the creation of numerous inflatable items: from furniture and air mattresses to temporary pavilions and circus tents. To promote this material in Spain, in 1971, the company Aiscondel gave students, who had come from around the world to attend the ICSID congress in Ibiza, an unlimited supply of PVC film to build the *Instant City* designed by José Miguel de Prada Poole.

Finally, we should also mention polystyrene and polyurethane, both invented in the 1930s. In its expanded version, polystyrene is ultralight and the superb packaging material known as Porexpan. Meanwhile, the foam version of polyurethane was often used in the 1970s to make soft single-piece furniture. Today, it is used for cladding, as an insulation and as filler.

7 Isabel Campi, Marta Gonzalez and Pilar Mellado. “Pasión por lo sintético. El objeto pop en la Barcelona del ‘desarrollismo’”, *Inmaterial. Diseño arte y sociedad*, vol 4, no. 7, 2019, pp. 95-123.

8 Philippe Decelles, Diane Hennebert and Pierre Loze: *L’utopie du tout plastique 1960-1973*. Brussels, Fondation pour l’architecture, 1994.

Melamine is a plastic widely used in laminate sheets as a decorative covering. Known by the name Formica, it was introduced at the Hogarhotel shows in Barcelona in 1966, 1967 and 1968, in a series of stunning installations by the Bonamusa-Tomàs studio. The Formica company donated the material on the condition that all the furniture and stands at the event were covered in melamine. The philosophy of "everything in Formica" synthesized perfectly with the colourful and artificial aesthetics of pop.

In conclusion, the trajectory of plastic, from its invention to is current omnipresence, reveals both its undeniable advantages and the environmental dangers it poses. Initially celebrated for its versatility and economy, plastic became of symbol of modernity and progress. However, plastic's slow decomposition time and its contribution to global pollution have transformed this chemical marvel into a serious ecologic threat. The solution to this dilemma does not lie in the absolute elimination of plastics but rather in sustainable innovation and eco-friendly management of plastic waste.

* Isabel Campi is PhD in Design History. President of Fundació Història del Disseny (History of Design Foundation).

Chair
Moulded fibreglass and polyester
Jordi Galí Camprubí, 1963–1964
Manufactured by Plásticos Trallero, L'Hospitalet de Llobregat
Donation Jordi Galí Camprubí, 2023 MDB 15.803

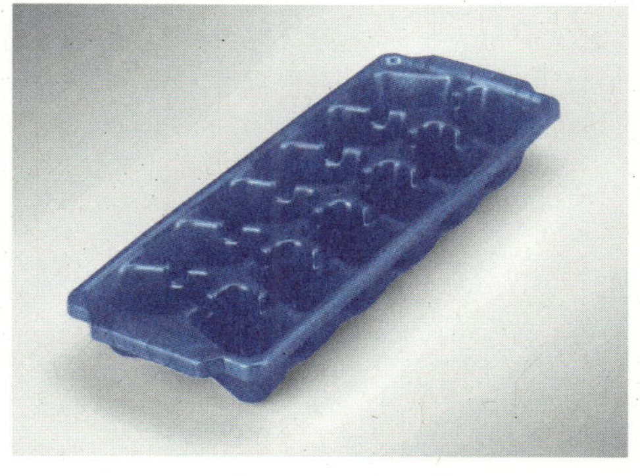

Ice tray
Moulded polyethylene
Manuel Jalón Corominas, Vicente Álvarez, Julio Cejudo, 1976
Manufactured by Manufacturas Rodex SA i Curver Rodex SA, Zaragoza, Spain
Donation Curver Rodex SA, 1995 MADB 135.781

Brisé fan
Painted and gilded ivory, tortoise shell and ribbon
Europe, 1720–1730
Bequest of Carlos Pirozzini i Martí, 1946 MADB 40.876

Brisé fan
Machine die-cut and painted celluloid, cotton ribbon
Japan, 1920–1930
Donation, Antoni Coll Fort, 1954 MADB 135.018

FROM IVORY TO BAKELITE

Wooden balls were first used in billiards, a game that dates back to the fifteenth century, but with the colonial expansion of Europe they were replaced by balls made of ivory. The popularity of the game in the nineteenth century and the proliferation of salons in cities led to increasing demands for ivory, which was, however, too expensive a material and, as a result, would soon be replaced, first by primer celluloid, that was dismissed on account of its inflammability, and then by Bakelite, the first fully synthetic plastic. Invented by Leo Baekeland in 1907, Bakelite had multiple uses ranging from the manufacturing of radio sets and telephones to that of kitchen utensils, all of which took advantage of its heat-resistant properties and electrical non-conductivity. It was incredibly popular and even though it was abandoned because of its brittleness and lack of versatility, it marked the birth of industrial plastic.

Gina iron
Steel and moulded Bakelite
Santiago Pey Estrany, 1962
Manufactured by Electromecánica Faraday, Barcelona
Donation, Santiago Pey Estrany, 1994 MADB 135.566

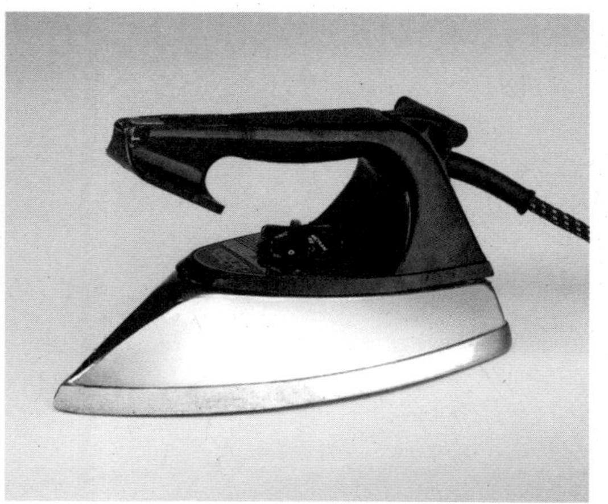

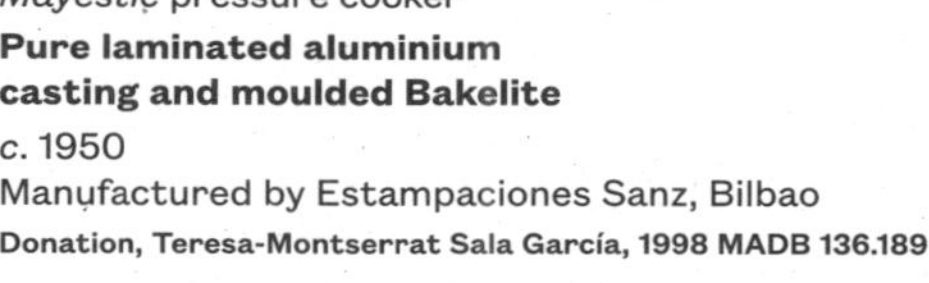

Mayestiç pressure cooker
Pure laminated aluminium casting and moulded Bakelite
c. 1950
Manufactured by Estampaciones Sanz, Bilbao
Donation, Teresa-Montserrat Sala García, 1998 MADB 136.189

THE APOTHEOSIS OF PLASTIC

The first plasticized PVC, polyvinyl chloride, was commercialized in 1926, characterized by its impermeability and fire resistance. Demand for the material grew during World War Two for military uses, and throughout the postwar period production steadily increased. The fifties and sixties saw the mass emergence of new plastics like polypropylene, that replaced expensive materials such as glass and wood, while in the seventies plastic replaced metal in light alloys. In the eighties, plastic production became a huge global industry. This exceptional development highlights the importance of plastic as a ubiquitous material. In 1950, world production of plastic materials amounted to two million tonnes. Today, over 450 million tonnes are produced annually.

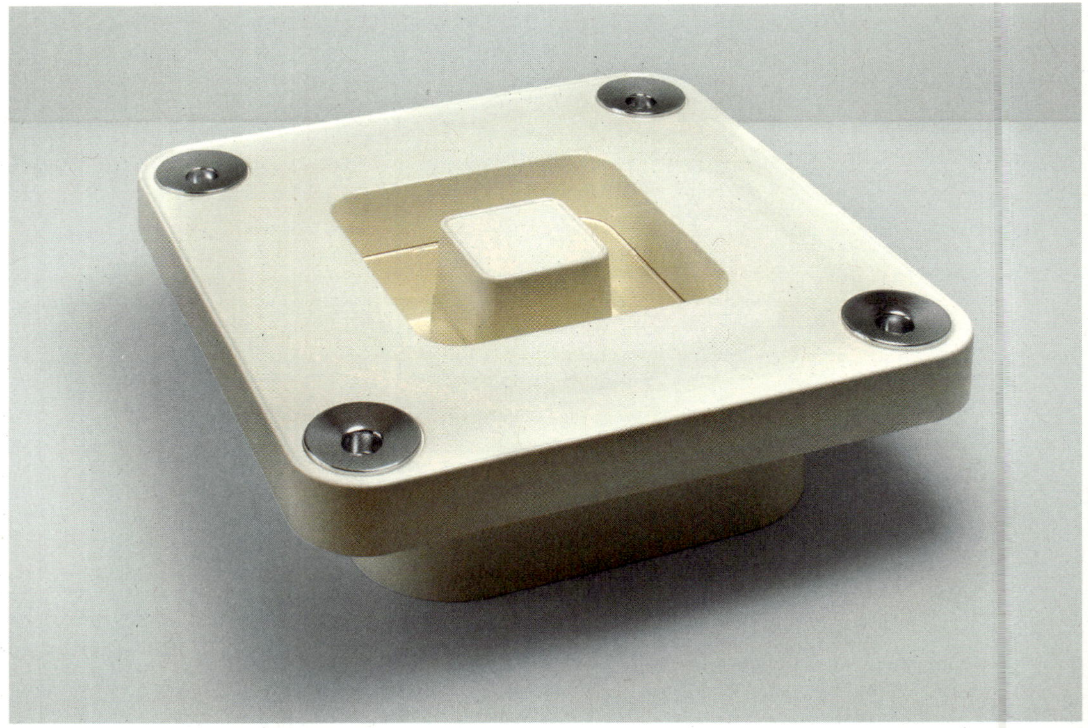

Mesa Bar (Bar Table)
Moulded resin and fiberglass and aluminium
Carles Fochs, Joaquim Prats Aragonés, 1970
Manufactured by DAI, Barcelona
Donation, Joaquim Prats Aragonès, 1995 MADB 135.888

Pila stool
Moulded polyester resin and fiberglass
Carles Fochs and Joaquim Prats Aragonés, 1970
Manufactured by DAI, Barcelona
Donation, Joaquim Prats Aragonés, 1995
MADB 135.889

Tossa ashtray
Moulded melamine
André Ricard Sala, 1970
Manufactured by Flamagàs SA, Barcelona
Donation,, 2001 MADB 136.697

Ashtray
Pressed melamine powder
José Juan Bigas Luna and Carles Riart Llop, 1969
Manufactured by Estudi i Botiga GRIS, Diseño y Forma SA (Disform), Barcelona
Donation, Mercè Castro Bonachera, Josep París Tomàs, 1998
MADB 136.289

Flod stool
Rotationally moulded medium-density polyethylene (ICORENE 3590)
azúamoliné (Martín Azúa and Gerard Moliné), 2007
Manufactured by Mobles 114, Barcelona
Donation, Mobles 114 Barcelona, 2014 MADB 138.921

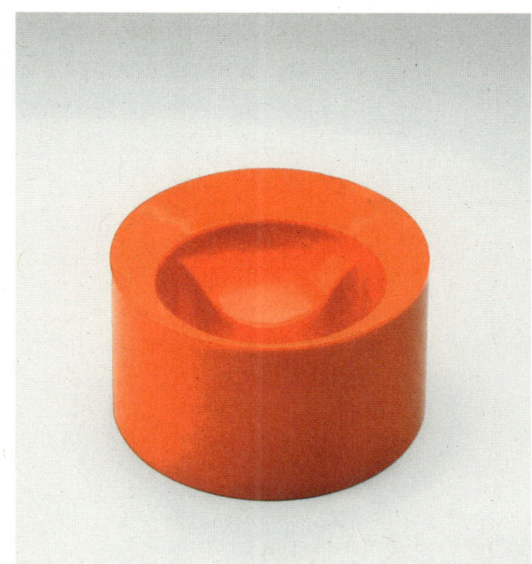

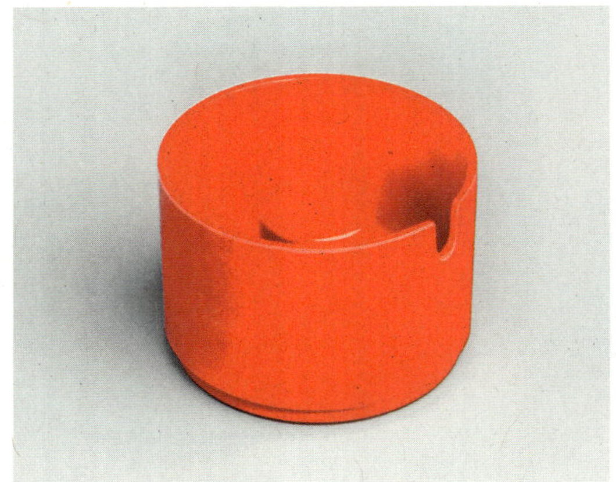

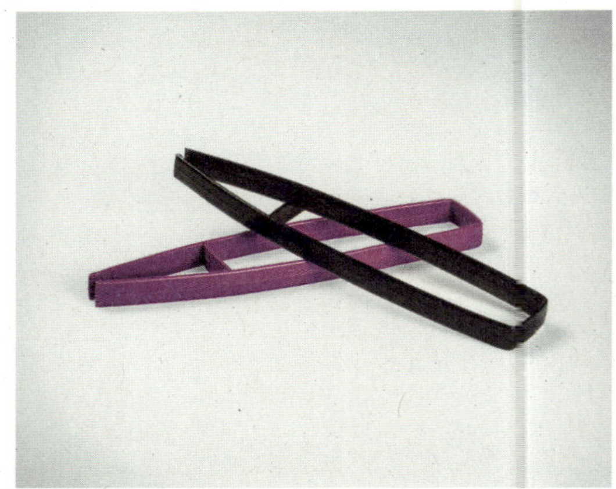

Ice cube container *Polar*
Moulded ABS and expanded polystyrene
Fernando Amat Ferré, 1974
Manufactured by Diseño y Forma SA (Disform), Barcelona
Donation, Carlos Javier López, 2015 MADB 138.941

Copenhagen ashtray
Moulded melamine
André Ricard Sala, 1966
Manufactured by Flamagàs SA, Annexa, Norda, Olivia Ricard & Cia, Mobles 114, Barcelona
Donation, Mobles 114 Barcelona, 2014 MADB 138.925

Cart
Laminated methacrylate and chrome-plated iron
Rafael Carreras Puigdengolas, 1971
Manufactured by Class, Barcelona
Donation, Rafael Carreras Puigdengolas, 1994 MADB 135.449

RR201 stool
Moulding expanded polystyrene
Andreu Carulla, 2018
Manufactured by Roca Recicla, Girona
Donation, Andreu Carulla, 2022 MDB 15.746

Simplex stool
Rotationally moulded polypropylene
azúamoliné (Martín Azúa and Gerard Moliné), 2005
Manufactured by Industrias Cosmic, Caldes de Montbui
Donation, Industrias Cosmic, 2007 MADB 138.631

Ice tongs
Moulded ABS plastic
André Ricard Sala, 1964
Manufactured by Arce, Norda, Acinox, Olivia Ricard & Cia, Mobles 114, Barcelona
Donation, Mobles 114 Barcelona, 2023 MDB 15.775

Pink Stool
Recycled plastic
Youngmin Kang, Seoul, 2021
Loan, Side Gallery

A FLEXIBLE ORDER: "INFLATABLE" AND IBIZA'S *INSTANT CITY*

ANTONIO COBO*

"Inflatable at Ibiza," by artist Josep Ponsatí, was a work of inflatable art built in the cove of San Miquel during the 7th ICSID Congress (International Council of Societies of Industrial Design) held in Ibiza, in October of 1971. Sponsored by the ADI/FAD Industrial Design Association and plastics manufacturer Aiscondel, the project consisted of a series of 11 x 3.5 metre white PVC (polyvinyl chloride) modules inflated with helium gas. Together the modules formed a giant mobile sculpture measuring 41 metres long.

Ponsatí's creation is an excellent example of ephemeral art highly sensitive to the surrounding conditions and human interactions. Its development and morphology did not conform to a rigid plan but rather arose from "a way of behaving,"[1] substituting a preestablished design on paper for a participatory strategy which determined the action in a specific place. In this way, Ponsatí created a unique experience using simple materials with a fleeting presence, in contrast to traditional art forms.

The project was implemented within a framework of openness to movements that questioned societal norms and proposed new lifestyles. The *Inflatable* distanced itself from static art, offering an immersion in a playful and transformative experience, qualities shared with various cultural phenomena that were beginning to challenge any form of conventionalism as a response to the rigidity and superficiality of the dominant culture.

In an essay entitled "Filosofías del *underground*" (Philosophies of the Underground), published in 1977, philosopher and urban planner Luis Racionero explained the different currents of thought that came together in a movement which, starting in the 1970s, expanded throughout the West. In the introduction, Racionero establishes as a common denominator all the so-called irrational philosophies, thus named not because they are opposed to reason but because they operate "against the rationalist monopoly on the forms of knowledge".[2] This starting point can help us to understand some artistic expressions which, as in Ponsatí's case, could be perfectly structured and coherent but were not interested in the search for a defendable truth, seeking instead an experience associated with energy, vitality and pleasure.

Racionero was at the centre of another countercultural statement associated with the ICSID Congress. Along with the self-named ad hoc committee, he signed the manifesto entitled *Instant City*, which called out to students around the world to attend the conference:

> The people, the youth of the New Culture will meet in Ibiza to be together, to listen to music, to dance, and to build the space in which we will live for a few days. We ask designers from the world over to help us create the instant city that our minds will shape over those several days. In an event centered around environmental design, behavior and form can come together over a week of design, construction, music, mime, fair, festival, and improvisation.[3]

Following the unexpected success of the call, architect José Miguel Prada Poole was commissioned to devise a plan that would bring this city to life. In the words of Prada Poole, "a City of Freedom not anarchic, because the greatest freedom is always found within a superior order. Not the unique order that is typically found in the city, but an order of non-anarchic freedom."[4] In other words, a flexible order capable of giving rise to more possibilities within a preestablished horizon. An architecture transformed into a mechanism in which the architect is simply another actor who participates in its configuration. For this, the inflatable city took as its basis a general plan and grammatical form which its inhabitants had to adapt to their needs following the assembly and construction manual. This approach entailed a collaborative process that faced various technical and logistical challenges that were overcome with a stapled-joint construction system and a pyramidal learning process. It also represented a departure from established rules, proposing a new paradigm in which architecture gains more value the less durable it is: an architecture of the event, the celebration and the party, where the specific qualities of each place ultimately define the project.

1 Alexandre Cirici in *Ponsatí, el Hinchable de Ibiza*, Cultural edition of Monsanto Ibérica and Aiscondel, 1971.

2 Luis Racionero: *Filosofías del underground*, Barcelona, Kairós, 1977.

3 Luis Racionero and the *ad hoc* committee for the *Instant City*. Manifesto published in the promotional brochure for Ibiza's *Instant City*, distributed internationally.

4 José Miguel de Prada Poole: "Instant City, Changing City", *Arquitectura: Publicación Mensual del C.O.A. de Madrid*, no. 157, 1972, pp. 23-36.

Ponsatí made a social and symbolic impact through a work of art neither bought nor sold but rather experienced. Similarly, in the Prada Poole project, ownership of the architecture is not linked to the ground on which it sits. Both cases challenge the social status of the artist and the architect, developing more collaborative models open to participation of the public and the inhabitants, one in which interaction with the natural environment of the cove of Sant Miquel adds an extra dimension where nature, architecture and art uniquely come together.

The same manufacturer provided the PVC that the students needed to build the instant city. Plastic, which then was common in the manufacturing of all kinds of daily objects, symbolized the integration of material innovation with more transformative sociocultural expressions. Thus, it was particularly fitting for the type of pneumatic construction that Prada Poole wanted, a perishable material whose breakdown would serve as the temporal measure of its life span. With this, he sought a city of the future, immaterial and free of inertia: "an accumulation of foam whose bubbles had to appear and disappear according to the different needs."[5]

The recreational nature of both projects transformed them into tools for play which sought to overcome the artificial dichotomy between the principle of pleasure and the principle of need. Within this context, plastic stood out as a basic material in art and architecture due to certain unique characteristics: flexibility, resistance and lightness, ideal qualities for building modular structures that require a high adaptive capacity.

The connection between the irrational philosophies to which Luis Racionero refers and Prada Poole and Ponsatí's projects can be summed up in the idea of a break with traditional structures to open new avenues of expression and experience. Two years later, the world faced the first major energy crisis in history. The 1973 oil crisis signalled an inflection point in the global perception of energy, revealing the vulnerability of an economy dependent upon oil and spurring the search for more sustainable alternative energies and materials. Although they were built with petrochemical-based compounds, both projects anticipated the need to experiment with new materials and to find more sustainable alternatives, decreasing our consumption of resources and reducing our reliance on heavy support structures to create a more adaptable and ecological future.

5 José Miguel de Prada Poole: "La arquitectura perecedera de las pompas de jabón", *El Urogallo*, no. 27, 1974, pp. 12-19.

* Antonio Cobo is PhD in Architecture. Professor in the Department of Science, Materials and Technology of Design at the Madrid School of Design.

CITIES ARE TOO HEAVY

The *Instant City* designed by Prada Poole was the world's first ephemeral pneumatic city, a call to the imagination and an experiment in collective living that welcomed the hundreds of attendees at the 7th International Council of Societies of Industrial Design, held in Ibiza in the months of September and October 1971. Volunteers, a million staples, and thousands of square meters of polyvinyl chloride of different colors shaped a unique experiment of community life. At the same time, with the assistance of a few students Josep Ponsatí raised an inflatable mobile sculpture out of huge white plastic modules that was approximately forty meters high.

These inflatable constructions triggered research in architectural cladding such as the Ethylene Tetrafluoroethylene (ETFE) used in Barcelona's Media-Tic Building, which gives the façade a cushioned appearance with a minimum thickness, solar filter, and thermal insulation suggesting the utopia of inhabiting a bubble.

Instant City, ICSID Congress at Sant Miquel cove, Ibiza
Polyvinyl chloride plastic
José Miguel de Prada Poole, 1971

Inflatable at Ibiza
Twelve white plastic modules
Josep Ponsatí, 1971
Loan, Josep Ponsatí

Media-TIC Building

Thermoplastic polymer covering Ethylene-TetraTetraFluoroEthylene (ETFE)

Enric Ruiz Geli / Cloud 9, Barcelona, 2010

Photographs: 1. Enric Ruiz-Geli; 2. José Miguel Hernández; 3. Enric Ruiz-Geli; 4. Luis Ros; 5. Enric Ruiz-Geli; 6. José Miguel Hernández; 7. Luis Ros

PLASTIC JUSTICE: PEDAGOGY AS ACTIVIST DESIGN PRACTICE

RAÚL GOÑI FERNÁNDEZ*

Can students and teachers learn and work with the challenges that microplastics pose to our common global assets? How should we teach environmental issues to design students? Can we build learning spaces, formal and informal, for environmental activism through design? The European project Plastic Justice, a pan-European educational collaboration between five art and design academies in The Hague, Reykjavik, Barcelona, London and Vilnius, emerged in this context.

Along with several NGOs and scientists committed to the environment, the educational initiative included different outreach and activism efforts that made up the digital platform Plasticjustice.eu, focused on the long-term impact of invisible microplastics on the human body. Its objective is the creation of new knowledge through intra-academic exchange and field research to encourage education in mindful design for the next generation of designers.

This new space for learning was created as an ideal setting for activism, co-producing knowledge between professionals and students who use progressive teaching strategies, promoting social change and introducing activist practices capable of upsetting the uniformizing education system that teaches standardized skills contrary to diversity. These processes involve the transformation of material and forms, without having to pay heed to preexisting models, or use them as paradigms, thus decolonializing the academy and activating education as a self-selection process that shuns elitist trends.

Microplastics

In 2019, not much was known about microplastics. The first articles and research that appeared at the time mention the presence of microplastics in human foetuses. That these small pieces of plastic can get into our food, water and even our bloodstream is an incredibly frightening and incomprehensible prospect. This almost invisible and ubiquitous environmental problem was a powerful and highly necessary incentive for young students, researchers and new storytellers to pay more attention in the educational field. The challenge was and is immense, demanding physical presence. But can materials have a voice and agency? Can design be a vector of critical social reflection that citizens can use to communicate and protest in society?

Visual communication is a tool that transforms reality, allowing us to formulate a critique and condemnation of a given situation. It's part of the process not the end. In Plastic Justice dissemination actions were carried out to raise awareness and encourage discussion about the problem that led to specific actions.

These actions were organized in a teacher's manual through the publication *A Teachers' Guide*,[1] talks,[2] workshops,[3] an exhibition[4] of student projects and different counter-information and guerrilla actions. The actions sought to build visual tools for social debate to make the causes visible and tangible.

Power becomes the ability to do something, and design empowers, makes visible, gives voice to, enables proposals and generates controversy, giving expression to personal and group concerns. This potential body of knowledge invites us to question our epistemological certainties, to establish disturbing dialogues across differences and form a political ethics capable of creating connections and recognition.

By involving the participants in political and social struggles, we build bridges within communities and help people to process their experiences in a positive and constructive way. In doing so, the main function of activist communication allows us to mobilize and put pressure on industry, corporations, governments or any kind of institution with power to change their approach and educational policies.

A Souvenir From The Colombian Coast

An example of a student project is the one by Natalia Soto. In it, the local community collects its own raw material, microplastics, on the beaches of Santa Marta, in Colombia, transforms them and gives life to a reinterpretation of the iconic Paco Rabanne[5] dress,now handmade and created from modular pieces that form the new garment. This scalable prototype restores the ecosystem and restimulates the economy by offering the local community an employment opportunity throughout the entire production process.

1 *Plastic Justice Teachers Guide*: https://plasticjustice.eu/repository/plastic-justice-teachers-guide/
Topics covered in this downloadable guide include: activism and policy change, policy letter writing, sustainability, and student projects. Environmental issues in the art and design academy. Theory and practice: environment and design curricula. Addressing socio-political challenges in the academy.

2 https://plasticjustice.eu/repository/?material_type=video

3 https://plasticjustice.eu/repository/?tag=workshop

4 https://plasticjustice.eu/repository/plastic-justice-exhibition/

5 https://www.cultura.gob.es/mtraje/colecciones/indispensables/vestido-rabanne.html

A Souvenir From The Colombian Coast
Recycled plastic
Natalia Soto, 2022

Little lessons

Plastic Justice is therefore a reflection on alternative pedagogical systems based on a new creative paradigm that encourages evolution toward educational cooperation. It is a response to counteract the competitive educational practices of late capitalism. It is an eco-centric and creative perspective on education, in contrast to an anthropocentric definition. It is a non-reductionist way of learning, as opposed to obsolete reductionist educational models of teaching.

Materialized and shared research allows us to build thinking artifacts and question-asking machines as opposed to the notion of the auteur designer or the designer as producer tied to industry. This is one of the main lessons of Plastic Justice. The designer bound to the ego, to virtuosity, versus the mediating designer who talks to us about strategies, tactics, field studies and the shift from producer to mediator, to facilitator, and from the individual to the group.

Design is positioned as a key agent of renewal in the world. Its goal should be to materialize processes and practices that turn it into a new kind of responsive knowledge in which methodologies and methods are as important as communicating findings with conceptual, analytic and aesthetic rigor. To protest is to be a witness. Idealism is the new realism. It's time to act. It's time to take risks and make mistakes.

* Raul Goñi Fernández is interdisciplinary designer, researcher and PhD in Design from the University of Lisbon.

MICRO-PLASTICS: A HEALTH ISSUE

Non-biodegradable or non-compostable plastic residues can take between 500 and 1000 years to decompose; indeed they never disappear completely, they just become smaller and smaller. Measuring less than 5 mm, these micro-plastics are formed when larger plastic items such as pneumatic tires are degraded. Increasingly present in oceans, soil, foodstuffs, and drinkable water, they pose serious biodiversity and health problems, as they can trigger inflammatory responses in the human body and lead to illnesses. The latest studies indicate that the average weight of microplastic waste consumed by each person in the world per week is five grams, equivalent to the weight of a credit card.

A person collecting trash in Citarum River, one of the most polluted rivers in Bandung, Java, Indonesia
Photograph by Sony Herdiana

Plastic Rivers no. 6 Ganges carpet
100% recycled PET
Álvaro Catalán de Ocón (Madrid, 1975), 2021
Manufactured by GAN, Ontinyent, Valencia
Donation, GAN (Gandia Blasco Group), 2024

RIVERS OF PLASTIC

Each year, nine million tonnes of plastic waste end up in the seas and oceans. They are transported fluvially, and are concentrated in the large rivers of the world and their main affluents.

Plastic Rivers, a rug designed by Álvaro Catalán de Ocón, is a handcrafted representation of one of the most polluted and polluting rivers of the planet – the Ganges. Hand-tufted, the rug s made of 100% PET (polyethylene terephthalate) recycled plastic fibers, material that takes on new meaning and reveals the paradoxical beauty of its origins: rivers that have been transformed into garbage dumps that drag thousands of tonnes of plastic to the oceans.

SINGLE USE

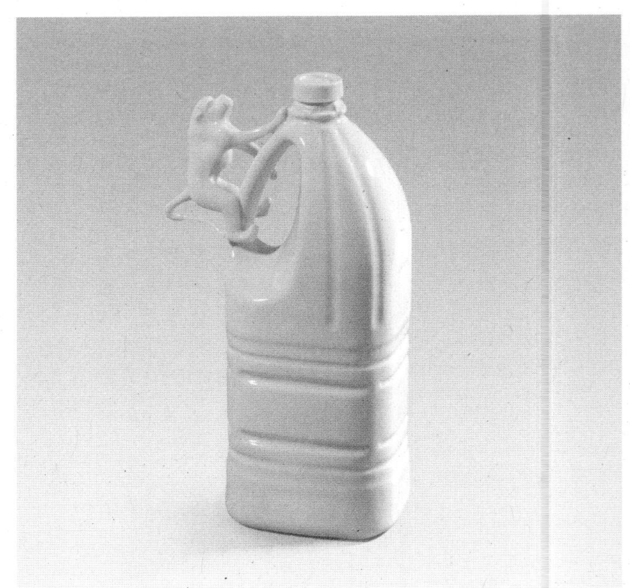

Half the amount of plastic made is designed for single-use purposes. In 2015, 380 million metric tonnes of plastic were produced; 55% of this amount was discarded, a further 25% was incinerated, and only 20% was recycled, figures that indicate high pollution rates. Between 2006 and 2020, the number of recycled plastic containers in Spain increased by 133%, and refuse deposited in disposal sites was reduced by 43%. The 2019 European Union directive concerning the impact of certain plastic products in the environment is clearly insufficient. The solution involves reducing the production of single-use plastics, improving waste management, increasing recycling and designing reusable packaging to shift from "single-use" to "multi-use".

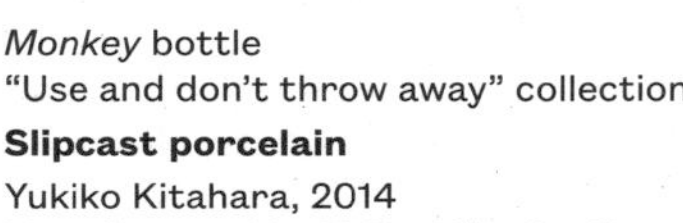

Monkey bottle
"Use and don't throw away" collection
Slipcast porcelain
Yukiko Kitahara, 2014
Manufactured by Taller Kúu, Seville
Donation, Yukiko Kitahara. Taller Kúu, 2020
MDB 12.170

Oil cruet
"Use and don't throw away" collection
Slipcast porcelain
Yukiko Kitahara, 2014
Manufactured by Taller Kúu, Seville
Donation, Yukiko Kitahara. Taller Kúu, 2020
MDB 12.171

Ramón bottle
"Use and don't throw away" collection
Slipcast porcelain
Yukiko Kitahara, 2014
Manufactured by Taller Kúu, Seville
Donation, Yukiko Kitahara. Taller Kúu, 2020
MDB 12.172

Clipper Classic lighter

Plastic, metal and stone

Enric Sardà, 1970
Manufactured by Flamagàs SA,
Llinars del Vallès

Donation, Rossend Casanova i Mandri, 2019
MDB 7.038

Agatha Ruiz de la Prada bottle

Moulded polypropylene and natural blown, lacquered and silk-screened glass

Ágatha Ruiz de la Prada, 1992
Manufactured by Perfumería Gal, Madrid

Donation, Ágatha Ruiz de la Prada, 1995
MADB 135.824

Rocky 747 pen, mechanical pencil

Moulded ABS resin

Equip de disseny Inoxcrom, 1984
Manufactured by Inoxcrom SA, Barcelona

Donation, Inoxcrom SA, 1998
MADB 136.268

Nenuco bottle. *Sage foam*

Moulded and silk-screened plastic

Albert Isern, 1984
Manufactured by Nenuco, Barcelona

Donation, Albert Isern, 2018
MDB 2.802

MENSTRUAL REVOLUTION

Half the world's population menstruates for an average of forty years and consequently consumes single-use products made of petrochemical materials such as plastic, rayon, polyester, and polypropylene, toxic and harmful both to our health and to the environment. Single-use menstrual products leave a carbon footprint that is five times higher than that of the silicone cup. Despite not being biodegradable and taking 400 years to disintegrate, silicone is an inert and hence non-toxic material and is therefore a better choice for reducing waste and environmental impact.

Leona Chalmers patented and commercialized the first menstrual cup made of rubber and latex in 1937, although its widespread usage came later, in 2002, thanks to the use of silicone that increased its lifespan to five years. *Enna Cycle* is a silicone menstrual cup and applicator designed by Ernest Perera Duran in 2016.

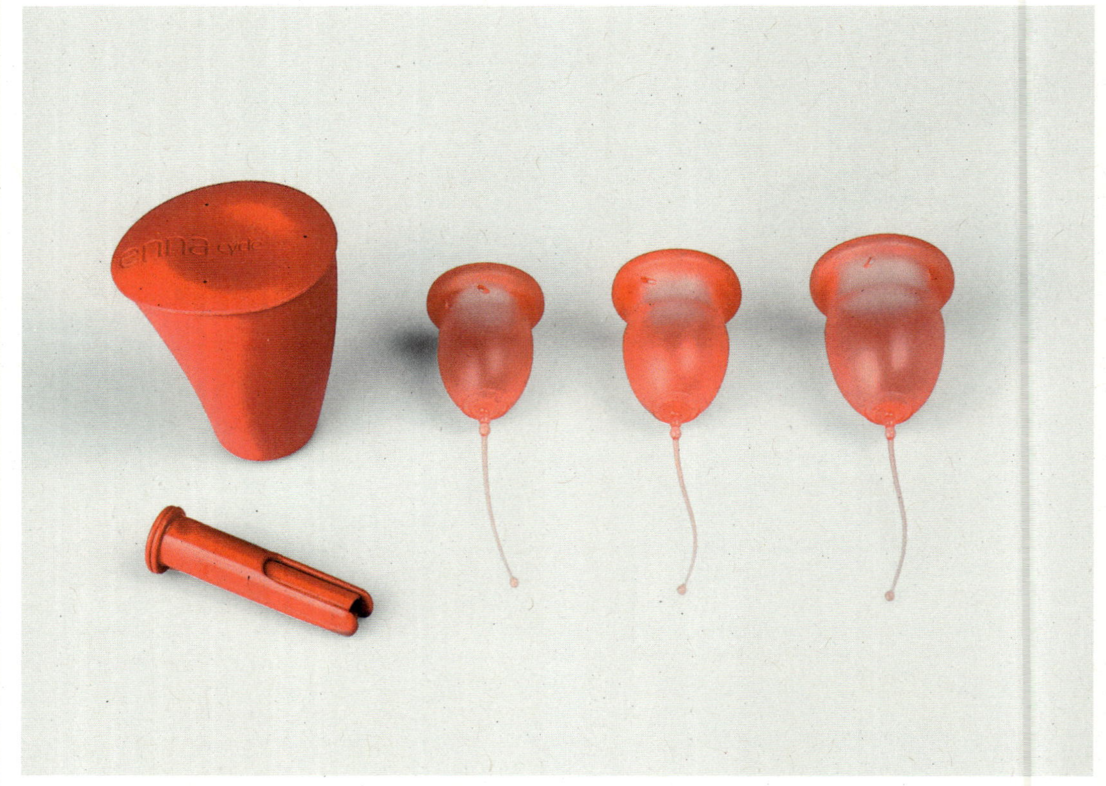

Enna Cycle menstrual cup
Moulded silicone
Ernest Perera Duran, 2016
Manufactured by EcareYou Innovation SL, Sant Cugat del Vallès
Donation, EcareYou Innovation SL through ADI-FAD, 2019 MDB 8.990

Evax pack
Flexographic plastic
Mario Eskenazi, 2012
Manufactured by Arbora & Ausonia,
Procter & Gamble, Barcelona
Donation, Mario Eskenazi, 2018 MDB 3.115

Evax Cottonlike pack
Flexographic plastic
Mario Eskenazi, 2012
Manufactured by Arbora & Ausonia,
Procter & Gamble, Barcelona
Donation, Mario Eskenazi, 2018 MDB 3.116

Evax Fina y Segura pack
Flexographic plastic
Mario Eskenazi, 2012
Manufactured by Arbora & Ausonia,
Procter & Gamble, Barcelona
Donation, Mario Eskenazi, 2018 MDB 3.111

Evax Fina y Segura Maxi sin alas pack
Flexographic plastic
Mario Eskenazi, 2012
Manufactured by Arbora & Ausonia,
Procter & Gamble, Barcelona
Donation, Mario Eskenazi, 2018 MDB 3.114

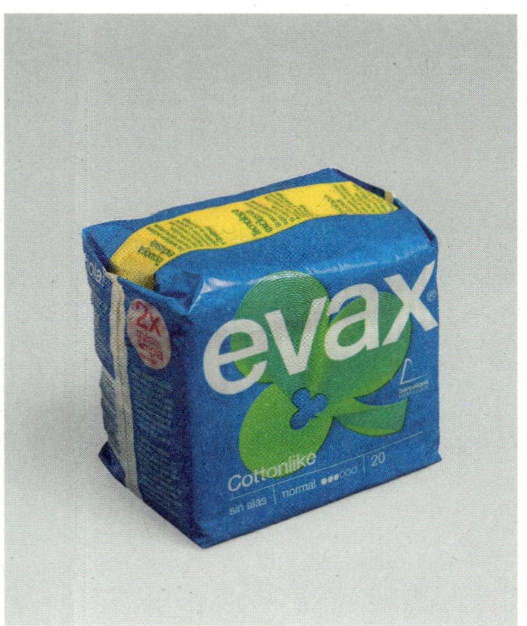

Pink chair
Polypropylene
Guillermo Santomà Bagaria, Barcelona, 2015
Loan, Guillermo Santomà Bagaria

IS THERE AN IDEAL CHAIR?

Monobloc, a lightweight stackable chair made of polypropylene, usually white in color, is considered the most ordinary of plastic chairs. Created by Henry Massonnet in 1972 , it is manufactured in one piece thanks to injection molding, a method that was very popular in the twentieth century. The chair is an example of large-scale economic design, democratic, useful, and resistant that must be valued and respected, to quote designer Martí Guixé. Guillermo Santomà, artist and designer, has reinvented Monobloc, transforming it into a unique object that expresses its petrochemical nature. Free Wheelchair Mission has supplied over 1.4 million *Monobloc* wheelchairs in ninety-five countries, as well as the Kigali Chair Project, thus giving dignity and hope to many people. The *Monobloc* chair is a symbol of global ubiquity reinterpreted in numerous ways.

Respect Cheap Furniture chair
Monobloc plastic chair from Turkey. Inscription with acrylic paint
Martí Guixé, Barcelona, 2009
Loan, Martí Guixé. Photograph by Inga Knölke

THE PITCHER GOES SO OFTEN

Water is essential for life and mankind has always had the need to transport it. Over the course of history this vital task has been performed using different materials and technologies. At first, the bottles and receptacles used to carry water were made of glass or ceramic, materials, which were useful yet heavy and fragile, making long-distance conveyance complicated and hazardous.

In the twentieth century, however, plastic revolutionized the packaging and transportation of water. Lightweight, cheap, and much more resistant to impacts than glass or ceramics, plastic allowed for large-scale mass distribution of water at much lower costs, making it much more accessible to people around the world. Plastic solved many logistical difficulties, although it also created a whole series of new problems.

Pitcher
Varnished terracotta over engobe
Barcelona, 1650–1710
Excavation, Antic Hospital de la Santa Creu, 1951 MCB 62.918

Pitcher
Incised and painted terracotta with engobe and *sgraffito*
Pablo Picasso, 1952
Manufactured by Poterie Madoura, Valauri
Donation, Pablo Picasso, 1957 MCB 64.669

Pitcher
Enamelled terracotta
Miguel Milá, 2019
Manufactured by Gómez y Gómez, Caldes de Montbui
Donation, Museu del Càntir d'Argentona, 2020 MDB 12.114

Bottle
Earthenware decorated with oxides
Albisola Superiore, Savona, 1600–1699
Old collection MCB 142.098

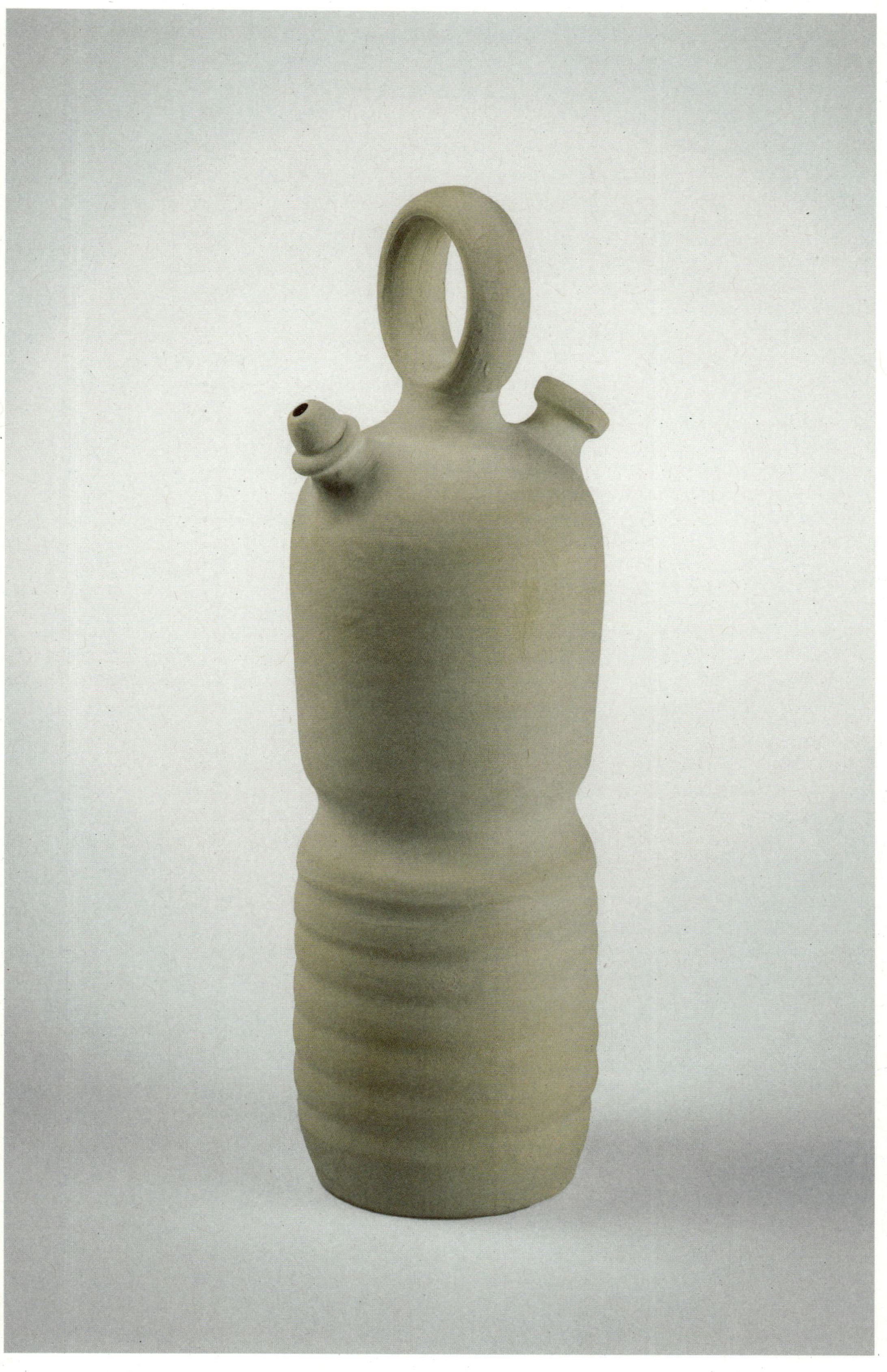

Pitcher *La siesta*
Terracotta
Héctor Serrano, Alberto Martínez and Raky Martínez, 2000
Manufactured by La Mediterránea, l'Olleria
Donation, la Mediterránea, 2006 MADB 138.560

MILLIONS OF PLASTIC BOTTLES A DAY

Nowadays, one million plastic bottles are sold per minute around the world, each one of which will take approximately 500 years to disintegrate (1000 years if not left outdoors). Every hour, over fifty-five million plastic bottles are consumed worldwide, and 1,300 million are thrown away every day, which equals almost 500,000 million per year. In order to reduce this impact we must urgently adopt more sustainable alternatives, such as reusable bottles made of stainless steel or glass, that are long-lasting and do not emit harmful chemical substances.

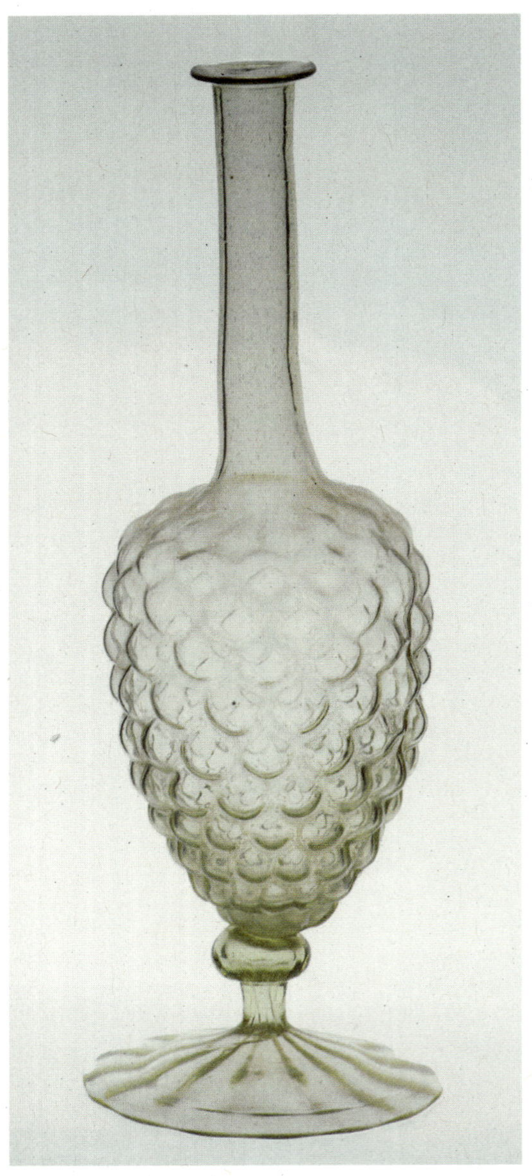

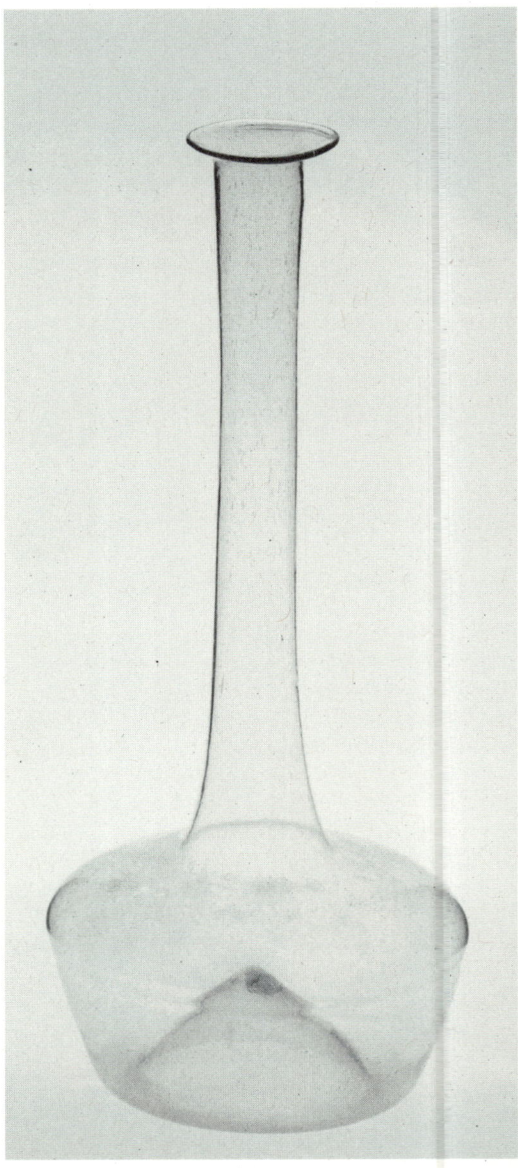

Bottle
Air-blown and pressed glass
Catalonia, 1600–1699
Purchase, 1905 MADB 23.333

Bottle
Air-blown glass
Catalonia, 1550–1650
Purchase, 1895 MADB 23.686

Bottle
Air-blown glass with lacticinium threads
Catalonia, 1700–1799
Purchase, 1932 MADB 4.940

Malavella Original bottle
Moulded glass, paper and metal cap
Lluís Morillas, 2005
Manufactured by Aigües Malavella, Caldes de Malavella
Donation, Lluís Morillas, 2018 MDB 2.323

Casa de família bottle
Moulded glass
Josep Maria Jujol i Gibert, 1912
Manufactured by BD. Ediciones de Diseño SA, BD Barcelona Design, Barcelona
Donation, BD Barcelona Design, 2020 MDB 12.541

Fuensanta bottle
Moulded glass, paper and sheet metal
Pati Núñez, 2008
Manufactured by Fuensanta, Asturias
Donation, Pati Núñez, 2022 MDB 15.330

Bottle
Air-blown glass with lacticinium threads
Catalonia, 1700–1799
Purchase, 1895 MADB 23.672

Vilajuïga bottle
Moulded glass, paper and sheet metal
MOS. More on simplicity, 2018
Manufactured by Aigües Minerals de Vilajuïga SA
Donation, MOS. More on simplicity through ADI-FAD, 2021 MDB 14.163

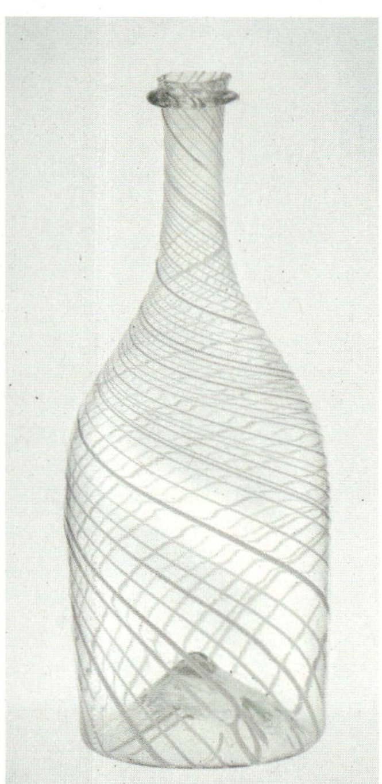

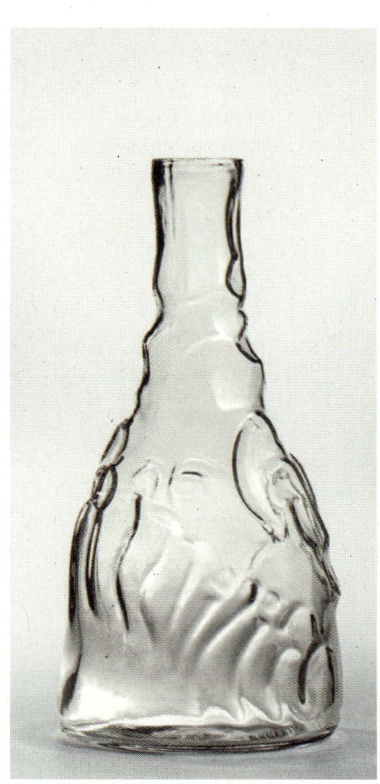

DREAMING OF A SUSTAINABLE FUTURE

RAMÓN ÚBEDA*

Take a journey through time. Go back to the 1980s, when design in this country was experiencing its boom and designers could do whatever they wanted, without having to worry about the consequences. Nobody had explained to them yet that what they were doing then, could have a direct influence on the world that we live in today. I'm not referring to what the twisting of the legs of a stool, for example, might have meant. I'm talking about how they were made, and this is true for everything manufactured during that time, when our industrial and material culture was as immature as our environmental awareness. Someone from outside had to come along and tell us it was insane to cut down a tree to make a chair. That someone was Phillipe Starck, but no one paid much attention to him.

Far removed from the world of design, in a village in the province of Tarragona called Móra d'Ebre, somebody else thought the same way, although in a less glamorous sector. The family of Silio Cardona, a chemical engineer, owned a coffin factory. They made them from wood, as was the tradition in our culture. Silio Cardona also didn't like that a tree had to be felled to make a coffin, much less that such high-quality material would end up rotting beneath the ground. This led him to invent an alternative material from an agricultural derivative: a simple almond shell, the inert material that is discarded after the edible fruit has been removed. This waste material also contains lignin and cellulose, the two basic components of trees.

He could have used another nut like a walnut or hazelnut, even olive pits, because the foundation was the same. But he chose almonds because Spain is the leading almond exporter in the European Union and in the Tarragona region of Catalonia there were factories devoted exclusively to husking tons of these nuts. Heaps of almond shells littered the landscape, with no purpose other than to be burned for heat. Silio was determined to find another use for them. In 1980 began experimenting with the possibilities offered by moulding a paste made from the shells, previously crushed and turned into powder, mixed with resins. For more than a decade, he developed and perfected the technology needed to solidify the paste by applying pressure and temperature.

The resulting composite had the appearance and properties of natural wood, as well as the manufacturing advantages of moulded plastic materials. It was like a plastic wood that could be used to manufacture any coffin industrially, no matter how many mouldings and filigrees it had. Silio called the new material Maderón, a name that was impossible to translate, although this wasn't an obstacle to arousing everyone's interest when we wanted to introduce it in the design sector. The advantages of using Maderón, apart from ecological, were financial. In 1994, Alberto Lievore redesigned his iconic Rothko chair, originally manufactured by Indartu, using this material, reducing costs by 50%.

The new technology offered unbeatable advantages in terms of time and production capacity compared to traditional woodworking. We created the publishing company Gauhaus to make the Batlló chair and the Calvet mirror designed by Antoni Gaudí affordable, while simultaneously meeting requests from designers and companies from all over the world, including Starck, who had finally found a way to create "wooden" chairs without having to sacrifice a tree. We began to work specifically with two models, Miss C.O.C.O and Cameleon, designed by the renowned Italian brands Cassina and Driade, respectively. All these projects came to a halt suddenly when, in October of 1997, Silio Cardona unexpectedly died in a traffic accident.

Plastic wood and vice versa

He was a unique individual, a member of a local rock-and-roll band and on the board of Pompas Fúnebres Europeas, who didn't consider himself an inventor. He said all he'd done was concoct an *allioli* in the right proportion. The problem was he did it all himself and when we tried to continue without him, the chairs broke. He'd taken the secret of his formula with him to the grave and along with it, a dream that could have a paved a new way towards sustainability came to an end. Luckily, things were already changing and trees were beginning to feel more secure when in the nineties, the Forest Stewardship Council, better known by its initials FSC, was created. A non-governmental, independent and international forest certification system, it was established to identify responsibly manufactured wood-based products.

Like the ones made by Andreu World, the first company in the world to have 100% of its catalogue with an FSC seal, the maximum level and in full. These aren't just occasional pieces manufactured for appearance's sake, as other companies that engage in ecological posturing, also known as greenwashing, often do. Even today, just a few manufacturers use exclusively wood resulting from reforestation and forest audits, from the tree to the final product, through the Chain-of-Custody of the Societé Générale de Surveillance (SGS). This is why Starck, who hadn't worked for a Spanish company since making his debut with the now defunct company Disform during the ebullient 1980s, wanted to pair up with the Valencia company to make at last, wooden seats and tables without feeling guilty about it.

Meanwhile, over the last few decades, all sorts of new materials produced from natural resources have appeared. They include animal leather substitutes made from banana crop waste, like Banofi, and from pineapple, specifically from the cellulose fibre extracted from its leaves, like Piñatex, created in the United Kingdom by the Asturian Carem Hijosa; and fabrics made from hemp waste, like LOVR by Revoltech, which, although it might appear to be new, isn't. The use of hemp fibres to make ship sails dates to the 5th century BC. In the 20th century, synthetic fibres began to replace hemp, among other reasons because the prohibition on marijuana affected the latter's cultivation in industrialized countries. Nor are corn-based bioplastics new. There are many more examples that inspire optimism. And yet the reality is it's very difficult to bring them to the market, not only because of the trials they must pass, but because of all the requirements that manufacturers demand from suppliers.

Plastic is fantastic, Ross Lovegrove said when in 2000, we designed for BD Barcelona, the first furniture collection made with rotationally moulded polyethylene to appear on the market, while the ubiquitous Starck was creating his own collection with Kartell. Since then, we've witnessed industrial plastic production grow exponentially. Greenpeace estimates that today the amount is close to 400 million tons per year. Beverage companies alone produce, also annually, 500 billion single-use polyester bottles (PET). A good chunk of it ends up in our oceans. We're aware of the problem but we continue needing plastic because there isn't another material to replace it. The alternative is to reuse it or reinvent it.

To minimize plastic's environmental impact, we must recycle more. Andreu World, again, has set an example with the development of proprietary materials. In addition, all its products are made from a thermopolymer called Pure ECO®, which is 100% recycled, not a small percentage as in most cases, and is 100% recyclable at the end of its life cycle. For upholstery, they have their own fabric, Circular ONE®, made from thread manufactured with packaging and fish net waste found among marine rubbish. In the fashion world, Ecoalf was a pioneer in introducing the upcycling of this type of waste, a practice which thanks to their efforts and that of a few others, is now common in other sectors such as the automobile industry and has a solid base of suppliers through such actions as the Seaqual initiative.

And what doesn't exist can be invented. The same determination that led the ingenious Silio Cardona to obtain a wood-based derivative that could be moulded like plastic allowed Andreu World to create a new natural thermopolymer that doesn't come from fossil fuels and is biodegradable, like wood. Another dream. The Nuez Lounge BIO® armchair, designed by Patricia Urquiola, is a world first. Its biological base is derived from fermentation processes through living microorganisms and it doesn't leave any waste because its remains can return as nutrients to nature through composting. These are just two examples of the past and the present that invite us to dream of a more sustainable future.

* Ramón Úbeda is designer, curator, journalist and sustainability consultant.

THE MYSTERY OF ALMONDS

Maderón is an innovative ecological material based on nut husks (almond shells), created in the nineties by Silio Cardona, and developed in collaboration with Ramón Úbeda. Made of lignin and cellulose, the shells are mixed with resins to obtain a malleable paste that has the properties of natural wood and is biodegradable. *Maderón* can be painted, varnished and shaped into complex forms, and is ideal for reproducing items of Art Nouveau furniture like the *Calvet* mirror and the *Batlló* chair by Antoni Gaudí, or the *Rothko* chair by Alberto Lievore. Its use allows the manufacturing of a wide range of products with no need to cut down trees. Unfortunately, however, the formula that made it possible disappeared with the death of its inventor, leaving a legacy of potential ecological applications in contemporary design interrupted, which is now being revived by innovative creations such as the *Nuez Lounge Bio*™ armchair.

Gauhaus. Handcrafted gilding of the *Calvet* mirror designed by Antoni Gaudí in 1900
Manufactured with *Maderón* for Gauhaus in 1996
Photograph by Jordi Cuxart

Nuez Lounge BIO® armchair
Thermo-polymer BIO® shell
Patricia Urquiola, 2021
Manufactured by Andreu World, Alaquàs
Donation, Andreu World 2025

Rothko chair

Lacquered *Maderón*

Alberto Liévore, 1989

Manufactured by Indartu (Simeyco), Guipuzcoa

Donation, Indartu (Simeyco), 1995 MADB 135.898

AFTER THE PARTY

The boom of plastic production since the fifties was a party of possibilities and boundless impacts. It is now time to come up with sustainable alternatives. Bio-sequins – biodegradable sequins made of nanocellulose derived from wood, plant dyes and gold leaf – keep the party spirit alive without affecting the environment. Makeat studio transforms food waste into functional bio-designs, offering creative alternatives to objects like bowls and dishes which are difficult to recycle and are transformed into innovative three-dimensional materials that release us from our dependency on plastic, paving the way for more sustainable partying.

Bio-sequins
Fanni Stafford, 2024
Johanna Naukkarinen / Fanni Stafford

Alternative headband
Bio-sequins (NFC, vegetable dye), cotton wool, mercerized cotton thread, Murano glass pearls, plastic headband, silk thread, organza and silk taffeta. Embroidery
Fanni Stafford, Finland, 2024
Loan, Fanni Stafford

Biond coasters
Food waste from the culinary sector: coffee, orange, eggshell and mussels
Makeat, Barcelona, 2024
Loan, Makeat

Wicked Hope dress
Silk chiffon dress embroidered with plastic sequins and braided patent leather buttons
Ángel Vilda, Barcelona, 2005
Donation, Ángel Vilda, 2014 MTIB 4.172/14

2

P

MATTE

ANT

NEW CRAFTS

The concept of craftsmanship or manual creation is opposed to that of industrial labor. Not until the late nineteenth century did the convergence between artisans, artists, and designers favor the development of an avant-garde and experimental craftsmanship, based on the expression of ideas and attitudes that challenged its own history and the social imaginary, in search of a new paradigm.

Leandro Cano's dress has been created using the knowledge that Pedro and Enrique Blanco have of the eleventh-century carpet-making technique, made of a fiber found in the leaves of agaves in Almería.

The legacy of artist and milliner María Mazás has taken the wide-brimmed straw hats worn by day laborers to the category of sculpture, produced by Eliurpi manufacturers. Contemporary creation is also a story of collaboration and the transmission of knowledge between master craftsmen and designers.

Boater hat
Braided straw and cotton ribbon bow
Cristóbal Balenciaga, 1940–1949
Manufactured by EISA, Madrid
Donation, Asociación Española de Productoras de Fibras Químicas, 1981 MTIB 109.945

Sculptural Head Object
Straw, wood, silk sinamay. Mixed technique
Elisabet Urpí Ràfols and Nacho Umpiérrez Fripp, 2022
Photograph by Nacho Umpiérrez Fripp DDA / ELIURPI
Loan, ELIURPI, 2024

Luto dress, *Corrida Collection*
Esparto grass
Leandro Cano, Jaén, 2018
Loan, Leandro Cano Luque

6 H_2O + 6 CO_2 + LIGHT. PHOTOSYNTHESIS: PAST, PRESENT AND FUTURE

CLARA GUASCH*

1. Transisting

Energy transition, from fossil fuels to renewable sources, and the digitization of life, entail intensive use of the periodic table. The metallization of our society is a new limit we have overstepped. We are heading towards exerting maximum pressure on planetary limits in the pursuit of the remaining mineral and fossil resources in the ground to avoid having to change anything.

The idea of finitude does not sit well with us. We do not like physical limits on technological development, as exponential as it is biased and unequal. But our environment, in the state in which we know it, is finite, even though we act as if this fact did not affect us. Then who does it concern? Those that come after us? We agree that the sustainability of human life on the planet consists of meeting our current needs without compromising the needs of future generations. Let's take a moment to see what we mean by this.

For one, exergy, energy, distortion. Increasingly more energy is needed to obtain a unit of precious fossil material to satisfy our insatiable desire for energy. More energy is needed to obtain some of the elements in mobile phones, circuit boards, batteries, servers, and the multitude of technological derivatives that seek to occupy more and more space and mediate life in its entirety. So, increasingly we need more energy to obtain the same amount of energy... to be able to continue, in turn, consuming more and more energy. This deceptive game has environmental, economic and social consequences on an interplanetary scale, not to mention the anthropological impact.

Fossils. Minerals. Both belong to a geologic time that is not ours. It is not time on a human scale. It is Greek *chronus*. It exceeds us on all sides. With the use of fossil fuels in materials for new technologies, as well as in old infrastructure, we are confronted with a physical limit and a significant energy impact. We continue to live in a paradox of Promethean dimensions. Continuing to dig for fuel is not an option. Renewable transition without a drastic reduction in energy consumption also is not viable. Efficiency becomes a deceptive mantra, and the paradox of economist and philosopher William Stanley Jevons (1865) is more relevant than ever: the greater the efficiency with which a resource is used, the more we consume it and the sooner we reach the point where we have exhausted it and face the consequences we hoped to avoid through increased efficiency.

2. Photosynthesize

Photosynthesis means something like composition triggered by light. The Greeks always got it right. Photosynthesis is the mechanism that generates and multiplies organic plant matter throughout the planet, and along with it breathing. The future needs a lot of photosynthesis to grow.

Luckily, the most unalloyed and rare vital resource on the planet is its vast biodiversity. Our gravest sin is neglecting this rarity. Biodiversity is heavy. Biomass is its weight. It is the sum of all life together, including us. If we group biomass by taxonomic categories according to its estimated weight, as Yinon M. Bar-On, Rob Phillips and Ron Milo have done in *The Biomass Distribution on Earth*,[1] we see the predominant place of the categories which photosynthesize, especially plants, but also algae and bacteria. Along with them, fungi that coexist in an ongoing exchange of fluids and goods care for us from the subsoil. Creative interdependencies.

Plants are skilful producers of cellulose, as are some bacteria. Of all the polymers, cellulose is the most abundant, the most enveloping and the most present. Cellulose is part of everything: food, celluloid, paper, wood and cotton, for example. Or what amounts to the same thing: the kitchen, the cinema, a book, a house, a table, music and a coat. Even windowpanes contain transparent cellulose. A renewable house. Everything renewable.

To sustain our life on the planet we need more natural photosynthesis. It is another paradox to have to think of synthetic photosynthesis to subsist on a planet where plants have the greatest importance.

Renewable materials depend critically on photosynthesis. And all serve as CO_2 reservoirs, either temporary or permanent, depending on what we do with them.

3. Cultivate

Our material future on this planet depends greatly on renewable materials. Not only because of their renewability but the systemic services they provide as part of the biosphere we inhabit. Agriculture, forestry and other cultures contribute an inventory of different materials capable of satisfying many of our needs provided they are viewed as regenerative cultures.

Regenerative agriculture is within our reach to recover soils and preserve interdependencies. We need to leave behind the tunnel vision of industrial monoculture agriculture and appreciate farming for what it is, i.e., culture. There is no culture without diversity. If there is no diversity only one result is possible: to end up inevitably languishing until we die out. Single-crop farming represents a way of thinking limited to a single thought. The Jevons paradox can also be applied to thought.

1 Yinon M. Bar-On, Rob Phillips and Ron Milo: *The Biomass Distribution on Earth*, Proceedings of the National Academy of Sciences of the United States of America, PNAS, 2017.

Plant-based cellulosic fibres are of critical importance in the catalogue of renewable materials for a resilient future. From wood to hemp, cellulose fibres are an inexhaustible pantry of materials in different formats with an infinity of applications. Specifically, cotton, which is basically cellulose, is a versatile fibre with unique properties scorned nowadays in favour of other, apparently more sophisticated manufactured fibres such as polyesters.

Between 45 degrees north and 35 degrees south, cotton is a crop that involves more 300 million people around the world. It is abundant, and more than 25 million tons are produced every year, in addition to other coproducts such as vegetable oil. However, the returns that cotton generates are not evenly distributed.

Out of an annual global fibre production of 105 million tons, wool (an animal-based renewable fibre) represents 2 million tons, often underused because of the gradual dismantling of this industry; polyester, in contrast, represents upwards of 65 million tons. In total, 15 kilograms of fibre per person are produced annually if we add up all the varieties, renewable and non-renewable. Today, the latter carry more weight. Ancient, cherished and easy to process both manually and industrially, cotton has been spurned for decades. It is reviled for consuming water in large quantities and generating emissions in its cultivation, as well as for contaminating the soil with fertilizers and pesticides. It is also blamed for serious human rights violations. Yet it is not the fibre but the agricultural model that is exploitative. The so-called *conventional* model based on maximum *performance* at the lowest cost ignores the externalities associated with the activity and pays little attention to the systemic impact. The same fibre can be grown respecting planetary limits and human rights, even if this is not yet the norm in most cases. For the *opposing* polyester industry, there is an incentive to call attention to and magnify figures that are easy-to-remember because of their impact yet difficult to understood without their full context. We have seen them repeated *ad nauseum* (in the form of the t-shirt) and very infrequently contrasted with reality, which is highly varied and complex regarding textile materials and their derivative products. Polyester has gradually usurped the place cotton used to occupy as a preferential fibre, diverting our attention conveniently towards recycling. Recycling is important in an economy that seeks to prolong the life of material resources, but fibre-to-fibre recycling does not exist, only bottle (plastic) to fibre, which interrupts an already established chain (from bottle to bottle). Additionally, recycling should never be the first option. We need to promote the reuse of resources already in circulation as envisioned in the hierarchy of waste. Until the progression proposed in this hierarchy is adopted, recycling is just another way of not changing anything at all.

All in all, cotton has very important initiatives in place regarding better farming practices. These initiatives seek to reduce the negative effects associated with single-crop farming and a bad economic model that fails to account for human beings, does not value the common goods its uses, and does not assume the cost of the externalities it generates.

Cellular agriculture lab-grown cotton remains. Perhaps this new type of farming is a complementary solution to prevent the loss of the material diversity we need, allowing for industrial scaling, without touching the ground, producing only when necessary, or farming in areas where it is not possible to do so now, in urban settings, for example. And yet, Jevons' shadow looms over any technology that holds out the promise of a solution.

* Clara Guasch is consultant in sustainability, materials and innovation. Professor in Elisava's Master in Design through New Materials.

FAIR FASHION TRADE

Avoiding the accumulation of unnecessary clothes and only purchasing garments produced ethically and sustainably is to practice fair trade in the field of fashion. The best options among fabrics of plant origin are linen, hemp, and organic cotton. Linen, that has been used since the year 7000 BC, is outstanding for its durability. Hemp, which has similar properties to those of linen, grows quickly without needing too much water or pesticides, thereby improving quality of soil. In its turn, organic cotton, free of chemicals, needs less water than conventional cotton and enforces ethical labor practices. The "organic" stamp promotes sustainable fashion with less environmental impact and better working conditions.

Espadrilles
Esparto grass sole and hemp fabric
Carmela Rodríguez, 1995
Manufactured by La Manual Alpargatera, Barcelona
Donation, Carmela Rodríguez, 2021 MDB 14.057

<
Vest with backpack.
Dones Mula Collection

Cotó Roig organic cotton (Catalonia) and ribbons

Miriam Ponsa, Manresa, 2014

Donation, Miriam Ponsa, 2024

Coptic textile from a shawl

Linen taffeta with wool tapestry decoration

Egypt, 650–850

Purchase, 1918 MTIB 37.682

Coptic textile

Linen taffeta with wool tapestry decoration

Egypt, 400–499

Purchase, 1913 MTIB 32.879

Coptic textile from a shawl

Linen taffeta with wool tapestry decoration

Egypt, 300–499

Purchase, 1918 MTIB 37.708

Armchair

Oak wood and braided twine

GATCPAC, Grup d'Arquitectes i Tècnics Catalans per al Progrés de l'Arquitectura Contemporània, 1936-1937
Manufactured by MIDVA (Mobles i Decoració de la Vivenda Actual), Mobles 114, Barcelona

Donation, Mobles 114 Barcelona, 2014 MADB 138.936

CORDAGE: ROPE AND RUSH

The earliest evidence of rope making was found in Neandertal archeological sites and dates back 50,000 years. Before industrialization, workers in Southern Europe only had simple pieces of furniture made of pinewood, olive wood or cypress wood, and cordage seats made of rope or rushes. In Majorca, the roper trade was still common in the fifties, before the rural exodus and mass production marginalized the craft. A few master craftsmen continue to keep the tradition alive working with materials like pita, raffia, wicker, and hemp. Contemporary design studios like 2monos and Studio Jaia have retaken and innovated the craft with new colors and geometric patterns.

Puput stool
European oak and cord (90% cotton and 10% recycled PET)
Studio Jaia, 2020
Manufactured by Studio Jaia, Mallorca
Donation, Studio Jaia, 2024 MDB 17.087

Chair
Turned pine wood and cattail seat
1915–1936
Manufactured by Silleros, SCCL, Catalonia
Purchase, 1994 MADB 135.386

Shibui stool
Metal rod and hand-woven pita (agave) cordage
2monos (Nicoletta Mantoan and Alejandro Dumon), 2019
Manufactured by 2monos, Mallorca
Donation, 2monos. Nicoletta Mantoan and Alejandro Dumon, 2024 MDB 17.085

WOOD FROM THE COLONIES

MÓNICA PIERA MIQUEL*

"Ehe veracht als gemacht" (It's easier to criticize than to create) was the maxim that cabinetmaker Ulrich Baumgartner wrote in the most secret recess of his remarkable *Pommerscher Kunstschrank* (Pomeranian Art Cabinet). Built for Phillip II, Duke of Pomerania-Stettin in Augsburg, from 1611 to 1617, the cabinet was the result of a complex team effort. Designed according to an ambitious iconographic plan, its drawers contained objects that exemplified the knowledge European civilization had acquired up to then. The *Wunderkammer* (wonder chamber) housed a magnificent collection of delicate tools, precision instruments that demonstrated the ability to apply scientific advances, materials from abroad transformed into works of art, games and crafted pieces using surprising techniques. Of course, ebony was the wood chosen for the cabinet's structure, combined with silver, hard stones, rock crystal, marble, enamel and paint, among other beautiful things.

The German cabinetmaker's words reflect the pride of a wood craftsman who viewed himself as belonging to a more elite professional category than a carpenter, one who was an expert in using high-quality wood to embellish furniture intended for a luxury market, which demanded knowledge, innovation and beauty in equal parts.

Ebanista, *ébéniste*, *ebenista*, cabinetmaker, *Küstler* are words that appeared in the 17th century to identify specialists who worked in the main artistic centres of Europe and used wood from the colonies and other refined materials in their pieces. This fresh style of decoration developed alongside intercontinental trade that offered new and surprising materials. From the very start, the high cost of quality wood required inventing a new construction method to take maximum advantage of the material. Thus, while the frames continued to be made from local trees, they were hidden beneath glued coverings of imported wood. Therefore, in the language of the modern age, to speak of cabinetmaking is to speak of veneers not solid wood.

In Spanish, the word for cabinetmaker is *ebanista*, which comes from the word *ébano* (ebony), a hardwood in the genus *Diospyros*. Black, metallic bright, heavy, finely textured and of high quality, it had been imported since antiquity to Europe from Africa for small objects. In the modern period, the Portuguese brought it from Asia and Africa while other ebony species visually akin to the genus *Dalbergia* were brought to Spain from Santo Domingo, Cuba and Puerto Rico.

"Who will say, or can count the beats of the instruments that resounded ceaselessly at the same time in the mountains of Cuenca, Toledo, in many mountain ranges of America and in the Pyrenees mountain chain."[1] The construction of the monastery and palace of San Lorenzo El Escorial was a milestone in the use of wood from the colonies. To build the sprawling residence required felling scores of pine trees, fruit trees, walnut trees, white poplars, black poplars, ash trees, and oaks, extracted from forests in many different parts of the Iberian Peninsula. However, "not long after the woodworking tasks were underway, perhaps due to insufficient drying time, it became clear that much of the wood being used rotted quickly. This led to speculation over the possibility of using wood from the vast American forests which, because of their hardness and near indestructibility, promised better results."[2]

Thus, from 1575-1595, different types of wood from the Viceroyalty of New Spain were brought in large quantities and for the first time to Europe, demonstrating their outstanding benefits, far superior to those of local species, and making possible highly innovative construction methods. Mahogany, acana, cedar, terebinth and ebony, which were not easy to transport, were brought by sea to the Port of Seville and then by land to the worksite. Furthermore, *angeli*, or wood from chinaberry trees, from eastern India and sent from Lisbon, was also used. The quality of these species and their exquisite execution is apparent today in the impeccable state of preservation of the library cabinets, the drawers in the sacristy and the choir stalls at the monastery.

Of course, the planet's natural riches are not distributed equally. Europe is small and poor in terms of resources, consolidating its power and interests through innovation, discovery and conquest. In the case of trees, experience passed down through generations made possible taking advantage of available species at any given time. Roots, fruits, leaves, bark and of course, wood have all been used in perfumes, medicine, food, herbal tea, cork and raw materials to produce objects that make our lives easier. For many centuries, wood has been an essential resource because of its characteristics: a material hard enough to withstand weight and much easier to work with than stone. In fact, until the development of grey iron in the 19th century, wood was the basic material used for buildings, bridges, machinery, means of transport, weapons, and furniture. As a result, demand for it was constant and massive, while the sources from which it was obtained were limited.

Contact with other continents introduced vast territories with a diversity of high-potential resources. While silver and gold were the most prized materials, the biological diversity of the trees in tropical and equinoctial forests meant that wood was not far behind. For, in addition to representing more raw material, wood from these trees enabled transforming everyday objects into artistic items made with materials and techniques that had never been seen before.

1 Baltasar Porreño: *Dichos y hechos del señor Rey Don Felipe Segundo el Prudente, potentísimo y glorioso Monarca de las Españas, y de las Indias*, Madrid, 1663, p. 120.

2 María Paz Aguiló: *Orden y decoro. Felipe II y el amueblamiento del Monasterio de El Escorial*, Madrid, CV FII, p. 12.

The European powers set in motion the machinery to secure their possession and beat the competition. It was not only about controlling resource exploitation and trade but knowing how to sell the products at luxury prices to balance the books. *Swietenia* (mahogany) and different *Dalbergia* species like rosewood, *Dalbergia frutescens*, Brazilian kingwood, and *Guaiacum* (lignum vitae) became a desired raw material, especially with the appropriation of indigenous people's knowledge to take advantage of these resources, which were expensive to obtain and transport.

In the 17th century, other countries began to compete with Spain and Portugal in the race to dominate the world and extract hitherto unknown natural goods and manufactured products. Holland, France and England founded the East and West Indian companies to supply a European market, now extensive, interested in consuming quality goods. Just as important as wood was lacquer, made from the sap of *Rhus vernicifera*, a tree cultivated in the East. In the 16th century, the first objects made from this fascinating resource arrived in Europe. The result of the overlaying of "layers of light," lacquer is hard, water-resistant, and to Westerners' surprise, dries quickly despite high humidity.

Consumers of luxury products insisted on technical expertise, ingenuity and aesthetic refinement, as these high-end goods indicated their social and cultural status. The best wood craftsmen vied with each other to meet these needs with veneers, marquetry and lacquers in constantly changing types and forms. Imported wood was therefore the answer to the scarcity of European wood, after centuries of overharvesting, but also the beginning of a global problem caused by an exponential growth in demand.

Starting in the 19th century, industrialization, demographic growth and an increase in the quality of life among the European middle class only added to the untamed and abusive exploitation of ecosystems, without regard to their fragility. Now, in the 21st century, not only must we acknowledge quantitative and qualitative decreases of species but also deforestation, which requires taking drastic measures and foregoing the most prized wood. Since 1973, the Convention on International Trade in Endangered Species of Wild Fauna and Flora (CITES) has protected endangered species by regulating trade. Keeping in mind this harsh and dire reality, the only viable way to stop the exploitation of forests is a strategic plan at the international level that fights for their sustainable use. We have begun to reverse the situation but greater social awareness is still needed.

At the same time, it is essential that we reuse what is already built or at least take advantage of preexisting components. This alternative is the only way to reduce consumption of natural resources, time and energy. We are so irrational that we shed tears over the felling of a tree yet refuse to own furniture made from its wood. The paradox is, while we are aware of the problem, day after day we destroy objects fashioned out of these treasured wood species – mahogany, rosewood, palo santo, cedar, ebony – usually for purely aesthetic reasons. A good example is the many solid mahogany and rosewood Isabelina style chair sets and tables in perfectly good condition that go unsold due to lack of demand. The reality is we fill our mouths with beautiful words like sustainability, yet we are the only ones in the history of humanity to disdain inherited objects, including the last pieces of furniture that could be made from wood species from the colonies that are now protected.

* Mónica Piera Miquel is PhD in Art History. President of the Associació d'Amics de l'Estudi del Moble (Association of Friends for the Study of Furniture).

WOOD FROM OVERSEAS. COLONIAL DEFORESTATION

For colonial traders in the sixteenth and seventeenth centuries, cypress, mahogany, rosewood, jacaranda, and ebony were the most coveted types of wood; the latter was highly valued as its sheets of intense black are the ideal for inlaying copper, pewter, bone, ivory, and tortoiseshell. The term "ebonist", derived from ebony, first appeared in the eighteenth century to distinguish it from carpenter. The extensive use of ebony and other exotic wood species contributed to the deforestation of the Antilles and of other tropical regions with serious consequences for biodiversity and for local populations. The sustainability of its exploitation is a crucial challenge for guaranteeing the availability of a valuable resource without endangering the ecosystems it comes from.

Desk
Ebony and cabinetwork, embossed silver, mirror, ivory on the handles and iron hinges
Belgium, *c.* 1650
Acquisition, Museu de les Arts Decoratives, 1931 MADB 8.433

Box
Pressed bamboo, lacquer, red and gold pigment
Japan, 1848–1868
Donation, Carme Artigas Alart, 1935 MADB 13.901

Dresser
Mahogany wood, pine core and mirror
Catalonia, 1780–1810
Purchase, 2009 MADB 138.676

Sentada chair
Laminated sycamore wood and stainless-steel tubing
Enric Miralles i Carme Pinós, 1988
Manufactured by Artespaña, Madrid
Donation, Artespaña, 1994 MADB 135.530

Armchair

Cut rosewood, ebony and *tipuana*. Upholstered in silk damask

Catalonia, 1850–1860

Donation, Joan Coma-Cros, 1970 MADB 106.348

Calvet coat rack
Cut and turned oak, iron band
Antoni Gaudí, 1899–1901
Manufactured by Taller Casas i Bardés, Barcelona
Loan, Cátedra Gaudí, 2018 CGEX0022

Press it! Sandwich maker
Hornbeam wood
Ernest Perera Duran, Amor de Madre, 2008
Manufactured by Serra Quintana, Vilanova i la Geltrú
Donation, Sociedad Mercantil Estatal de Acción Cultural SA, 2017 MDB 1.449

TURNED WOOD

The lathe dates back from approximately the year 1000 BC. Over the centuries, it has evolved to encompass today's lathes operated with Computer Numerical Control (CNC). In the fourteenth century, the abundance of wood in the Guilleries Catalan mountain region began to favor turnery work. Between 1965 and 1990, towns like Torelló or Sant Hilari Sacalm experienced their own industrial revolution thanks to the production of the decorative wood known as black gold that would have a huge economic impact. During the industrialization process, woodturning contributed to the transformation of the textile industry. Despite competition and changes in demand, the woodturning industry shifted its focus to furniture manufacturing, and to the creation of toys and decorative objects in order to restore its standards of quality and creativity.

The 7 Deadly Sins cup
Oak, aluminum and silicone
Iñaki Remiro & Adrià Guiu, 2013
Manufactured by Mugaritz, Guipuzcoa
Donation, Sociedad Mercantil Estatal de Acción Cultural SA, 2017 MDB 1.481

RATTAN, OR FANTASY WOVEN BY FASCINATION AND POWER

ROSSEND CASANOVA*

The Peacock Chair is the type of furniture piece that stands out for its seductive nature. Visually powerful, it exudes an influential personality. It is the exact opposite of the conventional chair – the one we use every day, that we don't pay attention to – exhibiting an unusual extravagance thanks to its almost sculptural structural exuberance. Today considered an iconic piece, one of its great virtues is how it was able to carve a place for itself in society and in the history of furniture without having a creator or manufacturer on record. In fact, the Peacock chair owes its existence to the experienced and callused hands of anonymous craftsmen. Also unknown are the different companies that have distributed these chairs around the world.

The chair generally features an hourglass-shaped drum base. Its design is mostly tribal and not very Western-looking. The armrests suggest a relaxed and restful use. But its true peculiarity is the backrest, which often towers above the head in the shape of a fan or an unfurled peacock's tail – hence its name. Due to this magisterial and disproportionate shape, the Peacock chair has acquired the status of a ceremonial seat of honour. Consequently, the person sitting in one does not do so casually but out of a desire to be noticed. For this reason, when displaying its seductive power, the chair focuses its charm on its occupant with artful ostentation, imbued with vanity.

Traditionally, its basic material is rattan, both for the structural and fastening parts. Rattan is a natural climbing plant, sustainably grown, that grows faster than most tropical wood species. It is flexible, conducive to the fashioning of complex, rounded shapes difficult to achieve with other materials. Rattan is also light and can be moved easily. It comes in various shades, a characteristic that offers different chromatic possibilities. And it is very sturdy, and therefore durable.

As a plant material it has features that make the Peacock chair a cozy and comfortable object, as rattan allows for an open structure that contributes to its breathability. Aside from the necessary verticality, its curve is an identifying feature, as well as its visible assembly, with intertwined fibres holding the structural pieces together. All these factors contributed to making it ideal for use in tropical, warm and humid places, far from the bourgeois European establishment and its stately furniture. Oddly enough, and despite its suitability for outdoor space, when the chair was introduced to the West in the early 20th century, it entered homes as an uncommon and fascinating object, quickly assuming its place in our visual culture. The Peacock chair is neither heavy nor bright, nor is it upholstered. While not opulent, its lavishness derives from the simplicity, transparency and docility of subdued nature.

George A. Malcolm, Associate Justice of the Philippine Supreme Court, seated on a Peacock Chair. Picture probably taken in Los Angeles, in 1926.

The Rattan Road

It seems impossible that such a chair, one that conveys enormous strength and is so enthralling because of its woven fantasy, has such a tragic and obscure origin dating back to the colonization of the Philippines, in Southeast Asia. In 1521, Ferdinand Magellan conquered the territory on behalf of Spain and, three centuries later, following the Spanish-American War of 1898, it became a subject of the United States, until its independence in 1946. Rattan grew abundantly and was used to manufacture furniture and other everyday utensils. The Peacock chair was born under North American colonial rule at Bilibid prison, in Manila, where prisoners made and weaved them as part of a rehabilitation programme. The reintegration programme was a source of local pride and eventually was used to organize visits to the prison as if it were a tourist attraction. Many North American tourists visiting the island went to the prison and bought the chairs, which they sent home as a souvenir, perhaps suggesting a

This 1968 poster shows Huey P. Newton seated on a Peacock chair. The text bellow reads: "The racist dog policemen must withdraw immediately from our communities, cease their wanton murder and brutality and torture of black people, or face the wrath of the armed people."

fictitious splendour from the islands. Thus, a constant trickle of chairs filled North American homes during the first quarter of the 20th century.

One of the oldest images of the chair is from 1914. Its title is revealing: *Jail Bird in a Peacock Chair*. It shows a mother seated on a chair holding her child in her arms. Convicted of murder, the woman was serving time for killing her husband who, apparently, made chairs like the she is sitting in.

Decades after ornamenting homes, the use of the Peacock chair waned though never disappeared. As an iconic furniture piece for the summer, it gained popular momentum during the 1970s and became a symbol of the Black Power movement in the United States when Huey P. Newton, co-founder of the Black Panther Party, had his picture taken in one with a spear in one hand and a rifle in the other. At the time, during the civil rights struggle, this empowering image transformed him into a leader seated on a throne, as if he were Black royalty. The message was not lost on many Afro-Americans, who unhesitatingly incorporated the Peacock chair into their homes. As a result, it became part of the decorative aesthetics of Black culture and an identifying symbol of Black identity, simultaneously evoking the traumatic experience of the Black diaspora. The Peacock chair also gained popularity in those years due to its appearance in the media, movies, magazines, posters, and even on album covers. As an accessory that revealed personality, it matched perfectly with the enigmatic, daring and sensual people who had themselves photographed sitting in it. Iconic actresses such as Elizabeth Taylor, Marilyn Monroe, Katharine Hepburn, Diana Ross and Donna Summer, even president John F. Kennedy, were photographed sitting in a Peacock chair, images which transcended borders. This role model was quickly incorporated into the European imagination, which adopted the Peacock chair as a symbol of modernity. In the movie *Emmanuelle*

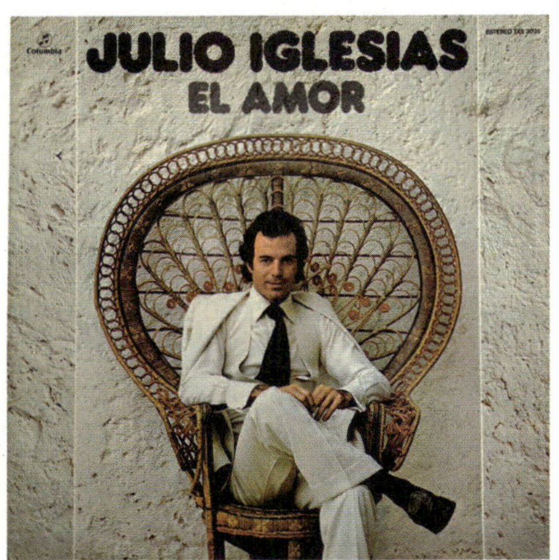

Album cover of the record *El amor* by Julio Iglesias. Discos Columbia SA, Madrid, 1976

Emmanuelle
Photochrom
Columbia Pictures, 1974

(1973), Sylvia Kristel, sitting in one, is the embodiment of eroticism, an image that was burned onto the public's retina. Julio Iglesias posed in a Peacock chair for the cover of his album *El amor* (1976), as did James Brown for *The Original Disco Man* (1979). Its evocative quality has persisted with other noteworthy examples, from Dolly Parton to Cher, who recently appeared in a Peacock chair for an advertising campaign.

Like the material touched by Tarzan

Even today, the Peacock chair connects us to a particular place and moment in time. A product of colonialism, its plant material, wild and domesticated, evokes the African forest as well. While originating in Asian, this material is reminiscent of wicker, or raffia, traditionally used to make baskets in Africa. And it is in Africa where the adventures of young Greystoke – or Tarzan (1912) – take place. Like apes, he moves through the jungle at great speed swinging from vines. So, while not the same material, rattan reminds us of other plant substances that are long and flexible, such as reeds or bamboo.

In the 1960s, the chair's shape was also adapted to the rise of plastic, when furniture made of fiberglass yarn became popular. Innovative traditionally based designs were manufactured in the United States (attributed to designer Russel Woodard) and Europe, where they were made with backrests of variable heights. These filled many hotels on the Mediterranean coast and the Canary Islands, as well as many entertainment venues where they can still be seen.

And because everything is cyclical, a few years ago, the Peacock chair and other rattan furniture pieces (made of reeds as well) were used to decorate relaxed contemporary atmospheres and environments with boho aesthetics that evoke a nomadic, free and hippy lifestyle of the past. An excellent example is the Valencia company Expormim, whose products include natural rattan pieces designed by Miguel Milá, Jaime Hayón, Mario Ruiz, Benedetta Tagliabue, Oscar Tusquets and the studio MUT Design, all part of the Design Museum of Barcelona-DHub's collection.

Even though today the chair hearkens back to that past and we view it as vintage, the truth is that the Peacock chair inspired new furniture pieces, authentic sequels to the original. Designer Patricia Urquiola offers two examples: the Crinoline armchair (2008), made by B&B Italia, also part of the museum's collection, woven with plant-based horsehair but with a backrest that evokes a peacock's tail; and more recently, the Pavo Real (Peacock) chair (2011), unmistakably named, made by Driade out of synthetic rattan (polyethylene).

Thus, what was a colonial product became a countercultural symbol, a frame of reference for messages of empowerment, and an icon of such cultural importance that its evocative capacity has not diminished over the years. More than 100 years later, the "material-object" pairing lives on.

* Rossend Casanova is PhD in Art History and conservator at the Museu del Disseny de Barcelona (DHub).

THE *PEACOCK CHAIR*: THE MOST SENSUOUS OF SEATS

The *Peacock Chair*, made of rattan, was invented in Bilibid Prison in Manila, where it was woven by Filipino inmates during the United States occupation of the colony. The first known image of the chair dates back to 1914 and shows a prisoner and her son, seated. The chair represented presumed modernization of the colony and attained maximum prominence in the seventies, first as a photograph on the covers of music albums. In 1967 the Black Panthers made it a symbol of Black Power and resistance. After having appeared in the film *Emmanuelle*, the chair would be associated with female sensuality and eroticism. Today, designer Patricia Urquiola and architect Benedetta Tagliabue revisit the chair.

Pepe sofa
Rattan, pith, steel and plastic
Benedetta Tagliabue – EMBT, 2013
Manufactured by Expormim, Valencia
Donation, Expormim, 2018 MDB 3.060

Crinoline armchair
Seat and backrest with braided aluminum frame with natural fibre twine and polyethylene cushion
Patricia Urquiola, 2008
Manufactured by B&B Italia in Novedrate, Milan
Donation, B&B, 2022 MDB 14.447

HEMP: FROM MANILA TO PRIORAT

Manila hemp (abaca) is one of the strongest known fibers. Used in the paper industry and also in the making of hats, carpets, clothes, and furniture, abaca fibers are traditionally woven in the Philippines into highly resistant fabrics.

The main countries producing this raw matter worldwide are Philippines and Ecuador, where working conditions are precarious. Consequently, the *Cesta* lamp designed by Miguel Milà and first made out of Manila hemp in 1962 is now made out of local cherrywood. Designer Joan Vellvé uses local hemp from the Priorat region to create rugged works, at once rigid and delicate, and standardized electrical accessories, all characterized by imaginative, artistic and local craftsmanship.

Casitas Margarida brochure
Ink on paper
Ribas and Creus, *c.* 1970
Indústries Gràfiques Francisco Casamajó, Barcelona
Donation, Ramon Ribas i Pere Creus, 2014 GAGB 9.694/14

Riuet floor lamp
Sant Joan de La Vilella Baixa cane, Priorat
Joan Vellvé Rafecas, 2021
Manufactured by Joan Vellvé Rafecas, Barcelona
Donation, Joan Vellvé Rafecas, 2024 MDB 17.108

Wilson mirror
Natural rattan and mirror
Marc Morro, 2019
Manufactured by TRENAT, Valencia
Loan, TRENAT

Cesta table lamp
Manila cane and polypropylene globe
Miguel Milá, 1962
Manufactured by Tramo, DAE, Polinax, Santa & Cole, Ediciones de Diseño, Barcelona
Donation, Xavier Larrea Cruces, 1994 MADB 135.398

WE CAN'T SEE THE TREES FOR THE FOREST
A SHORT ESSAY ABOUT THE FUTURE OF RELATIONSHIPS

CRIS NOGUER*

7 October 2023: the most brutal genocide in recent history begins. For some, Israel wants to reclaim the Promised Land; for others this is an assault to gain control of Palestine's oil and natural gas reserves.[1]

War atrocities occur in many places and in general, are connected to the exploitation of useful natural resources that generate the energy needed to produce the imaginative spectrum of objects that surround us: diamonds, metals, rare metals, oil, gas, fertile soil, water and wood.[2]

Being able to see beyond the object and drawing a line between land, material and thing is not something obvious and in everyday life there are no spaces to reflect on it.

Where is the cotton that fills up all the clothing stores farmed? Where is the oil extracted from that we need to produce all the plastic and textile products we use every day? What is the social and environmental impact of the extraction of metals to produce electronic devices? Which sandbanks are destroyed to obtain the raw material for cement, the basis of all modern construction? What is obliterated to procure the wood used to make numerous objects and in construction?

When we stop and follow the chain of processes, we arrive at places where violence against human and non-human lives prevails, a violence in *frictioned* territories where transnational complexity turns nature into spoils,[3] a violence that perpetuates the colonial model and is still justified and normalized in the name of money, progress and freedom.

Over and over, we hear from different points of view that resources are limited and that the Earth is finite. In the prevailing neoliberal logic, power is and will be held by those who control natural resources. This control remains primarily in the hands of agents of the global North, who extract and exploit the riches of the global South. In his book *Limits*, Giorgios Kallis explains his opposition to this idea, stating that "the science of modern economics was founded on the myth of an eternal dearth that calls for perpetual growth."

It is interesting to note Kallis' suggestion that the economy, not ecology, feeds off the idea of dearth and that lack of resources is necessary for the economy to continue functioning. This an economic system that feeds off the continuous search for novelty: new artifacts and new technologies, all in the name of efficiency, more investment and strategies that lead to a new push to exceed the threshold. In this way the longing for a more prosperous future in the dominant regions is preserved.

Progress:
m. The act of moving forward.

Longing:
1 To yearn or vehemently crave to achieve something.
2 In disuse.Laboured breathing.

But what happens if we move forward but stop yearning? Maybe we will find a way of engaging with the land and objects from a horizontal place without hierarchy, without a desire to rule.

We are now in Barcelona:

We breath peacefully
We look around
We observe
We listen attentively,
hearing the place

We are surrounded by young forests that cover a vast area and are highly vulnerable to wildfires. The reason for this fragility is the disappearance of an economic connection to the ecosystem of pine, oak and holm oak trees. These forests are not wild, as in the pre-agricultural era, but are the consequence of the relationship between humans and nature. They are socio-natural forests.[4]

In Barcelona's Montnegre micro-region, research is being conducted on whether ancestral and traditional knowledge of the area[5] is a good road map for recovering activities beneficial to low-growth species, improving the wealth of the forest and avoiding wildfires. To this end, close relationships are being established with local economies that highlight the region's biology. First, the value of local wood from dead trees or trees felled to facilitate the growth of others is now being emphasized. The quality of the wood from these trees is poor, containing woodworms and fungi, as well as being irregularly shaped, and generally this wood becomes biomass. Yet, on a closer look, it becomes apparent that what is considered "poor quality" reflects the industry's biased perception, one in search of a homogeneous wood for the industrialization of resources. Quality takes on a new meaning, however, when this parameter is set aside. Pine cones, birds, resin, mycelia, mammals, infestations, weeds, branches, rocks, mud, bark, bacteria, invasive species, moss, etc. all become part of a quality and vital ecosystem in a lush landscape.

1 UNCTAD: *The Economic Costs of the Israeli Occupation for the Palestinian People: The Unrealized Oil and Natural Gas Potential*, 2019. https://unctad.org/system/files/official-document/gdsapp2019d1_en.pdf Más información en: https://www.offshore-technology.com/projects/gaza-marine-gas-field/.

2 UN: *Conflict and natural resources*. https://peacekeeping.un.org/en/conflict-and-natural-resources.

3 Anna Lowenhaupt Tsing: *Friction. An ethnography of global connection*, Princeton, Princeton University Press, 2005.

4 Anna Lowenhaupt Tsing, *op. cit.*

5 TEK means *Traditional Ecological Knowledge*, or ancestral traditional knowledge. Julia Watson: *Lo-TEK Design by Radical Indigenism*, Colonia, Taschen, 2020.

Meanwhile, in the city we're surrounded by mountains of materials purposely burned every day. These are materials that once were a symbol of progress: tropical wood from species now in danger of extinction;[6] technological artifacts manufactured with rare metals; clothing; household appliances; and an entire ecosystem of seemingly inert objects – all once fleetingly and profoundly necessary.

If I immerse myself in the forest and the city, I sense the abundance that Kallis is talking about. I feel how we live in exorbitant affluence and how at the same time, we want more.

Kallis suggests this when he states that "until we accept the world as abundant, we won't be able to behold the limitations of our longing and the delimitations of a safe space for our freedom."[7]

Jane Bennett, in her book *Vibrant Matter*, explores a similar idea. She proposes engaging in dialogue with everything inert and non-human and seeing ourselves as another element in an ecosystem that is in constant movement, one in which our ability to do and to be, and the ability of the woodworm and a household appliance to do and to be, are on the same plane. Bennet defines and explains how "vital materialists" compared to environmentalists are the ones engaged in a dialogue with the Earth and who live *like* the planet, not *on* it, and thus "pay more attention to their own abilities and limitations as materials."[8]

Sensing that everyone and everything are material compositions, the author asks herself how we can be more receptive to the activities, feelings and effects of non-humans. Looking for ways of relating to each other, searching for bonds and generating new ecologies, she proposes new relationships, interconnections and networks between what is human and what is non-human, what is alive and what is inert.

> Can we imagine a culture of objects free of violence?
>
> Can we progress without longing?
>
> Can we feel the capacity to be and to do of everything that is non-human and inert?
>
> Can we accept territorial abundance and regional wealth?
>
> Can we rethink aesthetics and redefine the condition of quality of what surrounds us?

Perhaps then we would be able to understand that violence is not necessary, that it is not natural but rather cultural. That we can move forward through care, community and regeneration instead of destruction.

Author and paediatrician Michel Odent approaches the idea of understanding the source of human violence from an interesting perspective. After studying the evolution of civilizations through the mother-child relationship, Odent reaches the conclusion that civilizations have systematically created rituals to disrupt the initial relationship between mother and newborn. These rituals, Odent notes, "seek to obtain violent beings, ones capable of defending the social group in which they are born."[9] According to the author, as a result, a peaceful civilization tends to disappear.

6 Convention on International Trade in Endangered Species of Wild Fauna and Flora.

7 Giorgos Kallis: *Limits: Why Malthus Was Wrong and Why Environmentalists Should Care*, Stanford University Press, 2019.

8 Jane Bennett: *Vibrant Matter: A Political Ecology of Things*, Durham, Duke University Press, 2010.

9 Michel Odent: *Le bébé est un mammifère*, Paris, Editions L'Instant Présent, 2014.

For Odent, this violence is the cause of the current climate crisis, where humans fail to recognize Mother Earth as their own mother. In his opinion, a revolution focused on the new genesis of an ecological human is necessary to reverse this situation. A revolution that starts by tending to the relationship between baby and mother.

In the context of the *Matter Matters* exhibition, I suggest we radically alter how we think, changing everything around us and freeing it from violence. We need a collective imagination for children that creates a bond and fuses with Mother Earth, with what is human and non-human, with what is alive and inert.

I thus have re-signified the Delta stool from 1964, designed by Jordi Vilanova. This multi-function piece turns into two small children's chairs, adapted to their height, a table, and ultimately into a stool for an adult. A radical piece at the time, it is made of wood from a pine species common in Catalonia and consists of simple shapes.

The exhibited piece consists of four surfaces, with an experimental quality for children, made with holm oak bark, cork, pine tree bark and pine tree wood from the Montnegre area, thanks to the forest organization Singular Wood.

The proposal seeks to dethrone and de-hierarchize the child, to create a space for play that becomes part of the ecosystem at ground level, a space for pleasure enjoyed with the mother while exploring what is inert.

The four pieces are the material representation of the reedited stool in 32 x 32 x 32 cm format, and are presented on a pallet of recovered mahogany.

Montnegre, 2017
Photograph by Jordi Miquel Riera

* Cris Noguer is independent designer and researcher. Lecturer in the Master's Degree in Design Research at BAU, Barcelona.

DISSIDENT MATTER

Young forests are vulnerable to fires, plagues, and hydric stress, and need to establish connections to abolish the separation between human beings and nature. We are nature.

The Singular Wood cooperative in the Catalan region of Montnegre, and researcher Cris Noguer value local wood over and above biomass, taking advantage of trees that have either fallen or have been cut down. Cris Noguer creates unique imperfect works out of wood that has holes and fungi and is therefore rejected by traditional industry. In his works, Jordi Vilanova, a pioneering industrial designer in Spain, combines the functionality of the Mediterranean with Scandinavian simplicity. Noguer revisits the Delta stool designed by Vilanova, incorporating a post-natural, post-human perspective that highlights the connections with the transformative living matter produced locally of a singular and dissident beauty.

Stool
Wood
Cris Noguer Guardiola, 2024
Donation, Cris Noguer Guardiola, 2024 MDB 17.088

Stool
Wood and cork
Cris Noguer Guardiola, 2024
Donation, Cris Noguer Guardiola, 2024 MDB 17.089

Delta stool
Pine
Jordi Vilanova i Bosch, 1964
Manufactured by Jordi Vilanova SA, Isist Leather Bcn, Barcelona
Donation, Jordi Vilanova SA, 1994 MADB 135.66

Coat rack

Steamed beech and iron

Manufactured by Hijos de Ventura Feliu (attributed), Valencia, 1924

Acquisition, Museu de les Arts Decoratives, 1998
MADB 136.279

Rocking chair

Steamed beech and wickerwork

Manufactured by Hijos de Ventura Feliu, Valencia, *c.* 1916

Donation, Fundació Joan Brossa, 2012
MADB 138.848

In the late nineteenth century, the heating of wood allowed it to be bent and maintain its *magical* newly curved shaped. The production and consumption of items of furniture made of curved beechwood spread across Europe thanks to companies such as the one founded by Michael Thonet, and the firm set up by the Kohn brothers, Jacob and Josef. In Spain, Valencian manufacturers led a production that in Barcelona, and, by extension, throughout Catalonia, enjoyed great success in well-to-do families and in popular coffee houses. Today the magic of curves is valued once again, this time in imported rattan wood, and prestigious designers are revamping a traditional product.

Bed
Steamed beech, pine and iron
Unknown manufacturer, Valencia, *c.* 1900
Donation, Moragas-Spà family, 2018 MDB 3.070

WOOD URBANISM. FROM MOLECULAR TO TERRITORY

DANIEL IBAÑEZ ET AL.*

From small-scale thermal properties to large-scale forestry, territorial, and carbon cycle issues, wood has latent propensities not well addressed in the current discourse on wood construction. Through a range of design research formats, from material testing to in-situ documentation to speculative urban projects, this book articulates and illustrates future architectural and ecological potentials of wood. From under-considered thermal properties to emerging manufacturing possibilities to forestry regimes to larger ecosystem and carbon cycle dynamics, wood is uniquely positioned for ecological urbanization in the twenty-first century yet remains inadequately characterized in architecture, landscape architecture, and urbanism. As the unique material properties of wood operate at multiple, simultaneous spatial and temporal scales, so should the discussions surrounding wood's role as a critical material for design today. This text is a synthesis of a book[1] that brings into conversation scholars and practitioners who focus on wood from a range of perspectives, from the working forest to the mid-rise building to the cell itself. The aim is to examine the implications and potentials of wood urbanism, drawing particular focus to the complex relationships between land-use, wood production, and wood construction. While relying on the inherent intelligence and depth of multiple disciplines, a more totalizing thermodynamic perspective on the role of wood in contemporary buildings, urbanization, and territories is needed: from the imperceptibly small to the confoundingly large.

"Wood Urbanism" is a concept that focuses on the intricate relationship between timber and urban development, exploring the profound impact of wood across multiple scales – from the molecular level to vast territorial landscapes. The concept is unveiled in six aspects, each addressing a distinct aspect of timber construction and its broader implications. By examining the unique characteristics of different wood species, their role in carbon sequestration, thermal properties, and ecological contributions, the book presents a comprehensive transcalar perspective. Additionally, it highlights the socio-political dimensions of wood and its potential to transform urban environments through sustainable practices. "Wood Urbanism" ultimately articulates a vision for the future where wood plays a pivotal role in creating sustainable, resilient, and ecologically integrated urban spaces.

1. Species

Different species of wood, their unique character according to their place and behavior in the forest & its use value in material, implement & value. Disregarding the material's diversity is to ignore the complex landscape entanglements, and unique strengths and opportunities it provides. Instead of following the current trend of mass plantation and harvesting of a single species to cater to the timber demand, the variety must be increased to promote biodiversity in the forests they are sourced from. This, combined with sustainable forest management strategies can be used to maintain a good balance in the natural ecology while also promoting the ecological services provided by the forest to create a sustainable built environment. This poses challenges that require new research and tests for undervalued species but will promote biodiversity and reliance on regional sources. It will also require a change in policy and educational level, to empower architects to make the specifications according to the species' availability in the region, and the structural and aesthetic requirements.

2. Carbon

Trees sequester carbon in their lifetime, absorbing carbon from the atmosphere and storing it in their mass until it burns or decomposes when the carbon is released back into the environment. 50% of wood's dry weight is carbon. Clear cutting forests for timber usage without replantation is not carbon negative. So, again echoes the importance of sustainable forest management strategies and maintaining the balance between taking from and giving back to nature. Selective harvesting of trees allows more space and resources to the surrounding trees – the extraction of locked carbon in the cut tree allows higher sequestration of carbon by growth of healthier trees. Forests have the potential to remove and store a significant amount of the excess CO_2 now in the atmosphere, and therefore play a significant role in our planet's ability to regulate warming and carbon emissions.

3. Thermal

Wood is an anisotropic material, with varying characteristics in different axes. Thermal talks about the latent thermal and hygrothermal properties of wood -- through the relationship of conductivity to specific heat, effusivity and density. It connects with other aspects of the Wood Urbanism concept when we stop seeing the thermal property of wood in isolation; the carbon cycle of buildings is affected by the thermal capacities of a timber building. Other than the thermal properties of wood as a construction material, Thermal also addresses its use as biomass for heating and cooling purposes. The byproducts generated from construction waste can be used for such purposes, minimizing waste and ensuring the complete use, reuse and recycling of all products which in the end go back to nature.

1 "Wood Urbanism – From Molecular to Territorial" is a project of Daniel Ibañez, Kiel Moe and Jane Hutton developed at the Energy and Environments Lab at Harvard University GSD, published by Actar Publishers, Barcelona/New York, 2018. Book synthesis by Disha Arora and Santwana Malakar, MAEBB 23 (IAAC).

4. Ecology

Ecology in Wood Urbanism addresses the social and biophysical complexity of wood production landscapes. The ecosystemic services that forests provide go beyond just the production of a single commodity – local wood. Understanding these services (provisioning, regulating, cultural services and supporting services for biodiversity) as complex and globally significant also makes it a strong basis for marketing within green capitalism. The socio-nature perspective of forest is also highlighted as social practices of human inhabitation in forests.

Looking at forests through the lens of two contrasting paradigms of "exploitation" and "pure nature" creates a division between humans and nature. Instead, incorporating indigenous people and their knowledge in managed rural forests and plantations could be a better approach. The concept of secondary forests as a balance between the two paradigms can be applied in different scales – as peri urban forests providing ecosystemic service and as a green public space in cities to promote biodiversity and connection with nature.

5. Urbanism

"Urbanism" talks about the city as an object vs. city as a process. There are climate benefits of sequestering atmospheric carbon within long-lived timber products – the different components of the cities like timber buildings as well as open spaces can act as carbon sinks. For example, delaying carbon emissions reduces cumulative climatic energy input, buys time for adaptation of both natural and man-made systems, reduces the possibility of reaching dangerous climate 'tipping points', and increases the potential for permanent storage through future technologies such as carbon capture and storage. Taking the idea of secondary forests and designing interactive green spaces as carbon plantations can be incorporated in urban reforms and making cities dual natured.

6. Metabolism

Metabolism talks about the city being a metabolic system – *how cities need a permanent flow of energy and material to perform their daily functions*. The entire book, about seeing wood in transcalar level and understanding its importance in different phases, can be understood as a metabolic process itself. The inputs from forests are the wood products and other ecosystem services fueling the construction and other activities in the city and finally the outputs again going back to nature, completing the circularity. The ecological interdependencies between neighborhoods, parks and cities are also highlighted – *looking at wood as a material flow deeply embedded in the socio-ecological metabolism of cities*. It also addresses the circularity of the material, from the woods to the wood through contexts of different scales and perspectives.

In conclusion, "Wood Urbanism" provides a comprehensive examination of the multifaceted role of timber in contemporary and future urban environments. By exploring wood from its molecular properties to its territorial implications, the text emphasizes the importance of understanding the unique characteristics and ecological contributions of various wood species, advocating for sustainable forest management to enhance biodiversity. It also underscores the crucial role of wood in carbon sequestration, highlighting sustainable harvesting practices and the potential of forests to mitigate climate change. Additionally, the thermal properties of wood and its potential for complete lifecycle utilization are discussed, promoting a holistic view of wood's environmental impact. The ecological and socio-political dimensions of wood production landscapes are examined, advocating for the integration of indigenous knowledge and managed rural forests to balance exploitation and conservation. Furthermore, the concept of urbanism is redefined through the lens of wood, suggesting that timber buildings and green spaces can serve as urban carbon sinks. Finally, the metabolic perspective of cities is presented, emphasizing the circular flow of wood as a material deeply embedded in the socio-ecological metabolism of urban systems. Overall, the concept Wood Urbanism articulates the architectural and ecological potential of wood, advocating for a sustainable and interconnected approach to urban development.

* Daniel Ibañez is PhD in Architecture. Director of the IAAC (Institute for Advanced Architecture of Catalonia).

García Márquez Library
SUMA, 2022
Photograph by Pol Viladoms

THE CONCRETE OF THE FUTURE?

The concrete industry generates up to 8% of the world's carbon dioxide (CO_2) emissions. Cross-laminated timber (CLT) has emerged as a transformative solution for sustainable construction. Made out of layers of solid-sawn lumber, this material has the same structural resistance as concrete, but its carbon footprint is much smaller.

Notable examples of the new technique include the headquarters of La Borda housing cooperative designed by LaCol architectural cooperative which, thanks to CLT, has reduced CO_2 emissions by 65%, and Barcelona's García Márquez Public Library, designed by Suma Arquitectura, a building five times lighter thanks to the use of this material instead of concrete. The Institute for Advanced Architecture of Catalonia (IAAC) has set up Valldaura Labs, a research center that explores innovative solutions in CLT, which is destined to become a key construction material to combat climate change.

La Borda
Lacol SCCL, 2018
Photograph by Lluc Miralles

The Voxel, a quarantine cabin
Cross-laminated timber (CLT) structure
Valldaura Labs, IAAC, 2020
Photograph by Adrià Goula

FROM CORK TO BUILDING

Every ten years, the cork oak has its bark – i.e. cork – trimmed, without any harm to the tree. The process, that could be described as a haircut, contributes to the preservation of Mediterranean silvo-pastoral landscapes, inhabited by people who depend on cork and are engaged in extensive cattle breeding and forest management, thereby avoiding rural depopulation. Cork is thermal insulating, hypo-allergenic, and naturally resistant to mildew, bacteria, and insects. Thanks to its ecological advantages, it offers a unique experience, which is why it is used in sustainable designs. Madrid's Reggio School by Andrés Jaque / Office for Political Innovation has a thermally insulated casing made of 14.2 cm of dense cork, that reduces heating requirements by 50%. The casing, that accumulates organic matter, becomes a habitat for fungi and other forms of life, demonstrating the potential of cork in ecological and sustainable construction.

Reggio School
Andrés Jaque / Office for Political Innovation, Madrid, 2022
Photograph by José Hevia

3

AN
MATTE

WARMING HOMES AND BODIES

Wool has the ideal natural properties to warm our bodies and our homes. The wavy structure of wool's fibers (crimp) and its texture, forming millions of small bends that trap in dry air, help keep body temperature stable.

The *10k House* project by TAKK architectural office to renovate a small apartment in Barcelona on a very low budget upgrades the idea of housing with new uses and environmental awareness in the face of the energy crisis and climate change, choosing layouts based on thermal gradients that maximize energy efficiency. The variety of materials is reduced to the minimum, and Catalan wood and natural lambswool are prioritized. The construction system is independent and dry assembly techniques enable plans to be performed, in part, by unskilled workers.

Bathing suit
Alpaca wool knitwear
Jantzen, United States of America, 1928–1930
Donation, Pere Sans Llopart, 2016 MDB 765

>
TAKK 10K House
TAKK, Barcelona, 2023
Photograph by José Hevia

WOOL AS ACTANT: EXPLORING THE PERFORMATIVITY OF MATTER IN THE CREATIVE PROCESS

PILAR CORTADA*

Serra de Collserola Natural Park, which occupies around 8,000 hectares in the metropolitan area of Barcelona, is an extensive green zone of immense ecological and social value that faces daunting challenges due to increasing demographic pressure and the intensive ways in which visitors use the park. Despite the efforts of different public institutions to mitigate this impact and promote conservation practices, merely providing information has proven insufficient to bring about significant changes in visitors' behaviour. In response to this situation, Fundació Eina has launched the initiative Lab Collserola, a platform dedicated to the research, production and dissemination of innovative methodologies not only to mitigate the abovementioned impact, but also to transform the community's interaction with this green space. It does so by establishing emotional connections with Collserola through artistic and design projects that motivate people to adopt proactive behaviours to protect and preserve the park.

Tornen les esquelles, led by artists Ana Vivero and Martina Manyà, is one of the projects that hopes to recover and revalue the use of wool as a raw material by exploring new applications, with the aim of creating a potential resource in rural areas and promoting ecological practices that benefit the natural environment. The initiative addresses the environmental, cultural and economic unsustainability caused by the disappearance of shepherding and transhumance in Collserola. Additionally, it establishes synergies with other initiatives that use art to reclaim rural areas as a physical and cultural space that offers alternatives for life and co-existence, like the para-institution INLAND-Campo Adentro, founded by Fernando García-Dory, and the initiative "La lana de Collserola no se tira" (Collserola wool isn't thrown away), promoted by the Larre collective.

The project focuses on questioning the conventional and reductionist notion of creativity, traditionally based on the exceptional nature of human beings. In contrast, we see creativity as an emerging phenomenon in an ecosystem of complex interactions, which includes not only humans but also extends to other entities, materials, technologies and natural and built resources. Consequently, we share a vision of situated, relational and distributed creativity, focused more on the reciprocal interaction between the individual and their surroundings than on the creation of decontextualized representations.

We began our work by trying to understand the interconnections of wool with different aspects of the environment: the park, shepherds, sheep, visitors, students... We then address this interlacing network from a range of areas, including ecology, economy, production, biodiversity, design and craftmanship. We also reflect on the interrelationship of livestock, landscape heritage and environmental benefits. We promote participation, co-learning and collaboration, establishing networks and seeking alliances between local actors – shepherds, cooperatives, associations, collectives and small farmers – and local governments. We also review studies about shepherding and wool, comparing these practices in Collserola with those of other regions that face similar challenges.

The result of these conversations is the video *Cuatro walkabouts con los pastores* (Four walkabouts with shepherds), which we produced collectively. Participants include Sabrina Comisso of Can Puig in El Papiol; Jordi Rodríguez and Juan Gómez, of Finca La Salut in Sant Feliu de Llobregat; Daniel Sánchez Llobera, a shepherd in La Font del Gos de Horta; and José y Carlos Montoya of Ca n'Oller in Montcada i Reixac. They discuss the challenges of shepherding in frequently visited areas, as well as the problems of co-existing with wild boar; the increasingly intense droughts that force them to keep flocks close to corrals to have access to water; the exhausting daily work, regardless

Ca n'Oller
Shepherding in Collserola, 2024
Photograph by Teresa Bastardes Mestre

of the weather; and the tremendous difficulties caused by the increase in fodder, storage, veterinary and fuel costs. They also describe the scarcity of pasture land in Collserola, the struggle to survive as small producers in a sector that privileges large volumes, the need to prioritize local projects over processed foods, and the lack of recognition and support from both the community and governments regarding rural industry, highlighting the urgency of adapting regulations to the current reality. Furthermore, they call attention to the fact that preventive measures are not being taken against forest fires. Despite their ability to help in cleaning forests, shepherds do not receive adequate financing for this work. The authorities have neglected this matter, and the shepherds warn that if action is not taken soon, the implementation of the necessary measures could come too late.

In Eina's courtyard, with the participation of teachers, artists, artisans, students from the school and other institutions and interested citizens, we carried out the entire artisanal wool production process. For three weeks, we washed, untangled, carded and dyed the seventy fleece that Ana Vivero and Martina Manyà had carefully selected during the shearing in Collserola. While the park's sheep are not raised specifically for wool production, but rather for meat or milk, the fibre that we obtained was soft and flexible. However, this wool is usually discarded because it is considered too coarse, which results in high costs for shepherds and contributes to generating waste.

With the wool that we produced, Vivero and Manyà taught us how to make felt, one of the oldest fabrics obtained from animal fibres. The process involves condensing the carded and dyed wool and exposing it to heat, acidity, moisture, agitation and friction. This causes the wool's cuticle cells or scales to open, which allows the fibres to gradually interlock until the fabric is formed. Ryder[1] suggests that felting may have been discovered by observing how sheep hair, when detached during shedding, tangles and thickens into lumps of felt before falling off.

As Deleuze and Guattari explain,[2] felt differs from traditional fabrics in that it is an "anti-fabric," since it is formed from the random entangling and condensing of fibres, instead of an ordered and linear interweaving of threads. This arrangement without a predictable or linear pattern, and probably discovered by observing clumps of felt on sheep, has become a useful example to illustrate a more expansive idea of the creative process: the performativity of non-human actants. Focused on our needs, desires and capabilities, we often overlook how the agency of the material and the environment influence the creative process, even though all human action, including creation, depends of this performative setting.

1 Michael L. Ryder: "The Evolution of the Fleece," *Scientific American*, vol. 256, no. 1, 1987, pp. 112-19.

2 Gilles Deleuze and Félix Guattari: *Thousand Plateaus: Capitalism and Schizophrenia*, Minneapolis, University of Minnesota Press, 1987.

Tapestry making II
Eina Bosc, Barcelona, 2023
Photograph by Javier Garriga

Reciprocity and mutual transformation between human and non-human actants occur in every interaction. As Anna Tsing states,[3] every encounter in which we participate transforms us while, simultaneously, we also cause transformation. Thus, active exploration and flexible and open application of the senses to the world are essential in our approach, enabling us to perceive and materialize possibilities beyond the conventional focus of attention. Instead of pre-determining the results, we allow the objectives and fruit of our research to emerge from our encounters with wool. We don't act *upon* it but *with* it, dampening it, agitating it, rubbing it, always attentive to its changes, adapting to its invitations and refusals. This openness to the material *with* which we work not only guides our approach but also constantly sheds light on the creative process. For example, on one of these occasions, we observed how the washing process removes the natural lanolin, a waxy substance secreted by the sebaceous glands of sheep to protect their wool and skin from water and bacteria, from the wool. In response, along with Vivero, new members of the Tornen les esquelles collective – Solange Dalannais and Florencia Toro – and Ana Otero from SILA Studio, we formed a research group to restore the antimicrobial, antifungal and waterproof properties of untreated wool to felt through the (re)application of lanolin. This effort has a double objective: to increase the value of "anti-fabric" as a raw material and to introduce to new applications for it, while also promoting the sustainability of the park and processing of fabric materials.

3 Anna Lowenhaupt Tsing: *The Mushroom at the End of the World. On the Possibility of Life in Capitalist Ruins*, Princeton and Oxford, Princeton University Press, 2015.

* Pilar Cortada is Doctor in Philosophy. Director of Eina Obra.

PASTORAL FUTURES

The *Tornen les esquelles* collective emerged from a call for proposals by LAB Collserola, promoted by Eina Obra. This collective uses wool to strengthen symbiotic relationships in Collserola, where shepherding plays a key role in the sustainable management of the park, promoting environmentally friendly practices and recovering traditional knowledge. They incorporate wool into artistic and educational projects to promote environmental awareness and value local biodiversity. The collaboration between humans and sheep contributes to recovering a valuable tradition that, in addition to providing wool for material exploration, helps prevent the risk of fires. Institutions such as INLAND Campo Adentro, CPNSC and Materfad have also collaborated in this initiative.

Sauceboat
Earthenware
1798–1825
Manufactured by Real Fábrica de Loza y Porcelana de Alcora
Purchase, 1965 MCB 100.302

Tureen
Earthenware decorated with oxides
1788–1825
Manufactured by Real Fábrica de Loza y Porcelana de Alcora
Purchase, 1909 MCB 18.329

Sauceboat
Earthenware decorated with oxides
1788–1858
Manufactured by Real Fábrica de Loza y Porcelana de Alcora
Purchase, 1965 MCB 100.427

<
Xai crib / play mat
Sheep wool felt, cotton, leather and oak wood
Genís Senén Gilabert, Barcelona, 2012
Loan, Genís Senén Gilabert

MARESME SILK IN THE COLONIES

JOAN MIQUEL LLODRÀ NOGUERAS*

Many travelers who between the 17th and 19th centuries visited the Maresme region – known until not too long ago as the Costa de Levante (East Coast) – recorded in writing the intense manufacturing and industrial activity in the area, aside from the usual farming and fishing tasks. The products of this activity not only supplied the rest of the principality and kingdom's markets, but other places in Europe and, particularly, the colonies as well. It would be an endless endeavour to try and list all the goods that left Catalan ports for overseas. However, within the scope of the Maresme area, some of the ones produced by the early textile industry – or pre-industry – that had just begun to develop and were in high demand across the Atlantic include: *indianas* (printed linen or cotton fabric), scarves, stockings and, especially, lace.

In the 18th century, Catalonia, and specifically the towns along the Barcelona and Girona coast, was already an important centre for producing lace, which was manufactured with bobbins. While this activity is today considered a craft, less than a century ago bobbin lace employed thousands of women in Catalonia and generated enormous revenue for the lacemakers who sold it. In general, keeping in mind it came in many different varieties, lace was a piece of luxurious art comparable to precious metal work: in other words, an object which due to its high cost, very few people could afford.

Despite this, it was widely used to decorate and embellish both civilian and religious wardrobes or vestments, giving rise to high demand in Europe and its dependent territories, that is, the colonies. Though thousands of kilometres away from the metropolis, the elite (the overseas upper classes), and the less well-off classes too, continued to live and interact in a Western way. Regarding women's clothing, well into the 20th century lace was, in today's terms, a *must*. In a study of lacemakers in Arenys de Mar, historian Josep M. Pons Guri explains that a large part of the local shops' production was exported. The same was true of nearby towns, from Blanes to Mataró. The writings of the above-mentioned travelers confirm this, as do contemporary documents preserved in archives.

Throughout the 19th century, and after the loss of many Hispano-American colonies, Cuba and Puerto Rico remained a market eager to acquire these delicate yarn creations. From the late 18th century and throughout the next, the ruling classes, especially in Cuba, invested more in luxury objects, including lace. One of the most famous novels in Cuban literature, *Cecilia Valdés o La Loma del Ángel*, by Cirilo Villaverde – in its definitive 1882 version –, provides an accurate depiction of women's clothing in Gran Antilla: lace, either present in dresses or as an independent accessory, is a ubiquitous feature.

The lack of specialized skilled labour for this product – which in some cases required a very meticulous production process – meant that some pieces, especially the most luxurious ones, had to be imported from the "Old World," since there were certain things that tailors and seamstresses could not imitate. Within the context of 19th century Hispanic women's fashion, and even though Paris and the United States were already starting to become trendsetters, some accessories were traditionally indispensable. This is the case, specifically, of the *mantilla*, a lace veil covering the head and most of a woman's body that was frequently used in social and religious events. The considerable dimensions of *mantillas* – the production of which was complex and required many hours of work – explain the high prices people paid for them.

The main raw materials used for lace were hemp, linen, cotton and, of course, silk, a premium material par excellence for this industrial handicraft. Its organoleptic qualities and price made silk an external mark of prestige and wealth, regardless of the material in which it was used. Àngels Solà has studied the importance of this animal-based fibre in 18th and 19th-century Catalonia, often insufficiently acknowledged given the amount of raw material produced. Historians have been more interested in silk production in the rest of the Iberian Peninsula, especially in prestigious centres such as Valencia, Murcia and Toledo.

The use of one type of yarn or another not only depended on the technique used – guipure, snood, Valenciennes, duchesse... – but also on how each piece of lace was applied. For Catalan silk lace, there were two techniques that, because of the beautiful technical and artistic results, brought fame to the lacemakers that sold them: Chantilly and blonde lace, both of French origin. Blonde lace, a technique from the Normandy region developed in the 18th century, owes its name to the pale yellowish colour of raw silk, *blonde*. This variety, with rich and varied tactile and visual results – bright or matt – was quickly adapted and imitated by Catalan lacemakers.

While the objective here is not to explain the distinctive features of blonde lace, we would like to emphasize that, while the lacemakers on the northern coast of Barcelona tended to produce white fine lace, those from the Southern area – what we call today Baix Llobregat – stood out and were noted for their black lace. Places like Hospitalet de Llobregat, Sant Boi de Llobregat, Sant Feliu de Llobregat, Sant Climent and Martorelles were known for their Chantilly and blonde lace, with some spectacular pieces like the *mantilla* chosen for this exhibition (MTIB 120.097).

In 1913, Adelaida Ferré Gomis (1881-1955), a scholar who studied lace production in Catalonia and Spain, published in the "La Pàgina Artística" (The Artistic Page) section of *La Veu de Catalonia* an extensive and detailed article devoted to blonde lace.

Regarding the silk material used, Ferré included ample information about its characteristics and mentioned its origin: depending on the type needed – whether the yarn was more or less fine – it tended to come from Valencia, Caen and other places in France, and even China.

In this sense, noteworthy is one of the most recognized Catalan lacemakers specializing in blonde lace, nationally and internationally, who was awarded in numerous exhibitions and was supplier for the Spanish royal household: Josep Margarit Lleonart. Between the 1820s and 1870s, the specialized press called attention to this lace industrialist's silk, although, regrettably, he has not been sufficiently studied. Either for financial reasons or because of quality control, he produced the silk himself. On an estate located in Castellví de Rosanes (Baix Llobregat), Margarit installed the necessary infrastructure to carry out the whole process of cultivating silkworms: from fibre production with different types of worms, to the final spinning. Margarit was so interested in obtaining high-quality silk that in 1871 he published a guide entitled *Guía sericícola o cría del gusano de seda* (Guide to sericulture, or breeding silkworms).

Another topic that Adelaida Ferré discusses in her article has to do with the design motifs in blonde lace. With a few exceptions here and there, the repertoire was traditionally floral: flower motifs with a degree of naturalist inspiration. Ferré even refers, correctly, to the "Spanish style" that enjoyed widespread commercial success. A great connoisseur of the lace universe, the historian suggests, however, that the designs were adapted to the markets: "Drawings meant for our nation were light and delicate, while those sent to the Americas were not as flattering given the taste of women in those countries, who preferred them to be more ornate."

Another type of design worth mentioning is one that, besides enriching blonde lace samples, illustrates the importance that fashion and aesthetic currents had in the world of lace: *chinoiserie*. According to Ferré, between the years 1850 and 1860, these motifs of Eastern origin – mostly depicting architecture and people – were in vogue and appeared in many other applied arts as well. One person who used these motifs in his blonde work was a lacemaker named Molet. Despite the predominance of plant- and flower-based garlands across its surface, the *mantilla* chosen for the exhibition features a central eye-catching band with schematic structures like pagodas and steeples. These rather simple designs, more suggestive than explicit, reflect the attraction of Europe to cultures and civilizations so alien to the West. It is yet another example of how for hundreds of years, fabrics continue connecting worlds.

* Joan Miquel Llodrà Nogueras is Art historian.

THE SILK ROAD

The origin of silk is ancient and dubious. The silk industry began in China before the third millennium BC. The earliest reference to the manufacture of silk in Barcelona by Jewish artisans dates back to the year 1200. The guild of silk weavers, *Velers* [Veil Makers], was set up in 1533, and in the nineteenth century Barcelona and Reus became important silk-producing centers. Catalonia exported silk lace, handkerchiefs, scarves, stockings, and socks to the colonies, while the Manila shawl was imported to Spain through Mexico.

While silk is still an expanding market, today there are vegan alternatives like Eri silk or Ahimsa silk (processed without killing the silkworm), pineapple silk and orange silk, and lab-grown and fermented fabrics, although the latter are still too expensive to be mass-produced.

Manila shawl
Embroidered silk fabric and macramé tassels
Canton, 1913–1933
Bequest of Joan Artigas-Alart, 1935 MTIB 21.149

Mantilla
Blonde lace
Barcelona, 1825–1899
Donated by the heirs of Manuel de Genovart, 1981 MTIB 120.097

Nightgown
Silk satin embroidered with silk thread and cotton lace, cotton piping appliqué
Barcelona, 1934
Donation, Dolors Alegre Santamaria, 2016 MDB 436

Silence Collection outfit

Silk bourelle blouse with elastic threads and silk bambula muslin trousers

Marina Pujadas, Barcelona-Paris, 2010

Donation, Marina Pujadas, 2014 MTIB 4.212/14-00

ANIMAL MATTER. FORBIDDEN MATTER

JOSEP CAPSIR*

Since time immemorial, different civilizations have found it necessary to create luxury objects, either of a utilitarian or symbolic nature or to adorn themselves or decorate the interiors of homes, palaces, castles and temples often devoted to public events. To produce these items, materials derived from animals were often used, either local, imported or the result of colonial exploitation. In the latter cases, the materials were highly regarded due to their scarcity in their final place of destination, as well as for often intrinsically conveying unique qualities, which gave them added value.

We will focus here on four animal-based materials that are part of the decorative arts collections of the Design Museum of Barcelona's heritage collections. All are species protected to a lesser or greater extent under current law, a consequence of the abusive hunting of animals that contain the coveted object of desire and greed. Capturing these animals reached such high levels that today most are in critical danger of extinction.

One of the better-known materials used for centuries in luxury objects is ivory, a material almost exclusively obtained from elephant tusks. Its characteristics made ivory ideal for cutting into plates used in the 13th and 14th centuries in al-Andalus and Sicily to manufacture chests adorned with delicate gilt motifs. Also famous are the 16th and 17th-century Neapolitan desks that combined ebony with plates of carved and tinted ivory depicting mythological scenes, as well as the small 17th-century desks from Augsburg that featured ivory plates over a wooden core. During the same period in Germany and Austria, because of the ductility of ivory, extraordinary artists created beautiful sculptures with mythological or religious motifs, among them the figure of Saint Sebastian.

Fortunately, or unfortunately, depending on the observer's point of view, ivory has many characteristics. One of the most surprising is that by using an extremely thin translucent ivory sheet as a base for the creation of miniature portraits, it often was possible to reproduce the natural colour of skin with very effective results, depending on the skill of the artist. In Catalonia, Lluís Vermell stood out in the 19th century in this regard, and many of his signed works have been preserved.

At the time, China was the major supplier of ivory items, highly esteemed in the West. The most emblematic examples are the exquisitely carved figures in elegant chess sets or lavishly decorated card holders. Japan rivalled China in the use of ivory for luxury goods partly intended for export. Clear evidence of this are the many finely crafted katanas and daggers with hilt and sheaths that reached much of Europe in the 19th and first quarter of the 20th century.

Another prized material is tortoiseshell obtained from the hawksbill sea turtle, a saltwater species that once inhabited the Gulf of Mexico and the Caribbean. Plates were extracted from the carapace that protects the turtle from other animals on the seabed – though not from the predatory hand of humankind – and then polished, revealing peculiar chromatic tones with translucent qualities that made them ideal for making different decorative and personal objects.

Desks manufactured in Europe in the 17th century, especially in Spain, which combined ebony and jacaranda wood with hawksbill tortoiseshell plates, are well known. The chromatic contrast endowed the furniture with great beauty. These translucent plates were usually set over a red background, highlighting their natural colour. The most emblematic pieces of cabinetmaking at the time were from France, the work of André-Charles Boulle, known for his furniture pieces with a marquetry finish that combined metal and hawksbill tortoiseshell with spectacular results.

This technique, typical of the French cabinetmaker, flourished in the second half of the 19th century, coinciding with the emergence of historicism. A good example is the work of Catalan craftsman Josep Antoni Cabanyeres, whose work includes, among other pieces, secretary desks and beds in which he applied this decorative technique.

It should be noted that hawksbill tortoiseshell has also been used for centuries as a raw material to manufacture many objects for personal use made entirely from this material, such as combs, cases, and brisé fans. In addition, it has been partially used in eyeglass frames, fans and pocket watches.

The third material we will mention, highly valued for its iridescence, a characteristic which makes it unique due to the reflective effect when infused with light, is mother of pearl. It is usually obtained by polishing the shell of certain molluscs. Used since ancient times, some of these shells could be found in the Mediterranean Sea, but many others came from overseas colonies.

While little known, the most remarkable case of massive use of mother of pearl plates to ornament an object is the wedding carriage that the Marquess of Castellbell brought from Genoa in 1798 for his eldest daughter's marriage to the Baron of Maldá, which took place in Barcelona. A Berline carriage whose body consists of boards completely inlaid with mother of pearl, it was exhibited between 1932 and 1936 at the Decorative Arts Museum in Barcelona.

In the 19th century, use of mother of pearl proliferated in Europe to decorate objects for personal use such as binoculars and opera glasses and in metalwork pieces for civil and religious purposes. At the time, many objects made from mother of pearl were produced in China – adapted to Western tastes – and exported. Engraved mother of pearl was commonly used in brisé and other types of fans, for example, to make their sticks and guards. It should be noted that not all mother-of-pearl mollusc species are in danger of extinction and thus protected, though some of them are.

Coral is another animal-based marine raw material that was widely used in civil and religious metalwork in Europe during the 17th and 18th centuries. Various pieces of high artistic quality were imported into Spain from the viceroyship of Sicily. The people of Trapani excelled in the arduous task of extracting the coral from the seabed and then using it to make luxury objects featuring the prized "red gold," a name by which it was often and still is known today.

The most unique object made from coral, of which many samples have survived, is what Sicilians call *capezzale*, octagon-shaped creations of religious metalwork finished with an original marquetry of gilded copper and coral. Usually, a devotional image made from the esteemed red gold presides over the piece. The edge is often finely decorated with white enamel over laced metal with coral inlays. The *capezzale* stand out for a chromatic combination that grants them a special appeal.

For centuries, coral was traditionally considered to have certain protective qualities, which favoured its use in personal objects such as jewellery and even charms intended specifically to protect children in times of high child mortality rates, which increased the demand for it.

Uncontrolled capture for long periods of some animal species to extract ivory, tortoiseshell, mother of pearl and coral has left these creatures today close to extinction. This has led world leaders to create a vast array of legislation to protect them from plundering, exploitation and unregulated commerce. The legal starting point was the Convention on International Trade in Endangered Species of Wild Fauna

Nautilus cup
Sea snail shell and embossed and engraved silver
Carl Haas, Vienna, *c.* 1891
Purchase, 1891 MADB 110

Flask
Tortoise shell with silver and applied mother-of-pearl. Embroidered silk fabric. Moiré silk interior
Europe, 1830–1870
Donation, Mercedes Paluzie, 1972 MTIB 104.459

Binoculars
Gilded metal, mother of pearl, glass and plastic
Europe, 1860–1900
Donation, Pilar Goula, 1972 MADB 106.377

Sculpture of Saint Sebastian
Carved ivory
Austria, 1600–1699
MADB 37.786

and Flora, signed in Washington on 3 March 1973.

From a contemporary point of view, museums that hold heritage assets created in the past from animals currently in danger of extinction ought to emphasise their educational purpose and stress the human error that resulted in practically irreparable damage to nature in their acquisition. However, we do not believe these objects should cease to be exhibited, provided they are accompanied by an explanation that places them in their historical context. Many are extremely beautiful, of high artistic and heritage value, and unique, made from animal material that is now forbidden.

* Josep Capsir is historian and conservator at the Museu del Disseny de Barcelona (DHub).

Small desk
Ivory on fir core. Golden metal handles
Inside, **lapis lazuli plates and fabric**
Augsburg, *c.* 1650
Purchase, 1956 MADB 64.184

The trade of ivory and tortoiseshell is deeply embedded in the history of colonialism and slavery. In Western Africa, European and African merchants traded in ivory, and slaves were forced to transport it long-distance. In the Caribbean, tortoiseshell was also gathered by slaves.

Baroque writing desks decorated with inlaid ivory were symbols of wealth much sought after, although the precious material would subsequently be replaced by bone, which was more affordable. The ban on their trade and the protection of the species from which they are obtained are essential to ensure destructive practices do not continue. Contemplating these historical ivory and tortoiseshell objects today is like revisiting one of the cruelest aspects of colonialism and slavery.

Miniature [Portrait of a woman]
Gouache on ivory and metal frame
Lluís Vermell, Catalonia, 1846
Bequest of Martí Estany, 1943 MADB 40.055

Miniature [Portrait of a man]
Gouache on ivory and metal frame
Lorenzo Barrutia, Espanya, *c.* 1810
Bequest of Martí Estany, 1943 MADB 40.024

COVETED MATERIALS

Red coral is essential to maintain the biodiversity of marine ecosystems. The importation of *capezzali* – religious objects made of precious metals, including red coral, that were placed near headboards – in seventeenth-century Spain, during the Spanish viceroyalty of Sicily, and the subsequent introduction of jewelry made it a precious commodity. In our days, coral reefs in the Mediterranean suffer on two counts: their exploitation and the increase in sea temperature. The mortality of the red gorgonian, a soft coral, has been documented north of Catalonia's Costa Brava, although after decades of overexploitation it is recovering in protected areas of the Mediterranean.

Capezzale
Gilded and engraved copper with coral inlay and champlevé enamelling
Sicily, 1600–1650
Purchase, 1956 MADB 64.190

HUMAN MATERIAL LOOP

ZSOFIA KOLLAR*

The unknown science behind our long hair

The mystery of why humans can grow their hair so long remains a puzzle that scientists have yet to solve. Unlike our closest animal relatives, such as chimpanzees, humans exhibit a unique concentration of hair primarily on the head, a trait shared only with horses.

One prevailing idea posits that human's ability to grow long head hair can be traced back to our early ancestors' transition from dense forests to open savannahs. In this new environment, regulating body temperature under direct sunlight became a crucial challenge. It's theorized that longer head hair evolved as a form of natural protection from the sun, akin to a built-in hat that shielded the scalp and helped prevent overheating.

However, the exact length of head hair that humans can grow raises intriguing questions. While shorter hair could potentially offer sufficient protection from the sun, the evolution towards longer hair suggests additional factors at play. Some researchers speculate that beyond mere sun protection, longer hair may have served social or sexual functions throughout human history, influencing mate selection and social status. This dual perspective – adaptive advantage in the environment and social signaling – underscores the complexity of human evolution and the multiple factors that could have contributed to the development of this distinctive trait.

While the reason to grow our hair does not yet have a scientific explanation, hair is an incredibly powerful material. It is fragile yet super strong, intimate in its feel, and grows directly from our skin, making it an integral part of us. Despite this close connection, hair often seems to have a life of its own: it may not behave as we wish, it can provoke reactions from others, even after being cut off, it retains a unique strength.

The cultural significance of our hair

Hair embodies care, race, culture, resistance, and punishment. It is shaped for display, revered as sacred, and guarded as private and intimate, yet it holds public and political significance. The hair industry thrives not only through products bought and sold, but also through the trade of hair itself.

In many religions and cultures, hair holds profound significance. Muslim women and Sikh men conceal their hair in public, while Orthodox Jews maintain distinct practices for men and women. Native Americans cherish their hair for its spiritual connection to nature and power.

Hair transcends mere physicality; it is performative and political. Its appearance, or its loss, carries complex meanings. Audre Lorde, for example, recounted how her dreadlocks barred her from entering the British Virgin Islands, an instance where unwritten norms were legally enforced. The debate over veiled hair in secular nations like Turkey and France underscores its contentious role in public life. The entry of Turkey's first female MP wearing a headscarf symbolized a pivotal political moment. Mahsa Jina Amini's death in Tehran in 2022 sparked Iran's largest uprising since 1979. In response to her arrest for showing her hair, Iranian women cut their hair, burned their hijabs, and protested in the streets. This bravery ignited global solidarity, inspiring women worldwide to cut their hair in support of Iranian women's freedom.

In Buddhism, shaving one's hair signifies devotion and humility, yet is also deemed necessary due to perceived impurity. Conversely, in 1950s Kenya, Mau Mau fighters upheld uncut hair as a potent political statement. Angela Davis's afro during her 1971 trial transcended a personal choice to become a defiant political act, later cemented as an iconic image. Davis reflected on how her hairstyle was reduced to a mere fashion statement, revealing the vulnerability of historical symbols in African-American history.

Hair has been wielded as a tool of subjugation throughout history. Post-World War II, French towns publicly shaved women accused of collaborating with Nazis, an act laden with political overtones and gendered implications. The act of forcibly cutting hair without consent has deep historical roots, entwined with notions of political and cultural authority.

Hair, charged with symbolism, speaks volumes about individuals and societies alike, embodying narratives of identity, power, and resistance across time and cultures.

Hair as a material

Hair, a remarkable biological filament primarily composed of keratin protein, exhibits a unique blend of structural resilience. Structurally, it consists of three layers: the outer cuticle, the cortex, and sometimes a central medulla. Despite its resilience, hair is considered "dead" beyond its growth in the follicle, lacking biochemical activity. It retains traces of substances from an individual's bloodstream, such as medications, drugs, minerals, and vitamins. However, without follicle cells, hair cannot uniquely identify an individual but can indicate shared characteristics within a group. Gender cannot be discerned solely from hair, as both men and women have identical structures.

Unlike shed hair, DNA is present in bodily sources like blood, semen, skin cells, and more, but not in hair that has been cut or broken off, which lacks nuclear DNA from the cell nucleus. This unique DNA, inherited from both parents, is essential for individual identification through forensic analysis. Therefore, intact hair with its follicle cells is necessary to yield usable nuclear DNA.

Human Material Loop fabric samples, 2023

Hair also demonstrates exceptional physical properties, such as a strength-to-weight ratio comparable to steel. Composed mainly of the cortex and matrix, hair can stretch up to one and a half times its original length before breaking. The cortex, with its parallel fibrils, provides tensile strength, while the amorphous matrix influences how hair responds to deformation. Under stress, hair undergoes nanoscale structural changes, transitioning from coiled alpha helix chains to pleated beta-sheets, allowing it to endure significant deformation without fracturing. Hair's resilience extends to its response to humidity, as it can withstand substantial deformation under high humidity due to water softening its structure.

Despite its biological and cultural significance, human hair presents environmental challenges as a byproduct of barber shops, accumulating as a significant pollutant. Its durability, stemming from disulfide bonds and molecular weight, makes it resistant to degradation by enzymes like pepsin and trypsin. Consequently, hair waste accumulates in urban areas, contributing to solid waste and potentially obstructing drainage systems.

Human hair, primarily composed of keratin, is an important biomaterial with unique advantages such as non-toxicity, high tensile strength, lightweight nature, thermal insulation properties and flexibility. These attributes indicate its potential integration into production systems, although it remains underutilized in global product cycles amidst energy and ecological concerns.

Hair, the regenerative material of the past and future

The concept of harnessing human hair as a sustainable biomaterial represents a forward-thinking approach to addressing the environmental challenges of today. For decades, global resource depletion has escalated due to extensive human activity, which has transformed 70% of the Earth's land surface and caused severe biodiversity losses. Key industries such as food and fashion contribute significantly to this issue through their consumption, processing, and transportation of raw materials, leading to environmental degradation.

To combat these challenges effectively, a paradigm shift towards circular and sustainable practices is imperative. This shift requires us to move beyond mere recycling efforts and instead embrace innovative solutions that rejuvenate and sustain our natural ecosystems, communities, and economies. Advancements in technology over the past half-century have greatly enhanced global connectivity and comfort. However, as we progress, it has become evident that a global-local approach, focusing on utilizing local resources, is essential for a sustainable future.

Considering the future implications of population growth and ongoing technological innovation, the idea of humans themselves becoming a source of materials is both provocative and pragmatic. Companies like Human Material Loop are leading this charge in material science by pioneering the use of human hair as an alternative fiber in textiles. Their technology efficiently transforms hair into fibers, demonstrated through numerous prototypes and textile samples. Beyond reducing the environmental impact of textile production, their mission includes addressing health concerns associated with conventional materials, such as toxic chemicals and microplastic pollution.

Human hair, often discarded as waste, presents a transformative opportunity. By recognizing its potential as a valuable biomaterial, we can establish a global standard for local sourcing and manufacturing. This shift not only supports sustainable practices but also draws inspiration from ancestral wisdom, where all available resources are utilized with ingenuity and respect for the environment. In reimagining human hair as a sustainable resource, we pave the way for a future where innovation and environmental stewardship converge for the benefit of all.

Human Material Loop

Human Material Loop, founded in 2022 by Zsofia Kollar and based in Geleen, The Netherlands, is at the forefront of material science, particularly in transforming hair waste into valuable materials. More than a scientific endeavor, the company embraces a philosophical concept: our responsibility towards the planet we inhabit. As we continue to consume Earth's resources, it begs the question – what are we giving back in return?

Annually, beauty salons in Europe alone generate an estimated 150 million kg of hair waste, a remarkably clean waste stream. Yet, the majority of this resource ends up in incinerators or landfills, despite hair being one of the strongest natural proteins ever created – keratin.

The textile industry, a cornerstone of our economy, is also one of the most polluting sectors today. While textiles are integral to daily life, their production and consumption take a heavy toll on the environment and human health, necessitating urgent reforms.

Human Material Loop aims to exemplify regenerative practices, demonstrating that advanced technologies and existing machinery can integrate new fiber into production systems. Human hair, fundamentally composed of keratin-like wool or alpaca fibers, has been utilized in textiles for centuries, often exploiting animals and lands. By reimagining waste as a resource, Human Material Loop seeks to lead by example in material innovation.

Looking ahead to 2050, when nearly 10 billion people will inhabit the planet amidst escalating global climate change and dwindling agricultural land, the imperative to rethink production methods becomes clear. Soil degradation poses a critical environmental challenge, compromising global food security and exacerbating climate change through CO_2 release.

The fashion industry, in particular, contributes to soil degradation through practices such as overgrazing for wool and cotton production, and deforestation for wood-based fibers. These unsustainable practices underscore the need for systemic change.

The solution lies in reimagining our production systems and embracing new materials like human hair. Unlike traditional fibers sourced from natural landscapes, human hair remains in human hands until it is harvested, challenging our perspective on waste and materiality.

Human hair, with its inherent strength, non-toxic properties, and renewable availability, represents the fiber of the future. By harnessing this abundant resource, we can forge a path toward a circular economy where waste is minimized, resources are reused, and environmental stewardship is prioritized. Human Material Loop envisions a future where waste is nothing else just raw material in the wrong place.

Txell Miras x Human Material Loop

The independent Barcelona fashion house Txell Miras, founded in 2004 by the namesake designer, is renowned for its atypical garments full of intricate details and visually striking presentations that rarely leave anyone indifferent. Txell Miras, an indefatigable worker with a restless mind, creates sober and austere pieces. The material result? In this new collection, clothing is perceived as a cave in which to curl up and protect oneself from a

Txell Miras collection, 2024

somnambulant state where, as in a portrait of Francis Bacon, one feels unfocused and disfigured.

Her designs are precise, and her construction techniques align closely with our body's natural ergonomics. They are enveloping, often incorporating a profusion of attached pockets as the main conceptual and decorative element, highlighting the intention to empty pockets and overly loaded backpacks, symbolizing a necessary change of skin, an undoing, and releasing of ballast.

In collaboration with Human Material Loop, Txell Miras explores the possibilities of new material – material that once crowned someone's head and has now transformed into fabric, embodying what it means to be human today and the materiality of fashion. This collaboration raises profound questions: Does fashion only come alive when we put it on, or does it begin with the life of the material itself? Through human silhouettes, monotone colors, and the sharpness characteristic of Txell's designs, this exploration delves into the future of fashion and materiality, the timeless identity we humans carry, and what designers can express and achieve.

After all, fashion is nothing more than a layer of our identity, a visible skin on our body sculpted from the flows of fabric. But this identity is not just about shapes and cuts; it is also about responsibility. Just as we live our lives, we should dress in a way that does not harm our surroundings. Perhaps one answer to being fully regenerative is providing material for this visible layer on our bodies from the very materials that come from us.

* Zsofia Kollar is designer, researcher, published author and founder of Human Material Loop.

HAIRCUTS

Although we cut our hair quite often, we are not aware of its potential. Rich in keratin, human hair is an abundant and highly renewable material with unique properties: it is non-toxic, extremely resistant, lightweight, thermally insulating, flexible, and furthermore absorbs oil. Using it in textile production could reduce the demand for cotton and synthetic fibers, favoring environmental sustainability. Hair is compostable and improves soil health; it contributes to recycling and to a circular economy that promotes a zero-waste society. Made of human hair, the jewel designed by Ana Mir challenges conventional perceptions of the body, while both the dog leash designed by Sanne Visser and the *Human Material Loop* project by Zsofia Kollar examine the waste hair collected from the floors of hairdressing salons and its use as a sustainable biomaterial.

Manuel Outumuro
Printed copy on **Hahnemüle Fine Art 325 g/m² paper**
For Pantene, Madrid, 2007
Donation, Manuel Outumuro, 2010 MTIB 3.713/10

Necklace
Human hair
Ana Mir, Barcelona, 1995
Loan, Ana Mir

Dog leash
Dog hair
Studio Visser, 2016
Loan, Valérie Bergeron

Clog

Cork sole lined with tooled goatskin, silk ribbon

Spain, 1500–1599

Donation, Manuel Rocamora i Vidal, 1969 MTIB 88.430

Ankle boots

Leather and leather sole

Sybilla, Madrid, 1987

Donation, Consol Demàs Camacho, 2022 MDB 14.551-0

PIGS AS WEALTH AND ALTERNATIVES TO LEATHER

Leather has been highly appreciated since ancient times, used for its durability and flexibility. *Guadamecí* [from the Andalusian word *gadamisí*, a reference to the Libyan city of Ghadamis, known for its work on decorative leather product] is the tanned leather painted or engraved in Spain in the Middle Ages and much used in decoration. An essential material for manufacturing gloves, furs and shoes, leather has traditionally been a symbol of luxury. Today, its popularity has decreased due to ethical and environmental reasons. The chronicles in Christien Meindertsma's book *Pig 05049* describe pig exploitation and the countless products into which these animals are transformed.

Among the alternatives that reproduce the qualities of animal leather are vegan leather, made by coating cotton or linen and glazing with tree sap, leather made from the residues of the leather tanning process coated on textile supports, and leather produced from cacti and other plants. *The Squeeze the Orange* project transforms orange residues into compostable bioplastic for dressmaking.

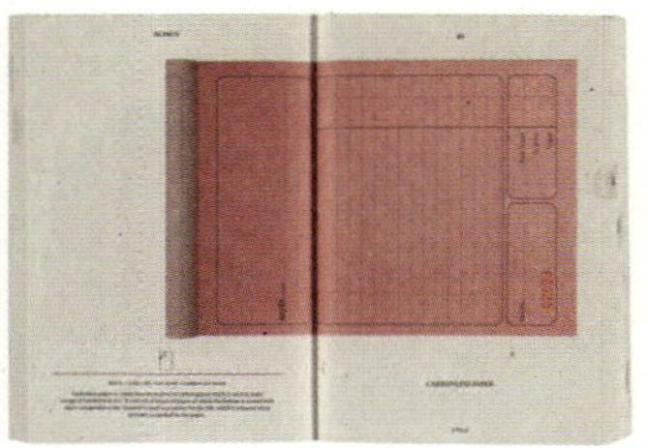
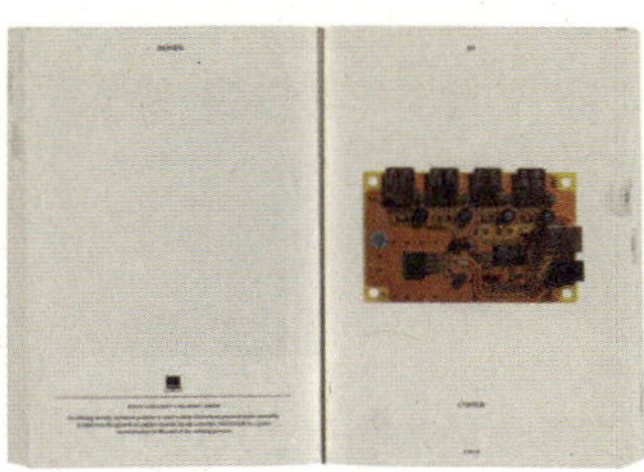
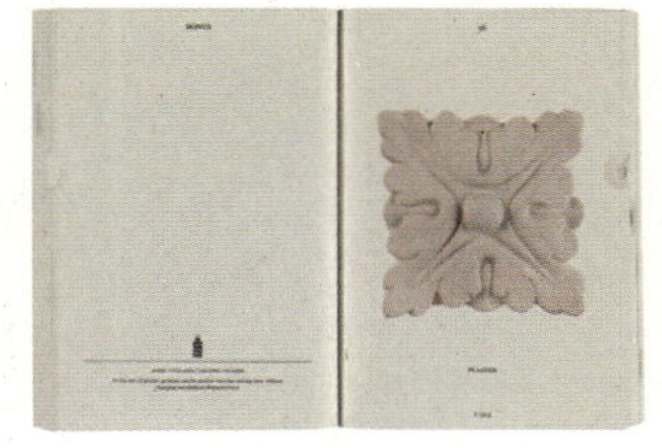
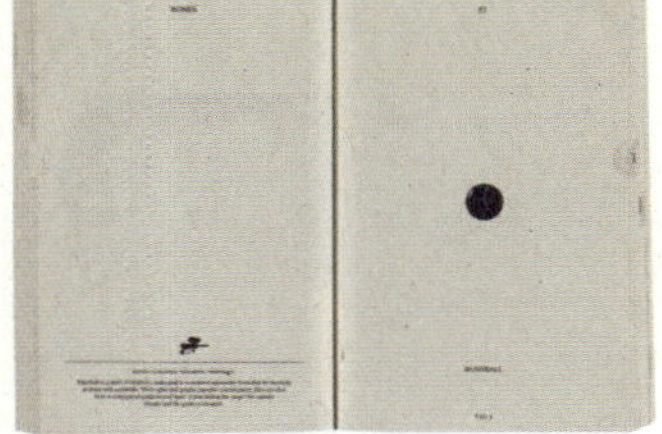

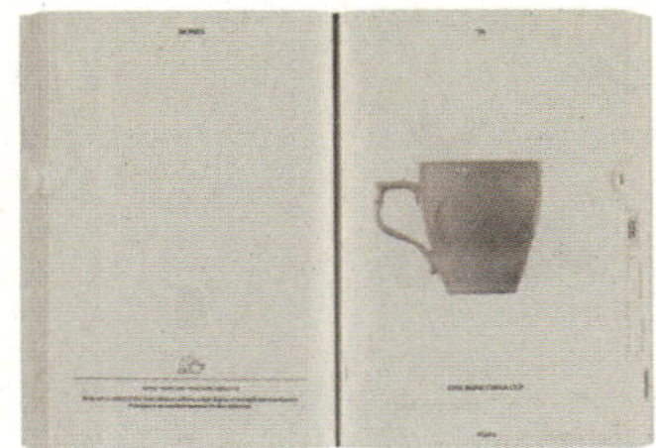

PIG 05049
Christien Meindertsma

Orange Trench Coat
Biomaterial from orange waste. Biodegradable leather
Squeeze The Orange - Susana Jurado and Elisenda Jaquemot, Barcelona, 2024
Loan, Squeeze The Orange. Biomaterials Fashion Design. Susana Jurado and Elisenda Jaquemot

4 MICR
BIOL
MATTER

O–
OGICAL

BIOPHILIC OBJECTS OR, NATURE INDOORS

The *PhotoSynthetica* Collection designed by ecoLogicStudio includes the *AIReactor*, a biotechnological desktop air purifier, the *Compostable Stool*, and the *Bio-Digital Ring*. The three works are interconnected: the biomass of micro-algae generated by the air purifier becomes the raw matter for the 3D printing of the seat and the jewel.

"This collection is born from the dream of growing the city of the future from the wasteland pollution of our current fossil civilization More than products these first three objects are tools to start a collective process of urban re-metabolization," states Marco Poletto, co-founder of ecoLogicStudio, an architecture and design innovation company specializing in biotechnology.

Photosyntetica Collection. *AIReactor*
Birch plywood components supports a photobioreactor hosting photosynthetic micro-algae cultures
ecoLogicStudio, Turin, London, 2024
Loan, ecoLogicStudio. Photograph by Pepe Fotografia

Photosyntetica Collection. *Compostable stool*
Biopolimer made of re-metabolized pollutants and carbon dioxide
ecoLogicStudio, Turin, London, 2024
Loan, ecoLogicStudio. Photograph by Pepe Fotografia

Photosyntetica Collection. *Bio-digital ring*
Algal biomass on a base of polylactic acid (PLA)
ecoLogicStudio, Turin, London, 2024
Loan, ecoLogicStudio. Photograph by Pepe Fotografia

HYDRA*

LAURA TRIPALDI*

From the three heads of Cerberus to the snakes writhing around Medusa's scalp, the idea that the seat of an organism's thoughts and consciousness might be located in more than one head has given rise to some of the most terrifying monsters in Western mythology. The most famous of these infernal creatures is undoubtedly the Lernaean Hydra, a highly poisonous sea serpent which, according to the myth, was confronted and defeated by Hercules in the second of his twelve labours. What made the Hydra a particularly fearsome adversary was not only its multiple heads – ranging from nine to fifty in different tellings of the story – but its ability to miraculously regenerate them if they were cut off, producing two new heads every time one was destroyed, thus making it impossible to kill. Hercules only managed to defeat the monster by burning the stumps of its severed heads, preventing it from continuing to multiply, and crushing the last remaining head with a boulder. In a sense the Hydra is the true nemesis of Hercules, who in turn embodies the archetype of the Western hero. His twelve labours, which involved battles with many monstrous creatures, tell a tale of the triumph of rational man: over the blind forces of brute matter, a matter which boasts an almost inexhaustible capacity to produce all shapes and sizes of abominable creatures in which the bodies of animals, men, and gods are mixed to produce frightening chimeras. Hercules can only have one head, the sole seat of consciousness that makes him a human individual, while the Hydra, a polycephalous organism capable of exponentially multiplying its heads, embodies a sort of metaphysical horror: it represents the disorder and multiplicity that constantly endanger the social and cosmic order, threatening to plunge it into chaos. But I should like to strike a blow in defence of the Hydra here: this fantastic polycephalous creature is not a blind, witless monster, although it certainly embodies a form of intelligence radically different from that its human antagonist.

Hercules's legendary struggle against the Hydra suggest the idea that precisely because it is less centralised, an organism with more heads is also necessarily less vulnerable. This is generally a valid principle when applied to any physical, biological, or social system, where a greater number of control centres guarantees greater stability in the face of environmental disturbances. Even our own organism, although endowed with a highly centralised nervous system, owes its ability to respond effectively to the environment largely to its 'polycephalous' nature – that is, its multi-cellular structure, in which various tasks are performed by specialised organs and tissues. There are however other organisms that have taken this delocalised structure to its most extreme consequences. In nature there are many animals capable of regenerating parts of their own bodies, from lizards to earthworms, but none of them have capabilities comparable to those of the legendary Lernaean Hydra. To find something that resembles the great Hydra, at least conceptually, we need to venture much further away from our particular branch of the tree of life.

In recent years a bizarre and apparently insignificant organism has begun to attract increasing scientific attention, and has even sparked widespread interest among the general public. It is *Physarum polycephalum*, also known as mucilaginous *mould* or *polycephalous slime*, a simple organism belonging to the protist realm, with an appearance similar to that of a yellowish mould, varying in size between ten centimetres and a metre in diameter. Unlike a fungus, however, *Physarum polycephalum* is capable of moving through its environment at a speed of one millimetre per second, deforming its body and forming strange 'tentacles' known as pseudopods which allow it to explore the world around it. Although it moves at a very slow pace for an animal, its amorphous body allows it to explore in search of the decomposing plant, matter upon which it feeds. From a morphological point of view, *Physarum polycephalum* is neither a monocellular nor a multicellular organism. In fact, during the main phase of its unusual life cycle, a polycephalous slime is made up of a very large number of cells which, unlike multicellular organisms proper, are fused together into a single membrane containing the endoplasm within which the nuclei freely float; for this reason, the organism has long been classified as acellular, i.e. lacking real cells. *Physarum polycephalum* is not unique in kind: the group of slime moulds to which it belongs, known as *myxomycetes* (literally muddy fungi, even though they have no real family connection with the actual fungí) contains numerous other similar organisms, each formed of a set of cells joined together to form a single indistinct agglomeration called a *plasmodium*.

This unique cellular structure is not the only reason *Physarum polycephalum* has received so much attention. As already mentioned, its exceptional nature lies in the fact that the plasmodium of polycephalous slime exhibits behaviour similar to that of an animal: it is able to move around its environment in search of food and protection from sunlight, even though it is a far simpler organism with no tissue or nervous system. This ability to move and change shape means that polycephalous slime exhibits a set of abilities that make it seem weirdly intelligent. Where does this intelligence come from? The movements of *Physarum polycephalum* are certainly not directed by any 'control centre', because its body is little more than an indistinct, homogeneous mass of endoplasm. But then how does it orient itself in space in order to find food? How does a brainless protean jelly direct its body into coherent and organised motion? Trying to answer these questions might give us some insight into how bodies radically different from our own express other forms of intelligence, and may perhaps even allow us to make peace with the polycephalous monsters that have populated our nightmares since ancient times.

In the early years of this millennium the behaviour of *Physarum polycephalum* began to be studied in the laboratory in an attempt to find an explanation for its ability to cope with a variety of different problems. In a 2010 experiment that became famous, a team of scientists from the University of Hokkaido grew a specimen of *Physarum polycephalum* on a reproduction of the Tokyo city map, placing oat flakes-the slime's meal of choice-at the nerve centres of the city. In a very short period, the organism had managed to optimise the routes connecting all the food sources, producing a network of 'tentacles' surprisingly similar to the city's rail transport network,[1] a result that is far from being obvious in advance: in computer science, the problem confronted by polycephalous slime here is known as the 'travelling salesman's problem', and it is known to be very difficult to solve with computational approaches. In order to optimise the most efficient route connecting *n* nodes of a network, it is necessary to individually evaluate all possible routes, the number of which multiplies exponentially as *n* increases, with a consequent exponential increase in the calculation time required by the algorithm. The fact that an extremely simple organism was able to find an efficient solution to such a complex problem immediately attracted the attention of scientists from a variety of different disciplinary fields. Information scientists Andrew Adamatzky director of the Unconventional Computing Laboratory at the University of the West of England, has extensively studied the behaviour of the *Physarum polycephalum*, extending the Tokyo experiment to a variety of other geographical territories and in each achieving very accurate reproductions of manmade transport networks. In one of the most curious experiments, a specimen of polycephalous slime was even placed on three-dimensional models of Moon and Mars to evaluate possible approaches to the colonisation of extraterratial planets.[2]

From this point on, a whole subfield of academic studies developed around the abilities of polycephalous slime to solve complex real-world problems, with Adamatzky hailed as the pioneer of a discipline known as 'Physarum computing'. The proposal is to use these living systems as real computational machines, exploiting their ability to optimise efficient pathways between different food sources.[3] These types of optimisation problems are particularly difficult to solve with conventional approaches, but occur often in our daily lives: not only in road planning but also, for example, in calculating the most efficient routes for city traffic. Even though polycephalous slime is very different from a conventional computer, it can do something that our computational machines are not capable of: it can be used to perform what in computer science is known as morphological computation, i.e. it is able to 'think with form', modifying its body to build complex networks that would require a prohibitive amount of calculation time for ordinary computation.

1 Atsushi Tero et al., 'Rules for Biologically Inspired Adaptive Network Design', *Science* 327:5964 (2010), 439-42.

2 Andrew Adamatzky et al., 'Physarum Imitates Explration an Colonistion. of Panets', in A. Adamatzky (ed.), *Advances in Physarum Machines: Sensing and Computing with Slime Mould* (Basel: Springer, 2016), 395-410.

3 Adamatzky (ed.), *Advances in Physarum Machines*.

Physarum polycephalum goes in search of food by expanding almost homogeneously into the surrounding environment, then retracting the parts of its body that are useless for providing nourishment, thus forming a network of little yellowish tubes that look like some kind of bizarre circulatory system. When it retracts from a surface, the slime deposits a substance that signals to its body not to expand in that particular region again, thus constructing a genuine spatial memory of its environment. This ability to remember what surrounds it, albeit in an unconventional way, combined with its ability to control the flow of its own endoplasm 'by exploiting a protein structure similar to that of our own muscles, allows the polycephalous slime to colonise its environment with an efficiency comparable to that of human beings, even without a brain and, as far as we know, without being aware of it. Since Physarum has no eyes or sense organs, it cannot coordinate its movement on the basis of a *representation* of the reality around it. Its intelligent behaviour emerges from a multitude of simple biochemical mechanisms acting locally in every part of its body.

Clearly, no one thinks that Physarum computing will in the near future replace the computational machines we are used to. The use of a living system as a medium for computation has obvious limitations, first of all the need to keep it alive and to reprogram it every time the need to perform a new operation arises. Even if there might be particular technological applications for the use of polycephalous slime as a problem-solving system, these studies, rather than aiming to develop a real technology, are more like a sort of thought experiment, making it possible to rethink computation and intelligence in new ways. Whereas in a traditional computer all information is processed by a *central processing unit* that performs a series of complex operations one at a time, one of the attractions of the possibility of using alternative materials for computation lies in their ability to perform a myriad of simple operations in parallel, yielding results which, in some case, can far exceed those possible with conventional computers.

* Text published in *Parallel Minds. Discovering the Intelligence of Materials*, published by Urbanomic.

* Laura Tripaldi is PhD in Materials Science and Nanotechnology from the Università degli Studi di Milano-Bicocca.

PARALLEL INTELLIGENCE: GEOBACTER AND BACTERIAL CELLULOSE

Geobacter is a genus of bacteria able to oxidize metals and organic compounds and produce electricity. Art and science go hand in hand in the *Geo-Llum* project designed by Samira Benini Allaouat to create public lighting without consuming energy.

In the textile industry, a new biodegradable thread – bio-cellulose – has been derived from bacterial cellulose (BC). This alternative to threads of animal and petrochemical origin has been developed by Cluster of Advanced Materials of Catalonia (MAV, for its initials in Catalan), in order to produce sustainable materials that will bring about a change in the textile industry, currently responsible for 20% of global clean water pollution, 10% of global carbon emissions, the incineration of 87% of clothes, and the release of micro-plastics in the environment.

Biocel
Bacterial cellulose filament knitted fabric
Elisava Research - Laura Freixas et al, 2023

Geo-Llum lamp
Geobacters, bronze, ecoresin, soil, electrical and electronic system
Samira Allaouat Benini, Barcelona, 2022
Loan, Samira Allaouat Benini

PROTEIN FIBER

Nowadays, the textile industry is exploring new approaches to favor the combination of conventional materials and fibers respectful of animals and of the environment. One of the most impressive examples of these new materials is Brewed Protein™ fiber, manufactured using plant-based ingredients as the primary feedstock through precision fermentation (brewing).

Proteins are essential components of skin, nails, and hair, and have evolved without human intervention for 3,800 years. Today, however, molecular engineering accelerates protein evolution to a few years or months.

As a result, the development of protein-based fabrics has also been speeded up, as in the case of Brewed Protein™ fiber produced by a microbial fermentation process, technologically designed to enable the customization of protein polymers. Such innovative examples pave the way for a future devoid of petrochemical and animal-based fabrics.

Yarn made from short fibres. Changing the fibre diameter and the percentage of protein content can produce different textures, from luxurious softness to bulky fleece
Spiber Inc., Japan, 2024

Material similar to fur
Spiber Inc., Japan, 2024

Material samples created by processing Brewed Protein™ polymer
Spiber Inc., Japan, 2024

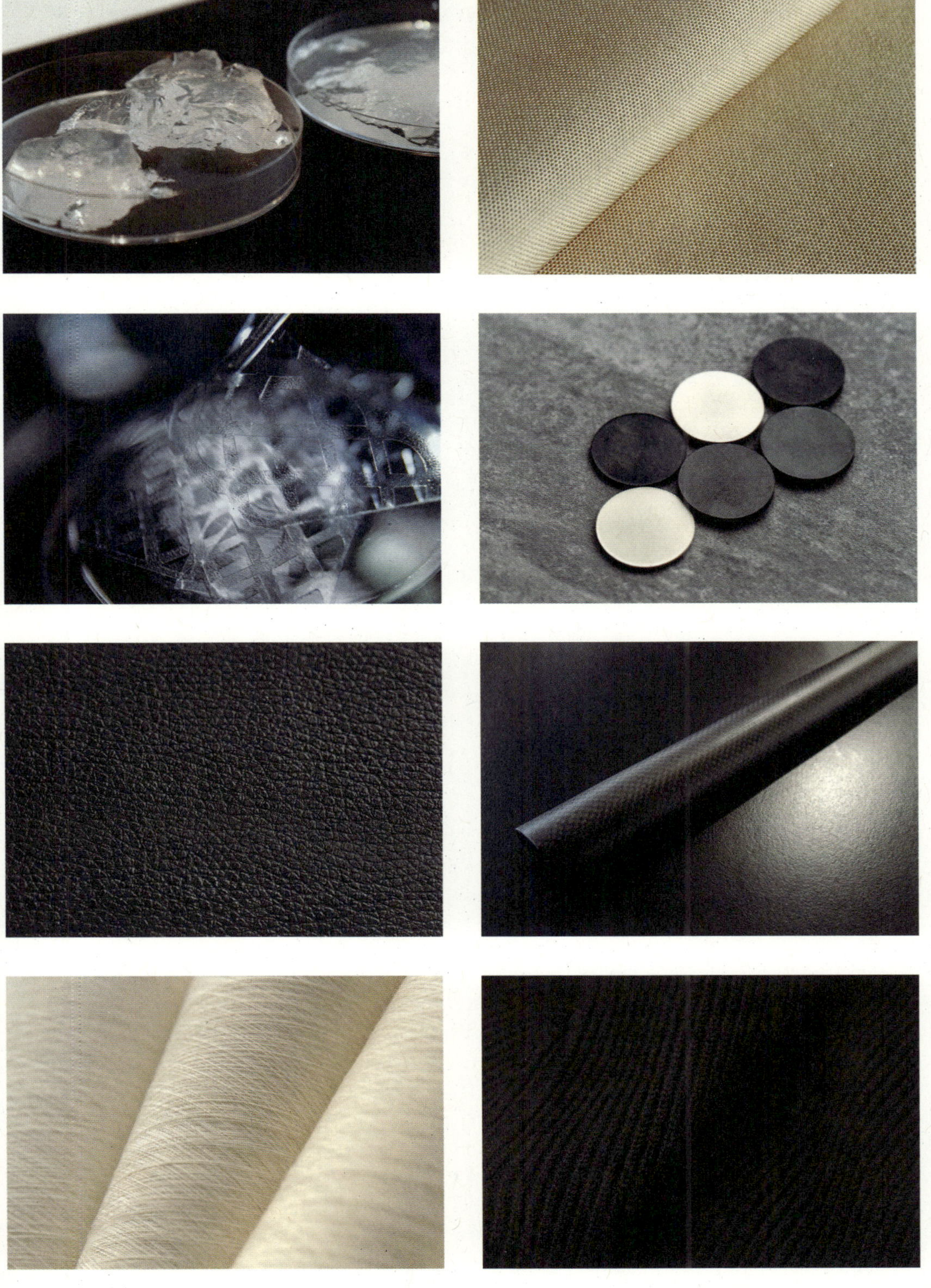

BIODESIGN. A SYMBIOTIC FUTURE

WILLIAM MYERS*

Imagine a future where you begin your morning tending to the hydroponic garden in your kitchen, populated with vibrant green algae purifying your air and replenishing part of your home-grown food supply. You are inspired by the cookbook *Cocina con Algas* and look forward to trying out recipes by the Barcelona-based chefs Oriol Castro, Eduard Xatruch and Mateu Casañas at dinner. Then, you take coffee while lounging on a chair 3D printed with bio-waste, while wearing soft, pliable leather made of bacterial cellulose dyed a deep cobalt blue. The concrete walls in your home appear slightly cracked, but it is of no concern as you know microscopic life inside them generates new limestone as a sealant. You cross a bridge supported by a network of living trees on your commute to work in a net-zero office building clad in surfaces that cater to birds and bees. This is a world lush with applied biodesign.

The speculative vision of such a morning harkens back to many childhood fantasies, especially those that unfolded in close contact with ecological systems. They are so abundant, beautiful, and generous, where each system links and provides for another one.

The impulses to build a treehouse, fashion clothes from leaves, or make habitats for insects can feel innate when we're young. So, where did it all go wrong? Was it mass urbanization, or fear driving a desire for control combined with the observations of philosophers like Descartes that deemed non-human life mere machines?

We believe it was a failure of imagination and the internalization of the logic of capitalism that makes a simplified notion of "growth" the answer to every problem. This is the foundation block of the myopic, extractive behavior of people and companies as the agents of markets.

We see *Matter Matters* as a rekindling of imagination and an examination of materials and practices from an emergent set of new values, made urgent in light of the climate crisis, goals of carbon neutrality, and our shared responsibility to advance social justice.

The good news: it seems that in the last 10 years there has been a marked shift in people's acceptance of and willingness to participate in the changes suggested above. In the words of many a marketer today: "consumers want this!"

And while this may not be the battlecry we're looking for, it may be the one we deserve and it will have to do. It points to a desire for biologically integrated approaches to making and building, while supporting ecosystems, even enhancing them whenever possible.

And in comes biodesign. Unlike biophilic design, 'green design,' or cradle-to-cradle, biodesign refers to the incorporation of living organisms or ecosystems as essential components or processes, enhancing the function of the finished work.

It moves beyond imitation to incorporation, establishing a more active collaboration between the natural and built environments to work with, not against, the innate inclinations of living things and natural materials.

Biodesign, like organisms, exists on scales from macro to micro, the visible to the invisible, drawing on life sciences and collaborations with biologists to fertilize a world of organic matter, natural integration, and sustainability.

This contrasts markedly with the industrial ideologies and mechanization which characterized the 20th century; the automation of functions to overpower, isolate, and control forces of nature.

The materials explored here illustrate how designing with biology lends itself to cross-field collaboration, sowing the seeds of a future ripe with cooperation and thoughtful design.

Bio-Structures: Cities Coexisting 'With' Their Environment

Vast cities (or at least neighborhoods) across the globe are beginning to embrace the function of native landscapes to coexist *with* the ebbs and flows of water and other resources. Sponge cities, a concept initially developed by architect Kongjiang Yu, are urban spaces inspired by the natural world to mitigate drought and flooding. The materials here are simple; a toolbox of porous concrete, green roofs, and swales of greenery with permeable layers of soil protect urban infrastructure and create a reservoir. Embracing ecological enhancement the resources required to maintain the urban landscape are reduced, recycling rain runoff in wet season and releasing water to cool the city in dryer months, creating a more temperate environment.

Fab Tree Hab, fabricated from living material by art, architecture and urban design research group Terraform ONE, is a collection of structures designed for human and animal cohabitation.

Aiming to prototype a dwelling that integrates seamlessly with the landscape, the firm replaced industrial materials with bio-based alternatives including cedar or jute sealed with beeswax or pine resin to prevent decay. Bioplastic tureens home to flora and fauna line the exterior of the structure, dissolving the boundary between outside and in.

These large-scale biodesigns are deeply ambitious, and often create pause. Is it possible to integrate these materials into our existing infrastructure, or do we need to build from the ground up?

Bio-Building: Living Materials for Architecture

Buildings, roads, sidewalks, and other urban infrastructure often suffers from shifting ground and unsustainable building materials. What if construction materials were more sustainably produced and flexible?

In Barcelona, the Biodigital Architecture program at UIC is bringing together natural and artificial intelligence to apply biological techniques to traditional architecture and design. They have produced Biodigital Architecture Bricks, 3D printed blocks with an inner structure of curves and squiggles like that of coral. Made from clay, the adapted inner structure allows for minimal material while still integrating into existing construction processes.

Concrete, another common construction material, makes up for approximately 7% of the world's CO_2 emissions. Two different sets of minds have created forms of bio-based concrete to address this issue. Snøhetta, a global transdisciplinary design practice, created Biocrete, a carbon neutral concrete substitute that combines wood waste and biochar into concrete, compensating for the CO_2 emissions of production. Dutch biologist Hendrik Marius Jonkers created a self-healing concrete that functions like traditional concrete. Incorporated with a limestone-producing bacteria, this bio-crete naturally heals itself, reducing the need for repairs over time.

Bio-Quotidianity: Redefining the Materiality of Objects for Daily Use

Biodesign beyond architecture may make you think of mushroom leather goods produced by Mycoworks, the integration of hydroponic gardens on residential rooftops, or fabric grown from a symbiotic culture of bacteria and yeast (SCOBY) used to make kombucha. These visible demonstrations of biodesign are but one facet of the work.

Biodesign is becoming more visible in our every day. ecoLogicStudio's AIReactor hosts up to 10 liters of living microalgae in a glass and birch structure to create a photobioreactor capable of absorbing carbon dioxide and pollutants while oxygenating the air. The AIReactor is one of several biophilic design products from ecoLogicStudio that embrace the true circularity of production and use, as the biomass grown from the air purification process becomes raw materials for the Compostable Stool and Bio-Digital Ring as part of the PhotoSynthetica collection.

The *Mycelium Chair*, by Studio Klarenbeek & Dros, is a 3D printed chair with living fungus growing within it, providing strength. Designed in collaboration with scientists at University of Wageningen, the team developed a new way of printing with living organisms, bringing together the natural and technical world. Klarenbeek believes this material could one day be used to make nearly anything in the future.

Bio-Future: Opportunities for an Ecological Life

Yet the costs of carbon emissions and climate change mount, and they will need to be addressed if a modern way of life, as we've come to know it, is to endure. Examples of biodesign profiled here anticipate this change: an accounting for, and eventual minimization of, what economists call negative externalities to the environment – the degradation of the air, soil, water, and life that does not figure into the end cost of manufacturing and building today. Only under new and sensibly designed constraints, such as a carbon tax on manufacturing, or incentives, such as a subsidy for structures that promote biodiversity, would projects such as Fab Tree Hab, Bio-crete, or matter from the Mycelium Chair become scalable.

Some of these works are brought together with many others in *Matter Matters*, staging dialogue with objects in the DHub's historical collection, both pointing the way towards a hopeful future and re-framing the older works.

By situating what 'matters' in a new light by proximity, we can see design in a different way, sometimes observing brilliance unrecognized in its time. Herein lies one of the keys to a brighter, more bio-integrated world: growing more sensitive to the limitations of our current conventions.

* William Myers is curator, author and lecturer based in Amsterdam.

Mycelium Chair
3D printing with organic matter from mycelium and wood substrates
Klarenbeek & Dros, The Netherlands, 2019

Geo-Llum lamp
Samira Benini Allaouat, 2022

TO SIT ON A TOADSTOOL

The designers in the Studio Klarenbeek & Dros work on methods of 3D printing with living organisms such as mycelia (branched filaments that constitute the nutritional apparatus of the fungi) and have created the *Mycelium Chair*. Inspired by natural growth, the design of the chair is a reflection on the possibilities of the technological avant-garde, innocuous production and the circularity of objects. To quote Klarenbeek, "It could be a table, a whole interior or even a house."

Mycelium Chair 3.0
3D printing with mycelium organic matter and wood substrates
Klarenbeek & Dros, The Netherlands, 2024
Loan, Klarenbeek & Dros, Designers of the Unusual

Hallucinogenic Mug set
Glazed ceramic. Turned and moulded
Lusesita, Barcelona, 2011
Donation, Sociedad Mercantil Estatal de Acción Cultural SA, 2017 MDB 1.508

Men's shoes

Velvet with silver thread embroidery, wooden heel lined with silk fabric, leather sole

France, 1643–1715

Donation, Manuel Rocamora i Vidal, 1969 MTIB 88.451-0

Women's shoes

Perforated cordovan leather, wooden heel, leather lining and leather sole

Spain, 1525–1574

Donation, Manuel Rocamora i Vidal, 1965 MTIB 88.428-0

TO SHOE IN NEW MATERIALS

The works by Sara González de Ubieta, an expert in new materials, imply that the present consumption model cannot continue. Determined to prevent the deterioration of ecosystems and environmental health, the artist experiments with biomaterials in her shoe designs. An architect and an artisan, in 2019 De Ubieta won the City of Barcelona Award with *Pràctica*, a project that summarizes her research on living materials such as the Scoby fungus, bacteria and algae. In her interdisciplinary practice, contemporary art, craftsmanship, shoe design, and research reveal a new form of production that strikes up a dialogue with the shoes in the Museu del Disseny-DHub.

Shoes made with moss
Sara González de Ubieta, 2019
Photograph by Rafa Castells

RESTROOM PAVILION

Conceived by Julia Montousse and Julia Rodríguez in 1953 and implemented by aeronautical engineer Manuel Jalón in 1956, the mop and bucket with a wringer are two of the most outstanding inventions in the history of Spanish industrial design. These were revolutionary utensils because they did away with the need to kneel down to clean floors, thereby dignifying housework.

The disinfection of contaminated matter has led to research in the area of hygienic materials and the design of sterile spaces and objects, all of which distance us from the fact that restrooms connect our bodies to the oceans thanks to designs ranging from washbasins and toilets to sewage systems.

The Restroom Pavilion examines the interconnections of matter in toilets, from bodies and structures to ecosystems, cultural rules, and regulations. It considers human beings as mobile ecologies with thousands of bacteria that interact with other organisms and introduces awareness of a new relationship between our bodies and the exterior, calling the traditional vision of architecture and design into question. The Restroom Pavilion also challenges discriminatory practices in these areas, revealing that we all share the same space.

The Restroom Pavillion at the Venice Architecture Biennale 2021
Matilde Cassani, Ignacio G. Galán and Iván L. Munuera, 2021
Image by Subliminal (Miguel de Guzman + Rocío Romero)

Doméstico bucket and mop
Iron bucket and wooden rollers; wooden stick, metal base and cotton scourer
Manuel Jalón Corominas, 1956
Manufactured by Manufacturas Rodex SA, Zaragoza
Donation, Curver Rodex SA, 1995 MADB 135785

5

MINE
MATTE

THE LIMITS OF MATTER

The detonation of the Trinity nuclear test, the first atomic explosion, took place in New Mexico on July 16, 1945. The ensuing high temperatures melted the desert sand and created Trinitite, a slightly radioactive glassy substance that was, however, safe to handle.

Artist and designer Teresa Estapé has used Trinitite in a jewel that interacts with a ring watch of 1800 in the Museu del Disseny-DHub. Both objects speak of time: while the watch is an allusion to normal time measured by timekeepers made of extracted metals, Trinitite refers to time encapsulated in matter that reminds us of the possibility of self-extinction of the human race. Trinity, and the 2,000-odd nuclear explosions between 1945 and 1996, have altered the composition of the atmosphere, shortening the hours of life on Earth. The trace of radioactive elements is one of the markers of the so-called Anthropocene.

Watch ring
Gold and engraved copper alloy, enamels, gemstones, steel and glass
Europe, *c.* 1800
Donation, Martí Estany, 1936 MADB 38.839

Watch ring
Gold and engraved copper alloy and openwork enamels, gemstones, steel and glass
Geneva, 1810
Donation, Martí Estany, 1936 MADB 38.846

Trinity ring
Trinitite, 18 kt Fairmined gold wire drawing and natural assembled pearls
Teresa Estapé, Barcelona, 2024
Loan, Teresa Estapé

THE DEMAND FOR CRITICAL RAW MATERIALS: CHALLENGES AND STRATEGIES FOR AN ECOLOGICAL TRANSITION

ALICIA VALERO DELGADO*

Today, we are faced with a monumental challenge: the transition towards a more sustainable and digitized economy, driven by renewable energies, electric vehicles, and electronic equipment, has created an unprecedented demand for raw materials. So far this century, we have extracted as much copper as we have in the entire history of humanity, and this trend is the same for most of the essential raw materials used today. Thus, between 2015 and 2018, more resources were extracted than in the entire first half of the 20th century.

Among these materials, crucial for the manufacturing of batteries, for example, are lithium, cobalt, nickel, manganese, and graphite. In addition, the so-called rare-earth elements, which include neodymium and dysprosium, are essential for the permanent magnets used in any motor, such as in wind power generators. Copper is indispensable for electrification: an electric vehicle requires four times more copper than a conventional internal combustion vehicle, and wind turbines need twelve times more copper than a thermal power plant. A cell phone can be made up of more than thirty different elements from the periodic table while an electric vehicle contains the periodic table nearly in its entirety.

This scenario has far-reaching implications for the economy, and many industrial sectors, highly dependent on increasingly rare raw materials, could be affected by the lack of supply. China dominates the production and processing of many of these critical materials. It is indeed the dependence of governments on the supply of a particular resource and its importance in the development of economies that determine if a material is considered critical. Thus, the European Union began to compile lists of critical raw materials, continuously updated since 2011. At that time, the list contained fourteen. Since then, more elements from the periodic table have been added to it. In the last 2023 update, the list included thirty-four critical raw materials, among them, groups of elements such as rare-earth elements, making the number of elements even higher. As can be seen, the current trend suggests in the medium term, that almost the entire periodic table will be identified as critical.

Supply risk predictions have caused the price of several raw materials to skyrocket. For example, copper has reached historic highs, exceeding 11,000 dollars per ton on the London Metal Exchange, in May of 2024. Price increases of raw materials encourage investment in exploration. However, discoveries of new deposits have decreased dramatically over the last decade. To meet the expected copper demand for 2035 would require discovering, each year, a deposit the size of the largest mine in the world, La Escondida in Chile, for the next twenty years. Yet, the average time needed for a mine to become operational is fifteen years, which means that supply interruptions will most likely be inevitable. Furthermore, as deposits are exhausted, the energy needed to extract the next ton increases exponentially, as do water consumption, CO_2 emissions, and landscape impact. It is not surprising, then, that societies refuse to open mines in their own countries, which has resulted in the increasing relegation of mining activity to third-world nations, predominantly in the global south, and in some cases with at best questionable social and environmental standards.

That said, the European Commission considers access to these resources a strategic priority. The recent enactment of the "Critical Materials Act" sets ambitious extraction, processing and recycling objectives within the EU, as well as aiming at limiting dependence on third countries. In short, Europe is promoting re-industrialization, as the mineral extraction industry, the heaviest and most contaminating, and, in general, the one with the least added value, has been gradually externalized to third countries. However, this industry constitutes the first link in the supply chain, without which the energy and digital transition is unfeasible. As a result, Europe finds itself in an extremely vulnerable position.

In addition to promoting domestic extraction, Europe wants to give an additional boost to the recovery of materials through recycling technologies. The current harsh reality is that the recovery rates for most essential elements needed for the transition are in many cases less than 1%. This is due to several factors: there are no reliable collection channels for these technologies and, in many cases, they do not reach the appropriate processing facilities. Moreover, these processing centres have specialized in recovering heavier and easier to recycle metals such as steel, copper and aluminium. But minor metals, such as tantalum, niobium, neodymium, silver, tin and many others, end up being discarded in landfills or mixed in alloys, and thus are no longer useful.

Clearly, technologies have evolved enormously in terms of reliability, safety, different applications and even energy efficiency. But this has been possible thanks to the use of a larger number and variety of materials. An LED bulb is ten times more efficient than an incandescent one, yet, while an incandescent bulb is made up of a tungsten filament, an aluminium bushing and glass, an LED contains indium, gallium, germanium and rare-earth elements, among others, which are not recovered. So, is it more sustainable? It is here where thermodynamics, which tells us that combining sugar and salt is easy but unmixing them requires such enormous amounts of effort it is better to discard the mix, comes into play. While materials are abundant and extracting them is inexpensive, as has been the case until now, this fact has not elicited much concern. Yet as we approach the physical limits of materials, the situation starts to become worrisome.

While we know that closing the circles completely is thermodynamically impossible, since there are always

Skutterudite
Consortium of the Museu de Ciències Naturals of Barcelona
Photograph by Joan Rosell Riba

Chalcopyrite
Consortium of the Museu de Ciències Naturals of Barcelona
Photograph by Joan Rosell Riba

Bastnäsite
Consortium of the Museu de Ciències Naturals of Barcelona
Photograph by Joan Rosell Riba

losses, we must strive to obtain a circular, or rather spiral economy. It is essential that the design of any product keep material scarcity in mind and that, in addition to using abundant local materials, products are designed to be robust, so that they last, and modular, so that their parts can be reused and ultimately recycled. Furthermore, standardization is crucial. Who cannot recall the number of mobile telephone chargers that used to exist due to a lack of standardization? All this generates more and more technological trash.

In a recent study we carried out in Instituto Energaia[1] along with Amigos de la Tierra, we found that in a transition scenario with improved recycling rates, 57% of the demand for critical materials could be met from now until 2050. This means that recycling is not sufficient to satisfy the enormity of the demand that awaits us in the future. Continuing to plunder the earth in search of the last few tons of concentrated resources will prolong the suffering for a few years, or decades at most.

1 https://www.tierra.org/wp-content/uploads/2023/12/informe_minerales_para_la_Transicion.pdf.

Monazite
Consortium of the Museu de Ciències Naturals of Barcelona
Photograph by Joan Rosell Riba

It is imperative and urgent that, once and for all, we face an unpleasant reality: the current pace of consumption and waste is utterly unsustainable. The natural resources that the earth generated for millions of years must be assessed fairly, since the greater a resource, the greater the debt we incur with nature and future generations, who will not have a concentration of resources at their disposal. Limitless desires have no place on a finite planet. The most effective solution to this problem hinges on drastically reducing consumption. Otherwise, we will only continue to fool ourselves.

* Alicia Valero Delgado is PhD in Mechanical Engineering. Head of the industrial ecology group at the CIRCE Institute. Lecturer at the University of Zaragoza.

WITH THE REBELLIOUS MOUNTAINS*

MARINA OTERO VERZIER#

For years plans for a massive lithium mine have been in the works in the Covas de Barros mountains of northern Portugal. Its image proliferates in blueprints, brochures, videos and reports. Documents commissioned by the mining company show this place of biodiversity and ancient traditions as terrain with neither details nor signs of life, a mere deposit of resources to be extracted. These abstract depictions coincide, too frequently, with the material imaginary behind architecture and design plans. Land transformed into lines or uniform shadings. Mountains and their intricate ecosystems reduced first, to discrete entities and then, to mines and quarries, material sources that give shape to our objects of desire. The cutting, detonations and extraction processes change the enclaves forever, sublimating them in heroic narratives of how human will and human technology can subdue nature.

The propagandistic images of companies like Savannah Resources challenge the stories of the inhabitants of Covas de Barroso who, leaving their daily lives behind to fight against extractivism, call attention to the impact mining has on the ecosystem and life of the creatures who inhabit it. The inverted mountain of Barroso has not yet been excavated, but the wound is already open, festering in the landscape, rupturing the social structures and mental ecologies that resist a scheme backed by the EU, the Portuguese government and outmoded dreams of progress. In addition to withstanding the pressure exerted by the powers that have designated this ecosystem, its inhabitants and ways of life as sacrificial ground, the community of Covas is accused of preventing the energy transition, the lithium-dependent post-fossil fuel green future. They are presented as uncultured, backward and selfish and are likened to animals.

So-called progress has been made historically at the expense of some lives in favour of others, through the abstraction and objectification of bodies and landscapes to place them in the service of work, the accumulation of capital and the gain of the few. The neoliberal green transition is not an exception. It continues to rely on the extractive industry to keep alive the promise of infinite growth and sustain unbridled consumption when the planet has reached a breaking point. Despite operating under the name "clean energy," lithium extraction in open-pit mines entails the destruction of deep layers of soil and the living things that live in and around them. Its activities have a long-term impact on the soil, water and air quality well beyond the pit.

The lithium that the mining company hopes to extract from the bowels of Covas will be exported to other regions where it will be processed and used as an essential component in mobile telephone batteries, laptop computers and electric cars. The polished surface of these technological devices makes us forget about the violence on which they depend. They are, in the words of philosopher Michael Marder, a product of "the disarticulation, the shattering of one totality at the behest of another – that of capital."[1]

Savannah Resources justify this kind of destruction by presenting a barren geography. But the mountains of Covas are not heaps of inert matter; they do not hold goods and products, designations that justify their extraction. A fistful of soil contains more lives than humans on the planet. Billions of bacteria and thousands of different species inhabit a single gram of fertile earth and are an intrinsic part of a living ecosystem.

In response to protests to the slogan, "No to the mine, yes to life," some people ask if not in Covas do Barroso, where? accepting environmental and social devastation as the inevitable cost of progress. The question, however, is if we are prepared to resist our compulsive desires and live appropriately on Earth. The so-called green transition will be in vain if it does not take place alongside a rethinking of the ethics of a society founded on extractivism and consumerism. Even when faced with the climate catastrophe, we tend to view as inevitable the need for more materials and energy, and we are confident that we will find new technical solutions instead of adopting alternative ways of living.

Meanwhile, the struggle continues in Covas. Every day, the inhabitants try to stop the construction of the mine that advances amidst the scandals of political and financial corruption that surround the licensing process. Covas is not alone. Lithium extraction has stirred communities in other parts of Portugal, Argentina, Bolivia, Chile, Spain, Democratic Republic of the Congo, and Serbia. I like to think that the citizen protests are joined by protests from all the elements of the ecosystem displaced by the digging of these giant inverted mountains. Thousands of videos of exploding lithium batteries that power mobile phones, hard disks, laptop computers and electric scooters and bicycles can be seen on the web. If most of our electronic devices are dying at the pace of planned obsolescence, sometimes they overheat and burn. It is precisely their high energy density that makes lithium batteries a trigger for dreams of progress, and for explosions. Their bursting becomes a metaphor of flammable nature and the potential instability of the society they serve, as well as the extreme limit to which certain bodies and ecosystems are subjected.

1 Michael Marder: "For the Earth That Has Never Been", *Stasis*, vol. 9, no. 1: *Terra, Natura, Matèria*, 2020, p. 61.

These protests and explosions, both of human organizations and more than human ones that make up these mountains, shake the Cartesian illusions established by abstraction processes, from the mine to consumer goods. They make clear the violence of economies of desires propelled by the market that encourage us to consume more objects and lead the unsustainable lifestyles prevalent in the Global North. In this volatile context of exploited and exhausted bodies and ecosystems, imagining new material and energy cultures and a new politics of representation is crucial for embracing a different way of being in the world.

As Marder argues, we think of energy as something held in the Earth or stored in our bodies and batteries that eventually can be released to be placed at the service of work.[2] We have a similar vision of matter, widely viewed as passive goods, something which must be manipulated and its properties instrumentalized and transformed into material, thereby exploring its economic potential. This notion of energy and matter also defines the design processes that, like mining, are based on abstraction and objectification of the environment. Architecture and design, moreover, play a critical role in channelling capitalist consumer desire and extractivism. However, design based on an understanding of the mountains, shared by many cultures, as beings instead of storehouses of energy and matter is possible. It is also possible to reshape desire and free it from market ambitions.

Every day, the Covas community mobilizes desire as a creative and collective energy that leads to alternative ways of life and systems of value and exchange. Its desire for life is not a compulsive longing for capitalist consumption that appropriates the imagination, land, bodies and relationships and encourages individualism and productivism. It is a transformational force capable of overcoming the violence of extractivism, a violence that fractures, disarticulates and disperses, that breaks the connections between each of the bodies that makes up the mountain, from its skyline to its utmost depths. In the rebellious mountains, the desire for life puts an end to the compulsive desires of capitalism.

2 Michael Marder: *Energy Dreams: Of Actuality*, New York: Columbia University Press, 2017.

* This article is based on research into lithium mining in northern Portugal. The results were made public in the exhibition *Compulsive Desires: On Lithium Extraction and Rebellious Mountains*, at the Galeria Municipal de Porto (2023), and in the book *Lítio. Estados de Exaustão*, Dafne Editora, 2023, co-edited with Anastasia Kubrak and Francisco Díaz. They were also included in subsequent articles in several publications, including *Aerocene Newspaper II* (2023) and the catalogue of the Venice Architecture Biennale *The Laboratory of the Future* (2023).

‡ Marina Otero Verzier is architect and researcher. Visiting Professor of the Graduate School of Architecture, Planning and Preservation at Columbia University, New York. From 2020 to 2023, Director of the Masters in Social Design at Design Academy Eindhoven. From 2015 to 2022, Director of Research at Het Nieuwe Instituut.

RED-HOT COPPER

Christian Herrera's *Calderilla Chair* is a contemporary chair, which is actually more discursive than functional.

Copper, the most conductive metal after silver, is a basic material in industrial and technological applications and one of the few metals found in nature in its pure original form (a native metal). Examples of its versatility can be found in ceramics of different periods in a range of green and reddish tonalities produced by its oxides and carbonates. There are more than 700 copper mines around the world, the largest of which are found in Chile, Peru, and Congo. Global consumption of copper has increased by almost 30% over the last ten years and demands are not expected to change.

Aerial image of Corta Atalaya mine, Huelva, 2024
Photograph by Atalaya Mining

Calderilla chair
5-cent soldered copper coins
Cristian Herrera Dalmau,
Barcelona, 2021
Loan, Il·lacions

Honey jar
Earthenware decorated with oxides
Manises, 1675–1725
Old collection MCB 9.224

Watch
Gilded copper alloy, gold filigree, steel gold filigree, steel, enamel and glass
Geneva, London, 1635–1684
Donation, Martí Estany, 1936 MADB 38.837

Watch
Engraved copper alloy and gold and gold finish, enamels, steel and glass
Le Roy, Paris, *c.* 1810
Donation, Martí Estany, 1936 MADB 38.784

Watch
Gold and copper alloy, gilded with filigree; enamel, gemstones, steel and glass
Europe, 1800–1840
Donation, Martí Estany, 1936 MADB 38.841

THE METAL THAT HAS FORGED HUMANITY

Some models of chests, fourteenth-century Gothic trunks, and the dyes used in the *Iron Uniforms* by Lucas Muñoz and Inés Sistiaga, made with nails from building material waste, are made of the hardest, most versatile and abundant material - iron. For three thousand years, ever since the onset of the Iron Age in Europe, this metal has been an engine of economic growth and progress. Catalan foundries underwent a great development during the sixteenth, seventeenth, and eighteenth centuries. Nowadays, iron and steel (carbon-enriched iron), of which over 2,000 million tonnes are produced each year, have yet to find an answer to the environmental challenge they face, as in order to make iron malleable it must be heated to extremely high temperatures that release huge amounts of polluting gases.

Trunk
Albero oak wood, cut, fabric appliqué, plastered and polychromed. Wrought iron, chiselled and applied
Barcelona, 1300–1399
Purchase, 1932 MADB 3.922

Chest
Wrought iron embossed and applied
Catalonia, 1475–1525
Purchase, 1932 MADB 5.256

Socarrat
Terracotta painted with oxides over lime
Paterna, 1400–1499
Purchase, 1932 MCB 5.549

Clar de lluna vase
Stoneware decorated with oxides
Josep Llorens Artigas, Paris, 1927
Purchase, 1932 MCB 8.679

Iron Shirts
Second-hand iron dyed shirts
Lucas Muñoz and Inés Sistiaga, Madrid, 2019
Loan, Lucas Muñoz Muñoz and Inés Sistiaga

XHOLOBENI YARDS. TITANIUM AND THE PLANETARY MAKING OF SHININESS / DUSTINESS

ANDRÉS JAQUE / OFFICE FOR POLITICAL INNOVATION*

I

I was born in Madrid in the 1970s, at the time when Mauritania, Morocco, and Spain negotiated their division of Western Saharan resources, as the Saharawi people were losing their hope for a prompt independence. Forty-seven years later, on March 16th 2022, Madrid woke up to a red sky. Something similar had already happened in Paris. The surface of buildings, cars, trees, sidewalks... They were all covered by a thick crust of red sand. A couple of days before, in the archipelago of Madeira, orange-level wind-gusts had given rise to an isolated depression at the Gulf of Cadiz. As a result, light particles of Saharan minerals, in concentrations that exceeded 200 μg/m^3, made their way to Madrid, suspended in rapidly moving flows of air. According to the Laboratory of Environmental Radiation at the University of La Laguna in Tenerife, this red sand contained high concentrations of radiocaesium.

Radiocaesium results from the fission of uranium 235, a material that is normally found in nuclear weapons. Only sixty years separate us from the last subterranean nuclear tests run by the French Government in Ekker. The presence of radiocaesium in the red sand brought to Europe a tiny part of the massive damage inflicted on the land, ecosystems, and bodies of indigenous and marginalized peoples during decades of material and nuclear colonialism.

Hudson Yards is the name given to the high-end redevelopment of the West Side rail yard, owned by the Metropolitan Transportation Authority on the west side of Manhattan in New York City. It was thought of as an opportunity to extend the midtown Manhattan Business District westward to the Hudson Riverfront. Since this yard is occupied by thirty railroad tracks that allow those living in the New Jersey suburbs to commute to midtown Manhattan, a $25 billion dollar steel platform was needed to bridge the tracks and provide a green-looking, landscaped podium to the Hudson Yards on top. There, sixteen shiny skyscrapers, with offices, apartments, hotels and restaurants would be marketed as Class A real estate products, due to their impressive views of the sunset, and a privileged access to clean air. Unexpectedly, it was the unprivileged residents of public housing in Harlem who made Hudson Yards possible. How could this be?

Since 1990, the United States EB-5 visa provides a speedy pipeline to US citizenship to foreign individuals who make a $500,000 real-estate-investment in the US. These wealthy US citizenship seekers are required to make a $500,000 investment in what is called a Targeted Employment Area (TEA). For a rural or urban area to be considered a Targeted Employment Area, its unemployment rate needs to be more than one-and-a-half times higher than the average unemployment rate in the US. In New York, the demarcation of Targeted Employment Areas needs to be approved by a public agency, called the Empire State Development.

This EB-5 fund is intended to use money from non-US citizens seeking US citizenship to subsidize the bettering of distressed areas. Since the Hudson Yards area would never reach this high unemployment rate, a deceiving urban aggregation was composed, by connecting the Hudson Yards with large underprivileged social-housing compounds in central and East Harlem, linked by non-populated parks.

In this way, the well-doing of Midtown would be rendered imperceptible when combined with Harlem's massive disenfranchisement. And this is how the super high-end Hudson Yards became a Targeted Employment Area. And it is also how Harlem's unemployed population made the construction of the hugely expensive Hudson Yards platform possible. But it is not only the unemployed Harlem residents who were involuntarily used to make this happen: Titanium was also needed to make Hudson Yards a reality.

Without titanium Hudson Yards would not exist. Once covered by the Hudson Yards platform, the track area would become so hot from quickly deaccelerating trains as they arrived that one could boil water on the tracks. For humans to survive as they board and leave their trains, and in order to grow trees on top of the platform, fifteen 40-foot-long jet engine blades were installed inside the podium that separates the railroad tracks and the Hudson Yards piazza.

In an installation equivalent to having seven jet airplanes with their engines permanently on in the middle of Manhattan, these fifteen jet engines drive the air at the speed of forty-five miles an hour from the tracks up through chimneys allocated inside the Hudson Yards buildings, to mix the hot air with the open air at a higher level. As a material, titanium alloys uniquely combine high structural resistance with the capacity to act as a heat barrier.

They resist temperatures of up to 1000 degrees Fahrenheit; and that is why they are needed in the fabrication of key components of the jet engine assemblies. Without titanium, both humans on the tracks and trees on the piazza would die. The fifteen titanium jet engine blades are the life support system of a society where humans and trees are involuntarily recruited to the overall project of multiplying the ground to accumulate value on top of more value.

At first sight, what is most striking about the Hudson Yards skyline is its shininess. Everything is shiny at Hudson Yards: the reddish surface of the Vessel, the carved surface of the inflated cushions in the Shed's façade, the self-cleaning glass of The Edge, the Louis Vuitton sign of the Louis Vuitton shop at The Shops and Restaurants at Hudson Yards mall. Everything shines at Hudson Yards.

In 2001, the multinational glass corporation Pilkington announced the development of the first self-cleaning glass: the Pilkington Activ, as an enhanced version of its premium product Pilkington Planar. By incorporating a series of titanium-dioxide-based coatings, the Pilkington Activ became a permanently shining building cladding solution.

Titanium dioxide has the capacity of photo-catalyzing dust in the sunlight. It facilitates the breaking down of dust particles. Its hydrophilicity properties force rainwater to form a thin layer instead of droplets. This thin layer washes away the molecules resulting from the breaking down of dust. As a result, titanium dioxide coatings keep surfaces dust-free and shining. Rapidly, the titanium-based coatings could also be applied to steel and aluminum building façades, inaugurating a new aesthetic regime for multinational corporate power: the global regime of shininess.

Since 1921, titanium has been the main component of the pigments used to produce white paint. White modern architecture was the result of titanium extraction. Titanium produced architectural whiteness. In the 2000s, titanium-made whiteness was replaced by titanium-made shininess. Hudson Yards is titanium-made shininess. Hudson Yards sublimizes modern whiteness through corporate shininess: the titanium global regime of shininess.

The politics of architecture are the way its materiality travels from bodies to landscapes, in time and space. The shininess of Hudson Yards is at the expense of the dustiness of places like Xholobeni, in South Africa.

The violence of Hudson Yards manifests in Xholobeni, 8,000 miles from New York. It is there, in Xholobeni, where the architectures of dissidence-to-shininess and resistance can be found. In Xholobeni's resistance is where the beauty of architecture can now be found.

II

"I am here to talk about our land. We love our land as it is. We love this land because it feeds us, it looks after us, it provides likely food for us. We are able to grow the food that we need in our homes, there are things, of course, that we buy from grocery stores such as cooking oil. We grow mealies, sweet potatoes, yams, beans, potatoes, cabbage, tomatoes, carrots, onions, everything that you can think of that we need in our kitchen, we grow it in these lands. But we also grow stuff to sell to the market. And the money that we get from selling some of our products is what we use to pay for school fees and university fees for our kids. And we are the people who would like to be independent and generate income or money on our own. Therefore, we become very angry when somebody talks about mining our land, because allowing mining to our land or bringing mining would rend our land impossible to produce."[1]

1 Mss Dlamini interviewed by Farah Alkhoury (Office for Political Innovation) in Sigidi village, Xholobeni (March 2023).

"The mineral that they want to mine in Xholobeni is titanium. Titanium is a heavy mineral. The heavy mineral makes the soils settled down. So if you do take titanium out of the soil, the soil becomes very light, and it could get blown away by the wind easily. Which would mean, once the mining happens here, we will be seating with a dust that will be flying all over, because the soil will remain very light and it can easily be blown by wind, we will be living among dust if we allow our land to be mined. Our land will be coated with dust, we would be eating the grass that is coated with dust. We don't want that to happen. And all our resources and the natural reserves that will experience a problem of dust flying around, which will take away even the tourists and we don't want it. The crops we have, we don't think they will produce well when there is dust flying around. So we are saying no to mining.

In Mpondoland, we compose songs to mark up history, to mark up events. But also songs that are composed to express the views about things that have happened in the community, or events that have happened, or people to express their owns views about how they feel about that. Something very sad has happened, so people compose the song and sing about it, and they will sing together. They clap hands; they dance, as a way of therapy to heal themselves of those bad things. So that's why those songs are very significant in our culture as a way to entertain, as a therapy, as recording of the history of events that have happened.

One of the songs was composed because of what happened a few years ago: people who were pro-mining were coming with a fleet of vehicles to the community because they wanted to take samples of the sand. Then, the members of the anti-mining community blocked the road. These guys who are pro-mining shot guns to scare these ones, but these people they didn't let go, they withheld. They therefore took

Ilmenite
Consortium of the Museu de Ciències Naturals de Barcelona
Photography by Joan Rosell Riba

Xholobeni Yards. Titanium and planetary creation of glitter / dust
Andrés Jaque / Office for Political Innovation, 2023

the empty cartouches of the bullets that were fired by these ones, and they invited the police, and they gave them those empty cartouches as evidence that these guys they shot these bullets. And then, the police took the empty cartouches away, which was going to be taken to ballistic assessment to determine whose gun fired those shots. But on the day of the trial, the police didn't have the evidence, those empty cartouches have disappeared. And now the community started to compose the song to say the police commissioner, or the police station commander, is actually one who has killed. He is against us because he is hiding away the evidence, so he is on the side of these guys who are causing problems on our community."[2]

"I'm born and bred in Mpondoland, in a village called Ntontela, and I'm one of the activists fighting against the mining in our land, in our ocean. Whatever happens to the ocean comes back to the land. So, it doesn't make sense to us to say no to mining to the land and yes to mining to the ocean. It does not make sense. Because ocean and the land is one thing, you cannot separate these two. We have to make sure that the mining in the ocean doesn't happen, because as soon as it happens, it will kill our lifeform and our lifestyle. Then we lose our own identity. We will be not able to feed ourselves, we will be not to live in an ecofriendly ecosystem. People, they see us a poorest people in our villages. All we know, we have clean oceans, and lot of food in our ocean, and also animals that actually protect ourselves and the ecosystem. Also we have the land, that means we are rich. It doesn't mean that because not living in a double-story hotel, or a double-story house then we are poor. We are not poor, we are rich."[3]

"I am the spoke person of Amadiba Crisis Committee. If you are going to destroy those caves there, it's the home of some other species. You destroy that ecosystem, because when you blast, you destroy everything that is sitting here. But we are born and bred here, we know the ocean as we know ourselves. The blasting is sound. The sound, you can imagine, the big flight or the jet, when it lands. That is the kind of sound that will be there in the ocean. And even if you are one kilometer away from the airport, the sound when the flight lands or when it goes up, this is the sound that is going to happen there. And you can imagine, the sound of a flight is also making a vibration and this is the thing that they the blasting they are going to do. That is why we say that the caves there are going to be shaken and be destroyed, because vibration will be there and the sound. Animals will move immediately, those that will survive."[4]

2 Sinegugu Zukulu interviewed by Farah Alkhoury (Office for Political Innovation) in Mpondoland, Amadiba, next to Xholobeni (March 2023).

3 Siyabonga Ndovela interviewed by Farah Alkhoury (Office for Political Innovation) in Mpondoland, Amadiba, next to Xholobeni (March 2023).

4 Nonhle Mbuthuma interviewed by Farah Alkhoury (Office for Political Innovation) in Mpondoland, Amadiba, next to Xholobeni (March 2023).

* Andrés Jaque is PhD in Architecture. Dean and Professor at the Graduate School of Architecture, Planning and Preservation, Columbia University.

R&D GLASS

Glass is a versatile material that is very present in our daily lives and plays a key role in contemporary design. Traditional techniques such as glassblowing coexist with highly precise and complex technologies.

The manufacturing of blown glass in Catalonia was recognized as Intangible Cultural Heritage in 2023. Although the technique had been perfected by the fifteenth century, the finest material samples were produced in the sixteenth century.

Daniel Steegmann's *Chandelier* and Pròsper Riba Vilardell's *Touchstone*, made out of recycled glass from the automotive industry, reveal the vibrancy of the tradition. Recycled glass maintains its properties and enables an energy saving of 38% throughout the process: glass once again becomes glass. The combination of innovation and creativity of the works by Cricursa, a Catalan company founded a hundred years ago specializing in curved glass, is another example; its collaborations with architects of international renown like RCR and Rem Koolhaas on works made of curved, laminated glass continue to pave the way in the fields of architecture and design.

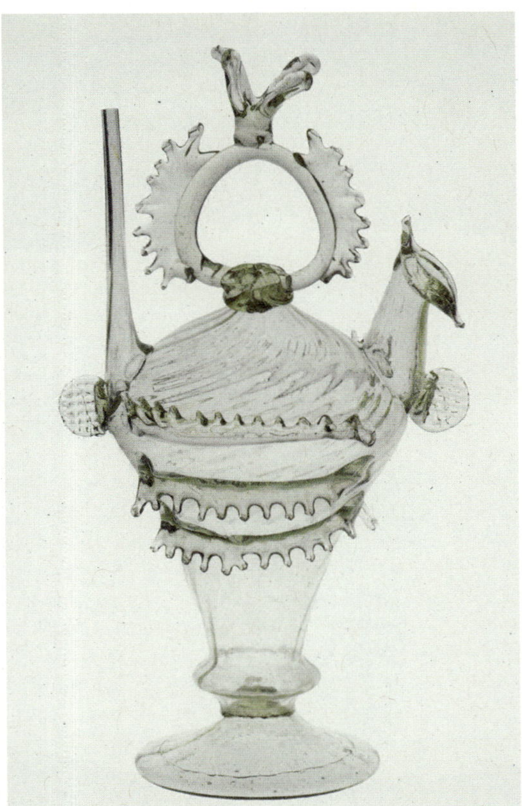

Pitcher
Air blown and pressed glass, stretched, pinched and stamped
Catalonia, 1700–1799
Purchase, 1932 MADB 4.709

Taipei Performing Arts Center
Curved glass *Crisunid*
Rem Koolhaas / OMA, Taiwan, 2019
Manufactured by Cricursa
Loan, Tvitec | Cricursa

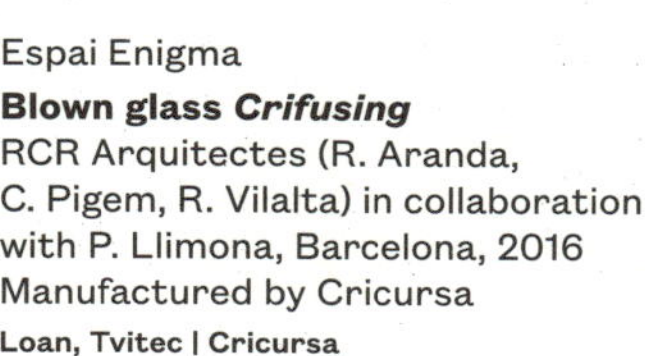

Espai Enigma
Blown glass *Crifusing*
RCR Arquitectes (R. Aranda, C. Pigem, R. Vilalta) in collaboration with P. Llimona, Barcelona, 2016
Manufactured by Cricursa
Loan, Tvitec | Cricursa

Touchstone vase
Hand-blown glass
The Glass Apprentice, 2022 for Mobles 114, Barcelona
Donation, Mobles 114, 2024 MDB 17.086

Lamp *Untitled (Speech Bubbles)*

Blown glass

Daniel Steegmann Mangrané, Barcelona, 2021

Loan, Collection Esther Schipper and Florian Wojnar
Photograph by Andrea Rossetti

Jug
Air blown and pressed glass, enamelled, gilded and pinched
Catalonia, *c.* 1500
Bequest of Emili Cabot i Rovira, 1924
MADB 23.280

Tray
Air-blown and enamelled glass
Catalonia, 1575–1625
Bequest of Emili Cabot i Rovira, 1924
MADB 23.307

COLORED ENAMELED GLASS

The sixteenth and seventeenth centuries were the golden age of enameled glass in Catalonia, an age that produced works which would survive wars, moves, and breakages. Thanks to the interest of nineteenth-century European collectors, these works are now in museums and art collections the world over, thereby ensuring the conservation of a heritage that is now accessible to the public.

They are objects that reveal a blend of styles, a reflection of the wealth of cultural exchanges. Traces of Islamic art can be found in decorative plant elements and geometric motifs, while material lightness and formal diversity betray the influence of the Venetian technique. Catalan glassware was decorated with green, white, yellow, and blue enamels, depicting flowers and green leaves, human figures and animals, showing the richness and variety of local production.

Pitcher
Air-blown glass, enamelled and stretched
Catalonia, 1550–1600
Bequest of Emili Cabot i Rovira, 1924 MADB 23.287

Sweet jar
Air-blown glass, enamelled and stretched
Catalonia, 1550–1600
Bequest of Emili Cabot i Rovira, 1924 MADB 23.290

FROM TRANSLUCENT PORCELAIN TO OPAQUE *CHINOISERIES* THE IMPACT OF ORIENTAL PORCELAIN ON EUROPEAN POTTERY

MARIA ANTÒNIA CASANOVAS*

Origin and inflection point of Chinese porcelain

The discovery of porcelain was not an accident but the result of a gradual technological evolution that took place in Chinese pottery workshops in the 8th century where the use of common clay was eliminated in favour of porcelain stoneware, fired at 1200°C. With this new material, ceramic objects ceased to be porous and the thick walls of pots and other receptacles became thin and delicate, occasionally as fine as an eggshell.

Ceramicists gradually developed and improved the recipe for this proto-porcelain – not found in other countries – until they realized that adding a larger proportion of kaolin to the quartz and feldspar mix resulted in a highly exclusive clay: porcelain. Among porcelain's unique characteristics are its pure white colour and translucence; its impermeability and sound; and its hardness and malleability. These singular features were immediately prized by Chinese emperors and the first European missionaries and merchants who in the second half of the 13th century, travelled to China.[1] The first white and blue porcelain objects were made during the reign of the Mongol-led Yuan dynasty (1278-1644) emperors, yet they reached their peak in the Ming dynasty (1368-1644). Throughout these four centuries, China experienced a social, economic and cultural transformation as its leaders opened the country's borders to the world, revitalizing the network of maritime and land routes along the ancient Silk Road.[2]

Henceforth, trade was revived with other Asian countries, the Middle and Near East, Mediterranean Europe and the east coast of Africa. China exported precious stones and metals, silk, amber, marble, lacquer, porcelain and spices, among other products, and imported European horses, dogs and other animals, furs, honey, grapevines, fruit, glass and wool fabrics.

European fascination with "white and blue" porcelain

The blue colour with which the Chinese made famous the first porcelain exported to Europe was obtained with cobalt oxide, originally from ancient Mesopotamia (today's Iraq). Potters from this country decorated earthenware[3] dishes with this colour, which reminded them of the semi-precious stone they prized the most: lapis lazuli. The Chinese imported cobalt until they discovered numerous mines in their own country. This was well timed as they required large amounts of the compound to meet the growing and obsessive demand for white and blue porcelain. The kilns in Jingdezhen, the largest Chinese ceramic centre, were lit twenty-four hours a day, and the city's strategic geographic location near the sea facilitated the transport of ceramic items. Large amounts travelled in the holds of ships belonging to Chinese and European maritime companies.[4]

The trade was highly lucrative and long-lasting.[5] Collecting porcelain was synonymous with prestige, refinement and elegance. The wealthiest kings, nobles and bourgeoise coveted these rare and exotic objects, and the Chinese jealously guarded their secret formula without sharing it with anybody. It was big business and they had a monopoly. Meanwhile, Western potters only mastered the technique for earthenware[6] which they used to make a wide variety of objects and tableware. These were noteworthy not for their delicateness and refinement but their simple shapes and popular, spontaneous and vibrant decorative qualities; nonetheless, they were affordable for most of their customers.

The great Italian patron of the arts Francesco de' Medici – more interested in science, art and alchemy than politics – commissioned the creation of a porcelain workshop in Pitti Palace, in Florence. Between 1575 and 1582 (the year of his death), the workshop produced about eighty pieces identical to Italian Renaissance gold and silverware yet decorated with floral motifs reminiscent of Chinese designs. The Grand Duke of Tuscany was the first European to happen upon the formula for an imitation porcelain known as Medici porcelain. It was a soft-paste porcelain, very different from authentic Asian porcelain despite the resemblance to it, and like the latter, prohibitively expensive. In the 17th and 18th centuries, other European centres also manufactured soft-paste porcelain objects whose production costs remained exorbitantly high.[7]

1 One of the first Westerners to travel along one of these routes to China was the Venetian merchant Marco Polo (1254-1324), who described the porcelain production process in his *Book of the Marvels of the World*, written between 1298 and 1299.

2 Created in 138 BC by the emperor Wu Ti (Han dynasty, 206 BC – 220 AD).

3 Earthenware covered with an opaque glaze that makes it waterproof and enables polychrome decorations.

4 The East Indies companies had their warehouses and factories in the Port of Canton, except for Spain and Portugal, whose galleons docked in Macao.

5 The East Indies companies were active until the mid-19th century.

6 Technique implemented by Syrian and Egyptian potters in Al-Andalus, which through Spain spread throughout Europe and, from the 16th century, to the New World.

7 Saint-Cloud, Vincennes, Bow, Chelsea, Alcora, Capodimonte, Doccia and Buen Retiro are some examples.

In the 17th century, in the Netherlands, a new genre of painting, still lifes with flowers and fruit, flourished. They featured faithful representations of Chinese ceramic pitchers, plates and bowls. Painters often included in these works more coveted objects, ones which were more fashionable and could endow their customers with greater dignity. Porcelain receptacles – the exuberant flower bouquets and the richness and variety of fruits that appear in these paintings – are associated with luxury, the exotic, and fragility, a quality that symbolizes the fleetingness of earthly life.

In addition to painters, European potters made earthenware imitations of Ming dynasty porcelain. Noteworthy are examples from Delft, Turin and Talavera de la Reina, in which the plants, birds and radial panels characteristic of the Wanli series (1563-1620) can be seen. While not porcelain, they had the same appearance and were affordable; they were like placebos.

However, the zenith of Chinese porcelain in Europe was in the 18th century, a period in which it was referred to as "white gold." The number of collectors increased dramatically. Of Augustus II the Strong, it was said that he suffered from the *maladie de porcelaine*[8] because he ultimately owned more than sixty thousand pieces. China could not keep up with production to meet European demand. Yet, what it exported to Europe did not appeal to all Chinese. In fact, there were two types of production: one for the Chinese market and another exclusively for Westerners. In many cases, Europeans sent to China designs, shields and other items to their liking so that the Chinese could produce customized table settings.

In 1709, an important event occurred: the recipe for porcelain was discovered in Europe, specifically, in Saxony, in the court of Augustus II. The first productions in his Meissen factory were identical copies of the Asian porcelain in his own collection. Orientalism remained the trend. In 1823, Charles Fourier coined the term *chinoiseries*, an allusion to 18th-century Chinese objects – porcelain, lacquerware and wallpaper – and the copies, reproductions and recreations of Chinese motifs produced in Europe. *Chinoiseries* (lit. "China style") are one of the most emblematic expressions of the Rococo style. They are characterized by a vocabulary of figures, flower bouquets, phoenixes and insects, which in some cases were faithful imitations of Chinese objects, while in others they were product of the artisan's imagination. In any event, all complied with Asian ornamental protocol: harmonic asymmetry. The manufacturer Alcora,[9] for example, produced a large amount of tableware adorned with China-style motifs in blue, polychrome and gold highlights. Alcora earthenware was of such high quality that leading experts have agreed it is the best European earthenware of the 18th century. In fact, the main objective of its founder, the Count of Aranda, was to manufacture porcelain. Yet, due to the lack of kaolin, the company could only produce soft-paste porcelain and highly delicate and refined earthenware.

8 Porcelain sickness.

9 Founded in 1727.

Dish
Earthenware decorated with oxides
Miguel Soliva, 1713–1755
Manufactured by Real Fábrica de Loza y Porcelana de Alcora
Purchase, 1932 MCB 4.466

Dish (detail)
Earthenware decorated with oxides
Miguel Soliva, 1713–1755
Manufactured by Real Fábrica de Loza y Porcelana de Alcora
Purchase, 1932 MCB 4.466

Blue and white porcelain was not a passing fancy but continued to form part of the ornamental repertoire of European potters. Proof of the longevity of this trend, which had such a large impact in Europe, are the objects produced by the Galician factory Sargadelos (active between 1806 and 1875).[10] The company mass produced decorative earthenware using new British mechanical processes such as chalcography and transfer-printing.[11] Thanks to their moderate price, printed table settings were used in middle-class households instead of Oriental or European porcelain tableware which, due to its high cost, was not affordable.

10 Founded by Antonio R. Ibáñez, forward-thinking engineer and entrepreneur who always looked to British industry as a model.

11 Chalcography was also used at the Alcora factory and in the factories Pickman and San Juan de Aznalfarache (Seville) and La Cartagenera (Murcia).

***** Maria Antònia Casanovas is historian. From 2004 to 2016 she was conservator in charge of the Museu de Ceràmica in Barcelona.

CHINOISERIE: WHITE GOLD

Chinoiserie is the term used to define a decorative style in Western art characterized by the appropriation of Chinese motifs and techniques. The Silk Road brought Chinese porcelain – known as white gold – to Europe. In the mid-sixteenth century, Spain began to import large amounts of such works, trading by sea with China from Manila. In the early eighteenth century, the Royal Factory of China and Porcelain in Alcora produced high quality china tableware decorated with chinoiserie motifs like lush vegetation and Oriental figures. It met the growing demand for such dinner services by the bourgeoisie, and could well rival luxury porcelain tableware at a lower cost. In the eighteenth century, the Buen Retiro Royal Porcelain Factory only produced *chinoiserie* porcelain for royalty, thereby establishing the Chinese aesthetic as a symbol of prestige and economic competition in Europe.

Orange tree vase
Porcelain decorated with oxides
Antoni Serra i Fiter, 1907
Manufactured by Fàbrica de Porcellanes i Gres d'Art, Barcelona
Purchase, 1907 MCB 1.576

Vase
Porcelain decorated with oxides
Xavier Nogués and Antoni Serra i Fiter, 1906
Manufactured by Fàbrica de Porcellanes and Gres d'Art, Barcelona
Purchase, 1967 MCB 71.918

Jar
Earthenware decorated with oxides
1727–1760
Manufactured by Real Fábrica de Loza y Porcelana de Alcora
Purchase, 1965 MCB 100.063

Sugar bowl
Earthenware decorated with oxides
1727–1760
Manufactured by Real Fábrica de Loza y Porcelana de Alcora
Purchase, 1932 MCB 4.158

Magnolia vase
Porcelain decorated with oxides
Antoni Serra i Fiter, 1906
Manufactured by Fàbrica de Porcellanes i Gres d'Art, Barcelona
Purchase, 1982 MCB 112.996

Vase
Porcelain decorated with oxides
China, 1790–1799
Old collection MCB 9.177

Tova. *3D Print House project*
Clay
IAAC, Valldaura Labs, 2022
Photograph by Gregori Civera

CLAY

Clay is a sedimentary rock composed of hydrous aluminum silicates obtained from the decomposition of stones that contain feldspar, like granite. It can appear in various colors ranging from orange-red to white, according to its impurities.

Over the course of history, the techniques of forming clay have ranged from press molding to modeling on a potter's wheel. The use of clay in 3D printing combines age-old techniques with modern technology. The Institute of Advanced Architecture of Catalonia (IAAC) explores the building potential of local materials by means of 3D printing. Clay is a viable and ecological solution for contemporary construction projects as it enables the creation of complex customized forms with global applications to emergency housing situations.

THE COLOURS OF CERAMICS: MINERAL PIGMENTS, NATURAL COLOURS

ISABEL FERNÁNDEZ DEL MORAL*

Ever since antiquity, humans have endowed objects and our surrounding spaces with properties that contribute to our wellbeing and give us pleasure, sometimes for their powerful symbolic connotations, other times with an aesthetic purpose. Colour is a fundamental part in the quest to achieve visual comfort, and in the past, to attain it, it was necessary to have knowledge of pigments and how to use them. The first pigments were found in natural settings and could be organic and mineral. However, in the context of ceramics, not all pigments work. Applying colour to clay is a complex task, since the substances need to be able to withstand high temperatures, as well as the chemical reactions and physical transformations that occur inside the kiln.

The choice of colour for a piece of pottery can reflect aesthetic, artistic and allegorical goals or the desire to signify luxury and power. But it also involves other issues such as the use of readily available minerals or, on the contrary, ones that have acquired a certain prestige and must be imported from far away. In addition, the technical and technological knowledge and developments achieved in different societies also influence the choice of colour. Firing temperatures, atmospheres and the important role of oxygen in combustion, as well as knowledge of different compositions and mixes of various elements, can result in virtually endless combinations of colours, ranges and hues.

Ideal results are attained when colours are applied over a white surface. Kaolin, a white clay essential to produce porcelain, served this purpose. Worthy for some of the designation "white gold," porcelain has been the object of desire and greed for its special characteristics: hardness, translucency, sonority and whiteness. Since the arrival in Europe of the first tableware brought by Marco Polo from China, finding the formula for porcelain became a priority for the European powers. While many did not achieve the desired result, the process itself resulted in numerous productions appreciated to this day for their high quality.

The first attempts at porcelain were made in Egypt and Mesopotamia, about 5000 years ago. However, the turning point in the use of colour over white ceramic surfaces came in the 8th century, in the Near East, and from there the technique reached Al-Andalus.[1] This was revolutionary and led to the production of enamelled pottery covered with tin oxide, a white colour with an opaque quality, resulting in new decorative outcomes and complex methods to obtain finishes that clearly enhanced the aesthetic effect of objects.

These colours added brightness and liveliness to buildings, both in façades and interiors. The use of ceramics applied to architecture reached its apogee with the technical improvement of glazed tiles. These provided a hygienic quality and thermal insulation ideal for construction, while at the same time they became the perfect medium for colourful and bright adornments.

The diversity of colours used in ceramics can be, as previously stated, quite rich. When using oxides, a vast colour range is possible, depending on how much are used, their combination with other minerals, the atmosphere in the kiln and temperature, among other factors.

Green hues obtained with copper are very common, although this mineral is also used to achieve red and golden tones. Copper is one of the most used minerals since prehistory. Very abundant in nature and easy to reuse, copper is appreciated for its ductility and because its high thermal and electrical conductivity enable the manufacturing of fibre optics and a wide range of electronic devices. When applied as an oxide in ceramics, copper can be a strong colourant. Egyptian turquoise paste was produced in ancient Egypt, but copper was commonly used to obtain a wide range of greens. Surprising results can be achieved if the firing is done in a reduction atmosphere (without oxygen inside the kiln). Depending on the glaze base, the chemical reaction can produce a metallic finish or a bright red called oxblood, highly valued in Chinese porcelain.

The combination of copper and manganese oxides (to obtain black) produced colours that resulted in the most emblematic Al-Andalus pottery: the green and purple of the Caliphate period which, later, in the medieval period, would be duplicated by Mudejar workshops under the Catalan-Aragonese crown. Infused with enormous symbolism, these colours illustrate the caliph's power and the Muslim religion. White is the colour of the Umayyad dynasty, green denotes Islam, and black its prophet Muhammad.

Copper was also the primary mineral in the new alchemical formula that arrived from Syria and Egypt to Al-Andalus workshops where pottery with a golden finish or metallic lustre was made. This material requires a complex technique in terms of mineral composition, temperatures and firing atmosphere. A mix of silver, copper oxide, cinnabar and red ochre diluted in vinegar was applied to the fired and opacified (with tin oxide) piece. The latter would be fired a third time to a low temperature in a reduction atmosphere.

1 Area of the Iberian peninsula under Muslim rule during the Middle Ages, between 711 and 1492.

Cobalt
Photograph by Adobe Stock

This complex technology gave rise to a luxury industry that substituted, and often imitated, gold and silver tableware.[2] These products were highly sought after by wealthy families in all the Western Mediterranean during the 15th century.

Blue, the quintessential colour in ceramics, can be achieved with cobalt. Specifically, it is obtained with cobalt oxide, a much prized mineral that endows objects with a high degree of prestige. It was used first in China, by way of Persia, to manufacture the precious porcelain pieces that started a trend in Europe in the late 14th century. There, ceramic workshops made this blue colour fashionable and filled European markets with their productions, replacing the previous ones.

Cobalt oxide produces ceramic surfaces with a wide range of blue tones depending on the mix of the glaze: from azure to marine, from bright blues to greyish ones. It is a highly stable element that always produces intense blues regardless of the firing atmosphere, although when mixed with other elements, other colours can be achieved such as pink, violet or red.

2 As a result of the Pragmatic Sanction of 2 June 1600, which prohibited the manufacture and use of gold and silver objects.

Even though this is a powerful colourant – even used in low percentages it manages to produce blue hues –, obtaining it has been difficult throughout history and thus application of this blue pigment was limited to valuable and luxury objects.

Usually, cobalt is found next to nickel, arsenic, iron or manganese. It is toxic, and handling and collecting it is dangerous. Extraction of mineral ores combined with arsenic makes it a high-risk activity. The German mining tradition contains many legends referring to evil spirits of the underworld named *kobold* that are lethal.[3] Even today, the same connotations apply to the mines in the Democratic Republic of Congo, where thousands of people work in exploitative and risky conditions detrimental both to their health and the environment.[4]

Nonetheless, mining for this raw material will not stop as it is a basic metal used in many of today's technologies (it is one of the elements required to manufacture lithium batteries for cars, phones, computers and electronic cigarettes).

In the ceramic sector, several projects are underway aimed at reducing cobalt extraction. The American Chemical Society has recently published the results of a research project in which a stable and reliable ceramic pigment was obtained from a barium, aluminium, silicon and cobalt compound heated at high temperature, thus reducing the amount of cobalt needed.[5] Meanwhile, the Instituto de Tecnología Cerámica (ITC), a research institute affiliated with Jaume I University, is conducting a study of the recovery of cobalt from electronic waste and its use in ceramic pigments.[6]

Other more abundant and easier to obtain minerals offer very versatile results, as is the case with iron. Iron oxide, frequently found in soils, has been the most common colourant since ancient times, including in ceramics. These oxides offer a wide array of hues ranging from yellow, ochre, brown, reddish and orange in an oxidation atmosphere, and grey, celadon green and black in a reduction atmosphere.

Finally, once the behaviour and results of these pigments are understood, all that remains is to blend them to obtain wonderful polychromatic effects. In the 16th century, Italian Renaissance artistic trends influenced the use of colours that had not been common in ceramics up to that time. One of the most characteristic was yellow, achieved using lead antimonate, also known as Naples yellow. With the addition of this final colour, the ceramic palette of mineral pigments was now complete and fully capable of producing the most beautiful pieces imaginable.

3 Laura Perryman: *The Colour Bible: The definitive guide to colour in art and design*, Ilex Press, 2021.

4 Kara Norton, *National Geographic*, 27 December 2023. https://www.nationalgeographic.es/autor/kara-norton.

5 Zhiwei Wang *et al.*, "Application and Properties of Co_2+-Doped $BaAl_2Si_2O_8$ Blue Pigments in Glazes", ACS Appl. Opt. Mater., 2 (2024): 313-322. https://doi.org/10.1021/acsaom.3c00419.

6 COBAT. https://www.itc.uji.es/el-itc-recupera-cobalto-de-dispositivos-electronicos-usados-para-fabricar-pigmentos-ceramicos/.

* Isabel Fernández del Moral is historian and conservator at the Museu del Disseny de Barcelona (DHub).

THE MATERIALITY OF COLORS. PIGMENTS IN POTTERY

With its combination of beauty and utility, pottery has captivated human civilization for centuries. Classified as metal oxide and synthetic pigments, they are essential as color is an expressive element.

Josep Llorens Artigas considered his work *Clar de lluna* one of his masterpieces. Acquired in 1932 by the Board of Museums of Barcelona, it is a fine example of the style that dominated his works, inspired both by tradition and by East Asian models, and characterized by his experiments with enamel resulting in high quality glazes and tonalities and depth.

The Museu del Disseny-DHub encompasses works by other artists who explored the field of pottery pigments, albeit in different ways, like Josep Puig i Cadafalch, Pablo Picasso, and Antoni Cumella and his firm, whose frequent collaborations with artists, designers, and architects were of international renown.

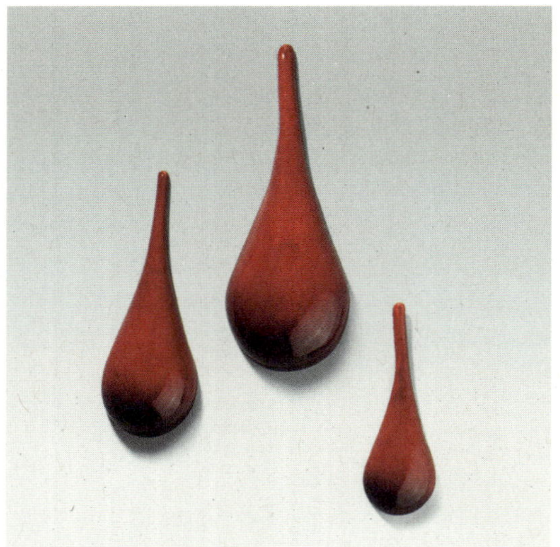

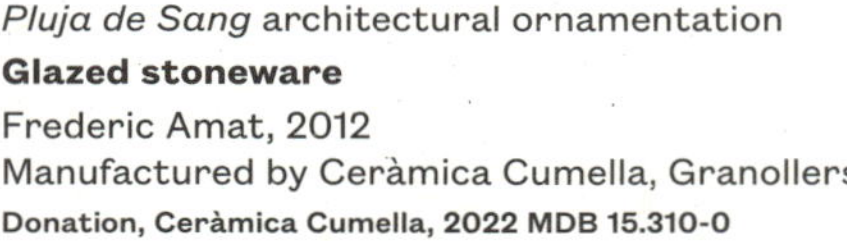

Pluja de Sang architectural ornamentation
Glazed stoneware
Frederic Amat, 2012
Manufactured by Ceràmica Cumella, Granollers
Donation, Ceràmica Cumella, 2022 MDB 15.310-0

Vase
Stoneware decorated with oxides
Josep Llorens Artigas, Gallifa, *c.* 1952
Donation, Isabel Escalada, vidow of Xavier Nogués, 1969 MCB 107.774

Vase
Stoneware decorated with oxides
Antoni Cumella, Granollers, 1981
Purchase, 1982 MCB 112.997

Bourrache vase

Terracotta with engobe and wax reserves, painted and glazed

Pablo Picasso, 1952

Manufactured by Poterie Madoura, Valauri

Donation, Pablo Picasso, 1957 MCB 64.660

Vase
Stoneware decorated with oxides
Josep Llorens Artigas, Gallifa, 1972
Donation, Mariette Gardy Artigas, 1991 MCB 154.633

COBALT BLUES

From ancient Egypt to dynastic China, cobalt has been valued for its ability to create bright, long-lasting colors in glass, enamel, and ceramics. Originally black in color, it turns blue when oxidized, an aesthetical feature that can be contemplated in a fifteenth-century tile produced in Manises (Valencia), in dishes, and in modern artworks by Joan Miró, Antoni Cumella, and Josep Llorens Artigas.

While the *New Majolica* bottles by Gerard Moliné criticize the consumption of plastic containers, the telephones designed and produced by the Fairphone company cause minimum harm to people and the planet. This is because they are made of cobalt from artisanal extraction cooperatives dedicated to fair trade in Democratic Republic of the Congo, country that produces 70% of global cobalt.

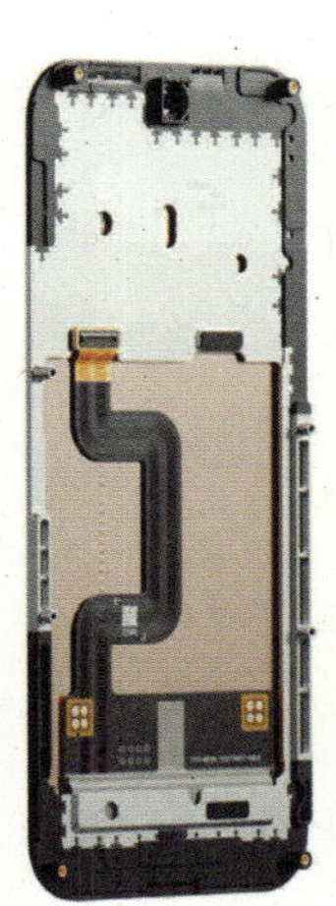

New Majolica 1 L #4 bottle
Hand-glazed porcelain
Gerard Moliné, 2014
Manufactured by Estudimoline, Barcelona
Donation, Gerard Navarro, 2024

Fairphone 5, 2023
Exploded view of a Fairphone, a smartphone designed and produced with minimal harm to people and the planet
Photograph by Fairphone

RECKONING WITH CONCRETE*

DAVID HOWE#

Iron, steel, aluminium, copper, glass, concrete, stone, brick and almost every bit of material stuff in our man-made world started life as a rock or mineral vein of one kind or another. As you look around any house, office, town or city nearly everything started life below the surface of the earth. The plastic casing around computer screens, steel radiators, aluminium-framed windows with their panes of glass, the copper wiring carrying the electricity to laptops, the rare earth metals that enable mobile phones to perform their wonders, the bricks to build houses. Before they all became this material stuff, they were the end-product of some geological process, some rock-forming activity, some rock-weathering breakdown, some human intervention.

Nowadays, we mine, quarry, pump, cut, blast and crush billions and billions of tons of the rock that lies beneath our feet every year. We are digging into and scraping away the surface of our planet at an unprecedented rate. We are shifting so much of the Earth's crust, and to such an extent, that we are now far outstripping nature's annual capacity to move mountains and fill oceans through wear, tear and weathering. And when all of this rock has been crushed and carried to the furnaces and factories, the cunning of men and women reworks these earthly treasures into new, marvellous things. We transmute nature. With cunning and chemistry, skill and ingenuity we weave our rocky resources into the very fabric of the modern world in which we live, work and play.

Let us look at one rock-based material in a little more detail. Concrete. It's no surprise to learn that concrete is the single most widely used man-made material in the world. The building industry has an insatiable appetite for concrete.

For thousands of years limestones have been used to build temples and cathedrals, palaces and pyramids, houses and castles. The ancient

Egyptians, Greeks and Romans had also learned that by heating limestone you can make quicklime or calcium oxide. And if you mix the lime with ash or similar materials you can make cement. Modern-day production involves crushing the limestone which is mainly made of calcium carbonate, then heating it to very high temperatures in a rotating kiln to drive off carbon dioxide, grinding it to a powder, mixing it with clay, heating it again before subjecting it to one final pulverisation to produce the cement powder. To make concrete the cement is mixed with water, sand and other aggregates. After being poured the concrete sets hard.

It's unlikely that the poet William Wordsworth or the polymath John Ruskin would have much good to say about concrete. They both believed that buildings, especially in the countryside, should blend sympathetically with their environment. Ruskin also felt that buildings and their form should remain true to the inherent character of the materials out of which they were built. Brick should appear as brick, stone as stone, wood as wood. Materials shouldn't dissemble.

But what is the natural form of concrete? What is it that architects are supposed to remain true to when they build with concrete? What architects slowly began to appreciate was that concrete's true character was its ability to take on any shape or form. In concrete, anything became possible.

In the hands of the best architects concrete can be beautiful. The sensuous sinuous flow of Zaha Hadid's Heydar Aliyev Centre in Baku, Azerbaijan; the billowing sails of the Sydney Opera House; the ethereal Millau Viaduct in southern France. Concrete can also be unapologetically functional: dams, sea defences, bridges. Concrete has built the modern world. It's everywhere. In skyscrapers and office blocks, high-rise housing and underground sewage systems, foundations and multi-storey car parks, tunnels and train stations, airports and docksides. But all too often, designs in concrete go astray. This is when concrete gets a bad press. It doesn't always weather well. It ages badly. It crumbles and discolours. Dystopian cityscapes feel dark, dank and dangerous. Millions of people live and work in concrete jungles.

But we are now paying a price for our love-affair with this most versatile of materials. Huge quarries and pits are dug to mine the billions of tons of limestone, sand and gravel needed to feed the factories and satisfy the material appetites of those who design and build. The extraction industries cut into hillsides, eat away mountains and scar the landscape. "The transformation of the Earth's land surface by mineral extraction and construction,' writes the geologist Anthony Cooper and his colleagues, 'is on a scale hugely greater than natural erosive terrestrial geological processes... Humans are now the major global geological driving force and an important component of Earth System processes in landscape evolution.'"[1] We are modifying the Earth to such an extent that we are creating a new geological epoch. As we degrade, pollute, re-shape and globally heat the planet causing climate change we are creating the beginnings of a new geological epoch. We have named it the Anthropocene.

1 Anthony Cooper, Teresa Brown, Simon Price, Jonathan Ford, Colin Waters: "Humans are the most significant global geomorphological driving force of the 21st Century", *Anthropocene Review*, 5 (3), 2018, pp. 222-229. https://doi. org/10.1177/2053019618800234.

It is in the manufacture of cement itself that we see one of its greatest environmental impacts. The very high temperatures needed to turn limestone and clay into cement are still mainly achieved by burning natural gas, coke or oil emitting vast volumes of the greenhouse gas, carbon dioxide, in the process. In order to produce one metric tonne of cement, approximately one metric tonne of carbon dioxide is generated. Burning fossil fuels, turning limestone into quicklime, and allowing the cement to set contribute 8 per cent of the world's annual emission of anthropogenically generated carbon dioxide, the greenhouse gas.

Emissions of carbon dioxide, whether from power stations, cement kilns or car engines are implicated in global heating and climate change. In turn, this leads to melting ice caps. For example, a study led by the geophysicist Ingo Sasgen[2] found that in 2019 the Greenland ice sheet had lost a record amount of ice, equivalent to a million tonnes per minute across the year. In 2020, a large section of the Greenland sea ice shelf, known as N79, broke off and broke up as it slipped into the ocean. Ice loss has tripled since the turn of the twenty-first century, as documented by NASA. Melting ice leads to rises in sea levels. Higher seas flood low-lying coastal areas. They alter the geography and shift the pattern of sedimentary movements and deposition. All of these geomorphological changes will appear in the geological records of the future.

As well as producing carbon dioxide and other noxious gases, burning wood and fossil fuels releases smoke and soot. These tiny particles of fly ash and black carbon eventually settle over the land and fall into lakes and rain down on the sea. Trace layers of these particles have been found in recent sedimentary deposits worldwide. This global footprint of human activity is now regarded as another key signature of the Anthropocene.

With this picture of global heating and climate change in the background, concrete's story is one of both virtues and vices. It has transformed our world. Our complex infrastructures depend on it. Concrete has allowed us to build big and high, solid and strong, quick and cheap. Its flexibility and versatility have helped engineers, designers and architects create ever-more breath-taking structures.

But concrete has its dark side. Billions of tons of concrete are produced annually. As well as cement production's huge carbon footprint, at the end of its working life, concrete hangs around. It too often fails the environmentalist's four virtues test: *renounce, reduce, reuse and recycle*. Unlike glass, aluminium and iron, concrete is difficult to recycle. When its days are over and buildings are demolished, the crushed concrete doesn't disappear. It is left as rubble, landfill and urban waste. Just like natural sediments, it gets dispersed and buried. It accumulates in pockets and layers, where, in a million years' time or more, it could still be present as a strange calcareous, limey geological layer sandwiched between bands of sand or beds of shale or solidified seams of household rubbish and industrial waste. Concrete's poor recyclability means that it could be recognised as one of the signature 'rocks' of the Anthropocene

"In *The Story of Stuff*,[3] Annie Leonard reminds us of the sheer wastefulness of the way we organise our materials economy. The system is linear. We go from extraction to production to distribution to consumption to disposal. Every stage has implications for people and the environment.

2 Ingo Sasgen, et al.: "Return to rapid ice loss in Greenland and record loss in 2019 detected by the GRACE-FO satellites", *Communications Earth & Environment*, 1 (8), 2020. https://doi.org/10.1038/s43247-020-0010-1.

3 Annie Leonard: *La historia de las cosas*, Fondo de Cultura Económica de España, 2010. Accessible in: https://www.storyofstuff.org/.

Linear systems will not work forever on a finite planet. Modern economic systems of deregulated capitalism demand that we make consumption our way of life. Capitalism requires that we buy, discard and replace at an ever-increasing rate. It demands perpetual growth. Its appetite for the planet's resources knows no limits. But the world's resources, geological and biological, are ultimately limited. We live, says the French thinker Bruno Latour, in a narrow zone on the Earth's surface. He calls this the 'critical zone,' with a band of air above and surface crust below, a zone that supports all life. 'In the critical zone,' he says, 'we must maintain what we have because it is finite, it's local, it's at risk and it's the object of conflict.'"[4]

"Yes, we are technologically clever, but all too often we can be environmentally stupid. We shall continue to mine and extract, manufacture and make, use and consume, but we have to listen to what environmental scientists have to say and heed the warnings of the ecologically wise. We have to consume less. The footprints we leave on the planet have to be smaller. Our economies have to be circular and not linear. Whatever we do, the Earth will still be here. But whether we will be around to see it will depend on us."

4 Interview by Jonathan Watts to Bruno Latour in *The Guardian*, 6th June 2020, https://www.theguardian.com/world/2020/jun/06/bruno-latour-coronavirus-gaiahypothesis-climate-crisis.

* Extracts and adaptations from *Extraction to Extinction: Rethinking our Relationship with Earth's Natural Resources* by David Howe, Saraband: Salford, UK, 2021.

‡ David Howe is professor Emeritus at the University of East Anglia, School of Social Work.

Zeleste table lamp
Alabaster
Santiago Roqueta Matías and Àngel Jové, 1973
Manufactured by Santiago Roqueta and Àngel Jové, Snark Design, Santa & Cole, Ediciones de Diseño, Barcelona
Donation, Santa & Cole, Ediciones de Diseño SA, 1994 MADB 135.656

ALABASTER. DISASTER

The story behind an alabaster souvenir covers thousands of kilometers traveled between Spain and China or India. 80% of the world's alabaster is extracted in Spain, Italy, Egypt, the United States, Mexico, and China. Alabaster is a microcrystalline variety of chalk resembling polished marble. Its fragility explains why only 15% of it is commercialized. The exploitation of open-pit quarries has a huge environmental impact, and exportation to countries like India for the creation of manufactured works prevents added value being derived from the region of production.

The *Zaida* side table by si.atelier and *Zeleste* table lamp by Santiago Roqueta and Àngel Jové are examples of local artisanal alternatives to this exportation of resources. Both objects reflect local alabaster's potential in the production of mono-material objects that take advantage of its ductile and translucent properties for high-quality design.

Zaida table
Alabaster cut and varnished
Si.Atelier (Sonia Michalopoulou and Isabel Francoy), 2021
Manufactured by Si.Atelier, Barcelona
Donation, Si.Atelier (Isabel Francoy and Sonia Michalopoulou), 2024 MDB 17.027

MARÉS SANDSTONE, WOOD AND MARINE PLANTS

CARLES OLIVER*

The 6th IPCC report (2023)[1] indicates that currently implemented policies are leading to global warming scenarios in which the temperature increase will be above 3°C, meaning that the Paris Agreement's goal to keep the temperature rise between 1.5°C and 2°C will not be met.

What can we do in the field of architecture to contribute to changing the model immediately?

In general, protection of local ecosystems in richer countries involves the delocalization of production processes and negative impact on the ecosystems of poorer countries. To adapt to climate change, without depending on future technological developments whose efficiency and viability are unknown, architecture can search for production models that prioritize global social justice, within a paradigm of degrowth. In other words, we can reduce resource consumption, minimize the impact of manufacturing processes on people and places globally, and increase levels of comfort and well-being, always seeking the highest degree of energy and material self-sufficiency possible.

How can architecture address these challenges every day?

One option is for architecture to provide habitability and comfort as passively as possible, with the aim of minimizing the:

a) Total energy demand for heating and cooling of spaces.

b) Embedded emissions of the building methods used.

c) External energy dependence.

d) High maintenance costs that result in the planned obsolescence of current technology.

In the Balearic Islands, a proposal has been collectively developed based on these premises which defines habitability according to a "local resources map." In addition to social (housing emergency, lack of skilled labour, etc.) and atmospheric factors (temperature, humidity, solar exposure, rain, wind, etc.), it includes the use of low environmental impact materials, preferably local ones, whose characteristics comply with both European and regional laws. For example, in the Balearic Islands, regional climate change law states that "local governments shall incorporate eco-friendly building materials, preferably of local origin" (BOIB 27, 02/03/2019).

In addition to the materials used in sectors undergoing an ecological transition, we also have at our disposal another set of resources, those used in vernacular architecture,[2] which have the added value of constituting the cultural heritage and landscape of each geographic area. With few exceptions, they are materials used in the self-building sector (and therefore exempt from obligatory EC marking) or produced by small family businesses that lack ecolabels but whose proximity allows for in-person inspection of production processes). The combined use of local available resources and imported ones with environmental certification seals represents a model that enables reducing by more than 60% the CO_2 emissions generated during construction work and complying immediately with the European Commission's "Fit for 55" reduction target for 2030.

The work of recovering and developing the know-how of each resource must include learning the skills and constructive tradition associated with the material to dispel certain aesthetic preconceptions that could complicate the projects in terms of costs, maintenance and durability. Working from the premise of optimization of the mechanical and constructive capabilities of vernacular materials such as raw earth, stone, lime, glue-free sawn lumber, marine plants, etc., enables reducing incidental expenses and gives rise to building, spatial and formal solutions specific to each one.

It is difficult for individual studies to undertake singlehandedly the research, collection, updating and dissemination of knowledge of traditional techniques adapted to the means available to us today. Consequently, the involvement of the local governments of each region, with their own map of resources, will be necessary.

One example could be reuse of marés[3] sandstone which, after years of disuse and relegation to a merely decorative function, has been recovered as a material for load-bearing structures and walls in social housing projects promoted by the Balearic Islands Regional Government.

In the planning and execution of four projects in the period 2018-2023, the refinement of the building technique in which such elements as the type of mortar between blocks, the anchorages between double walls, the type of roof, and unreinforced lintels is noteworthy. The latest project to date involving this material is the construction of six publicly subsidized housing developments in Santa Eugenia.

1 *Sixth assessment report*, published by the Intergovernmental Panel on Climate Change (IPCC), the United Nations (UN) body that provides regular scientific assessments on climate change and proposes adaptation and mitigation strategies, approved by the 195 member states (IPCC, 2023).

2 Vernacular architecture is an architectural style based on the ancestral building tradition of each place, generally executed without architects. It was popularized by Bernard Rudofsky at the MoMA exhibition *Architecture without architects* in 1964.

3 Local sandstone found in Mallorca, Menorca and Formentera.

In terms of design, repetition and standardization were key factors in significantly streamlining the building process and compensating for cost overrun of traditional materials compared to conventional ones, making their use in construction work more feasible and viable. In the six public housing units in Santa Eugenia, ensuring that the distance to shafts between the pillars was always the same, regardless of the project and use, was a priority. Thus, in addition using a mini crane, pillars were raised with a template formed by a metal framework, while the structural unit consists of two 40 x 80 cm pillars thickened with a 10 cm wall, on which the stone lintels rest on the ground floor and the wooden lintels on the first floor. The vault arch is also always uniform.

In the six public housing unit project, "urban mining" was carried out with building elements from a preexisting farming warehouse: marés sandstones, tiles and two wooden exterior doors. In addition, solid wood formwork panels were reused for inclined slabs on the first floor while all interior woodwork consists of beams salvaged from a demolition.

Only high-quality well-preserved wood was chosen, which can be seen in the distance between the knots: the closer they are together, the better the wood, as this indicates slower growth.

The main advantage of using wood predating the 1970s is, in general, that the felling and drying process was carried out properly, allowing for natural growth with an ideal proportion of heartwood and sapwood. It is important to choose boards without high levels of woodworm or xylophagous insect infestation, as these can spread to the rest of the house.

The rest of the wood is imported, preferably from the peninsula, with an FSC or PEFC forest management seal as a necessary condition.

The Santa Eugenia public housing project proves the viability of incorporating stone vaults into group housing projects to ensure thermal inertia and execution of the vertical and horizontal structure using the same local low-carbon material. The stone necessarily works through compression forces, which translates here into barrel vaults that passively cool these buildings in summer and cope with the increasingly intense heat waves.

One of the most eye-opening discoveries made during the design process with the planners was that while the vault makes a lot of sense in the ground-floor ceiling, the first-floor ceiling requires structural overexertion, as the horizontal pressure is very high, and consequently for a two-story building type, a slightly inclined roof appears to be the most efficient solution in P1, even though currently the truss wood must be imported from outside the island. Interestingly, by designing without aesthetic preconceptions and without imposing a predetermined result, the same structural solution that had been developed over centuries of vernacular refinement in typical traditional Mallorcan architecture was reached.

Another building element that might appear to be secondary, such as the type of thermal insulation for the roof, can also be a significant factor when determining the building's volumetrics. If natural fibres are used,[4] again, accumulated experience suggests opting for an inclined roof, both to facilitate the construction of the roof itself during the rainy season (for some reason, it never rains in the Mediterranean, except when the roof is being built!) and to complete the installation with a breathable waterproof layer.

The insulation in the six-unit public housing project consists of dried dead *Posidonia oceanica*, commonly known as Neptune grass, a protected Mediterranean marine seagrass species. Although it cannot be sold and its use requires permission from the responsible authorities, Neptune grass is a good example of how each context has resources that can constitute a production model that respects surrounding ecosystems.

Neptune grass does not rot once it is dry if proper humidity levels are maintained and, after being extracted from the sea, no insect, bacteria or mammal eats the plant, thus guaranteeing its durability. Samples more than six hundred years old and in a perfect state of preservation exist.

This project is only one instance in a series of examples recently developed in the Balearic Islands that demonstrate the viability of a production model in the construction sector that reduces the externalities it generates.

The sum of these proposals represents an architectural language based neither on style nor form, but the incorporation of environmental and social priorities. Thus, the recovery of cultural heritage becomes a tool both for meeting decarbonization objectives and reviving the notion of the city as the sum of anonymous and silent contributions.

Self-sufficiency in building processes blurs the limit between productive space in the city and productive space in the country, as the city is built with materials from adjacent rural areas.

The model can be replicated and is adaptable within each context and to its map of local resources.

4 For example, cork, wood, recycled cotton, wool from sheep, dried dead Neptune grass, etc., depending on the resource map of each region.

* Carles Oliver is architect and director of the 'Life Reusing Posidonia' project at IBAVI, awarded the LIFE 2021 prize for the best environmental project by the European Commission.

INHABITING AN ECOSYSTEM: *MARÈS* [MAJORCAN LIMESTONE]

The need to save energy resources and scarce assets like the water used in building materials such as bricks and concrete has led the construction industry to consider reintroducing local stone. This is the case of Majorcan limestone in the Balearic Islands.

The use of local materials and traditional techniques in the 6HPP Santa Eugènia design of six social houses in Majorca significantly reduces carbon dioxide (CO_2) emissions and construction waste, while improving energy efficiency. The building, developed for the Balearic Housing Institute (IBAVI, for its Spanish initials) by architects Carles Oliver Barceló and Xim Moyá Costa, employs local materials: its structure is made of Majorcan limestone, its insulation is made of seagrass and recycled wood. This project doesn't only provide environmental benefits, but also promotes a better quality of life, proving that we don't only inhabit homes, we also inhabit ecosystems.

6 publicly subsidized housing units in Santa Eugènia
Carles Oliver, Xim Moyá, 2021
Photograph by José Hevia

6 publicly subsidized housing units in Santa Eugènia
Carles Oliver, Xim Moyá, 2021
Photograph by José Hevia

6

DIGI
MATTE

Hortensia armchair
Pink petals made of 100% polyester (PES) on moulded foam covering metal structure
Andrés Reisinger (digital artist) and Julia Esqué (design), Barcelona, 2019
Loan, Andrés Reisinger / Reisinger Studio

Bikini
Lycra knit fabric, synthetic fibre for the daisies
Encarnació Domènech, *c.* 1969
Manufactured by Kuny, Barcelona
Donation, Encarnació Domènech, 1982
MTIB 143.086

THE NEW VIRTUAL

A new generation of creators is using 3D modeling and tools of artificial intelligence (AI) to represent different worlds, often in a dreamlike aesthetic. Some of these designs that arise in the virtual world end up becoming new realities. The formal exuberance of the *Hortensia* chair by Andrés Reisinger captivated social media and went viral, which led to its materialization. Designer Júlia Esqué was in charge of its material development, in which 20,000 pieces of polyester in the shape of rose petals transform a virtual concept into a commercial piece of furniture and a cult object.

THE NEW VIRTUAL. A GLOSSARY*

BIKA REBEK / MARLIES WIRTH#

In virtual space, visionary designs and fictional scenarios for architecture and urban planning can be imagined and distributed beyond the limitations of the real world. Widely accessible computational tools and the socio-technical aspects of Internet use have not only revolutionized the creative process and concept development in architecture and design, but have also expanded our understanding of how we shape, experience, and navigate space.

Over the last decade, a new generation of imaginative creators from a range of backgrounds and disciplines – including architecture, landscape design, interior and product design, urban planning, visual arts, game design, and film – has emerged. This new manifestation of The New Virtual addresses the challenges and potentials of virtual worlds, as well as the associated social, ecological, political, and infrastructural effects. These creators feature critical, interactive, participatory, playable, and hyper-realistic works from younger generations in a variety of media, such as renderings, CGI visualizations, 3D animations and prints, digital films, virtual reality, blockchain projects, and video games.

Interconnected terms from 3D modelling to worldbuilding are essential to navigate the New Virtual. Here is a non-exhaustive glossary generated by Chat GPT-3, reviewed and refined by human editors.

3D Modelling

3D modelling is the process of creating three-dimensional digital representations of objects, buildings, spaces, or scenes. It involves the creation of geometry, textures, lighting, and materials to produce a realistic or stylized model. 3D modelling is used in various fields such as film, game development, architecture, product design, and virtual worlds.

3D scan

3D scanning is a technology used to convert physical objects, architectures, or landscapes into digital 3D models. For this purpose, special scanners with cameras and sensors are often used to capture objects based on their shape, texture, size, location in space, etc. In this way, millimetre-sized components or even entire planets can be digitized without having to reproduce them using laborious → ***3D modelling***.

AI model

AI models are specific applications of → ***machine learning***. An AI model is a computer program developed by training machine learning algorithms based on a large amount of data that is capable of performing specific tasks or making predictions, such as image recognition, speech recognition, or automated decision-making.

Algorithm

An algorithm is a step-by-step procedure for solving a problem. It consists of a sequence of instructions that can be executed by a computer or other device. Algorithms can be used to process data, perform complex calculations, or make decisions. Text-to-image algorithms such as → ***Midjourney***, Dall-E, or Stable Diffusion have become increasingly popular with creators. In this context, the question of authorship is currently being debated: While human designers still provide the original idea or concept in the form of the text prompt, the interpretation and realization of the visualization is performed by the algorithm. Who is the actual creator of the work and what role do cultural, social, and technological factors play in its creation? Certainly, the use of algorithms can open up new and surprising possibilities of co-creation and collaboration and expand the creative process.

Cappricio

Capriccio (Ital. caprice) is a term in architecture that refers to a fantasy or dream representation of a building or landscape. Different architectural elements and styles can be assembled in fictional and often fantastic combinations to visualize architectural visions that are beyond the realm of the possible and do not serve any practical function. Architectures created with AI-based software such as → ***Midjourney*** or as → ***Dreamscapes*** are often capriccios.

CGI (Computer Generated Imagery)

CGI refers to images and animations (series of images) produced using computer software. They are often used in the film and video game industries to create complex effects and scenes that would not be possible using traditional methods. There are different reasons for using CGI, which can range from having more control of a situation or retouching mistakes to recreating images from past times.

Chat GPT

Chat GPT (Generative Pre-trained Transformer) is a powerful text-based → ***AI model*** based on the GPT architecture. It is designed to simulate humanlike conversations and can be used for a variety of applications such as chatbots, text generation, and automatic translation. It does this by tracing its way word by word through the text that is being generated.

CNC fabrication

CNC fabrication refers to the computer-controlled production of parts, entire component groups, or models from a variety of materials. However, the name CNC (Computerized Numerical Control) says nothing about how materials are processed. Rather, it is a collective term that refers to the fact that a machine is given positions in space with the help of a sequence of numbers, at which certain work steps are then to be performed. CNC fabrication methods such as 3D printing and 3-axis milling are techniques used to turn digital models back into physical objects.

Digital twin

A digital twin is a digital replica of a real object or system. Various data and sources are collected and located in a virtual model. This can be used to simulate different scenarios and configurations. Digital twins are often created on the basis of → ***3D scans***.

Dreamscapes

Dreamscapes are digital environments that merge reality and fiction with the help of technological tools such as → ***rendering***, → ***CGI*** or by using → ***AI models***. In these utopian virtual places and spaces, the laws of the physical world are suspended. They can combine utopian, dystopian, bizarre, and surreal elements, rendering surfaces, textures, light, and materials with a degree of realism almost indistinguishable from a "real" photograph.

Game engine

A game engine is a software platform that enables developers to create computer games faster and more efficiently, manage the user interface, control the interaction with the computer's hardware, and optimize the game's performance.

Lore

Lore is a body of knowledge, traditions, and stories that have a certain meaning within a culture or group. It can include myths, legends, history, and customs that have been passed down through oral or written tradition. In the context of → ***worldbuilding*** and the → ***metaverse***, "lore" can refer to the narrative and backstory of a virtual world or game. The lore of a virtual world can include information about the setting, such as the geography, technology, and political structure, as well as details about the different factions and characters that populate the world. Lore can help create a sense of immersion and depth in a virtual world. Lore is often created and maintained by the developers of the virtual world, but it can also be shaped and expanded upon by the community of players who inhabit it.

Machine learning

Machine learning refers to a type of artificial intelligence that allows computers to recognize patterns in data and make predictions without being specifically programmed. Instead, large numbers of reference datasets are used to train the machine. This means that the machine learns "on its own" from the given data. If these data contain certain world views and opinions, these are also transferred to the AI, which is often referred to as "data bias", a bias resulting from the processing of data based on historically accumulated data.

Metaverse

The metaverse is the idea of an immersive virtual world that can be visited and experienced by different users simultaneously. It is often considered the next stage of the internet (→ ***Web3***) and offers the possibility to integrate different applications, games, and services in a common virtual environment. The term "metaverse" was first used by science fiction author Neal Stephenson in his novel *Snow Crash* (1992), describing his vision of how a virtual reality-based internet might develop in the future. The term has been adopted in modern times by Meta (formerly Facebook).

Hortensia armchair
3D digital rendering
Andrés Reisinger (digital artist)
Barcelona, 2019

Midjourney

The Midjourney → ***algorithm*** is an → ***AI model*** that can turn text into images. The algorithm can be activated by entering text prompts with the command "/imagine:". Based on the descriptive text, the algorithm generates four variations of images from which users can select and instruct the algorithm to generate further variations and refine them. Precise visual specifications can be defined to achieve different lighting or weather conditions, materials and textures, colours, environments, and stylistic references to specific architectural models (e.g., "in the style of John Lautner"). Midjourney learns from the users' choices and feedback, and improves its results over time.

Normal maps

Normal maps allow computers to detect the direction in which a surface is oriented or a surface normal is pointing. This allows for details to be defined or added to a surface without the need for compute-intensive geometry. They are often used in game development and architectural visualization to clarify the rendering of textures on 3D models and optimize the performance of computer games and applications. The colour concept of the exhibition design is based on the colour spectrum used in normal maps to specify the computer's representation of volumetric depth.

Portals

Portals are a concept in virtual space that refers to the transition from one virtual environment to another. They can serve as visual or physical separators or connections, helping users with orientation in → ***virtual space*** and allowing them to move from one environment to the next. The key visual of the exhibition poster features Space Popular's manifesto for the future of portals and virtual travel – *The Fabric of Civic Teleportation* – which outlines the key qualities needed to create a meaningful, fair, and civic infrastructure for the Immersive Internet → ***Web3***.

Rendering

Rendering (literally "to represent") refers to the process of creating images from digital data. This often involves visualizing a 3D model with special software (so-called render engines) using simulated material properties and effects. It is also possible to use digitized textures of real objects, obtained, for example, from photographs, to represent surfaces.

Virtual space

Virtual space is a computer-generated environment that can be explored by users. It can be a virtual space displayed on a computer screen or an augmented or virtual reality (AR, VR) experienced with VR goggles or on a screen. Virtual space is used for games, simulations, architectural visualizations, the → ***metaverse***, and more.

Web3

Web3 is the idea of a future version of the internet based on decentralized organization. Web3 uses blockchain technology to enable a new generation of decentralized applications and services that are not controlled by central authorities. Control over data, content, and applications will shift from individual large companies to users and communities.

Worldbuilding

Worldbuilding is the process of creating a fictional world or environment in books, movies, video games, or other media forms. It includes designing geography, landscape, architecture, cultures, physical laws, characters, mythologies, → ***lore***, and (background) stories. In gaming, it also includes creating game mechanics and objectives.

* These glossary terms were specifically chosen for the exhibition */imagine: A Journey into The New Virtual* (2023, MAK – Museum of Applied Arts, Vienna), a contemporary exploration of the evolving nature of virtual space over the past decade, re-examining questions of culture, ecology, and politics in the post-digital world.

* Bika Rebek is an architect, curator, educator and founder of Some Place Studio. Marlies Wirth is Curator of Digital Culture and Head of the Design Collection, Museum of Applied Arts and Contemporary Art (MAK), Vienna. Both curators of the exhibition 'The New Virtual' at the MAKK in Vienna.

THE GAMIFICATION OF MATTER

Storytelling is as old as humanity, and stories can be formulated in countless ways. A shiny brass plate illustrates the oldest of tales, the expulsion of Adam and Eve from the Garden of Eden, and the *Endling. Extinction is Forever* video game by Herobeat Studios imagines a post-apocalyptic world. A basin of yesteryear chiseled with the figure of St George becomes the heroine of a fantasy world in the *Gris* video game by Nómada Studio. From copper to bytes, such changes in material reveal an evolution of means that nevertheless preserves the same desire.

Basin
Cast copper alloy, embossed, chiselled and punched with stamp
Germany, 1500–1599
Purchase, 1922 MADB 3.792

Gris

Videogame

Nomada Studio, Barcelona, 2018

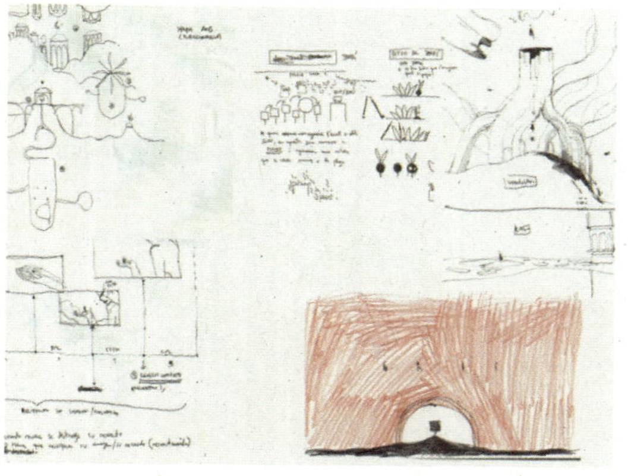

Endling. Extinction is Forever
Videogame
Herobeat Studios, Barcelona, 2022

TYPOGRAPHIC DEMATERIALIZATION

ANDREU BALIUS*

The shapes of the letters that make up the Latin alphabet have been with us for more than two thousand years. The evolution from handwriting to virtual auto-generated writing provided by programming and artificial intelligence took centuries. Compared to such an extended timeframe, the step from the physical to the intangible and virtual constitutes a fleeting wisp of air in time.

Although the letters in our alphabet have stayed basically the same since the Romans created them, their design and visual representation have changed dramatically while expressing our ideas and thoughts through text. Today, with a computer keyboard or directly by touching the screen of our mobile phones, we can access these archetypical shapes that, regardless of their design, represent the sounds of the language we speak.

Typographical writing emerged with the printing press, a true cultural revolution made possible by the perfect coupling of art and technology. Taking advantage of the technical possibilities of the moment, this innovation helped transfer manuscript calligraphy – the codex – to a new format: the printed book. Typography meant the mechanization of writing by means of a combination of movable types, each one reproducing, in a raised metal block, the shape of one or several letters. This is what is called a block letter or print.

This year marks the 550th anniversary of the first printed book in Spain, entitled *Obres o trobes en lahors de la Verge Maria*, a collection of poems printed in Valencia in 1474.[1] Since the middle of the 15th century, typography, as a printing technique[2] and way to write, has contributed to the large-scale production of books and printed material, facilitating the expansion of knowledge. Typography, therefore, is a form of writing, just like handwriting. What's specific about it is that the letters – the graphic signs we use to represent language – are not created manually with strokes performed by hand, but have been previously designed and manufactured to be reproduced in the composition of a text.

The materials used to manufacture a letter types, as well as how they are reproduced on a medium, have varied depending on the technology of the time. At first, types were made of lead,[3] which was used to make the physical mould of the typographic form. In the early 19th century, however, wood – lighter and cheaper than metal – enabled the production and distribution of larger fonts, suitable for the printing of posters. While the first letter designs were intended for reading text on pages, starting in the 19th century, more attractive and impactful designs appeared with these new, larger-size media in mind. The growing demand for printed material and the technological possibilities that stemmed from the Industrial Revolution applied to graphic arts brought about significant changes in typographic printing and composition. The invention of Monotype and linotype machines in the late-19th century signalled a new revolution for typesetting, especially benefitting periodicals such as newspapers and magazines because texts could be set at a much faster pace. Before the emergence of Monotype, typographers had to set the texts by manually situating each lead type, one after the other. However, the new machine's keyboard allowed the typographer to cast letters from molten metal while typing. With linotype, the metal was melted by lines of text, instead of letter by letter.

In the mid-20th century, typographic printing began to give way to offset printing, and typesetting adapted to these changes by introducing photographic procedures in the preparation of a master for printing. While in the traditional system, the letter shape appeared on the paper by applying pressure to the tinted type, with phototypesetting the text was created on photographic paper that needed to be developed as if it were a photograph. In this case, the type is not a relief, as with lead types, but the image of each typographic character is represented on a disc or negative film.

During this transition phase, when the cast slowly loses its physical properties, typographic designs were available in transferable letters used in lettering with brand names such as Letraset and Mecanorma, in plastic or cardboard stencils, or as types engraved in rubber polymer, thus replacing wood and metal.

1 *Obres o trobes en lahors de la Verge Maria* was the first book printed in the Crown of Aragon, and the first of a literary nature in the Iberian Peninsula. German printer Lambert Palmart published it in Valencia in 1474.

2 The word typography has several meanings. It is a printing technique, different than other techniques such as lithography, woodcut, or silk-screen printing, but also refers to the composition of a printed text.

3 Types were created with an alloy of lead, tin and antimony in different proportions.

Several materials have been used to manufacture the casts used to print typographies when typesetting. Yet it wasn't until the 1970s, with the arrival of digitization techniques,[4] that types stopped being physical elements and became a succession of coordinates to be interpreted by programs and operating systems that make their designs visible. Fonts ceased to be a collection of movable types and became a set of mathematical instructions contained in a digital file that a computer or printer was able to interpret and make visible on a screen or a printed page. The cast, the master used to reproduce the type through a keyboard, wasn't tangible anymore, but became virtual. The transformation of a drawn letter into a digital type required storing all the information that defines its designs into mathematical instructions. It's still astounding how when we strike the key for the letter A, that same letter appears on the screen. In addition, we are also able to choose among a variety of typographies, each representing the same letter A with different designs: *Futura*, *Helvetica*, *Times New Roman*, *Univers*...

The emergence of *PostScript* in the mid-1980s was a turning point in the use and design of typography.[5] This format ensured that fonts and designs were represented consistently in different output devices, a crucial innovation for the publishing sector.

In the early 1990s, typography underwent a genuine revolution thanks to the possibilities digital technology offered to new generations of designers, also influenced by postmodern thought. The expressive possibilities of digital tools applied to typography made possible the achievement of a plethora of graphic solutions, both static and dynamic. The programming languages applied to typography and typesetting have considerably increased possibilities both in the definition of letters and typographic writing. Computer programs such as Glyphs or FontLab are excellent for vector drawing an entire alphabet and then exporting it as a digital font. Soon, the use of artificial intelligence to design digital fonts promises not only to increase the efficiency and flexibility of the design process, but also to improve the quality, personalization and adaptability of fonts to meet the needs of any situation, including users' needs. Typographic casts might have faded, but they haven't disappeared. Rather they've been transformed. Matter has become something intangible. Block letters, now digitized, circulate through networks or remain inactive in the computer's memory, waiting for the user to activate them to make them visible again.

4 Peter Karow, a computer programmer, introduced the IKARUS system, a program that converts typographies into a digital format. His contribution was crucial for the transition of fonts from a physical format to a digital format.

5 *PostScript* is a page description language that Adobe Systems developed in the mid-1980s. It revolutionized desktop publishing because it allowed users to design and produce high-quality documents using personal computers and laser printers.

* Andreu Balius is PhD in Design from the University of Southampton. Founder of Typerepublic type foundry.

THE DEMATERIALIZATION OF TYPOGRAPHY

Typography, an art and technique for the graphic arrangement of type, has evolved hand in hand with technology, influenced by artistic and cultural movements over the course of history. The Gutenberg press used metal molds made of alloys of lead, antimony, and tin, to create movable types for printing. Other materials such as wood and plastic would subsequently be used, and the printing process was accelerated by the introduction of new machinery. The definitive change came about with the arrival of offset printing. Thanks to the digital revolution of the eighties, typography in the computer age witnessed the creation of thousands of digital fonts (sets of letters with specific designs) and the democratization of access. Artificial intelligence has created new opportunities for generating customized fonts starting from textual descriptions. The interaction between the immediacy of artificial intelligence (AI) and human creativity opens up a whole new age for typography.

Gran Canon movable type
Steel punches. Copper dies. Metal, lead and tin alloy type
Jerónimo Antonio Gil, 1766–1778
Manufactured by Imprenta Real, Madrid
Fund Imprenta Real. Depósito del Ministerio de Cultura

Gòtic Incunable movable type
Punches made of steel, copper and lead matrices
Eudald Canibell, Barcelona, 1904
Donation, F. T. Neufville, 1987

Tipografia Seat BCN font
Digital typography
Andreu Balius, 2022
Manufactured by Seat, Barcelona
Donation, Andreu Balius, 2024

Εύκολος ανεφοδιασμός
تصميم السيارة الإسبانية
КАТАЛОНСКИЙ ДИЗАЙН
Driving pleasure
הדרך תמיד תהיה שלנו
Ένα καλύτερο αύριο ξεκινάει τώρα
Alhambra
Надаємо форму мріям
تحركك إلى الأمام

Ella font
Digital typography
Laura Meseguer, Barcelona, 2022
Donation, Laura Meseguer, 2024

CALLIGRAPHY
Ella Roman Regular
Pens and Béziers
Ella Uncial Bold
Aesthetics
Ella Rustic Regular
BRUTAL
Ella Brutalist Bold
Texture and color
Ella Brutalist Regular
STYLE
Ella Rustic Bold
REGULAR & BOLD
Ella Uncial Regular
Inspiration
Ella Roman Bold

Super Tipo Veloz font
Paper
Joan Trochut i Blanchart, 1942
Manufactured by Fundició Tipogràfica José Iranzo, Barcelona
Donation, Pierre Trochut i Blanchard 1999 MDB 12.880

UPCYCLING WASTE WOOD WITH INDUSTRY 4.0 TECHNOLOGIES

MARTA MALÉ-ALEMANY / TONY SCHOEN*

The complexity of wood: its rising value and the challenges for creating cost-effective recycling solutions

Wood embodies many attributes that align with circular construction principles. Its renewability, carbon storage capacity, easy disassembly, reuse and recycling potential, make it an essential material to create sustainable and resilient buildings. Wood construction is rising, with the development of various engineered wood systems like CLT (cross-laminated timber), wood frame construction and modular factory-built units. Some municipalities are encouraging this trend by requiring a percentage of new housing to be built in wood. Yet, in general, wood use in the building sector is still considerably low. In this context, circular applications for ceramic elements (i.e., bricks, rooftiles) are now common practice, and the reusability of cement-based elements is being explored despite all economic and logistic challenges. Rooftiles find their ways to new buildings. Concrete and masonry are being crushed and sorted on-site, to become road filler or feedstock for new 'circular' concrete.

Even though wood waste amounts are still relatively small, its material versatility and pressing economic factors are propelling sustainable wood harvesting and reuse solutions, especially from building renovations and demolitions. Beams, planks, and wall cladding are the largest wood waste streams from building demolitions. While harvested in small quantities, major demolition companies are initiating 'circular material hubs', where harvested wood (predominantly beams) is manually cleaned for reuse, including metal removal. In renovation projects, solid doors, window frames, and wall cladding are the most valuable wood sources, and the largest fraction to be harvested. Yet their reclamation is still limited because they contain considerable deformities and contamination. Besides, old window frames were designed for single glazing only, which hinders their 1:1 reuse. Thus in total, of the 435 kton wood extracted annually from buildings, only 55 kton are harvested by demolition companies, the rest is brought to waste collection sites. Once turned to waste, virtually all wood is burned (66%) or turned into chipboard (34%).

Nonetheless, the potential of reusing wood and the need to overcome its technical challenges has not gone unnoticed. Research efforts and pilots are being developed and implemented by various consortiums of partners (i.e. various EU funded projects), involving municipal, commercial and knowledge parties.

Upscaling wood reuse presents great challenges. Each waste wood piece is different, with varying topology, notches, holes, cracks, and other deformities, requiring the technical capabilities to evaluate material properties and deterioration. Moreover, this wood is often surface treated (i.e., paint, varnish, oils) and can contain metal. These contaminations are currently removed by hand, by people who are challenged to enter the regular job market. However, research shows that an alternative and scalable workflow for wood inspection and processing can benefit from industry 4.0 technologies. Given the (technical) bottlenecks and lack of cost-effective solutions for upscaling wood reuse, this workflow is key and needs development.

Digital production and circular wood: new technical means and creative opportunities

Computer-aided design and manufacturing (digital production) have radically expanded the creative and production opportunities across all design-related industries. Alongside, the advent of smart industry (including robotics) supports a paradigm shift from standardization to mass-customization, where a high-volume production of objects with unique features is now a reality.

The use of industrial robots for timber construction is an emerging field, involving many leading researchers and innovative practices in engineering and architecture. This technology enables manufacturing complexity (i.e., angled and composed cuts, surface milling, others) in an automated and scalable manner. Work by Svilans *et al.*[1] presents an overview of digital workflows for timber structures, including material properties and behavior, 3D scanning, and the production of large scale, freeform glulam parts. For design, several parametric *toolkits* for designing and constructing structures from beams (including manufacturing instructions) exist. The same is true for integrated design tools that generate specific joints and related toolpaths for robotic manufacturing, which are used to make structures from engineered timber plates.

1 Tom Svilans *et al.*: 'New Workflows for Digital Timber', *Digital Wood Design. Lecture Notes in Civil Engineering*, 24, 2019, pp. 93–134.

These digital processes, while focused on virgin (standard) wood, also apply to residual (non-standard) wood streams. This opportunity requires new design methods that encourage adaptive reuse of circular materials, involving material inventories and algorithms that can align the data of available wood and the product characteristics, with the most optimal correspondence. For production, it needs a flexible production set-up that can process a continuously varying material stream, with manufacturing instructions that vary piece by piece. Industrial robots are effective, versatile and inexhaustible tools, which can be programmed and equipped to perform wood working processes on (non-standard) wood pieces, which would otherwise be discarded.

Research at Robot Lab: Innovating the reuse of wood with Smart Industry principles

Applying digital production for wood reuse is therefore an emerging research area. Since 2018, the Robot Lab at the Faculty of Technology of the Amsterdam University of Applied Sciences has consistently focused on applied research connecting the potential of smart industry technologies to upscale the circular reuse of materials (especially wood), exploring both industrial leftovers and waste streams. For wood, this objective varies in complexity, depending on the harvesting source: residual wood from the manufacturing industry is mostly clean wood, while wood waste from building renovation or demolition is often contaminated with paints and metal. The Robot Lab explores these opportunities, conscious that impact can be created at various levels of wood cascading.

This applied research involves wood inspection processes, design-from-availability methods, customized production with robotics based on smart factory principles, the development of custom handling tools for uneven wood streams, and developments for informed assembly with mixed media (MR). It is done with a wide network of partners, including municipalities, housing corporations, contractors, demolition companies, suppliers and technical experts from smart industry, and wholesale companies, furniture makers, window manufacturers and other partners from wood industry, who aim to find alternative futures for waste wood, to create meaningful applications with a positive impact for society.

In 2020, this question led to creating a reception desk for the VIP lounge of the Johan Cruyff Arena,[2] fabricated with 300+ left-over pieces of massive (residual) wood. This case study first demonstrated that given a specific wood batch, it is possible to generate a unique design, which in fact takes advantage of the material differentiation. It also helped envision how smart industry processes could support the fabrication of these unique wood applications. This workflow, involving design from availability and custom robotic production, has become a core methodology of all Robot Lab's circular wood related developments.

2 In collaboration with Amsterdamsche Fijnhout (wood wholesaler), Heineken Design Group (Interior design) and Nijboer (contractor).

As a follow up, the project *Circular Wood 4.0* (2022-24) focuses on the development of an upcycling wood factory, a robotic set-up capable of working with variable wood streams (in a continuum) to produce outstanding, bespoke objects for the hospitality sector. In this project, wood waste from manufacturing is turned into customized systems for horeca interiors, including wall and ceiling panels, room dividers and furniture pieces. This is done with a specific design tool (linked to a wood waste inventory), which can generate unique decorative tiles, matching the geometry of an existing wall, ceiling or other architectural element. These bespoke interiors, made of high-quality waste wood are not only beautiful, they are also meaningful applications for hospitality: they embody the core values of front running hotels towards circularity, and help decrease the negative impact of their high turnover of interior redesigns and renovations (every 7 years on average).

In parallel, the project *Circular Wood for the Neighborhood* (2020-22) explored the possibilities of reusing waste wood from residential building renovations and demolitions to create valuable applications, by digital production means. This project generated hands-on experience with wood harvested on site, combined with a detailed material flow analysis from the survey of various renovation projects by major housing corporations. Potential valuable wood was projected into the design of three case studies, including physical prototypes fabricated at the Robot Lab.

In conclusion, Robot Lab projects show that upcycling waste wood with Smart Industry approaches can offer a promising solution to the challenges of sustainable construction. Wood's recyclability and low environmental impact make it an ideal material for circular construction, but its varied conditions require advanced technical solutions. To enhance the value of waste wood and propel its effective reuse, computational design and smart production setups can help efficiently handle these complexities. By adopting these innovations, it is possible to reduce construction waste, lower carbon footprints, and support sustainable building practices, towards more resilient and circular urban environments.

* Marta Malé-Alemany is PhD in Architecture, researcher and curator specialising in the relationship and integration between design and digital production. Founder and leader of Robot Lab. Senior lecturer in Digital Production at the Amsterdam School of Technology.
Tony Schoen is a mechanical engineer at the Urban Technology Circular Wood for the Neighborhood research program at Amsterdam University of Applied Sciences.

Cup
Open Source 3D drawing
Olga Subirós Studio, 2024

Cup
Air blown glass
Catalonia, 1575–1625
Purchase, 1932 MADB 4.989

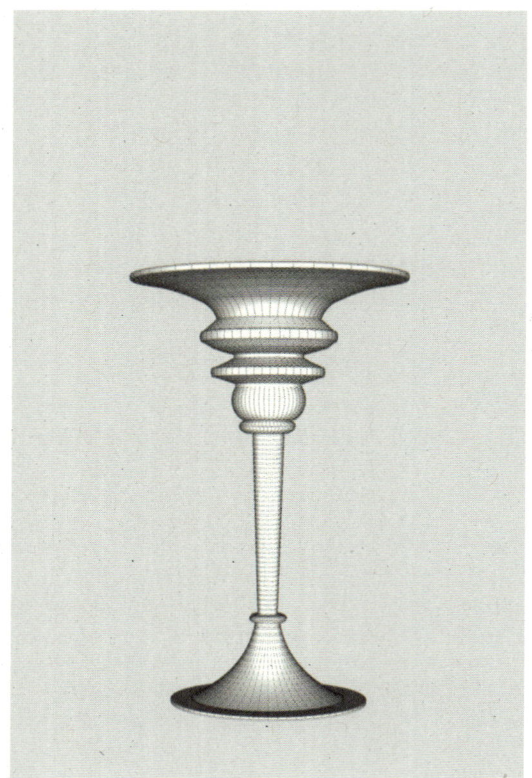

THE DEMOCRATIZATION OF DESIGN

3D printing has the potential to revolutionize society, being as it is a fairer, more democratic form of printing. As a result of the expiry of patents and the creation of RepRap, the first open-code 3D printer, over the last twenty years everything has changed. The new technology enables small designer firms and entrepreneurs to freely create works, and on a global scale share their projects and innovations, ranging from medical supplies to printed corals for reefs. The selection of historical cups in the Museu del Disseny-DHub made by Martí Guixé has been scanned, generated the open source file and printed. Barcelona's Manufacturing Atheneums provide residents of the city access to this technology, offering them public spaces and resources, and promoting the democratization of technology and heritage.

Aleu protective mask

TPE thermoplastic elastomer material for injection moulding and PA12 polyamide with 3D-HP MJF printing and elastic band

Eurecat. Centre Tecnològic de Catalunya and other participating companies, Girona, 2020

Donation Centre Tecnològic Eurecat, 2021 MDB 14.011

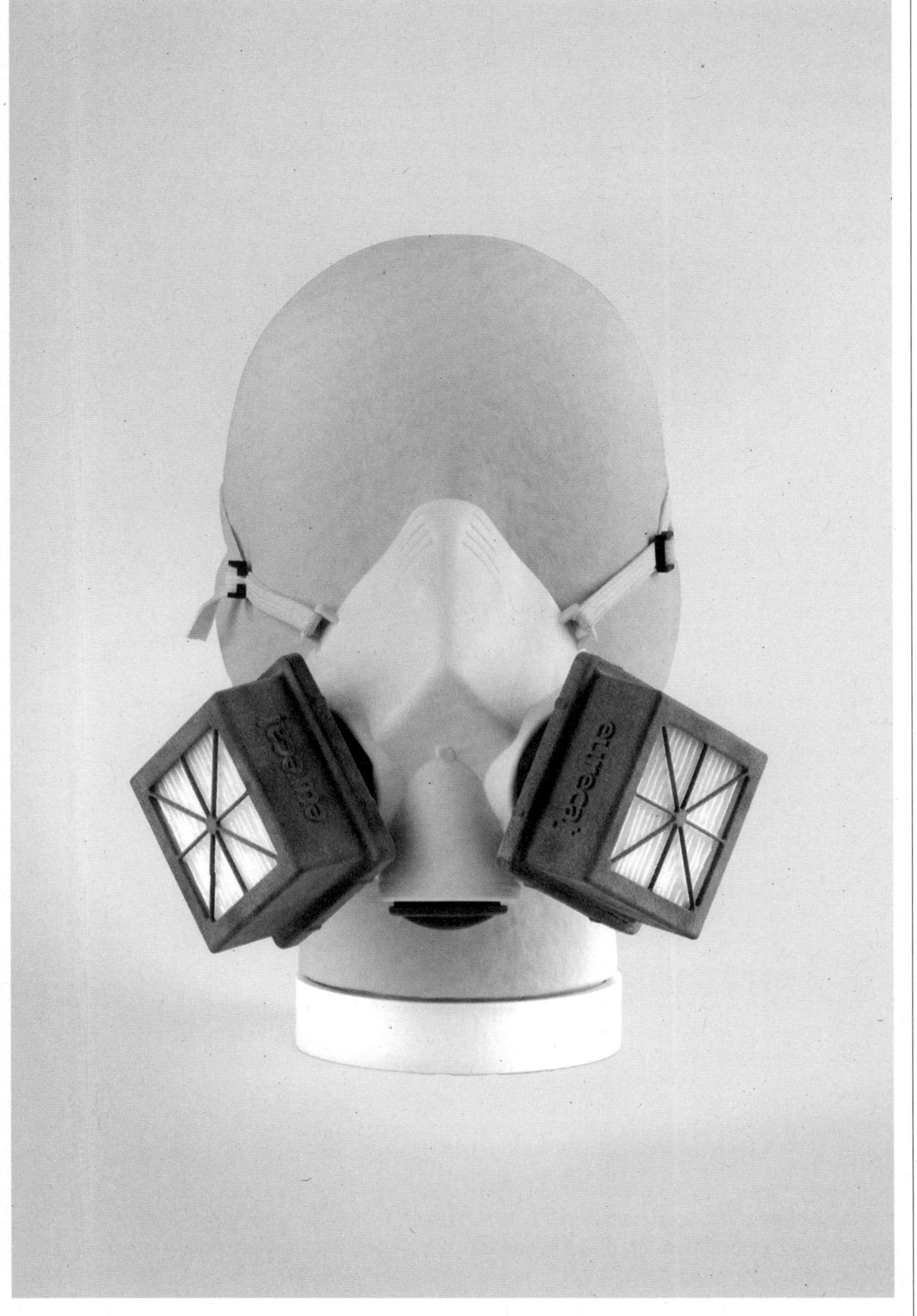

Punchbag bag
Polyamide with selective laser synthesized laser synthesis (SLS)
Freedom of Creation (Janne Kyttänen and Jiri Evenhuis), 2005
Manufactured by Freedom of Creation, The Netherlands
Accession, Museu de les Arts Decoratives, 2011
MADB 138.771

Cell Cycle bracelet
Nylon and polyamide with Selective Laser Sintering (SLS)
Nervous System (Jessica Rosenkrantz and Jesse Louis-Rosenberg), 2009
Manufactured by Shapeways, The Netherlands
Accession, Museu de les Arts Decoratives, 2011
MADB 138.768

DIGITAL CRAFTSMANSHIP

Digital technology and traditional craftsmanship come together to create new forms of design known as digital crafts. Artisans and designers use technology as a complement to traditional methods to produce unique works. Knowledge of traditional techniques connects us to the past, while digital technology opens the door to innovations and endless possibilities. 3D printing, that enables the precise creation of complex structures, can be considered a new craft form. *Farcell* portable lamp by Banzai Turba is 3D-printed and acquires its final appearance by hand modeling.

Hatillo (bundle) table lamp
3D printing with PLA (polylactic acid) coloured with wheat residue
Banzai Turba and Curated by, Barcelona, 2021
Donation, Curated by through ADI-FAD, 2023 MDB 16.337

OPEN DATA, OPEN CITY

300.000 KM/S*

In the 1970s, Barcelona's Plaça de les Glòries was defined by a road network intended for automobiles cutting through it in all directions, creating interstitial spaces for green (and very brown) islands where it was hoped that citizens would find a respite from the dense city, amidst the noise, exhaust fumes and speed barriers. Probably at the time, the image of the future that awaited the city was very different from what it really is today, fifty years later. A quick look at science fiction or even what some urban planners drew up suggests that the Barcelona of the future should be filled with cars and fumes, coloured lights, huge screens and flying contraptions. However, today this space is an enormous park devoid of vehicles, a place where trees, flowers and cool shade have emerged. The greenness is all over the place even if today we must contend with the first onslaught of climate change.

The current city of the future that nobody could imagine is a garden. Technology appears to be absent from Plaça de les Glòries, which is also the location of Disseny Hub Barcelona. We don't see screens or coloured lights or much less, flying cars. Nor do the buildings appear to be transplanted from New York, Tokyo or the Los Angeles of *Blade Runner*. Rather, they're friendlier, softer, more domestic and good-natured. This new slice of the city, even if it not apparent on the surface, is the result of the intense application of computer technology, extensive telecommunications networks, satellites that provide a daily X-ray of the ground, the miniaturization of electronic components (which among other things have given rise to cell phones), and so many other technological advances that have changed the way we observe and describe the world, as well as how we decide and then act upon it.

The new city centre is the result of a drastic reduction in the use of private vehicles. This has ceded public space for traffic to other uses not connected to mobility, taking the opportunity to transform these areas into spaces where nature, play, rest and wellbeing can thrive once again. At the same time, this reduction has not been detrimental to the number of trips that citizens make throughout the day. Instead, it has contributed to an increase in the use of public transportation and other mobility systems which no science fiction film dared to imagine, such as bicycles and scooters.

The mobility transformation has many causes. Probably the one with the most impact recently is the dramatic increase in the number of people working from home. Because of the same above-mentioned technologies, we no longer need to commute (and all at once) to work every day. Rather we can choose when to go to the office to meet with colleagues or talk about complex matters more intensely in person.

The decrease in time and travel has resulted in an increase in short trips that connect the home to a mosaic of activities related to daily needs (going to the supermarket, picking the kids up from school, visiting relatives) and other adjacent activities (meeting with friends, going to the cinema, playing a football match and other activities that have nothing to do with the productive city).

According to figures from the Embarriados[1] study (which analyses the series of mobility statistics of the Ministry of Transportation and Sustainable Mobility generated by tracking mobile devices), to date, the number of post-pandemic trips the city's inhabitants make is nearly the same as before. However, the distances covered are much shorter: the result is less kilometres travelled and, consequently, a decrease in the length of the trips.

The behavioural pattern of this emerging mobility is much less exact, however, more erratic, and varies from day to day (since we don't always go to the same cinema or meet with the same friends). It depends on the day of the week, the month of the year, the weather and many other still unknown factors. It's harder to measure and describe and thus more complicated to predict, plan and design, rendering obsolete certain methodologies used to configure a type of systematic mobility embodied by the privately owned internal combustion vehicle.

Consequently, this new mobility is tied to the possibility of measuring and describing it. All these new means of transport (buses, bikes, scooters and others) are equipped with sensors monitored by computer technology and telecommunications networks that digest floods of data nonstop without allowing a single byte of information to escape. For this reason, the future doesn't lie in hyperloops, drones and helicopters but in buses that arrive on time, that inform us about their route, that tell us exactly how much time we must wait, and that are interconnected with a bicycle network that enables us to make the act of moving around a pleasant and healthy ride as well.

1 The Embarriados project (https://embarriados.cotec.es/) analyses the potential risk of social segregation associated with the reduction in mobility, carried out by 300.000 km/s along with COTEC.

Nowadays, mobility is more complex, and so is the society that moves. It requires different modes of transport, with different operating mechanisms and several managing entities. This complexity can lead us to want to simplify, to make it easier to understand, and thus do without complex statistical algorithms in the search for patterns, correlation or causes that enable us to identify and propose improvements and readjustments. It isn't surprising that the tangle of interconnected agents and processes that support mobility systems today necessitates AI-based management systems capable of making autonomous decisions, processing the huge amount of data that the city generates, analysing situations and providing effective alternatives.

We embrace these new opportunities with enthusiasm but also distrust. We still don't know how these systems could malfunction if constantly fed (trained with) the same information they have generated based on their predictions. Or rather, if they only know how to manage what we have measured, it means they will likely end up reducing traffic jams but also allowing more vehicles to circulate in the city, as, for this reason, they're good at optimizing systems but not transforming or imagining possible new models.

A society whose care-taking duties are redistributed among all its members; one where there is daily time for leisure, in which the city not only ensures the basic operational flows of work but also those related to desire and emotions; and, ultimately, one that seeks the wellbeing of its members would be unthinkable without the technologies that make these processes possible.

But the same society that relies on these technologies to function smoothly is also at the mercy of those who provide them. That is, it depends on the reliability and trustworthiness of these technologies, that the benefits derived by those who profit from them don't exhaust the revenues of those who consume them, that they seek (or try to seek) the common good (and don't create problems which they themselves could solve).

In fact, all the technologies that gird this new mobility, and indeed all the processes that cities are automating and autonomizing,[2] are within the reach of any citizen. The large majority are open-code tools, transparent and documented. The cost is low (if they require a license) and the hardware they require isn't more expensive than that of computer used to play video games. In addition, they depend on public infrastructure such as GPS satellites and the Internet.[3] This might suggest that anyone could navigate the complex maze of urban decisions. But this isn't the case: the raw material that fuels them and that they also produce – data – is only accessible to a few agents who, in the end, will be the ones able to make the best decisions.

2 Kate Crawford and Vladan Joler: *Calculating Empires: A Genealogy of Technology and Power Since 1500*, 2023. Available at: https://calculatingempires.net/.

3 GPS, or Global Positioning System, is a global navigation system via satellite that provides information related to location, speed and time synchronization.

Companies like Google[4] can trace mobile devices and determine our location. Automobile companies monitor the routes of their vehicles equipped with GPS and transfer this information to other companies like INRIX.[5] Lots of mobile applications share users' geopositioning data with CUEBIQ,[6] which then sells them. Credit card activity is meticulously documented, enabling us to know the reason for every trip. We leave so many digital clues behind on our journey through the city that escape our knowledge, and we have less and less evidence of their existence. Behind all this is not a privacy problem, which we can assume is resolved if companies comply with the GDPR.[7] The real problem is not being able to access the data we generate (data that could be used to make seemingly banal decisions such as determining the best bus route or where a new parking space for bicycles is available). Consequently, we depend on a few companies that amass huge amounts of highly valuable information to understand and suggest ways the city should operate.

This lack of information risks handing over to large corporations the ability to understand the city better and implement new design proposals. It implies accepting that the massive urban complexity we have created together can only be deciphered by those who are not our neighbours, but who seek to make the most of the need and the attempt to make our environment better.

The data that public infrastructure generates must be reused by the same public institutions. It is imperative that such data, raw material of the decisions that will define our future, are in hands that defend the public good, not individual interests. Public governance of data is critical for a better future, but these data must also be presented and shown. They must be transparent to the public so that citizens are aware of the information flows in which we participate without knowing it. We need more awareness of the datafication of our surroundings.

We need the maps that guide our decisions, communicate plans to people, and evaluate the success of policies to be developed with data that the city has sovereignty over, so that the cartography that directs us towards a collective and prosperous future is our own.

4 Google provides real-time metrics of different places in the city. Available at: https://www.google.com/.

5 INRIX provides mobility data (traffic status) to other companies such as Google (https://inrix.com/).

6 CUEBIQ provides metrics of different places in the city while tracking consumers https://www.cuebiq.com/.

7 Regulation (EU) 2016/679 of the European Parliament and of the Council of 27 April 2016, on the protection of natural persons with regard to the processing of personal data and on the free movement of such data, and repealing Directive 95/46/EC (General Data Protection Regulation). Available at: https://eur-lex.Europe.eu/legal-content/es/TXT/?uri=CELEX%3A32016R0679.

* 300.000 km/s is a data analysis and consulting agency focused on cities, awarded in 2019 with the S+T+ARTS award and the CSCAE Spanish Urbanism award.

CITIES WILL BELONG TO THOSE WHO MAP THEM

The huge amount of data (telephony, mobility, bank transactions, demography, and income, among others), both public and private, generated by cities are essential for their analysis and planning. Data become information, and information is power. This power is exerted by companies and public administrations, yet it must be renegotiated in order to guarantee the common good. The maps of the twenty-first century, drawn up based on mass data, are fundamental tools for revealing that which is invisible in cities and for building cartographic evidences that may be transformed into public policies. This allows citizens to identify problems and gives them an opportunity to renegotiate the social contract. The flux of one year of cyclists using the municipal cycle-hire Bicing service in Barcelona has been visualized by 300.000 km/s town planning agency. Taking public open data, the agency provides an unprecedented analysis of the city.

Aerial view of Plaça de les Glòries in 2026 (render)
Barcelona City Hall, 2024
Barcelona City Hall

Bicing Barcelona 2023
Visualization and data analysis
300.000 km/s, Barcelona, 2024

Defooooooooooooooooooooooorest

Interactive installation

Joana Moll, Barcelona, 2016

Loan, Joana Moll

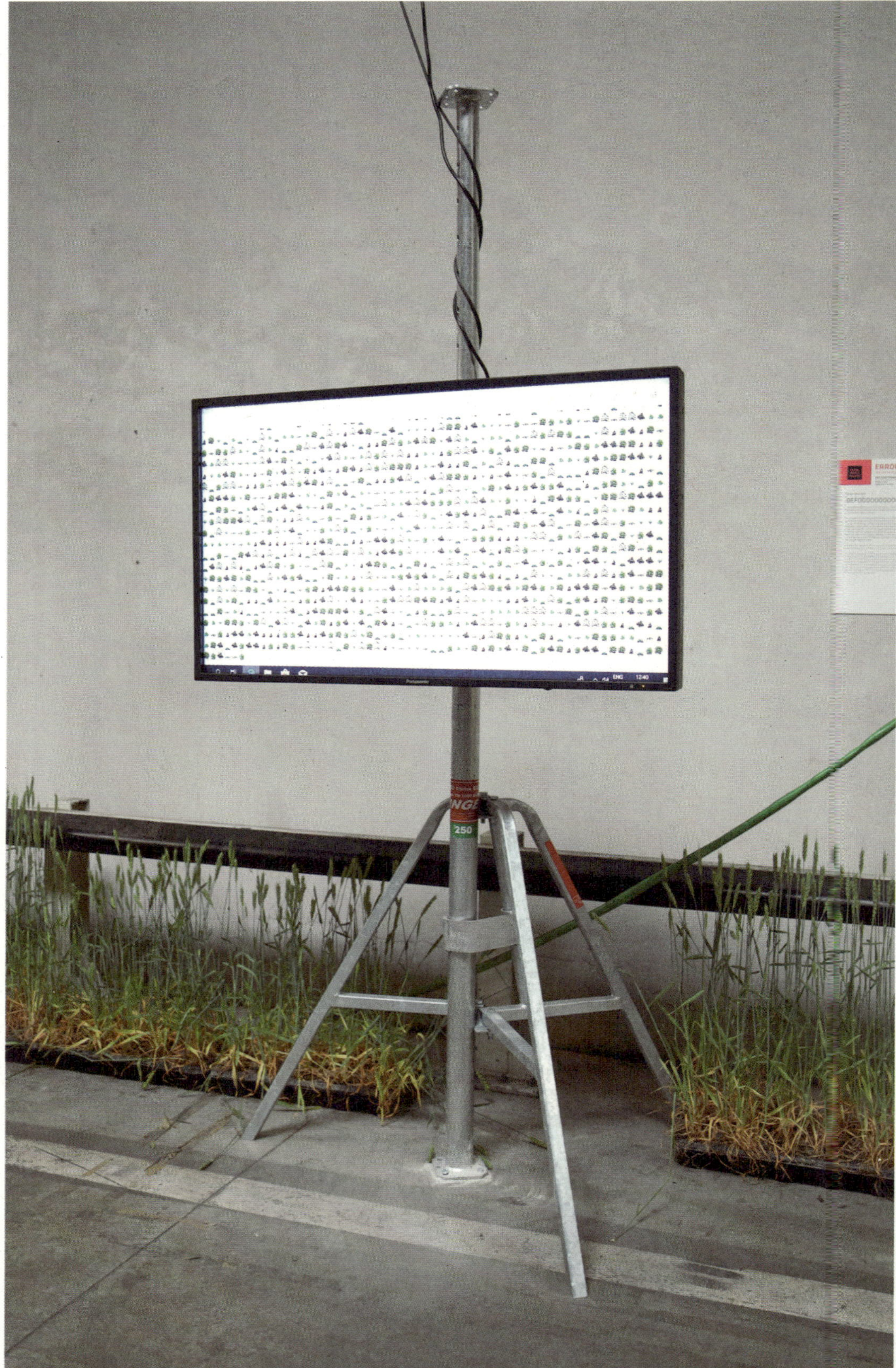

THE ECOLOGICAL AND SOCIAL IMPACT OF DIGITAL TRANSFORMATION

Defoooooooooooooooooooorest by Joana Moll and *Guest Images. Parasitology of Vision and Other Symbioses* by Estampa collective expose the ecological, social, and technological impacts of digital transformation. Moll's work draws attention to the number of trees needed to absorb the carbon dioxide (CO_2) generated Google visits every second, thereby revealing the relationship between our digital actions and their ecological consequences, while the installation by Estampa examines forms of artificial vision, and how digital images become starting points for processes of data extraction. Both works are invitations to reconsider the material connections between the digital world and the physical medium, and spotlight the need for a complex and critical understanding of the world in which we live.

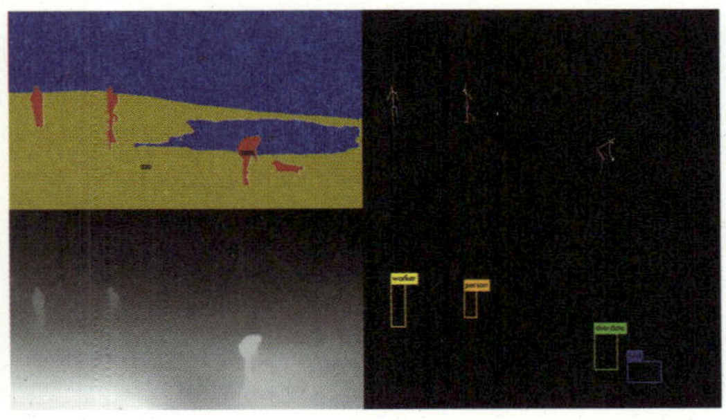

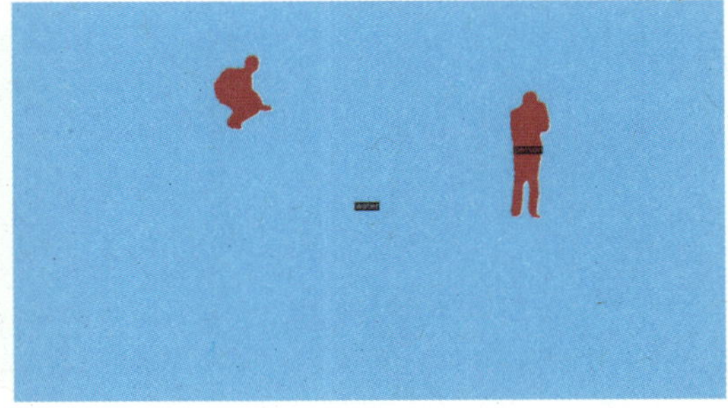

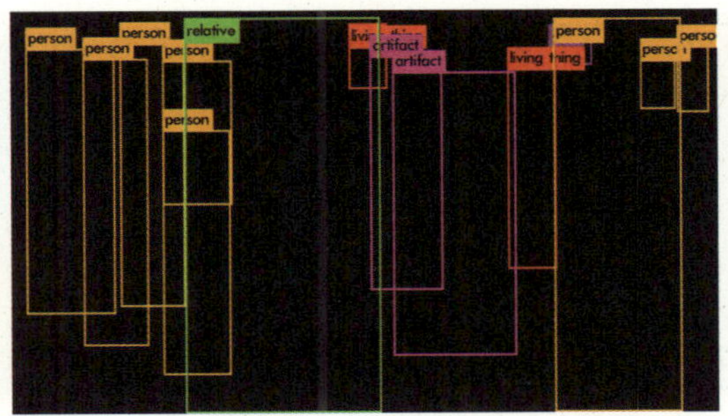

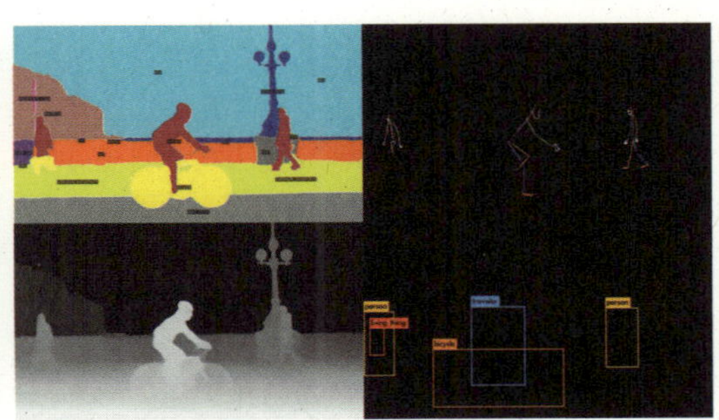

Host images. Parasitology of vision and other symbiosis
Multichannel audiovisual installation
Estampa, Barcelona, 2022
Loan, Estampa Disseny Il·lustració i Animació SCP

CRITICAL PEDAGOGY FOR ARTIFICIAL INTELLIGENCE*

ESTAMPA*

In recent years, news about artificial intelligence, machine learning and computer vision has begun to proliferate. We are told that machines can learn, see and create, giving rise to a discourse based on novelty and an apparently imminent future. At times, within this landscape, it is difficult to distinguish between real developments and fantasies or warnings. Yet without a doubt, this panoptic fog is part of the power we grant these tools, both in the present and the future, and is also part of the negative and positive concerns they awaken in us. Much of this discourse might be classified as false debates or, at least, the resurgence of old debates. Thus, in a classical artistic field, associated with discourse on creation and authorship, the status that should be given to the images created with these tools is discussed (neglecting much discourse about technologies such as photography or practices such as appropriation).

Metaphors are essential when talking about all digital tools and the power they wield. Are expressions such as "intelligence," "vision," "learning," "neuronal" and the whole array of similar terms the most adequate to define these tools? Maybe not, especially when their metaphorical nature is overlooked. We would not understand them in the same way if we designated them as tools for probabilistic classification, or if instead of saying that an artificial intelligence "painted" a Rembrandt, we said that it has produced a statistical reproduction of the style (which is itself also surprising). It would also be better if we refer to its essential nature as well, which is not "thinking" or "creating" but "automatizing." For these tools, this type of designation suggests an entity that endows them with apparent autonomy and independence, which is the basis of their supposed authority.

Because the crux of much discourse is constructing a characterization that legitimizes an objective capacity, or a non-human one, in data analysis. That is, it is an old magic trick of power where things are beyond our control and even – and this is cynicism, not magic – their control, becoming incarnate in a supposed objective and in independent operations. A typical example of this in an Anglo-Saxon context is the use of these tools to calculate the costs of medical insurance. While this neoliberal action presented as something necessary has not reach our shores yet, we understand the situation perfectly, one outlined as a scenario where no dialogue or discussion is possible beyond the imposition of the results of network analysis. As in a plethora of cases, perhaps this simply makes evident what is already happening: if a company employee calculates this cost, it is unlikely it will be done in the spirit of dialogue or will respond to certain criteria they wish to explain to us and which we are more than welcome to question. But it does not matter whether the calculation is made with formulas applied by employees or if it is the output of a neuronal network resulting from the insurance company's data and the data of the person taking out the insurance: in both cases someone has accepted that this method works, and this is where an opaque responsibility exists solely because we want to – in other words, the internal functioning of the network might be hazy but the decision to use one formula or another, and how the tool has been trained, should not be. Opacity is not the main feature of artificial intelligence but rather the nature of power.

While metaphors are one of these tools' fields of power, we must not forget the normative framework in which they are developed. The tools are created within the ideology of massive data, and they fully embrace it. By this we mean that everything must leave a trace and be archived automatically, and that as can be deduced from the expression "data mining," data are considered a natural resource available for use. This metaphor is significant as the expression of a capitalist fantasy: data is a natural resource which, contrary to already mined resources, will not dry up but in a typical delusional fantasy, grow while we gladly accept to live with and acquire more and more devices that monitor us. It is as if the system had constructed its own bottomless pit of fairy tales. AI techniques have been created within this context (they celebrate the aggregation of data and give them value by turning them into training datasets) and for this context, enabling the development of tools such as computer vision which greatly increase monitorization and extractivism on a massive scale.

The more these tools have been developed in an industrial framework, the more evident it is that we cannot refer to them as a technology but as infrastructure. This is so from a computational point of view, since the current large models – such as large language models like ChatGPT – could not be trained without large data centres and supercomputing equipment. In this sense, the ecological problem of the digital world becomes graver and compounds the more the deployment of these tools and their scale increases. However, they are not infrastructure only for this reason but also because of their dependency on a precarious and delocalized workforce that records the data to train these tools or is used to perform mechanical tasks related to the filtering and refining of the models.[1]

1 Regarding this question, see one of our latest projects: *Cartography of generative AI*, 2024 (cartography-of-generative-ai.net).

The Next Rembrandt
2021
CC BY 2.0. Source: Wikimedia Commons

In recent years we experienced what probably was the moment of the first cultural reception of these tools. From their development in the research field, we have moved on to their presence in public discourse and their first massive use. In this situation, where we still do not know the breadth and characteristics of these technologies (and in which, consequently, fears are more abstract and diffuse and thus more present and powerful), it is especially important to understand what we are dealing with, to take control of these tools and intervene in these discourses. Before their possibilities are restricted and solidified to the point where they seem inexorable, it is important to reflect on them and use them from the vantage of critical contexts to dispel the mystique that envelops them. In our work, we have sought to understand how these tools function and to use them against the grain, avoiding barriers to discourse as well as industrial barriers, which distance us from them and present them as foregone conclusions. This is why we believe that the title of our first AI project, "The Bad Student: Critical Pedagogy for Artificial Intelligences,"[2] still has programmatic value.

2 It is available on the collective's web page: tallerestampa.com/es/estampa/el-mal-alumne/.

* This is a shorter version of the article "El mal alumno" (The Bad Student), which we published on the website "CCCBLab. Investigación e innovación en cultura", on 18 March 2019.

* Estampa is an experimental artistic collective.

WE ARE DATA

Up until a decade ago, most data were produced by scientific, industrial, and administrative processes, a situation which changed with the explosion of mobile technologies and the popularization of social media services. Today, the routine activities of millions of citizens generate data. Our digital actions leave traces that capture our desires, fears, and hopes. Quantifying our lives has become an everyday practice that inspires new industries. Projects like *Sand Falls* by Domestic Data Streamers collective prove that art, technology, and the social sciences can converge to measure emotional impact, offering a new outlook on our interaction with data.

Sand Falls 01, installation
Estructura de ferro, vidre bufat i sorra
Domestic Data Streamers, Barcelona, 2015
Loan, Domestic Data Streamers

MANIFESTO IN FAVOUR OF TECHNOLOGICAL SOVEREIGNTY AND DIGITAL RIGHTS FOR CITIES

FRANCESCA BRIA / MALCOLM BAIN*

Our values and beliefs

1.
We believe in **technological sovereignty** for cities, for full control and autonomy of their Information and Communications Technologies (ICTs), including service infrastructures, websites, applications and data, in compliance with and with the support of laws that protect the interests of municipalities and their citizens.

Technological sovereignty helps cities protect citizens' rights through greater accessibility, transparency and accountability required for open government.

2.
We believe that **citizens' digital rights** must be placed at the centre of cities' digital policies and protected through the implementation of Technological Sovereignty and digital democracy policies.

Citizens' digital rights include the rights of privacy, security, information self-determination and neutrality, giving citizens a choice about what happens to their digital identity, who uses their data online, and for which purposes. Digital democracy enables more citizen participation in design and governance of cities and city services.

3.
We believe that **Free Software, Open Data** and **Open Standards, Document and Data formats and communication protocols** are the bases for technological sovereignty for cities and best support the digital rights of our citizens.

Free Software, Open Data and Open Standards, Formats and Protocols provide cities and citizens with tools enabling non-discriminatory access to and provision of digital services. This is not just a technology paradigm, but a culture that helps individuals and communities to protect their digital rights as well as to achieve innovation and reach goals that are beneficial for society in a collaborative manner.

4.
We believe that **Free Software** provides a solid foundation to achieve better levels of **efficiency**, **stability** and **interoperability** required for cities' ICT platforms, through source code ownership, collaborative development and sharing, all of which enable participation in digital services' security, validation and improvement.

Municipal investment and participation in Free Software projects help developing local skills and contribute to technologies which can reinforce citizens' digital rights while bringing benefits to the local economy. Free Software offers value for money in terms of long term sustainability and local economic development that is greater than any short term financial gains.

5.
We believe that **Open City Data** is a necessary element of technological sovereignty and must be managed and provided in an ethical, transparent, accessible and sustainable manner.

As well as supporting local innovation, Open City Data empowers citizens and enables better data-driven decision making in cities and, by providing visibility and accountability, induces more trust in local government and greater citizen engagement in policy making.

6.
We believe that the mandatory adoption of **Open Standards, Document and Data formats and Communication Protocols** will improve transparency, coordination between public authorities and collaboration with the private sector.

Shared, open cross-government standards, formats and protocols make services better for users and cheaper to run. Open standards simplify access to information by all organisations and individuals that want to participate in the City's development.

Thus our core values are

Technological sovereignty, including data sovereignty

Digital rights for citizens

Interoperability and accessibility

Collaborative development, through sharing and pooling of resources

Citizen and industry participation in technology design and governance

Transparency and auditability, security and privacy

Our goals

All municipal digital policies give priority to the protection of citizens' digital rights, reflect their wishes and are based on their participation.

Municipal ICTs implement and support citizens' digital rights, including privacy, security, accountability and neutrality by design; and give citizens the ability to decide what happens to their digital identity, who uses their data, and for which purposes.

All municipal digital services are implemented through Free Software and all hardware is under the control of the city and runs Free Software.

Cities publish the components of their ICT service infrastructures and share them with other cities, to allow for wider participation in improving these shared components, individually or collectively.

All components of city ICTs conform to open standards, document and data formats and communication protocols. All data processed and published by cities does not require the purchase and/or use of proprietary and/or closed source tools or services. Access and use of municipal digital services will not require members of the public to run any software that is not Free.

Cities benefit from and foster a local ecosystem of partners, providers and users with demonstrated experience in providing Free Software and Open Data based ICT services and infrastructures, using Open Standards, formats and protocols. All City tenders for ICT services can be fulfilled by members of the local ICT sector with skills in Free Software and Open Data.

Cities' ICTs enable citizens to access, visualize, and analyse public information, and promote greater civic engagement and participation, e.g. through documented APIs so that users can develop their own software to request city services. City web sites have no tracker tags, do not use resources from third party sites, and all their functionalities operate properly even if the user's browser does not execute Javascript code.

Actions to achieve our goals

Cities shall develop and implement a digital rights and equality agenda, track and monitor the respect for citizens' digital rights, and jointly create tools and resources to help advance this effort.

Cities shall procure ICT services based on Free Software and only consider non-Free offers when a Free Software based offer is not available. Procurement of components for Cities ICT infrastructures shall enable offers based exclusively on Free Software and shall award projects to Free Software based offers when submitted.

Cities shall review and publish as Free Software existing components of its ICT Infrastructure in which it holds the rights to do so. In addition, Cities shall identify those elements of its ICT infrastructure that are opportunities for implementing with or substituting by Free Software.

Cities shall use hardware resources controlled by the City itself adopting appropriate technical and organizational measures to ensure the protection of their citizens' and visitors' data and privacy.

Cities shall pool their ICT Infrastructure budgets for common procurement of Free Software technologies and services, and tools for publishing Open Data sets.

Cities shall develop internally appropriate Free Software and Open Data related skills to achieve autonomous management of their ICT infrastructures and services.

Cities shall promote and support local Free Software and Open Data based enterprise and community through developing skills, encouraging networking, supporting Free Software and Open Data enterprise, user groups and events, and providing financial and other types of resources.

Cities shall support and encourage the development of Free Software, Open Data and Digital Rights curricula in their municipal area educational institutions, to create a culture of openness and collaboration that will then support the cities' ICT policies for the future.

Cities shall review and publish as Open Data all non-confidential or private data generated by municipal ICTs and provide platforms for other entities to do the same, to promote a transparent and collaborative relationship between city government and citizens.

MareNostrum4 supercomputer at the Barcelona Supercomputing Centre
Vcarceler, 2019

* Authors: Francesca Bria (Chair), Malcolm Bain (coordinator).
Contributors (Advisory Board members): Richard Stallman, Javier Ruiz, Roberto Di Cosmo, Mitchell Baker, Renata Ávila, Marleen Stikker, Paolo Vecchi, Sergio Amadeu.
Francesca Bria is economist. Professor at the UCL Institute for Innovation and Public Purpose, London.

7

INTAN MATTER

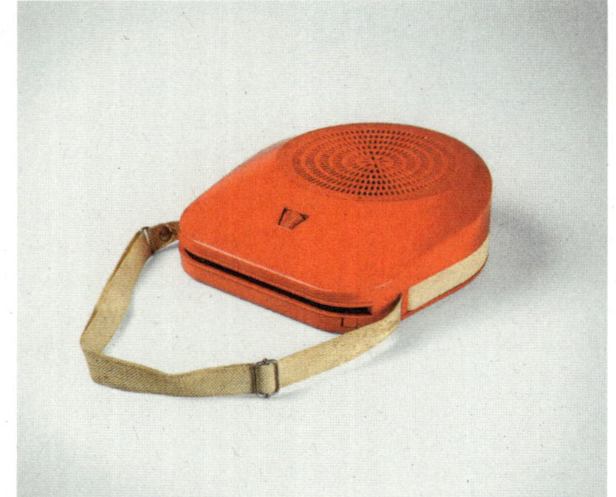

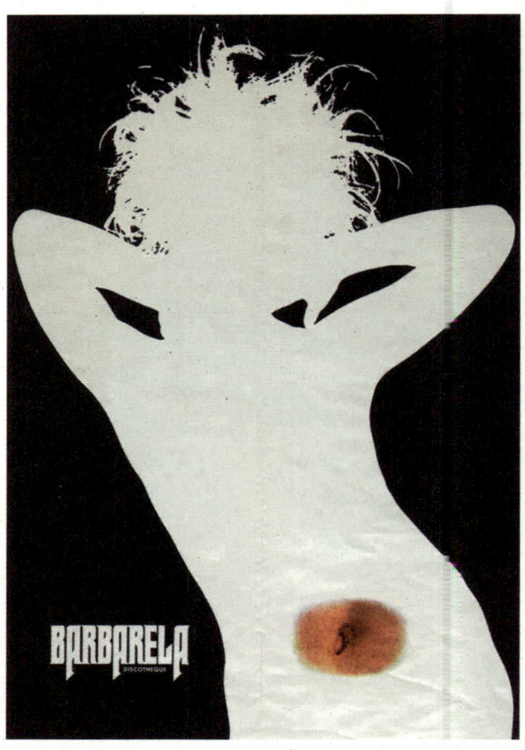

Comedisco Minitoc record player
Bianchi, 1975

Fountains of Montjuïc
Oriol Maspons, Carles Buïgas Sans, 1963 (later print). Museu Nacional d'Art de Catalunya, donation of the artist, 1999
Photograph, Museu Nacional d'Art de Catalunya, Barcelona, Spain © Oriol Maspons Photographic Archive, VEGAP, Barcelona, 2024

Exposició Internacional Barcelona poster
Chromolithography on paper
Josep Capuz i Mamano, Barcelona, 1929
Purchase, 2008 GAGB 19/08

Barbarela poster
Ink on paper
Carlos Rolando, Barcelona, 1969
Donation, Fundació Comunicació Gràfica, 2019 MDB 7.218

FARO 320 portable record player
Steel, wood, brass and polystyrene
Manufactured by Faro Española SA, Barcelona, c. 1970
Donation, Paco García, 2002 MADB 136.789

Over the course of the twentieth century, architecture and design developed from tectonic, tangible practices into atmospherical, multisensory, and ephemeral practices thanks to the introduction of electronic light and sound, and sometimes chemical technologies.

The Magic Fountain of Montjuïc, designed by Carles Buïgas for the 1929 Barcelona International Exposition, is an early example of such works that used the "waterlight" technique to create effects of form and color with skylights and prisms. Artificial lights, electronic sounds, and psychotropic substances were first used in the sixties as instruments of spatial regulation, as seen in Mediterranean discotheques. The mirror ball, a symbol of the age of disco, illustrates this transformation. Proposals like *Enviro-Pill* by Archigram illustrate how designers used drugs as tools to create new worlds starting from mind-body interactions that are now translated into digital environments.

Enviro-Pill, It's My Choice
Ron Herron, Archigram

INTANGIBILITY: A GENEALOGY

POL ESTEVE*

The opening of the 1929 Barcelona International Exposition not only consolidated the architectural language of Modernism in the form of Mies van der Rohe's pavilion. It also introduced Montjuïc's Magic Fountain which fascinated spectators with its kinetic and multi-coloured forms.

The Mies pavilion – meticulously examined in its materiality and spatiality – instantly entered the annals of architecture. Yet, the fountain, despite its popularity, was more of a footnote, relegated to the realm of popular culture, of mannered sensory languages, of the decorative disciplines. Still, Carles Buïgas i Sans' project signified the triumph of a new paradigm in design.

Since its emergence in the 19th century, electricity had had a profound influence on every facet of life. A spectrum of electrical devices, from street lights to refrigerators, gradually came to monopolize daily activities. This new energy source, originally intended to be the overriding motif of the 1929 Exposition, opened the possibility of including dynamic elements in design. Light, sound and movement could now be produced electrically, without human or animal power.

The 1929 Magic Fountain took the use of electricity beyond strict functionality and granted it an aesthetic dimension. It sought plastic, spatial and sensory expression. A lively design style developed over time, Eugeni d'Ors called it the art of *aiguallum* (water light)[1] while Buïgas would later deploy it in other projects such as *La nave luminosa* (The luminous ship). In it, the electrically activated and illuminated water acquires an architectural presence.

These first exercises in turning electrical power into multi-sensory experiences were interrupted during wartime, but they made a powerful comeback in the 1960s and 1970s, which saw a renewed interest in the concepts of mood and atmosphere, seen as the multidisciplinary design of the inhabited environment. Different materials, techniques and systems developed by the military were integrated into the world of design and their potential to transform the experience of the environment was explored.

Internationally, the new interest in space, technology and multi-sensory experiences found its expression in museums – for example, in MoMA, under the direction of Ambaz –, in universal exhibitions –Montreal, 1967, and Osaka, 1970 – and in Western art, design and architecture: Italian radical architects, the American counterculture, and the Center for Advanced Visual Studies at MIT, to name a few. In a context of technological optimism, though often also of political and social criticism, certain projects and experiments from that time still stand out today as radical proposals for the inclusion of new mood technologies.

Within the Spanish and Catalan context, the most interesting experiments in dynamic and multi-sensory designs were conducted by the leisure industry, more specifically, the nightlife sector, rather than the institutional one. The discotheque, which emerged in the 1960s as a new space for socializing while dancing to electronically produced music under artificial lights and the influence of drugs, became a testing ground. Discos in the Costa Brava were pioneers, as cultural critic Simon Frith noted in the 1970s.

On dance floors in towns like Platja d'Aro, multidisciplinary teams of architects and light and sound technicians, among others, worked together to create an experience based on trans-sensory effects produced by electronic and chemical technologies. Light and sound waves were now used as building materials shaped as desired to provide a high-intensity experience.

Tectonic materials, static and lasting, which assume their shape in response to mass and gravity, gave way to new fluid and fleeting materials which, like the water in the Magic Fountain, lack a shape of their own and flow in space. The result was new a materiality that expresses itself as a field of expansive waves intersecting with the surrounding bodies. New possibilities thus opened for design. Instead of being understood as the geometric composition of an object, it was now conceived as the body's relationship with an ever-changing environment.

It was during this period that the body took centre stage as a receptor and mediator in design practice. The use of chemical technologies that interact with the body's metabolic processes became popular. Psychotropic substances were seen as tools to modulate perception and, therefore, potentially design it. Acting on sensory and cognitive mechanisms, lab-designed molecules became, simultaneously, powerful instruments of design.

1 https://www.lavanguardia.com/edicion-impresa/20170626/423699552843/la-nau-lluminosa-de-buigas.html.

On the dance floor, psychotropic substances not only were the medium to enhance the experience of the setting, but their effect was a design referent as well. The psychedelic movement, particularly, impregnated all areas of design, shifting the entire range of the perceptive and sensory qualities of one's inner journey to objects, fashion, music and other areas. Outside of Spain, architects and designers even went so far as to use chemistry as the ultimate design tool. Archigram and Hans Hollein imagined inhabitable settings accessible by ingesting a pill.

Since the 1960s, the emergence of new electronic and chemical materials has gone hand in hand with the development of cybernetics. If the Magic Fountain had a control board and discos a booth where disc-jockeys manually regulated mood parameters, from then on, more sophisticated, reactive and autonomous systems would be experimented with to regulate the setting.

Put simply, the interaction between spatial design techniques and cybernetics that started in the 1960s led to today's digital media. Currently, 3D-design programs make it possible to represent objects and moods not subject to the laws of physics, but that exist only as digital codes. What we are witnessing, then, is the final dematerialization of design.

This summarized genealogy, based on experimenting with mouldable materials like water, and which with the help of electric and chemical micro-technologies ultimately was used to design and produce intangible settings, is not isolated from the technical and economic transformations of our culture. Rather the Montjuïc fountain can be seen as the aesthetic manifestation of the mechanical progress of the first Industrial Revolution; the disco as the aesthetic manifestation of the second technological era, which coincides with the liberalization of the economy, and digital settings as the aesthetic manifestation of the acceleration of techno-capitalism.

The transition of the world of design from tectonics to intangibility occurred while production systems were being transformed. The water rays in Montjuïc fountain heralded a process of dematerialization that invokes the unique experience of the individual as the central axis of design. Ever since, technologies and techniques of intangibility have made available to us the fluid, changing, transient and subjective environment characteristic of the post-industrial era.

* Pol Esteve is PhD in Architecture, researcher and university professor at ETH Zurich.

Space Oddity model
Foam board, black cardboard, methacrylate, ping-pong ball, tree, 12V digital RGB LED strip, 12V 120W transformer, control technology by Protopixel
Antoni Arola and Jordi Tamayo, Barcelona, 2024
Loan, Antoni Arola and Jordi Tamayo

IMMATERIAL COLORS

Light has no mass but it does have energy, a characteristic that enables designers like Antoni Arola to transform environments with technologies such as RGB LEDS, light-emitting diodes that can produce over 16 million different colors using the three primary colors, red, green, and blue. Flexible and creative, they can produce a variety of atmospheres in the same space thanks to the strategic position of fountains of lights and illuminated surfaces, thereby defining space and color in innovative ways that change over time. Antoni Arola's incorporeal architectural spaces place light in the center of contemporary design.

LIVING MATERIALS – RESONANT MATERIALS

JAVIER PEÑA*

"I don't understand why elements aren't taught like letters and numbers if they're necessary to interpret the world, our world, everyone's world..."
"It's a dream come true, numbers, letters and elements equally..."
"It's a dream come true, elements: a universal language..."

This is the beginning and two choruses of a song I wrote and of many talks and classes I've given. It's also, especially, the foundation of the information that has sparked in me the tenderness I feel for materials and the passion with which I have had the good fortune to share hundreds of adventures with my students, from the classroom to the infinite and beyond.

Dimitri Mendeleev's periodic table, which I learned about in school at the age of thirteen, fascinated me. It led me to university and showed me a world different from the one I'd known before. A different reality that taught me that all matter is electric and that electricity conditions all materials. It also taught me that the universe is insubstantial and consists only of the movement of electrical charges. And that pressure varies the movement of these charges, generating waves with their corresponding frequencies. I observed how, at different pressures, different movements and different frequencies of the related waves were produced. This is what I like to think the elements are: waves, vibrations and frequencies. This is the dream I allowed myself to have thanks to the lessons of the masters Walter Russell and Nikola Tesla. This a dream come true. The periodic table that we study is the effect. The cause is yet to be understood.

I believe that infinite molecules, infinite compounds and infinite materials are the infinite combinations of waves, with their corresponding frequencies, of the infinite states of pressure of our dear chemical elements. The ones that make up the periodic table! And what we long for as humans is to share our life always with resonant materials which, ever since I was introduced to them, I dare say are "materials that, being as alive as we are, are capable of generating a resonant and consistent interaction with the environment, with the planet, and with the living things that inhabit it." For the element that exists is not an element because it exists; it's also because it bestows existence.

It is widely believed that there is living matter and there is inert matter. That there are two worlds or two different planes, and one is known as inanimate. Minerals, stones, metals, materials in general make up this world. In the other world, or on the other plane, is what is alive, that which is consists of the essence of life, what is animate, and consequently moving and evolving. To put it very simply, this is part of the cultural alphabet with which we continue to build our way of thinking about the future and constructing our present realities: life is the essential property or quality of animals and plants, whereby they evolve, adapt to the environment, develop and reproduce. Meanwhile, we would say that a stone or steel or silver is not alive.

> But didn't we say the elements give rise to existence and that we believe that materials made up of elements, electrical charges in motion, are alive?

Around fifty years after the discovery of DNA, Austrian physicist Erwin Schrödinger, one of the creators of quantum theory, inspired an entire generation of scientists by posing, again, a timeless philosophical question: what is life?

Schrödinger believed that, despite our "obvious inability" to define it, life would eventually be explained by physics and chemistry. He believed that life is matter that replicates its structure as it grows, like a crystal, a strange "aperiodic crystal."

Many minerals grow like crystals, in addition to emitting waves with their corresponding frequencies. What a coincidence!

Years later, NASA, the leading United States space agency, defined life as "a self-sustaining chemical system capable of Darwinian evolution and considered the specific features of the one life we know – Terran life."

Yet another coincidence! If we set aside the part about Darwinian evolution and focus simply on evolution and, therefore, change and movement, we are faced with a beautifully integrating, holistic and universal instance of life that makes us see the world and the planet we live on as a being that by no means should we destroy.

The beautifully described cycle of life needs to broaden its horizons and start to include beings that we call inert, inanimate and dead. It should include the mineral kingdom and thus begin to vibrate in a resonant and coherent way with our material friends. Perhaps then we would understand a little better the concept of sustainability, the circular economy and the green colour of everything. All colours are equally important, although black and white have unique effects.

We know that getting there is important, but the journey is even more so. On my journey, I observed how the Greek philosophers never stopped searching for the principles and foundations that made up the matter all around them and with which they interacted. For Thales of Miletus, water was the origin of everything, while for Anaximenes it was air. For Heraclitus, it was fire. Democritus introduced us to atoms so that Aristotle could conclude that there are four elements that give form to what see when we look down and another, the so-called quintessence, the Ether that explains the heavens to us, what we see when we look up, thus defining the theory of the four elements.

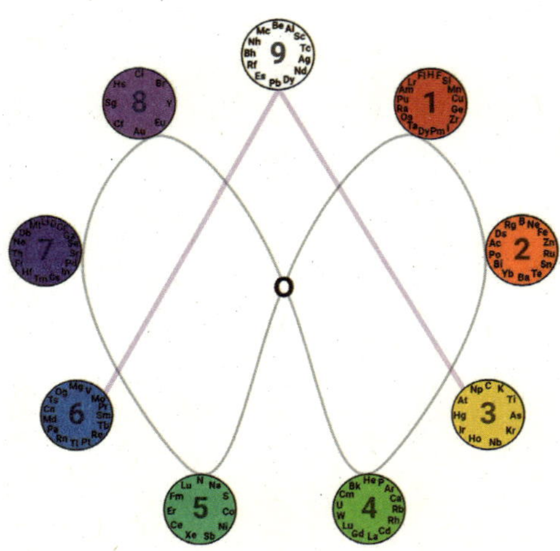

Resonant Organization of Chemical Elements
that connects numbers, letters
Javier Peña, *Elements 6. The Truth*, 2024

The Third Bagua, the Material Bagua
Javier Peña, *Elements 9. The Third Bagua*, 2022

I also observed, with some admiration, how in Chinese culture, having the same concerns, their vision of things shaped a different reality. Where the Greeks proposed one theory after another in relation to the basic components of physical objects – earth, air, fire and atoms, and everything else –, Chinese culture focused on the *phases* or changes that are constantly taking place. Movement, again, was the key, and the Chinese understood this very well. Albert Einstein also understood it when he said that "the measure of intelligence is the ability to change."

In recent decades, quantum mechanics (QM) has exceeded the limits of atomic and subatomic scales. This new science that tends towards unification has made it possible to create a model of the universe that recovers the holistic sense of the understanding of reality of ancient cultures. This is a universal system connected energetically, and one that is proving to be genuine and independent of the scale at which it is measured and observed. In this light, the mechanistic model that tells us that reality is made up of material entities with radically defined limits, between which there is only "emptiness," and that interact strictly on the local physical plane, governed by strict and immutable natural laws, becomes suspect. According to the quantum model, a human being is an energetic being in a universe being whose behaviour is fully integrated:

> The universe is a continuous whole, there are no separate elements. Quantum entities influence each other instantaneously, at any distance without force or energy exchange.
>
> All quantum entities share holographic information about the whole.
>
> Quantum energy fields are the essential elements of nature, not particles.

In these intense times in which we live, affected by what we call artificial intelligence, quantum modelling of reality entails the consideration of information and energy fields as essential elements of physical reality that connect us to everything and to everyone, with our cherished elements as generous bearers of all knowledge. In our reality, a field consists of a matrix or environment that connects two or more points in space, generally through the force of gravity or electromagnetism. This occurs because an electric and magnetic field, viewed as an area of influence capable of interfering with objects up to infinite distances, forms around any electrical charge. These fields aren't measured by forces but energy and information exchanges.

In 1656, physicist Christiann Huygens observed the spontaneous synchronization of inanimate objects for the first time. Synchronization remained a focus of several disciplines of knowledge, with the realization that it affected both biological beings and, consequently, human beings, as well as what we call inert or inanimate beings. These demonstrable discoveries prove that existence is an interaction of animate and inanimate systems.

The elements are alive and give life to the materials of which we are made.

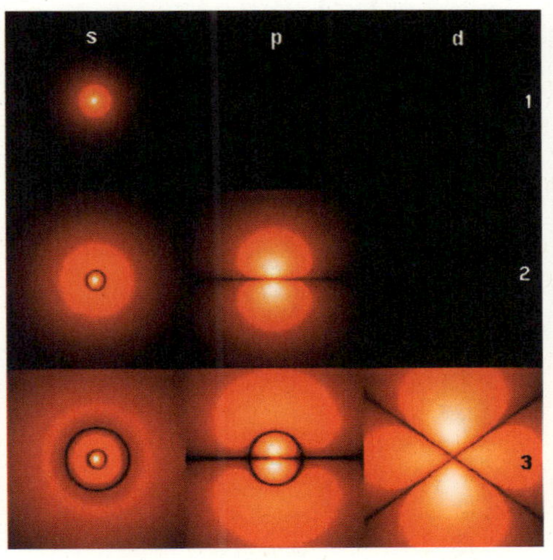

Probability densities corresponding to wave functions of an electron of a hydrogen atom with infinite energy levels (increasing from the top of the image down: n = 1, 2, 3, ...) and angular momentum (increasing from left to right: s, p, d...). Brighter areas correspond to a higher probability density in a position measurement

* Javier Peña is PhD in Chemical Sciences. Founder of Materfad in 2008. General Director of the Escola Universitària de Disseny Elisava (Elisava University School of Design) since 2016.

BECOMING A DISCURSIVE, MULTIPLE, STICKY AND REBELLIOUS MATERIALITY

LAURA BENÍTEZ*

The reduction of the ontological horizon to immanence is so radical that it represents the preliminary condition for defining the project of liberation.[1]

—Antonio Negri

In the contemporary context, the debate concerning the human condition includes numerous proposals to rethink ourselves in the face of what appears to be the end of the human species and how we have understood this up to now. From the implementation of capacities and conditions, to the tactical use of technologies to edit a body beyond an anthropocentric paradigm, one thing seems clear: Western humanity, with its modern heritage, appears to be in trouble and needs to be reconsidered urgently regarding the possibility of editing the body and regarding a mediated body that is no longer only human. The different options that technological implementation seems to offer are changing even the configuration of what up to now we have called subjectivity. The body as an edited element is one of the inflection points in this "new" articulation of what is possible. Yet what are the power relations in which this mediated body is inscribed technologically? Are we faced with an arrangement of possibility in terms of neo-liberal individualism? Or are we faced with a rearrangement of subjectivity in terms of multitude? These questions are posed as critical triggers to address what is at stake in the intersections between bio(info) technologies, the body, artistic practices, subjectivity(ies) and power relations, paying particular attention to Mary Maggic and Mai Ling.

Certainly, contemporary narratives about the human condition are filled with proposals that appear as lighthouses of salvation in a context of collapse, promising bright futures –futures in which bodies, human and non-human, appear as the culmination of the neo-Darwinian dream, materialities refined and *improved* by the much-acclaimed *advanced technologies*. However, technocentric and techno-fantastical promises conceal deep abysses of subjectivity, power and hegemony. Within this landscape, the work of Mary Maggic opens a crack of resistance and subversion, weaving intersections between biotechnology, artistic practices and existential activism. Thus, this brief paper[1] explores the discursive materiality of Mary Maggic's work, examining its trans-feminist, decolonial and trans-specific solidarity focus, as well as its embodiment of queer and design justice ethics.

Mary Maggic, an artist and researcher, inhabits a place *in between* biotechnology, artistic practices and biohacking, creating narratives, not just representational, that challenge the ontological borders between what is natural and what is artificial, what is human and what is non-human, as well as all manifestations of binary logic. Through their work, they question hegemonic narratives of gender, biopolitics and necropolitics, offering a critical and subversive vision of (com) posthuman bodies. One of their more well-known projects, *Open Source Estrogen*, a collaborative effort but developed mostly by Mary Maggic, combines biohacking practices with speculative design from a perspective of tactical subversion. Posing the question, "And if it were possible to make estrogen in the kitchen?", *Open Source Estrogen* opens the debate on hormone control and production and their consequences, as well on the silenced contamination by xenoestrogens.[2] The project addresses how xenoestrogen contamination causes disruptions and mutations in the hormonal system, given that xenoestrogens are hormone disruptors, that is, they create changes in the way the endocrine system functions, thus affecting hormonal balance. It is precisely in the context of this panorama, which the artist defines as molecular colonization, that the project seeks to open a debate on the sovereignty of the body beyond an anthropocentric notion and on the impossibility of continuing to think in binary terms. In fact, historical-pharmaceutic materiality makes clear that now nothing is binary because we have been "performed" by a molecular invasion. "If everything, human and non-human, is affected by hegemonic forces, from the project's perspective, and as a catalyst for critical thinking, we must share tools and knowledge and hack these hormonal colonization systems to create social mutagenesis."[3] The metaphoric nature of this mutagenesis allows us to think of pollutants not merely as inert waste but active agents that interact with bodies and the "environment" *through* complex dynamics, thereby inviting us to reconsider our relationship with matter, recognizing the agency of non-human elements. As a result, we can challenge, even if it is at the micro/nano scale, the colonial power structures that have exerted control over and exploited non-normative and non-human bodies.

1 Antonio Negri: *The Savage Anomaly*, Minneapolis, University of Minnesota Press, 1990.

2 Xenoestrogens are synthetic hormones created in the 1930s by the chemical and pharmaceutical industry.

3 Mary Tsang, Paula Pin, Gaia Leandra, Byron Rich, Carlos Gámez and Amanda Padilla: *Estrozine*. Mary Maggic, 2012. https://files.cargocollective.com/c781072/estrozine-1.1.pdf.

Open Source Estrogen defies the notion of technocentric *improvement*, revealing the material complexity and ambiguity of bodies. It is an allegory of the fluid and mutable nature of gender, shedding light on structures and devices that restrain and define bodies. Thus, all the procedures that the proposal implements are based on the commitment not only to open source the code but make it accessible and subject to re-appropriation, sharing publicly the methods for extracting, detecting and, perhaps, synthesizing hormones and asking the question, "What would happen if we synthesized open-source estrogens?" This question therefore becomes a critical trigger that unlocks biotechnological knowledge, believing in the creation of open, inclusive, participatory and equitable technologies. Mary Maggic's approach makes clear an ethos of care. Here "care" is understood not only as a practice but an epistemological framework through which to rethink our interactions with the *material world*.[4]

Becoming-Stickiness, a film by the collective Mai Ling,[5] also addresses this issue, exploring the racialized and gender-based logic of *ornamentalism*, taking as a reference Anne Anlin Cheng, who analyses how the European and United States collective imagination has constructed Asian femininity as a hybrid of a human being and an ornamental object, an aestheticization of the existence of *colonial subjects*. The film draws from the exhibition NOT YOUR ORNAMENT, presented at Vienna Secession, between September and November of 2023. In fact, it is in relation to the specific context of the founding of the collective that Mai Ling challenges this objectified condition and ornamental subordination through "decorative" and "invasive" plants. Taking the relationship of the Secession institution to Art Nouveau, in which ornamental floral and plant designs were very common, as a material-epistemic starting point, the collective steps in, placing its agency at the centre vis-à-vis the ornamental aestheticization which perpetuates the sexualization and dehumanization of Asian bodies in white colonial society. It is not inconsequential, then, that the kudzu plant plays a crucial role in relation to the exhibition and the idea of "stickiness" as an agency of resistance and pleasure.

> Introduced initially as a "ornamental" plant during the Centennial International Exhibition in 1876, in the United States, and subsequently used in agriculture to combat soil erosion, the vine is viewed today as an invasive species in most of the Western world. Native to East and Southeast Asia and some Pacific Islands, kudzu is known for its beneficial properties as a material for weaving and for its use in traditional medicine and cooking, as the starch in its roots acts as a thickening agent and sticky ingredient (Mai Ling, s.f.).

4 Maria Puig de la Bellacasa: *Matters of Care: Speculative Ethics in More Than Human Worlds*. Minneapolis, University of Minnesota Press, 2017.

5 Collective, founded in 2019, of which Mary Tsang (Mary Maggic) is a member. "Dedicated to fostering dialogues about experiences of racism, sexism, homophobia, and any kind of prejudice, particularly against Asian FLINT* (female*, lesbian, intersex*, non-binary, and trans*). Rooted in solidarity against patriarchal and racial discrimination, the group provides a protected space and an expanding network to give a voice to the many people affected by this discrimination and to encourage new forms of collaboration [...] The name Mai Ling refers to an eponymous 1979 TV sketch by German comedian Gerhard Polt that depicts sexist and racial stereotypes and prejudices against Asian women* in German-speaking society [...] Mai Ling challenges the Western patriarchal gaze and confronts the racist fantasies that continue to reproduce stereotypes about "Asia" and are still deeply rooted and internalized by society." Read more at https://mai-ling.org/.

The project begins with the search for kudzu, stickiness and pleasure through the body language of experiencing, cooking, eating, feeling, interacting with and embodying the *invasive plant*. It culminates in a collective choreography in which numerous bodies intermingle and end up becoming one with the plants, challenging binary thinking and the supposed dichotomies between subject and object, between decorative and invasive. Mai Ling and Kudzu as vibrating agency-charged matter, articulate a choreography of cocreation and transformation, exposing the morass of horticultural colonialism, exoticism, esthetization and migratory experiences. This attitude gives rise to *other realities* in which agents and entities neither pre-exist their interactions nor the narratives that define them, but are established together through becoming instances of *stickiness*.

"Stickiness" that distances us from the sterile and technocentric dreams of Silicon Valley and its gurus like Elon Musk. People who continue reproducing the creation of transcendent political devices, closely linked to the Modern State, becoming new techno-reductionist models. In contrast, proposals like those by Mary Maggic and Mai Ling seem to be closer to a notion of constitutive immanent power where individualities are presented as a multitude, a *becoming-with* mediated technologically but not techno-centred. Returning to the idea of multitude according to Toni Negri and Michael Hardt, we find a notion of constituent power as ontological principle, where being is presented as a movement of transformation, a transformation which has nothing to do with *being-in-transition* in terms of improvement but with a *being-with*, a transformative movement towards a *telos* of the common. Now, it is worth noting that there is something in Mary Magicc's conception which exceeds Negri and Hardt's multitude, a gesture that allows the outside to overflow the inside, bringing to light the question

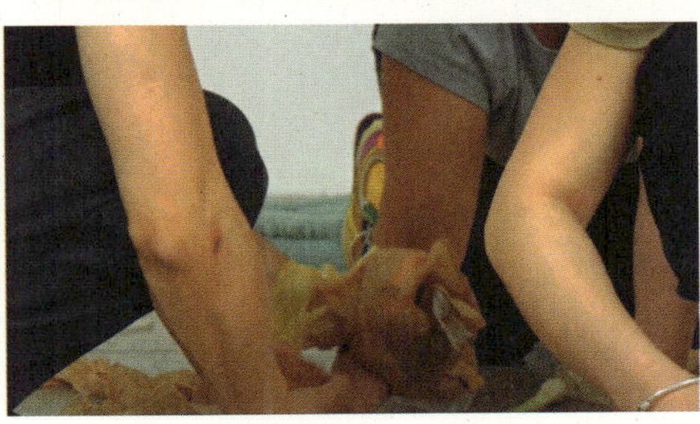

Mai Ling, *Becoming Stickiness*, 2023
Screenshots of the movie

of who "is permitted" to enter this majority, thereby giving rise to a radically contemporary emergency; in other words, that this majority can no longer be either merely an ethnocentric majority or anthropocentric. Perhaps what we have is a sticky and insurgent *telos of the common*, since as Negri and Hardt pointed out in *Imperio*[6] "there is something real which prefigures a coming future: the telos whose pulse we can feel, the multitude we construct within desire."

In Mary Maggic's projects something like what Michel Foucault noted in *Words and Things*[7] is at work, that is: a radicalization of the process of self-constitution. With the distinction that the body is not understood here as an autonomous agent but a node enmeshed in an extensive system of relationships. An "editable" mutagenesis as a site of amorphous re-meanings distributed in a network of bodies, not only human ones, in which constituent power is not so much related to a kind of undifferentiated continuity of an individual being but to its creative difference. Thus, Mary Maggic's work is understood as an affirmative practice in which relationships are seen as decisions of narrative multiplicities and, consequently, constituent. A place where power operates "as a dynamic and constitutive inherence of what is individual and of multiplicity" as "counter-power where power is a project to subordinate multiplicity, intelligence, freedom, potency," where anomalous bodies confront disciplinary and disciplined bodies.

Artistic practices such as Mary Maggic's represent the revolt of anomalous bodies, of material singularities that reappropriate technological mediation *as sympoiesis*, as an ongoing process of materialization. They hold out possibilities of rebellion *for-with* bodies challenging technocentric improvement narratives and opening new possibilities of existence. Both *Open Source Estrogen* and *Becoming-Stickiness* demand a careful approach and a commitment in terms of responsibility and hability, paying special attention to the symbiotic interdependencies that support our existence. These are practices which view bio(info)technological materiality not in terms of domination or control, characteristic of an anthropocentric and colonial legacy, but as power for thinking *through* the diverse materiality of bodies and subjectivities, respecting the complexity and multiplicity of differences regarding *life*. And the truth is Mary Maggic, through their critical and subversive approach, shows us how bio(info)technologies can be used to challenge hegemonic narratives, opening cracks of possibilities to bring about a discursive, multiple, sticky and rebellious materiality.

6 Michael Hardt and Antonio Negri: *Empire*, Cambridge, Harvard University Press, 2001.

7 Michel Foucault [1966]: *Les mots et les choses: Une archéologie des sciences humaines*, Paris, Gallimard, 1990.

8 Antonio Negri, *op. cit.*, 1993.

* Laura Benítez is PhD in Philosophy, researcher and independent curator.

Functionality, body, and design come together in the corset, an anatomical garment that was staple in women's wardrobes from the Renaissance to the twentieth century. In spite of the criticism sparked in the late nineteenth century due to the physical harm caused by corsets, women wear them as symbols of social status in keeping with beauty canons. Philosopher Paul B. Preciado has introduced the concept of *technobody* in his literature, according to which the body is redesigned by technology and can hence overcome the limits between natural and artificial. Transformed into a multi-connected techno-self, the body destabilizes gender polarity, creating new subjectivities. The conception of the body as a host of substances that can be modified by chemistry or by fashion still determines our ways of redesigning it.

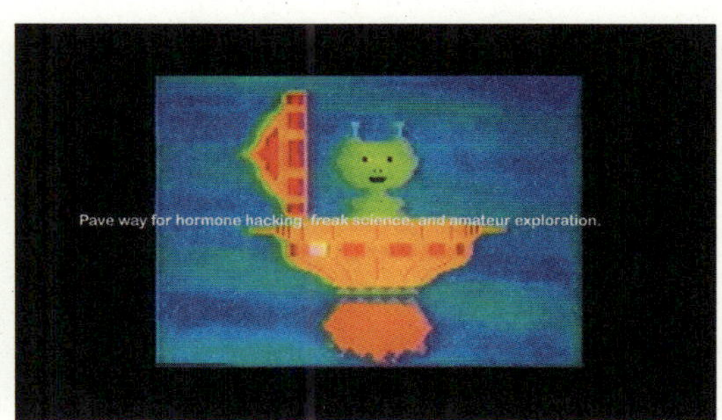

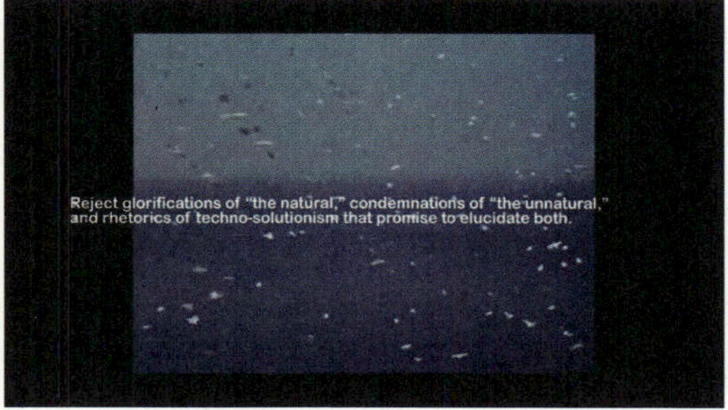

Open Source Estrogen: A Manifesto
Video
Mary Maggic, 2016–2017
Loan, Mary Maggic

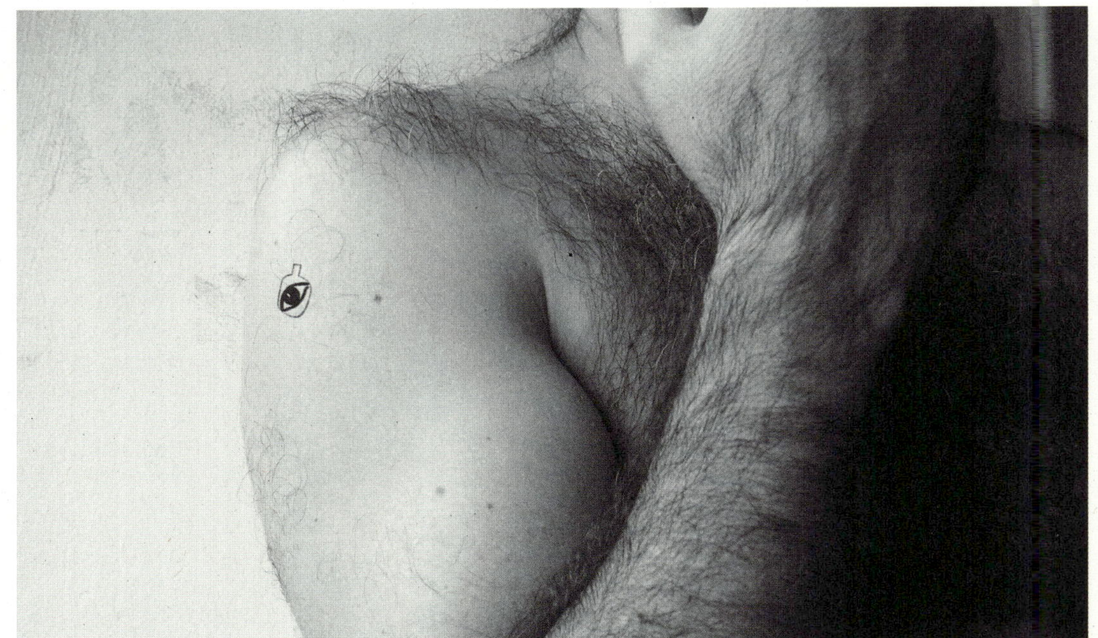

Visualize Stamp
Scented ink stamps to use on skin
Ana Mir, Barcelona, 2006
Manufactured by Antonio Puig
Loan, Ana Mir

Tonopán card
Ink on paper
Josep Pla-Narbona
Laboratorio Sandoz, Madrid, *c.* 1969
Donation, Pla-Narbona, 2013 GAGB 1038/13-03

Binomil Hipnótico card
Ink on paper
Antoni Morillas i Verdura
Laboratorio Uriach, Sant Adrià de Besòs, 1965
Donation, Lluís Morillas, 2013 GAGB 1182/13

>
Pharmacy pot
Earthenware decorated with oxides
1727–1749
Manufactured by Real Fábrica de Loza y Porcelana de Alcora
Purchase, 1932 MCB 4.134

Antim.
nium.

DESIGNING WITH/THE AIR*

NEREA CALVILLO*

Everyone and everything is in a constant exchange with air: absorbing, releasing, accumulating gases and particles. In and out. We breathe. Plants breathe. Factories breathe. Cities breathe. And yet, some industries and institutions ("security" departments, entertainment companies, weapons industries, etc.) design machines, devices, or infrastructures where air is put to work, where air is designed to carry out various (geopolitical) projects.

The most obvious one is warfare, where chemical laboratories collaborate with the military to develop gas bombs. For cultural theorist Peter Sloterdijk this is a form of "air design" – where mass destruction is achieved by poisoning the environment instead of individuals directly.[1] However, taking the notion of "air design" literally – that is, to change air's composition with a specific purpose, although not necessarily to kill – sheds light on an even wider range of implicated practices, technologies, and bodies. To be clear, the aim of looking through the weaponization of air is not to undermine the brutality of this bloodless and often invisible form of mass destruction – which is, for its apparent brutality, most often publicized. Instead, it is to connect us to other questions, histories, techniques, responsibilities, politics, affects, and effects mobilized through less visible air design practices and their impacts.

Air design is also used as a form of capture and control, intimidation and dispersal, like the tear gas used against protesters by police around the world. Other deterring chemicals are released to the air in the form of herbicides or pesticides, in a sort of warfare against weeds or insects. Reversely, other projects change the composition of the air by (trying to) remove some of its components. For instance, some carbon sequestration projects capture atmospheric CO_2 to transform it into energy, or compact CO to create ink or construction bricks. And yet, the benefits of these geoengineering projects are controversial. They might reduce some CO_2 from the atmosphere, but their construction and functioning consume energy, water, sand, often polluting water bodies, depleting mines, and so forth. And, of course, the benefit of CO_2 reduction is not evenly distributed. Large companies (often petrochemical ones) design air to profit off of their own pollution – with the aim of "cleaning" it.

Beyond violent acts of destruction, environmental management, and forms of demonstration or resistance, air design is also part of the everyday. In fact, the built environment was born *through* air design, stratifying indoor and outdoor air to protect and provide shelter. Buildings are intense air metabolizers, and architecture is deeply implicated in this process. Air's movement *through* buildings has been designed – usually by engineers – to create comfort or even permit inhabitation. Today, due to the high levels of air pollution across the world, the built environment has become organized around what anthropologist Jerry Zee names "architectures of air", which stratify breathers by income, and therefore race, class, gender.[2] For example, the wealthier you are, the "cleaner" or "purer" the air you are able to inhabit is – even if that inhabitation is temporary. Breathing clean air becomes a commodity that only a few can afford. Because as long as there is a "solution" for it, the cause of such pollution does not need to be addressed. As a consequence, the open, outdoor air evidences these inequalities.

The thicker the walls, the more sophisticated the filters and the more powerful the AC units, the worse the air quality is outdoors. And yet, cleaning the outdoors air is – at least for now – not a solution. The only "solution" is to stop polluting through a systems change. In the meantime – or in parallel – it might be useful to explore alternative and multiscalar forms of air design and intervention with/in it beyond solutionist approaches.

Air design can open up other forms of being together, and maybe designers can contribute to this. And they have. During the twentieth century the air, not in its chemical but in its physical conditions, was taken up as a structural element to create inflatable structures, to imagine other forms of politics and society. It can also become a tool for resistance through its capacity to shift conditions of transparency and visibility, like the smoke used during the Haitian Revolution, which became a symbol and a technology for Black and anti-colonial uprisings.[3] These two examples are a good opportunity to explore the liberatory potential of air design, and how air design can be operationalized in two ways: as designing *with* air (as a vehicle for something else) or to design *the* air (where the object of design is the air itself). So from now on I will refer to *designing with/the air*.

1 Peter Sloterdijk: *Terror from the Air*), Cambridge, London, The MIT Press, 2009.

2 Jerry Zee: 'Breathing in the City: Beijing and the Architecture of Air'. *Scapegoat* 8 (2015), pp. 46–56.

3 Rosa Aiello, Nataleah Hunter-Young and Michael Litwack: 'Smoking Out: An Introduction', *Public* 29, no. 58 (Fall 2018), pp. 6–21.

From experience designing and building three spatial design projects, Polivagina, Sticky Airs and Yellow Dust, where we designed with helium and smoke, I noticed how designing with/the air transforms design: from an attempt to control the capacities of a future building and regulate its inhabitants, to an experimental set-up that embraces uncertainty.[4] Design – understood broadly to encompass space, object, environment or graphic design – is no longer about deciding how to create a shape and assemble components, but rather it is a practice concerned with how to design the construction process as an experiment. It is concerned with how we design and build. So, to work with it, we need to learn to be affected. Because we cannot see it, therefore we need to feel it, holding, sensing, putting the body in. Because the air *requires* its own practices, which force (us) humans to adapt. The air unsettles what we know, and silently demonstrates that the design and building tools that we have been using until now to deal with wood or stone might be no longer adequate.

I have come to describe *Polivagina*, *Sticky Airs* and *Yellow Dust* as environmental mediations. They are technically not buildings or installations, they are environments themselves that at the same time mediate with the environment. In both projects the agency of air demanded not only different re-combinations of matter and humans, but different practices to do so. Because it was not about changing the order of materials (as in other accounts of architecture). In fact, the air made visible or brought to the fore that design is no longer a process that ends with the construction of a building, but a constant re-assembly of materials, humans, ideas. The agency of air not only shifted the order in which humans participate (as in practices of co-design, where users also participate in the initial design phases). It was about finding new practices of construction and inhabitation, such as horizontal and self-organized construction teams or playful spectatorship.

Thus designing with/the air through environmental mediations opens up other types of affects with material entities, like atmospheric attunements. But most importantly, it offers the possibility of designing desirable socialities with political and/or transformative capacities. Building with air calls for feminist or queer construction practices where anybody can contribute, and practices of assembly are substituted by practices of care.

4 Nerea Calvillo: *Aeropolis: Queering Air in Toxicpolluted Worlds*, New York, Columbia Books on Architecture and the City, 2023.

* This text is an excerpt of *Aeropolis: Queering Airs in Toxicpolluted Worlds*.

‡ Nerea Calvillo is architect and researcher. Assistant Professor at the Centre for Interdisciplinary Methodologies of the University of Warwick.

Yellow Dust
C+arquitectas / In The Air, 2017
Nerea Calvillo

AEROPOLIS

Air, the counter-mold of the city, is the intangible element that affects human beings and other creatures. Half the world's population lives in urban environments, and nine out of every ten people breathe air polluted above the air quality guideline levels marked by the World Health Organization (WHO). The climate emergency transforms cities into heat islands, and poor construction quality often prevents energy efficiency.

Nerea Calvillo addresses this problem in the project entitled *Yellow Dust*, a performative artifact designed to raise awareness of air pollution and monitor it. In its turn, the infrared termographic image of the Museu del Disseny-DHub illustrates the energy losses of buildings, showing revealing areas of inefficiency that need improvement. In unison, the work by Nerea Calvillo and the termographic study emphasize the need for architects and designers to deal with the invisible aspects of urban environments, such as the quality of air and energy efficiency.

Intra-connected matter
Thermographic image of the DHub building
Barcelona, October 2024
Droneit / Olga Subirós

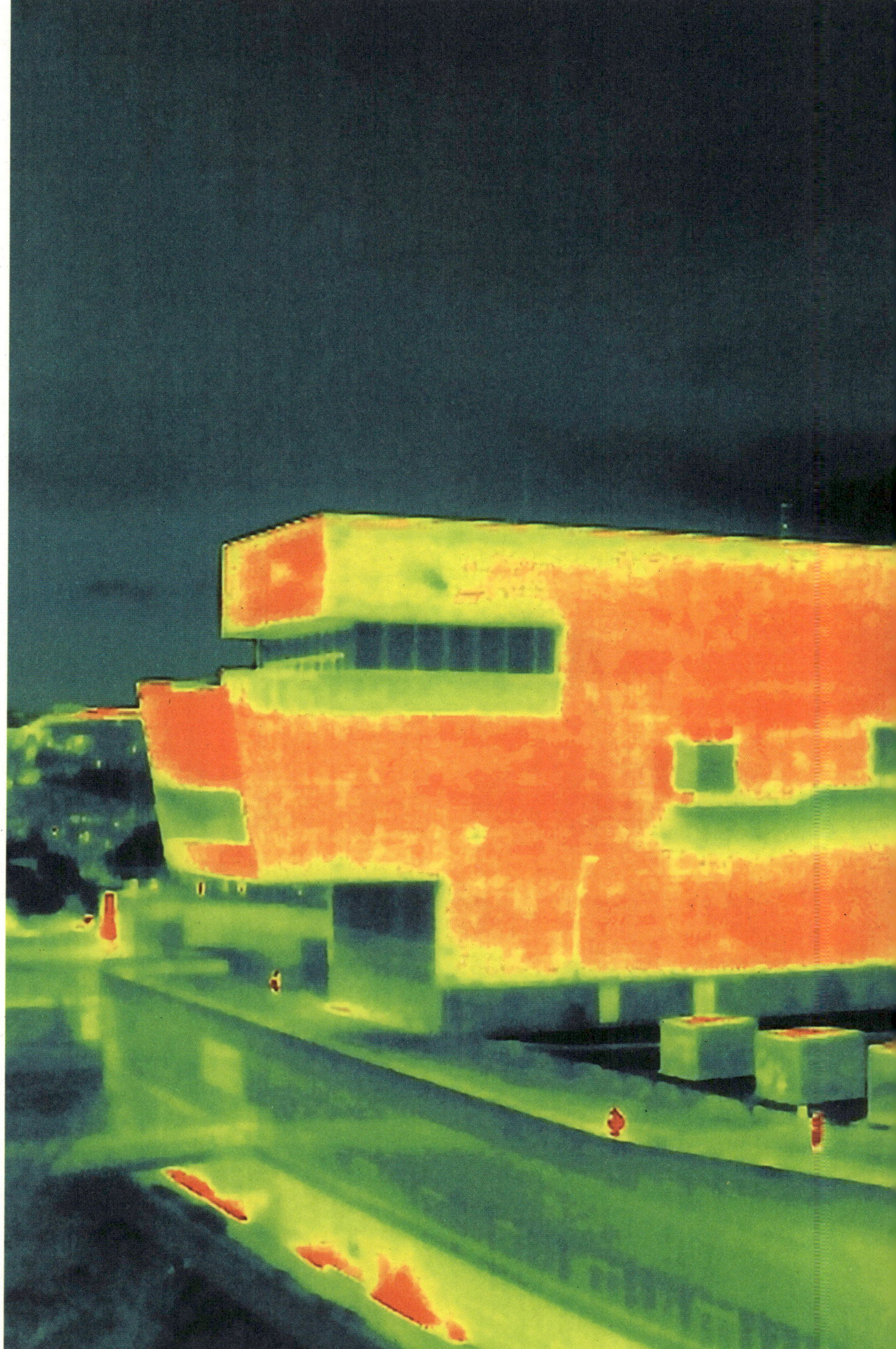

21.8°C
16.6°C

THE ANTHROPOCENE STYLE: TOWARDS A NEW DECORATIVE REALITY

PHILIPPE RAHM*

Ongoing since the beginning of the industrial era, global warming is having a significant impact on terrestrial eco- and climate systems and the distribution of land and sea surfaces. Given the amplification of these chemical, physical, and biological changes, which affect both the atmosphere and the lithosphere, some scientists have begun to discuss the change in terms of geological time, coining the term "Anthropocene" – the successor to the Holocene in the march of geological eras. The causes of this change in the era are no longer "natural," cosmic, or volcanic, as was previously the case, but human, a result of man's burning of fossil fuels, deforestation, and other industrial activities. This climate and geological-era change will have an enormous impact on human lives and activities, among them population migration following the disappearance of coastal areas, changes in climatically-based local economies, and an increase in the amount of extreme-weather incidents.

The need to slow down the rate of global warming has become an international priority, as evidenced by the Paris Agreement, thrashed out among 196 nations at the COP 21 summit in 2015. Architecture and construction are at the forefront of the fight against global warming because they are responsible for almost one-third of the emissions of greenhouse gases primarily through air and hot-water heating and air-conditioning. The construction industry's principal responses over the past decade have been an effort to reduce the energy consumption of buildings and the prioritized use of renewable energy. These new thermal regulations have important consequences for architectural design, rendering obsolete many 20th-century architectural strategies with respect to both the exterior shape of the buildings and interior design.

The necessity of enclosing a pocket of air which can then be acclimatized to human needs requires the use of solid materials to define a tight envelope which, at its most prosaic, consists in a floor, four walls, and a ceiling, which mark the boundary between an artificial and the natural climate. Assembling these materials to enclose this bubble of anthropogenic atmosphere generates specific problems linked to the weight, form, and dimensions of these materials, a process which subsequently induces, without its being desired at the outset, a set of recommendations and ways of doing things that for a long time constituted the major part of architectural treatises. Without consciously realizing it, we have witnessed, from the beginning of architectural history, a shift of interest and priority from space, interior volume, and climate towards the solid and the structural, these latter being in reality only secondary means for defining interior space as a vacuum more convenient for the exclusion of natural climatic hazards.

Our purpose today is to take up this history in the face of the new energy and climate challenges that dominate our era and which force us to establish a new stage in the writing of the solid. This began when architects were required to thermally insulate their buildings from the outside. What had always been the exterior expression of their buildings, namely the supporting structure and cladding materials, suddenly found itself hidden behind a soft, 20-centimeter-thick layer of fiberglass, mineral, or PET wool which would henceforth take on the role of defining external appearances. What emerges from this transition is that the external thermal insulation re-emphasizes the primary mission of architecture, which is to provide an interior void that is thermally modified in relation to the outside natural climate. Removed from the façade, the supporting structure takes on its true secondary role as the means of constituting the interior void.

Our drive for a new Anthropocene style is about not only the external shape of a building and its materials but also about the interior – the so-called "decorative" style. The interior styles inherited from Modernism take no account of energy consumption, constituted as they were in reaction to a series of technological developments based on unlimited fossil-fuel utilization. First came central heating in the first half of the 19th century, then electric lighting in the 1880s, followed by air-conditioning in the first decade of the 20th century; the stylistic consequence of these developments was to depreciate the value of the old decorative arts – panelling, tapestries, carpets, mirrors, chandeliers, etc., whose mission was to increase thermal and lighting comfort in a pre-industrial era when heating, cooling, and lighting had a low yield. Adolf Loos's *Ornament and Crime* (1908), Mies van der Rohe's "less is more," Le Corbusier's "Law of Ripolin," the Bauhaus's "needs of the people before the need for luxury" were new aesthetic programs in which the old decorative elements, which lost their legitimacy with respect to the augmentation of heat and light, were removed in favour of an empty white minimalism, without ornament or decoration, which was made possible by the propagation of electricity generation through the burning of fossil fuels. Modern systems of heating and air-conditioning, which significantly contribute to global warming, can no longer suffice in our Anthropocene age as the unique way to heat or cool our buildings. We need to harness thermal insulation, vapor barriers, double-flow ventilation, and other techniques, whose consequences include the invention of a new decorative language inside our homes and workplaces that will supersede the Modernist minimalism of the 20th century.

Our mission today is to re-evaluate domestic and work space, rethinking their decorative style to meet the new thermal regulations and in doing so invent the appropriate architectural language of the Anthropocene. The ambition is to offer a new style in the history of the decorative arts – after the Louis Quinze, Regency, Empire, Louis Philippe, or Mid-Century Modern styles comes the Anthropocene style of today. Rising to contemporary challenges with respect to sustainable development and the reduction of energy consumption and greenhouse-gas emissions, our task is to redraw the lines, patterns, and geometry of walls, ceilings, floors, woodwork, and mouldings according to the optical behaviour of solar rays to increase natural lighting, to reduce conduction of excessive heat accumulated on the ceiling, to increase the coefficient of wall insulation, and to impede thermal bridges. We must rethink our choice of materials on the basis of their specific physical properties such as optical, thermal, or acoustic absorption or reflection, porosity or impermeability with respect to air or water vapor, their factor of thermal conductivity, effusivity, or emissivity, prioritizing the non-toxic and the innovative. Materials must be reassessed in terms of colour and texture to reflect the infrared and absorb other wavelengths.

Modern central heating and air-conditioning made us forget the real value of pre-industrial interior design, which, despite the low efficiency of candles, oil lamps, and coal fires, acted as so many devices to improve thermal and luminous interior comfort. In northern Europe, for example, to fight against conduction of cold from soils and non-insulated floors, carpets were laid, while tapestry and wood panelling were hung on masonry walls to block the transfer of heat from the body to these chill surfaces. To counter low winter temperatures, fireplaces, stoves, and *braseros* provided intense but inefficiently distributed calories, in the process becoming decorative elements in their own right. Against the draughts let in by window and door frames, drapes and hangings were mounted, or screens set up to protect the sitting area around the hearth, while the poor thermal insulation of single glazing was countered at night through the use of heavy velvet curtains. Weak winter

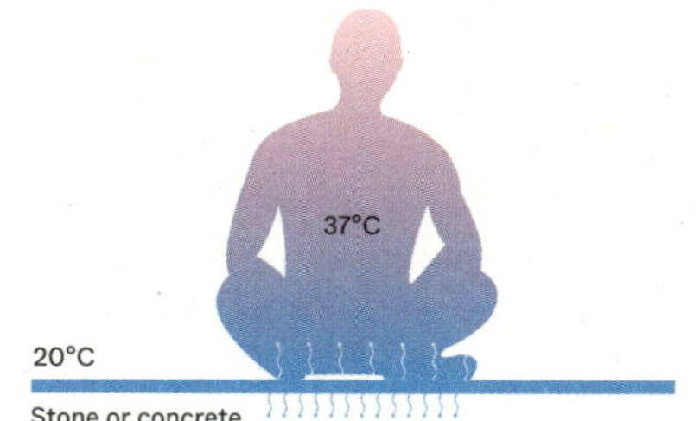

High-emissivity flooring cools the body.

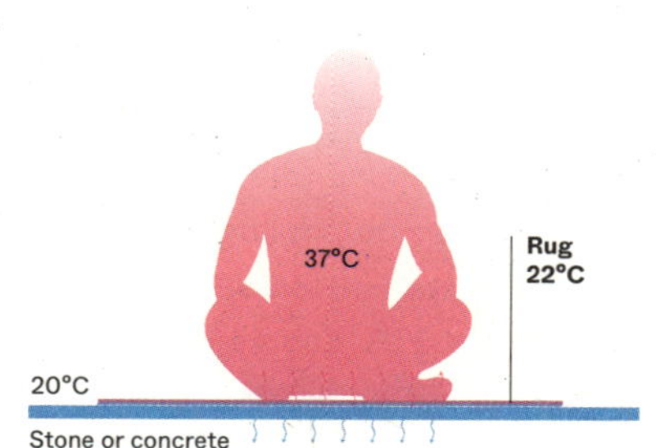

A low-emissivity rug blocks the cold emanating from the floor.

The Anthropocene Style
Philippe Rahm, 2023

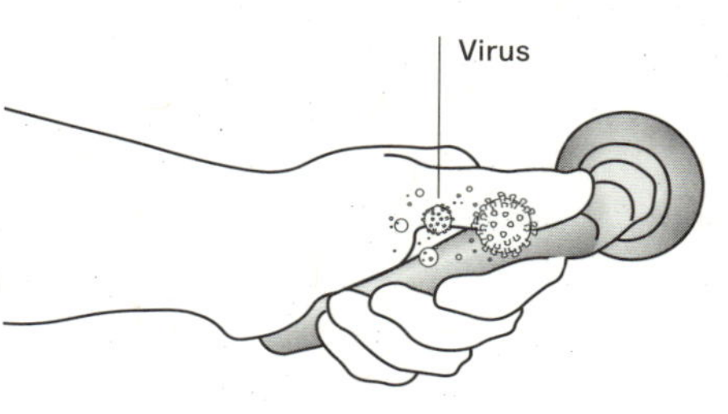

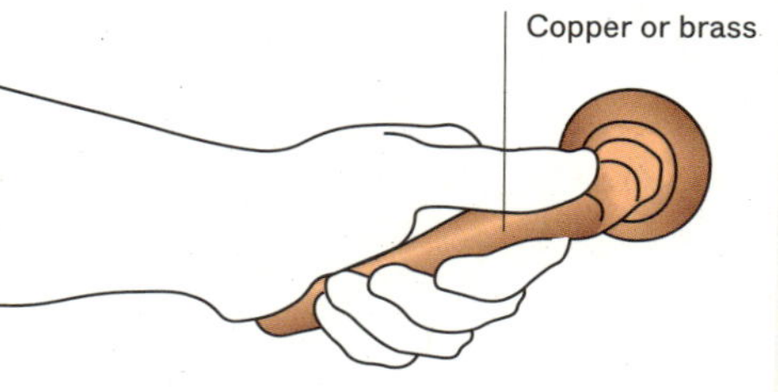

The Anthropocene Style
Philippe Rahm, 2023

daylight or night time candlelight was augmented through the use of mirrors, gilding, and the crystal drops and prisms of chandeliers which reflected, diffracted, and spread light throughout the space. The fundamental *raison d'être* of all these decorative elements – fighting the cold and augmenting luminosity – was lost with the arrival of gas and electricity, making of them mere ornament, stripped of any real function or meaning.

In renouncing the dominance of energy-guzzling industrial-age techniques, we must reconsider the old decorative strategies and analyse their relevance and efficiency, countering their deficiencies to improve them and bring them up to today's standards. The new 21st-century thermal regulations require complete and perfect thermal insulation, a vapor barrier, and double-flow ventilation. We must reduce energy consumption, improve the thermal envelope and air tightness, manage water-vapor movement and the risk of condensation, all the while ensuring proper ventilation. To help us to do this, new materials and techniques are making their appearance – mineral wool, Tyvek® rain screens, plastic air-tight membranes, to name but three –, whose aesthetic effect could be considered akin to decoration, generating a possible revival of a decorative language a century after it was banished by the Modernist white minimalism of the 20th century.

The Anthropocene style is renewing the materiality of the solid, conditioned by the climatic and energy stakes of today. We must strip the solid of the narrative structures stemming from Postmodernity, the discursive images, metaphors, and representations hitherto bound up with the choice of façade material. What we must bring into the definition of the solid – and consequently into the entire visual expressivity of the building – are physical, thermal and climatic values, such as those of reflectance, emissivity, and effusivity, in addition to conductivity, which is already being expressed through external thermal insulation.

* Philippe Rahm is PhD in architecture, researcher and educator. Founder of Philippe Rahm architectes.

Roselles curtain

Jute taffeta, printed linen taffeta and and cotton sateen lining

María Ángeles González, 1961
Manufactured by Tapicerías Gancedo for La Cantonada, Barcelona

Donation, Mateu Díez family, 2022
MDB 14.387

Casa Calvet handle

Brass metalwork

Antoni Gaudí i Cornet, *c.* 1902
Manufactured by BD. Ediciones de Diseño SA, BD Barcelona Design, Barcelona

Donation, BD Barcelona Design, 2020
MDB 12.540

Handle

Aluminum metalwork and turned wood

Antoni de Moragas i Gallissà, 1957
Manufactured by CIVE, Compañía Inmobiliaria de Viviendas Económicas, EDIBS, Barcelona; Polinax, Vilanova i la Geltrú

Donation, Albert Bastardes, 2000
MADB 136.679

Termoimpulsor fan and heater

Chromed metal, plastic and electrical wiring

Manuel Jalón Corominas, 1963
Manufactured by Manufacturas Rodex SA, Zaragoza

Donation, Juli Capella Samper, 2015
MADB 138.946

CES-25 air conditioner

Moulded ABS resin and steel

Ramon Benedito Graells, 1989
Manufactured by Compañía Roca Radiadores SA, Gavà

Donation, Compañía Roca Radiadores SA, 1995 MADB 135.779

THE ANTHROPOCENE STYLE

Philippe Rahm's manifesto "The Anthropocene Style" is a call to architects and designers to recover the decorative arts that in practical terms regulated aspects such as the temperature and salubrity of interiors. With the growing use of fossil fuels and air conditioning, carpets, tapestries, and curtains lost their functional roles. Faced with the need to reduce energy consumption and carbon dioxide (CO_2) emissions, the manifesto suggests a return to such practical decorative elements. A prominent example is the use of door handles made of silver, copper and its alloys like brass, that, unlike the plastic handles of today, have bactericide properties. "The Anthropocene Style" is an invitation to reconsider pre-industrial solutions to the challenges of our era.

A SYNTHETIC UNIVERSE*

BLANCA PUJALS#

Joanna Rose: What are Neutrinos, then? Olga Botner: Oh! I wish we knew what Neutrinos are! ... Neutrinossss aaaareeee amongggg these few fundamental particles which make up matter. And we know them from radioactive decaysssss, but what they really are, no one knows, no one has ever seen a Neutrino. Neutrinos have no electric charge, and we can only detect particles, which carry electric charge, and so we can only discover Neutrinos when they interact with something and produce charge particles. And this is how we know three kinds of Neutrinos but no one has ever seen the Neutrino itself.[1]

About one hundred trillion neutrinos pass through your body each second.[2]

Since the end of the Second World War, new architectures and infrastructures for containing and artificially reproducing the conditions present at the beginning of the universe have surfaced across the world. A synthetic replica of the early universe on Earth.

These sophisticated technospaces are composed of sealed chambers that recreate specific and non-existent physical conditions on Earth to reveal the origin of matter. Spread throughout a subterranean global chamber system, they constitute an invisible underground network.

The world's largest and most complex scientific instrument, the Large Hadron Collider (LHC) at the European Organization for Nuclear Research (CERN) in Geneva, is a ring twenty-seven kilometres in diameter buried one hundred meters under the French-Swiss border. At the Sudbury Neutrino Observatory (SNO) in Ontario,

Canada, a twelve-meter-diameter acrylic sphere detector is located two kilometres below the surface in Vale Limited's Creighton nickel mine. The IceCube Neutrino Observatory at the Amundsen-Scott South Pole Station is a one-cubic-kilometre array of sensors at depths between 1,450 and 2,450 meters beneath the Antarctic ice. Particle physics experiments require highly specific and controlled conditions, since the production of elementary particles is extremely difficult and their detection requires extremely sensitive equipment. Any small interference can skew the results.[3] The sensors used for this scientific work need to be placed deep underground, either in massive new holes, in old mines, in deep-sea waters, or under the Antarctic or Siberian ice to avoid the cosmic radiation that would interfere with the results. These laboratories are creating a new subterranean infrastructure – a material, epistemological, and ontological layer of contemporary science.

[15.312 trillion neutrinos have just passed through you.]

The tiny monastic laboratory of the seventeenth century has been replaced by a global technoscientific infrastructure spread across the planet. These major scientific spaces and networks have expanded the idea of the lone scientist's lab to large cities of scientists working on the same dilemmas. Experiments for studying the smallest particles of matter and their phenomena now involve massive urban complexes, buildings, and chambers designed to host the invisible. These sites constitute what I have termed *sensing infrastructures* amplifying new geopolitical and material interactions offering a multiscalar, entangled organism of scientists, particles, liquids, data, politics and technologies working together for the production of knowledge and to translate a world not directly perceptible to humans. As Donna Haraway states, "the human body is the prosthetic body par excellence. It relies on tools to evolve."[4] Scientific infrastructures became architectures of hybrid systems of transnational and more-than-human collaborations.

The notion of infrastructure acts as a revelatory of the "working" quality of this universe, opening into the perception of a whole world of invisible labours that are more than human.

—Maria Puig de la Bellacasa[5]

1 My transcript of an excerpt from the interview given by Professor Olga Botner, member of the Nobel Committee for Physics, to freelance journalist Joanna Rose, on the occasion of the 2015 Nobel Prize in Physics.

2 Neutrino is a particle that carries energy and information. The singularity of neutrinos is that they are the weakest, the smallest, the most abundant, and the most elusive of all the particles in the Cosmos. Neutrinos are mainly described as elusive because they have no electric charge, so they do not interact with the electromagnetic spectrum, which means that we cannot sense, register, or study neutrinos directly, we can only see its traces. It is a particle that defies the Standard Model of Particle Physics and intercepts a predictable way of understanding matter.

3 Some neutrino detectors, such as the SNO in Canada or Super-Kamiokande (or Super-K) built inside the now-closed Mozumi mine of Kamioka Mining and Smelting Co. in Japan, have reused existing extractivist infrastructures. The overlapping of infrastructural layers reveals the changes in economy and labour structures and the social problematic surrounding these specific sites when the mine closes. The substitution of a mine for a highly sophisticated scientific facility does not repair the social fabric of the surrounding villages, struggling with unemployment and its economic dependency on the extraction of minerals.

4 Donna J. Haraway, "A Cyborg Manifesto: Science, Technology, and Socialist-Feminism in the Late Twentieth Century," in *Simians, Cyborgs, and Women: The Reinvention of Nature*, 149–82 (London: Free Association Books, 1991).

5 Maria Puig de la Bellacasa, "Encountering Bioinfrastructure: Ecological Struggles and the Sciences of Soil," *Social Epistemology* 28, no. 1 (2014): 26–40 (here 27).

Contemporary laboratories are an assembly of parts: multiple teams, disciplines, and countries. Their machines are built and designed around the world, and scientific teams comprise large global collaborations of experts. These teams not only study phenomena at the smallest of scales but also look at large-scale phenomena, in the process participating in synchronized global networks supported by complex infrastructures.

As a large techno-organism, this transnational laboratory of observatories and colliders is simultaneously storing and processing the data it collects. It is an architecture of wire and sensor networks enlarging the physical space to an infrastructure of worldwide interconnections. Scientific infrastructures around the world are sensing and collecting data uninterruptedly. Earth itself has become a planetary laboratory, endlessly monitoring and being monitored by scientific infrastructures that are largely invisible.

The dimensions and sophistication of these new scientific laboratories increasingly require an excess of financial resources from the participating countries, with costs exceeding most national budgets – even more so if the countries are small – so fundamental science experiments are planned and sustained with shared public resources. Treaties, alliances, joint ventures, and collaborations through scientific infrastructures and knowledge are made on a planetary scale, where the geopolitical implications of the infrastructures of fundamental physics is expanded into global geoeconomics.[6] They have generated a new infrastructure combining political pacts with developments made in the scientific field. Science is participating actively in political treaties and agreements in the name of peace and scientific knowledge, playing a key role in countries' foreign relations, where scientific collaborations are used as a source of soft power which, in contrast to hard power, is the ability to attract co-opt rather than coerce.

[26.976 trillion neutrinos have just passed through you.]

In 1949, shortly after the Second World War, a group of scientists conceived the idea of a European atomic physics laboratory to avoid resource competition and war in Europe. It was the first postwar proposal for scientific collaboration among European countries.[7] The European physicists Niels Bohr, Edoardo Amaldi, Pierre Auger, Lew Kowarski, and the engineer and politician Raoul Dautry imagined the creation of a future physics laboratory to host the new fundamental physics knowledge, an architecture where physicists from different nations would work together to produce future facts across multiple generations. Eight years later, the European Atomic Energy Community was created at the same time as the European Economic Community (EEC).

6 Deborah Cowen and Neil Smith, 2009. "After Geopolitics? From the Geopolitical Social to Geoeconomics." *Antipode*, 41: 22-48.

7 The first signed treaty, the European Coal and Steel Community (ECSC), was proposed by French foreign minister Robert Schuman on May 9, 1950. It was formally established in 1951 by the Treaty of Paris, signed by Belgium, France, Italy, Luxembourg, the Netherlands, and West Germany.

Still from three-channel video installation 'A Synthetic Universe: The Unmaking of Microscopic Bonds in Transnational Space' Blanca Pujals, 2016
CERN's historical archive, © CERN

Neutrino detector at SNO+, SNOLAB cave experiment (Ontario, Canada)
SNOLAB

Still from three-channel video installation 'A Synthetic Universe: The Unmaking of Microscopic Bonds in Transnational Space' Blanca Pujals, 2016
CERN's historical archive, © CERN

The Euratom Treaty was signed for the coordination of research in atomic energy and the creation of CERN in Geneva.[8] CERN is a laboratory built to introduce nuclear research into society by decoupling it from nuclear weapons through the Atoms for Peace program, and also to prevent resource wars in Europe after the Second World War through the Euratom Treaty. That Geneva was chosen to host CERN, despite Switzerland not being a member of the EEC, was not by chance. The Swiss Confederation had maintained neutrality and remained a stable state during both world wars, and science, although is historically involved in military development, and after the wars in Europe, scientific experiments, national defences and energy resources increasingly merged, paradoxically needs long-term stable conditions to carry out experiments over long periods. CERN, an interstate organization that is not administratively linked to either country within which it is sited, became an enclosed space with particular, controlled conditions. France and Switzerland are the "host countries" but do not exercise sovereignty over CERN. A fence with checkpoints surrounds the laboratory, and one must be accredited to pass through. In the name of scientific knowledge and peace, the Euratom Treaty built a new architecture of the territory – a new political entity based on a multinational political union, a supranational political form with negotiated power. New supranational laboratories like CERN transformed physics into a force within politics, creating new spaces of negotiation and agreement.

8 The 'Euratom Treaty' was not included in the general ECC treaty due to the disapproval of the word 'atomic' within the civil society for its connotations after the War and the raising menace of nuclear weapons. In order that the collaboration in the research of atomic energy would not create suspicion about the European Economic Community, it was written in a separate document under its own conditions and still has a separate legal form.

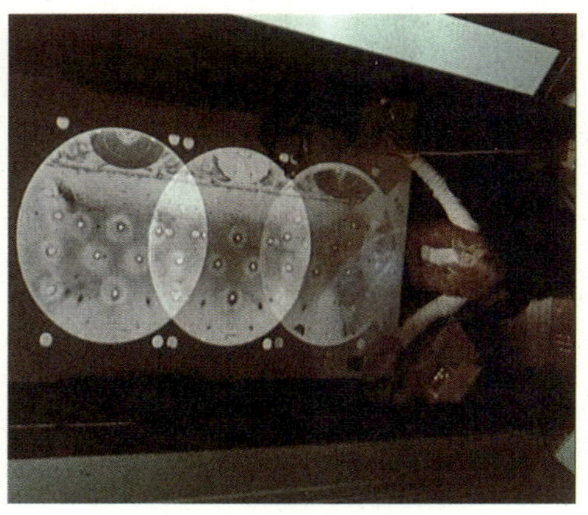

Still from three-channel video installation 'A Synthetic Universe: The Unmaking of Microscopic Bonds in Transnational Space'
Blanca Pujals, 2016
CERN's historical archive, © CERN

Atoms for Peace envelope and stamps
Author's personal archive

Although the LHC at CERN is imperceptible from the surface, it also organizes the land above it. Billions of subatomic particles cross the French-Swiss border about eleven thousand times every second. Twenty years after the first ground works started in Geneva, the construction of the first large accelerator, the Super Proton Synchrotron, crossed underneath the Franco-Swiss border, entering French territory, trespassing across the threshold of the nation-state. The free circulation of the elementary particles in 1983 predated by twelve years the Schengen agreement abolishing internal border controls in Europe (implemented in 1995) and predated Switzerland's incorporation to that agreement by twenty-six years.

During the construction of CERN, not only was the horizontal nation-state border surpassed, but it also challenged vertical private property laws. Although the experimental machine was built deep underground to avoid radiation and damage to the properties and land existing along the tunnel's path, in France a landowner's property rights extend from the surface to the earth's centre. Therefore, French authorities had to declare the land occupied by the future collider a public good and turn the underlying rock, down to the earth's nucleus, into "public property."

However, although political alliances made on the scientific field demand territories and transnational collaborations based on science for peace, bodies in some of these countries are still and increasingly locked within a regime of violence and systemic discrimination, which reveal different forms of structural differences, rights and conflicts.

[44.136 trillion neutrinos have just passed through you.]

"Science is a natural way to build bridges between cultures and nations, because of its common language."[9] This claim, made by theoretical physicist Eliezer

Rabinovici, celebrates a new elementary particle laboratory in the Middle East set up on the model of CERN. First proposed in 1993 following the Oslo Accords and the Israeli-Palestinian peace process, the Synchrotron-Light for Experimental Science Applications in the Middle East (SESAME) was inaugurated in May 2017. The new laboratory is based on the claim that regional peace can be achieved through science. Located in Jordan, SESAME aims to build "scientific and cultural bridges between neighbouring countries, promoting mutual understanding and tolerance through international cooperation, and fostering a regional community of scientific users who will work together."[10]

The founding members are Bahrain (not currently a member), Cyprus, Egypt, Iran, Israel, Jordan, Pakistan, the Palestinian Authority, and Turkey. "I don't know how many places there are where all these governments have representatives who have the opportunity to come and talk to each other," said Giorgio Paolucci, the scientific director of SESAME.[11] This collaboration made possible by scientific soft power reveals an inevitable paradox. Transnational collaborations to enable world-class research in the scientific field are built, but fundamental social structures are endlessly destroyed.

The transnational network of particle physics underground laboratories is constructing a new scientific architecture around the world: a sensing infrastructure, which amplifies new political and material interactions. A hybrid human-machine-liquid-organism-particle, where cables, bodies, rare earth metals, liquids, soil, subterranean critters, particles, atmosphere and cosmic events are increasingly interconnected in a techno-organism for unveiling the almost silent infrastructure of subatomic particles that are relentlessly trespassing us. Quantum Physics is not detached from our social and political structures; it is entangled by its spatial, territorial and material interactions and interferences, although it remains as an invisible infrastructure.

[52,632 trillion neutrinos have just passed through you.]

9 Eliezer Rabinovici quoted in Dennis Overbye, "A Light for Science, and Cooperation, in the Middle East," *New York Times*, May 8, 2017, https://www.nytimes.com/2017/05/08/science/sesame-institute-jordan-synchrotron.html.

10 "SESAME," UNESCO, http://www.unesco.org/new/en/natural-sciences/science-technology/basic-sciences/international-basic-sciences-program/sesame.

11 Kareem Shaheen, "Open SESAME: Particle Accelerator Project Brings Middle East Together," *The Guardian*, August 30, 2016, https://www.theguardian.com/world/2016/aug/30/sesame-particle-accelerator-project-middle-east-jordan.

* Revised and edited version of the text previously published in: Blanca Pujals, 'A matter of Matter. The Unmaking of Microscopic Bonds in Transnational Space''. In *Artnodes Journal on Art, Science, and Technology*, no 25, (2020), Dialogs Between Art and Fundamental Science, January 20, edited by Monica Bello and Andy Gracie: 1-10. Barcelona: UOC Scientific Journal.
This text is part of a larger project of research and film work called 'A Synthetic Universe: The Unmaking of microscopic bonds in transnational space' initiated in 2016.

‡ Blanca Pujals is PhD in architecture, researcher and associate professor.

8 AFFEC ONAL/ TIONAL

TI- IC- MATTER

Cañada Real Social and Community Center
Recetas Urbanas - Santiago Cirugeda, 2018-2019
Recetas Urbanas

Chairs in Town Hall Square in Logroño
Izaskun Chinchilla Architects, 2022
Josema Cutillas

Practices in participatory design ensure that resulting projects do not only provide communities with spatial solutions, but also strengthen social ties and the sense of belonging. The Recetas Urbanas collective, led by Santiago Cirugeda, exemplifies this emphasis on participation, on the fact of shaping cities and communities from the bottom upwards, and on self-building, with projects like the Cañada Real community center in Madrid, erected with the participation of over 1,200 volunteers. The project entitled *100 Chairs and 3 Urban Salons* by Izaskun Chinchilla presented at Logroño's Concéntrico Festival invited citizens to co-create multi-use foldable chairs through a participatory application. On the other hand, Top Manta is a brand created by the Sindicato de Vendedores Ambulantes de Barcelona (Barcelona Street Vendors Union) to improve the living conditions of street vendors.

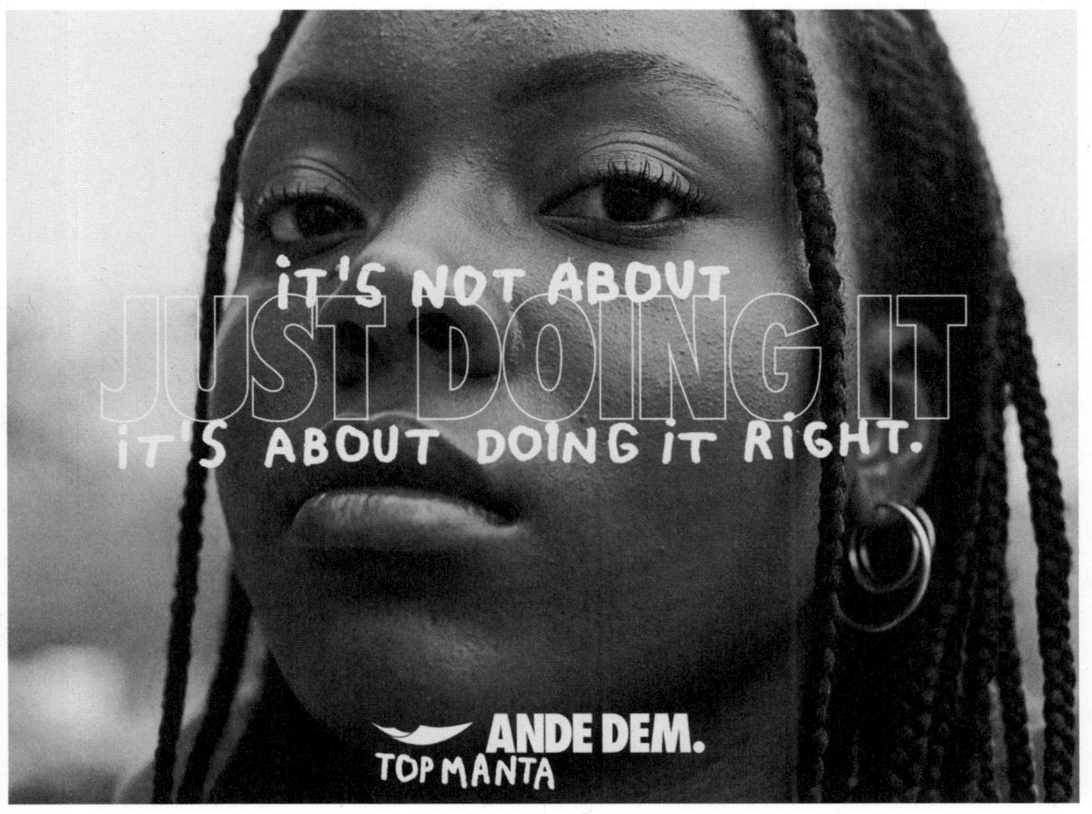

Ande Dem sneakers ('A walk together' in Wolof)
Advertising campaign
Top Manta and Emerson, Font & Pont, 2021

AFFECTION AS A FORM OF SUBVERSIVE ARCHITECTURE*

ELVIRA DYANGANI OSE / RAÚL MUÑOZ DE LA VEGA*

ELVIRA DYANGANI OSE: If the *Recetas Urbanas* projects didn't contain a space to be built, the setting would feel like being in a bar in the afternoon having a *carajillo* (coffee with liqueur). In each project there is a strange collective intimacy, a way to encourage community as a process. One would think that in the execution of this kind of architecture there is a defiant spontaneity, when, in fact, a meditated and wildly free orchestration lies behind it.

The formulation of any urban recipe implies an act of generosity – from the studio and each of the participants – turned into a political platform where to create a social space, the condition of possibility is established. A space which, defying what was originally imposed by political powers, reclaims our capacity to intervene and our responsibility to make decisions.

Their proposal of an *anarchitecture* could be interpreted in this sense as the enunciation of what Henri Lefebvre called a *differential* space,[1] insofar as it suggests that we must subvert the bureaucratic homogeneity that governs our cities and their user's manuals and empower citizens to take control of a politically dominated technocratic space. Their *recipes* imply that in managing our daily lives, in the act of participating, architecture can manifest itself as activism, as the source of a deep transformation of what is administrative, social, political, educational...

RAÚL MUÑOZ DE LA VEGA: I believe this act of participating, active at different levels, lies in a key concept. Like the analogy that Henri Sanoff establishes between democracy and representative design – delegates, indirect and inactive – and democracy and participative design – active and with direct involvement,[2] in the collective building processes of *Recetas Urbanas*, citizens must demonstrate an involvement and a commitment that goes much deeper than in other forms of architecture or urban planning. But perhaps they've never been offered so much in return. Their processes often act as catalysts: connecting desires, strengthening the silenced voices of communities, substituting unmet needs and giving prominence to demands. This transformative power isn't aimed at citizens alone but at authorities and governing bodies, seeking reflection on and a reassessment of their policies and actions in different areas. Although the studio must repeatedly operate within illegal, unregulated frameworks, or against public administrations, this isn't so much an act of resistance *against* authority. Rather, some of its strategies are implemented initially without cooperation, hoping to obtain support from the appropriate authorities at a later stage.

In this respect, the projects *Aula Abierta Granada*, *La Escuela Crece* and *Trincheras* serve as an example of an evolution in the reaction of different institutions to some of the studio's projects. *Aula Abierta Granada* (Open Classroom Granada) arose from students' desire to have a self-managed space for reflection and work at the Universidad de Granada. Although they'd convinced the rector's office, the possibilities of this initiative never materialized because of the university's inflexibility and bureaucratic procedures.

Taking this project as a reference point, the situation was later reversed. Both in the case of *La Escuela Crece* (The School Grows) and in *Trincheras* (Trenches), the directors of the Madrid School of Design and the dean's office of the Fine Arts Department of the University of Málaga began these projects providing the necessary guarantees and structures to be able to implement the theoretical and practical approaches generated during the collective construction processes with students.

The series of projects completed by the studio, which started with lack of support from government bodies and public authorities, constitutes a repository that Cirugeda calls *jurisprudencia construida* (built jurisprudence). This accumulation of precedents makes clear that other solutions are possible and effective to counteract mistrust and the stagnant culture of public administrations, while also serving as an antidote to citizen complacency and discouragement.

EDO: In this sense, *built jurisprudence* is an unlimited form of subversion that adapts to any new context and determines not so much the result, but the condition of possibility for new change. This repository represents the true exhibition of difference, but it also establishes a network of affections, generating a hidden humanistic revolution through the management of these desires as a destabilizer of administrative policies. This formulation of affection as political gesture and subversive architecture is, perhaps, for me, the studio's most important contribution to architecture, art and social policies.

In the architecture of *Recetas Urbanas*, both in projects arising from collective proposals without any initial cooperation from public administrations and in those that take place under the aegis of an artistic setting – i.e., *Prótesis Institucional* or *House of Words* –, there seems to be a manifestation of what AbdouMaliq Simone calls "people as infrastructure".[3]

1 Henri Lefebvre: *The Production of the Space*, New Jersey, Wiley-Blackwell, 1991, p. 231.

2 Henry Sanoff: "Integrating Programming, Evaluation and Participation in Design. A Theory Z Approach", London, Routledge Revivals, 1992.

3 AbdouMaliq Simone, "People as Infrastructure: Intersecting Fragments in Johannesburg" in *Public Culture*, vol. 16, no. 3, North Carolina, Duke University Press, 2004, pp 407-429.

According to Simone, cities could be more productive and effective spaces as a result of the social relationships that take place in them. Thus, social, political and economic practices are crucial in training social agents to articulate a possible transformation of what is urban. The recipes include collective experiences and memories in architecture and design... It's then that architecture becomes a questioning, a tekné, in which the position of citizens with respect to the legal framework is established, predisposing them to self-government.

Perhaps no other project better illustrates the idea of the recipe as a micro-stage for the reformulation of what is social as the Cañada Real Socio-Communal Centre – perhaps the most complex project to date. In it, the studio combines a proposal for a neighbourhood and associative meeting space in a neighbourhood that includes people of different origins and income levels, in a sustainable building that includes structures and other materials from prior projects. The biggest challenge is not the end use of the space by the communities, but creating a social space of care and affection during the construction process where these groups can coexist with the political powers involved in the project.

Meanwhile, in *House of Words* (Gothenburg, Sweden), more than seventy people from around the world contributed to designing and building a place they'd hardly use, one that would accommodate other people. The studio, in collaboration with artist Loulou Cherinet, created a space to participate, reflect and meet that would hold cultural mediation sessions, as well as the biennial's symposium. But its goal would also be to question and subvert the notion of outsider-ship (in Swedish, *utanförskap*) that the conservative party had already used in 2006 to label a certain category of foreigners as intruders, thereby identifying them as existing outside the legal *status quo*.

Cherinet created an open and pluralistic dialog where she examined the impact of this policy and rhetoric in the media in reference to those communities. However, emphasis was placed on the previous collective process, which gave rise to a space for the coexistence of these groups and the biennial's participants. This resulted in a temporary – and conceptual – "home" that would symbolize the shelter which the Swedish public administrations failed to provide: a network of affection, like some the studio's other projects, that uses organic and day-to-day informal strategies combined with in-depth research of the social and administrative policies of each situation to make proposing changes in legality possible.

RMV: And in the research into the political and administrative structure in which we live recurrent questions arise. What tools do citizens have to change the notion of legality? Who can propose new regulations? Which frameworks are used to understand the law? Projects like *Kuvas SC* and *Andamio* respond to Cirugeda's attempts to understand and test how citizens relate to government bodies and to what extent current regulations allow citizens to discuss the law and can be used to foster situations that public authorities hadn't anticipated but citizens needed.

In this respect, many of the *recipes* include a proposal for an amendment to the law. The subversive power of these recipes doesn't consist solely in questioning a specific *status quo*, but in the way the studio uses architecture, enabling new social situations which help reformulate legality both from the vantage point of theoretical criticism and practical action, contributing not just to questioning but to an already materialized possible solution.

EDO: That subversion of reality is a fundamental aspect in their work as well. On the one hand, in terms of developing new laws and new mechanisms that affect tenders and public calls, but on the other as a formula to question architecture itself and the way it's taught. Projects like

La Escuela Crece entailed questioning and later changing the school's curriculum. These initiatives expanded the ability of faculty and students to influence their school's governing body, making the limits placed on their ability to imagine alternatives more porous.

RMV: Maybe without being fully aware of it, when he was a student, alongside his academic training, Cirugeda was testing the educational methodology he would later develop in projects like *La Escuela Crece*. It was an alternative education, a horizontal approach that creates knowledge collectively and is based on practical research.

A lot of the lacklustre interest in the official education offered by the school of architecture in Seville - where he never completed his studies - had to do with the verticality of the teaching and "thinking" of architecture - from teacher to student, from student to citizen -, with the inflexibility of so many academic processes, the absence of a space for critical self-reflection, and the disconnect between the university environment and real life and the effective functioning of cities.

EDO: There is in all this a clear passion for cross-disciplinary work or, almost, a need to escape any kind of definition granted both to the studio and to Cirugeda. Before he became an architect, when was creating works of art, he didn't want to be considered an artist. His exhibitions weren't exhibitions per se, but meetings, happenings that took place when someone entered the space where he'd decided to have his atelier, like with the Finland pavilion project in Seville. The same thing happened if someone decided to spend the afternoon in *La Casita* (The Little House), during the time he occupied it as a member of several collectives. It can't be denied that in all this there is an aesthetic license that tilts towards art and its freedoms, rather than towards the rigidity Cirugeda repeatedly encountered in architecture school.

His solo projects were madness made reality due to the questioning of his immediate world: from a night table in his kitchen, to his friend Pepe's apartment, to imagining a house consisting of the empty rooms of his neighbours' homes. His architecture is, above all, an architecture of complicity. One that includes, besides his neighbours, volunteers of all sorts: social workers, artists, architects, educators, cultural agents, lawyers, association representatives, disenchanted citizens, members of underprivileged communities. All of whom constitute what he calls "the army of fools," thereby generating a map of affections as a defining strategy of subversion.

* This is a condensed version of the conversation published in *Usted está aquí: Recetas Urbanas*, Madrid, Ediciones Asimétricas, 2018.

‡ Elvira Dyangani Ose is director of the Museum of Contemporary Art of Barcelona (MACBA) from September 2021. Raúl Muñoz de la Vega is a contemporary art curator.

MATERIAL KINSHIPS

ETHEL BARAONA POHL / ANNA PUIGJANER*

"But the question of what composes the world around us drastically depends on how one is situated within that world, and in turn affects the who that one might be in relation with."[1]

In recent years, there has been an increasing interest in the topics of "care," "repair," and "maintenance," in such a way that they are rapidly becoming buzzwords in academic circles in the fields of architecture and design. Decades ago, the well-known *Manifesto for Maintenance Art 1969!, Proposal for an exhibition 'Care'* by Mierle Lademan Ukeles, in which she asked "After the revolution, who's going to pick up the garbage on Monday morning?", clearly emphasized two components related to maintenance. One is the labour of doing so – a gendered task – and secondly, the need of caring for the spaces we inhabit – not only to care for its inhabitants, but for all the materiality that form our cities and environments, historically driven by practices of repair and maintenance in ways that become so common that we tend to overlook them.

In that sense, operations of *care*, *repair*, and *maintenance* transverse different scales – from the planet, to the territory, to the community and to the body –. Therefore, this text delves into the concept of 'material kinships' as proposed by Clementine Edwards and Kris Dittel in their book *Material Kinship Reader*, and following their question: "What does it mean to acknowledge one's closeness to, enmeshment in or even kinship with the material world?." Material kinships are based on commitment and in the acknowledgement that everything is connected. In order to 'make kin' with something material, you have to take care of it, repair it, maintain it.

There is also an ecological and social impact on the concept of material kinships, as the notion of making kin with a thing is also a clear invitation to interrogate relationships and connections in the world at large and, hence, has an emancipatory potential. As Joannie Baumgärtner poses it, "If kinship usually fortifies the ways and conditions in which we inherit the world, then shifting its integration and performativity might allow us to change how we inhabit it."[2] Love can be expressed in diverse ways and the possibility to make kin with a thing is nothing new as it has a long tradition as an important component of our ancestors' knowledge of the world. However, material kinships have been somehow diminished or overseen within capitalist societies that reinforce the notion of the nuclear family, diminishing the value of all other understandings of kin. This is especially so if we talk about making kin with material things in such a way that is not related to consumerism and the monetary value of those things.

Interestingly, when talking about material kinships, often forgotten is our own materiality as creatures made of "stuff." Iron in the blood, in a rock or in a structural beam, we share – but do not always see – the patterns of our traces in the world. We are all participants in the rhythms of our planet. The ways in which we configure what is outside or not alien to us might be a first step in rethinking kinship, in addition to recognizing that material kinship is a relatively new name for something as old as humanity.

Through a set of examples, this text serves as an acknowledgement of former and existent material kindships, a journey through places, scales, and ways of understanding human and non-human relationships with different kinds of matter.

1. *Totora* and *kilhi*

Once a year, on Lake Titicaca, when the water level rises, the *totora* (from the Quechua *t'utura*), a bulrush commonly found in South American marshes and swamps, breaks apart, jettisoning part of its mass. This normally occurs in summer, when the *totora* root, or *kilhi*, entangled with the soil and other minerals at the bottom of the lake, becomes detached, forming masses of floating matter like cork. These surfaces of unsinkable matter are the foundation upon which for centuries the Uru people have built a floating settlement currently made up of about eighty islands inhabited by around two thousand people.

1 Clementine Edwards and Kris Dittel (eds.): *The Material Kinship Reader*, Eindhoven, Onomatopee, 2022.

2 Joannie Baumgärtner, "Family Value", a Clementine Edwards and Kris Dittel (eds.): *The Material Kinship Reader*, Eindhoven, Onomatopee, 2022.

Layers of dry bulrush are placed on top of the *kilhi* and stacked and intertwined in the form of a cross to form thicknesses of just over one metre. Due to the humidity of the lake, this thickness gradually decreases, forcing the inhabitants to rebuild different parts of the islands every three or four months. The *totora*, however, is collected regularly: the stems are cut thirty centimetres from the root to allow them to grow back, thereby furthering the gathering cycle, the growth of the settlement and care for the plant. The bulrush, meanwhile, along with fish and other living creatures, also oxygenates and enriches cyclically the water and land in the area. Perhaps the transient and fragile nature of the islands of the Uru people explains the complex interdependencies and care that take place on the lake, although this might be overestimating the capability of the architecture. In any event, the Urus understand that, to form part of the ecosystem of the place, their way of building and living must follow transient cyclical forms, just as with the tides of the lake itself and the growth of the organic material on which they depend.

2. *Quipus*

The Bolivian sociologist, scholar and activist of Aymara origin Silvia Rivera Cusicanqui refers to the woman weaver as a metaphor for interculturalism, explaining it in the following terms: "Women always weave relationships with the other, with otherness. With what is wild, with what is indigenous, with the market, with the dominant world." Weaving communally is an activity that transcends the act of sewing; it is also an instance of caring. Raising and tending to the sheep, llamas and alpacas that produce the wool, even the way in which traditional knowledge about weaving and caring for the objects and materials, including the looms, fabrics and yarns, is revived, are all practices with a social, political and cultural dimension intimately connected to local identities and indigenous epistemologies, as in the case of the *quipus*.

Quipus[4] (from the Quechua *khipu*) could be regarded as the equivalent of today's modern archives They are a rather sophisticated accounting and memory system of cords and knots used in Incan culture. According to historian Ariadna Baulenas, the twisting of the yarns, their colour, the distances between the cords, the position of the knots, and their form and direction, in addition to the number of knots, were variables that made it possible to record a vast array of data, much of which remains undecipherable. This grants the *quipus* an important element of timelessness, in which the preservation and transmission of knowledge spans several generations.

3. Thorn Houses

Curator and researcher Natalia Grabowska has expressed on many occasions[5] her deep love towards a tower, more specifically for a type of architecture misleadingly named Graduation Towers but also called Thorn Houses. Natalia, as many inhabitants of Poland but also of some areas of Germany and Austria, has a deep attachment to this type of architecture that is considered medicinal and therefore valued for its healing powers.

3 Silvia Rivera Cusicanqui: *Ch'ixinakax Utxiwa. Una reflexión sobre prácticas y discursos descolonizadores*, Buenos Aires, Tinta Limón, 2010.

4 Federica Zambeletti: "Cosmos, Computers and Quipus: An interview with Marina Otero and Locument", KoozArch, 29 January 2024. https://www.koozarch.com/interviews/cosmos-computers-and-quipus-marina-otero-and-locument.

5 Natalia Grabowska and Dominique Petit-Frère: "Being Realistic", *Prada Frames: Being Home*, podcast curated by FormaFantasma for Prada, produced by KoozArch, April 2024.

Originally, these were structures built for salt production but that indirectly also create an environment filled with tiny droplets of mineral-rich water believed to be highly beneficial for the respiratory system. They consist of a wooden frame stuffed with bundles of blackthorn. The salt water pumped from above partially evaporates when it runs down the brushwood thickets, where the salt crystallizes. The mist generated in this process is very similar to a sea breeze. This is an architecture to be breathed and which itself breathes symbiotically, within a space and materiality that heal and promote health. Today, they are no longer used for salt production but are still prized and maintained for their caring capacities.

4. From weapons to musical instruments

A friend[6] wrote to us recently wondering about Mierle Lademan Ukeles' thoughts on who's going to tidy up after the revolution. "I wonder," she wrote, "if it is possible to actually answer such questions by looking forensically into recent past conflicts and what happens to rubble and/or weapon debris after the war has moved elsewhere, in what ways those remains can be transformed into a useful material for rebuilding, and thus repurposing the effects of destruction into material for creation."

The works 'Imagine' and 'Disarm' by Pedro Reyes might be a good response. The artist transformed 6,700 weapons confiscated from Mexican cartels into musical instruments. We wonder if a project like this can help us understand that radical transformation is not only desirable but possible through the understanding that ultimately, everything is interrelational and that weapons are not only devices for killing. In the same way as they have embedded stories of violence, capitalism, extractivism, and colonisation, the minerals from which they are made also carry with them millennia of ecosystem evolution, traces of insects, plants, debris... and they vibrate in different frequencies that, in the end, can be also found in the very essence of music. Maybe a radical transformation can only be possible if we step back from our self-absorbed anthropocentrism and look at matter differently. But still a question will remain after that revolution, highlighting the inextinguishable cyclic nature of care and kinship: who's going to pick up the garbage on Monday morning?

6 Elena Arévalo Melville, author and illustrator of children's books, based in the UK.

* Ethel Baraona is Head of research of the Chair of CARE at ETH Zurich.
Anna Puigjaner is Director of the Chair of CARE at ETH Zurich.

GARBAGE DOESN'T EXIST

When we no longer want or need something, we turn it into garbage. This linear process of deterioration defines today's consumer society. Even so, recycling and reuse can prolong the life of materials. Basurama, a collective dedicated to cultural and environmental research, creation and production has promoted projects like *ReLabs*, that reuses local waste material generated in schools, or fallen trees resulting from the effects of climate change like the Filomena storm, to create play areas. These projects subvert the machine-based society of production and consumption, proving that everything has a potential for creativity and usefulness. An abandoned pneumatic tire can be waste or can be turned into a swing.

Shoelaces Jeans lamp
Prototype of lamp made with **reused denim** in the La Troballa workshop of Arrels Fundació, originally produced by the Back to Eco organization in 2018
Curro Claret, Barcelona, 2018

Filomena bench
Trunk, reused deck chairs and rope
Basurama and Nacho Bertola, Madrid, 2021
Loan, Basurama

Re-crea project on the playground of Francisco de Quevedo Elementary School, Leganés
Basurama, 2021
basurama.org CCBY-NC-SA 4.0

Temporary playground in Taipei
Basurama + City Yeast, 2016
basurama.org CCBY-NC-SA 4.0

RUS Lima: public amusement park
Basurama, 2010
basurama.org CCBY-NC-SA 4.0

RIGHT TO REPAIR

BLANCA CALLÉN*

"Don't despair, just repair"

—The Restart Project

All objects and materials, alive or inert, are subject to wear and tear, decomposition and deterioration associated with their use and the passage of time. Every object and material, ourselves included, are therefore fragile, finite and transitory.

These constitutional characteristics – fragility, finitude and transitoriness – have been understood, at times, as vulnerability. Connecting music and feminist theory, where Leonard Cohen sings "There is a crack, a crack in everything; That's how the light gets in",[1] Judith Butler holds that in vulnerability, as a condition of existence, lies a fundamental ethical and political power.[2] This is because this vulnerable crack hurls us inevitably into the social realm, enabling (and simultaneously necessitating) interdependence with others and mutual care – care thanks to which we endure and resist collectively in the face of threats and harm that make us fragile. In other words: because we are neither autonomous nor independent, because nothing exists in or for itself, because "there is a crack in everything," we resist.

Berenice Fisher and Joan Tronto, feminist theoreticians of the ethics of care, defined care as an activity that includes "Everything we do to remain, continue and repair the world so we can live in it as well as possible."[3] Repair (but also maintenance and even cleaning) then entails ways of caring which make possible the continuity of existence despite wear and tear, damage and fragilities, both those which are inevitable and avoidable, ordinary or provoked. This means that, while caring acts have been historically reviled and relegated to domestic and hidden places, and considered a merely reproductive, feminized and racialized task barely recognized or not acknowledged at all, we need them to continue: since time immemorial, for all matter and objects, and at all scales.

The first indication of human civilization, according to Margaret Mead, was a fractured and healed femur, as this was evidence of the time someone had devoted to caring for and being with the injured person until they recovered. Turning to the DNA evidence, when an injury is detected, the cell activates a series of mechanisms that halt its division to give it time to heal. If not done properly, the initial damage could result in cellular mutation, injury, cancer or other illnesses. Many trees, such as some pines, "self-prune," so that their lower branches gradually drop off as they grow. As a result, only high flames will reach their leaves in the event of a fire. In fact, forest fires are a specific kind of damage in the landscape which nonetheless act as a thermal condition for the germination of the seeds of certain bushes that were latent in the subsoil and whose emergence regenerates through self-repair of the burned land. All these examples prove that repair is not something exceptional but a basic and transverse vital activity, essential for the continuity (although never the same as before) of different life forms in the face of multiple damage, ruptures and deteriorations.

Judging by the environmental damaged caused by their activity – waste, pollution, exhaustion of natural resources, etc. –, one of the most dangerous human agents are designers.[4] At the service of industry and within a framework of economic and market capitalism, design (especially industrial design) has contributed to the mass production of readily disposable consumer goods transformed prematurely into waste. Technology and electrical and electronic devices are the paradigm for this voracious accelerationist logic and the kind of waste that has multiplied most in recent years, increasing five times faster than it is recycled.[5]

1 Leonard Cohen, "Anthem", on the album *The Future*, 1992.

2 Judith Butler: *Vulnerability in Resistance*, Durham, Duke University Press, 2016.

3 Berenice Fisher and Joan Tronto: "Toward a Feminist Theory of Caring", in Emily K. Abel and Margaret K. Nelson (eds.), *Circles of Care: Work and Identity in Women's Lives*, Albany, SUNY Press, 1990, pp. 35-62.

4 Victor Papanek: *Design for the Real World: Human Ecology and Social Change* [1971], London, Thames & Hudson, 1985.

5 International Telecommunication Union (ITU) and United Nations Institute for Training and Research (UNITAR). Cornelis P. Baldé, Ruediger Kuehr, Tales Yamamoto, Rosie McDonald, Elena D'Angelo, Shahana Althaf, Garam Bel, Otmar Deubzer, Elena Fernandez-Cubillo, Vanessa Forti, Vanessa Gray, Sunil Herat, Shunichi Honda, Giulia Iattoni, Deepali S. Khetriwal, Vittoria Luda di Cortemiglia, Yuliya Lobuntsova, Innocent Nnorom, Noémie Pralat, Michelle Wagner: *Global E-waste Monitor 2024*. Geneva / Bonn, 2024.

Some of the mechanisms and strategies that encourage this brisk conversion to waste include: small aesthetic changes which incite the feeling of being “out-of-step” among consumers, the use of less durable lower quality materials, the use of non-standard screws, the hiding of opening points on devices, the gluing of their parts (with their resulting inseparability), software discontinuance or incompatibility, the lack of access to repair manuals, the absence or high price of replacement parts and the loss of the warranty if the devices are opened or handled by non-officially authorized personnel. These latter obstacles impose a technological authority[6] that discourages users from knowing and repairing their own devices, thereby distancing them from technical knowledge which at other times in history they possessed. In the words of repair activists: “If we don’t know how to fix our own devices, can we continue considering ourselves their owners?”

Oblivious to this type of epistemic damage but aware of the environmental impact of such capitalistic logic, the European Union has recently approved two complementary regulations: the European Ecodesign Directive,[7] which introduces such requirements as the durability and repairability of products and the energy efficiency of resources; and the Directive known as the “right to repair”.[8] This directive applies to a very limited number of devices after the warranty has expired and, among other measures, obligates manufacturers to inform consumers of their right to repair and extend the warranty on repaired devices for another year. It requires providing access to spare parts at a “reasonable” price for a minimum period, not preventing independent repairers from using original or second-hand spare parts and ensuring that member States adopt, at least, a measure which promotes repair, such as repair vouchers, information campaigns, repair courses and support for community repair spaces.

While its adoption has been applauded as an action that protects consumer interests and an advancement towards a more sustainable society, a detailed analysis of the text raises some critical questions about its ambiguity and impreciseness (what does “reasonable” mean regarding a price?), about the way it will be implemented in each country, about its actual scope and even its possible “clash” with copyright law and patent rights. There is also the fear that repair could become a new market niche that ends up being monopolized by the same large technology manufacturers whose economic interests led to the premature obsolescence now being sought to be curbed.

6 Ernesto Oroza: *RIKIMBILI. Une étude sur la désobéissance technologique et quelques formes de réinvention*, Publications de l’Université de Saint-Étienne, 2009.

7 EU. European Parliament legislative resolution of 23 April 2024, on the proposal for a regulation of the European Parliament and of the Council establishing a framework for the setting of ecodesign requirements for sustainable products and repealing Directive 2009/125/EC (COM(2022)0142 - C9-0132/2022 - 2022/0095(COD)).

8 EU. European Parliament legislative resolution of 23 April 2024, on the proposal for a directive of the European Parliament and of the Council establishing common rules to promote the repair of goods and amending Regulation (EU) 2017/2394 and Directives (EU) 2019/771 and (EU) 2020/1828 (COM(2023)0155 - C9-0117/2023 - 2023/0083(COD)).

However, looking back to the notion of more basic repair set forth earlier and analysing the directive through an ecological and community prism, we find deeper and more general limitations. While repair is now institutionalized and recognized as an individual consumer right, we are not simply isolated consumers but creative agents with the ability to collectively resist from the position of vulnerability that connects us. Furthermore, more than a legal standard, repair is, as we have seen, a common need and inalienable basic activity to ensure that life can continue. Thus, while the law is a legal tool useful within a framework of widespread capitalism and commodification, it is not enough to appeal to institutions to defend the most fundamental rights (and capabilities) which at some point we lost or were taken away. The right to repair, as a basic principle of life, is best achieved by performing the activity itself: repairing. Because not even the best of laws can be implemented without the support of a solid cultural foundation – in this case, a collective culture of repair, universal and internalized, that embraces repair as something personal and a common cause to defend.

The right to repair would then be a collective political action that seeks to recover not only the ownership of things[9] but also shared skills and knowledge (DIWO: Do It with Others), as well as the collective agency needed to care for each other and sustain ourselves mutually, to "continue contending with the problem"[10] on a damaged but resistant planet, for example, through participation in community repair initiatives such as Repair Cafés and Restart Parties.

Seen in this light, repair is a socio-material act of caring that occurs in the "after" of design and production, and which by facing its damaging effects contributes to making them visible and making us aware of them.[11] This is essential if the purveyors of design and production are going to accept their responsibility. But in addition, in this disobedient[12] act of opening the "black boxes"[13] to try to repair them, we learn how things function... or how they could function differently. Knowing helps us to overcome the fear of technology and, consequently, while we repair, "we not only repair devices but our relationship with them," according to Restarters.

9 Aaron Perzanowski: *The Right to Repair: Reclaiming Control over the Things We Own*, Cambridge University Press, 2022.

10 Donna Haraway: *Staying with the Trouble: Making Kin in the Chthulucene*, Duke University Press, 2016.

11 Maria Puig de la Bellacasa: "Matters of Care in Technoscience: Assembling Neglected Things", *Social Studies of Science*, no. 41(1), 2011, pp. 85-106.

12 Ernesto Oroza, *op. cit.*

13 Bruno Latour: *Pandora's Hope: Essays on the Reality of Science Studies*, Harvard University Press, 1999.

Alongside material and relational repair is another type of economic and ecological repair. And the fact is that repair is a post-consumption practice that contributes to living from the abundance of sufficiency. Given that 80% of the energy used during a computer's entire lifetime is consumed in its manufacturing, it is easier to understand the slogan that "the best device is one that already exists". So, within a framework of degrowth, we would also have to claim the "right not to produce." This is in harmony with voices critical of design[14] which urge us to question and dematerialize it and turn designers into "undesigners".[15] In previous studies[16] we explained how a restorative design – both in its effects and its practice or teaching – must recognize the expertise of repairers and ally itself with their knowledge (situational and partial).[17] Because the position they are in, at the end of the useful life of things, grants them an epistemic advantage,[18] a privileged point of view on the damages caused by design.

Yet repair, like all care, has its limits: not everything is repairable, nor is repair always desirable *per se*. Repairing also requires recognizing and assuming finiteness and the possibility of an always transformational "death." Nor is repairability a property of things. Rather it is a relational condition achieved (or not) temporarily. At times repairing some things puts others at risk. For this reason, repair is only one possibility among others that requires careful and complex situational ethical-political analysis of those who are affected by it. As such it can be an obligation or an imposition. The challenge now is how to make the right to repair a practical alternative and collective political gesture capable of overcoming its institutional attachment, making us stronger and able to resist a socioeconomic order that weakens us and threatens the continuity of so many lives and resources on the planet.

14 Tony Fry: *Defuturing: A New Design Philosophy*, Londres, Bloomsbury, 2020; Tony Fry i Adam Nocek *Design in Crisis. New Worlds, Philosophies and Practices*, Londres, Routledge, 2021; Cameron Tonkinwise, «Is Design Finished? Dematèrialisation and Changing Things», *Design Philosophy Papers*, vol. 3, núm. 2, 2005, pàgs. 99-117.

15 Cameron Tonkinwise, "Before Design, More-than-Design: Elucidating 'Ontological Design'", *Design and Culture*, vol. 14 no. 3, 2022, pp. 341-359.

16 Blanca Callén and Melisa Duque: "'We Not Only Repair Our Devices, But Also Our Relationship With Them': Repair-led designing at the Restart Parties in Barcelona", in Eleni Kalantidou, Guy Keulemans, Abby Mellick Lopes, Niklavs Rubenis and Alison Gill (eds.) *Repair/Design: Place, Practice & Community*, London, Palgrave Macmillan, 2023, pp. 91-120; Blanca Callén and Melisa Duque: "Editorial: Repairing Design: Damage, Care, and Fragilities", *Diseña*, vol. 23, August 2023, pp. 1-14; Melisa Duque and Blanca Callén (in print): "Repair-led Learning for Design Education", in Adams, J. & Carr, Ch. (eds). *Designing through Planetary Breakdown: Locating Material Knowledge and Practical Skill*, London, Routledge.

17 Donna Haraway [1991]: *Simians, Cyborgs, and Women: The Reinvention of Nature*, London, Routledge, 2015.

18 Steven J. Jackson: "Rethinking Repair", in Tarleton Gillespie, Pablo J. Boczkowski and Kirsten A. Foot (eds.), *Media Technologies: Essays on Communication, Materiality and Society*, MIT Press, 2014, pp. 221-240.

* Blanca Callén is social psychologist. Co-founder and active member of the association Restarters BCN.

THE RIGHT TO REPAIR

Planned obsolescence, a concept that first appeared in 1932 as a way to increase the profits of manufacturers in times of crises, is the production of goods with short useful lives in order to boost consumption. Today, this economic model has serious environmental consequences. The European Commission estimates that the premature replacement of products generates 261 million tonnes of carbon dioxide (CO_2) emissions, and 35 million tonnes of annual waste. In its "Repair Manifesto"of 2009, the Plataforma 21 collective called to "stop recycling and start repairing". On April 23, 2024, the European Parliament passed a set of measures to reinforce the right to repair.

Model 560 iron
Aluminium, Bakelite and steel
Jata Technical Office, 1958
Manufactured by Electrodomésticos Jata, Eibar
Donation, Calvera Sagué family, 2008 MADB 138.639

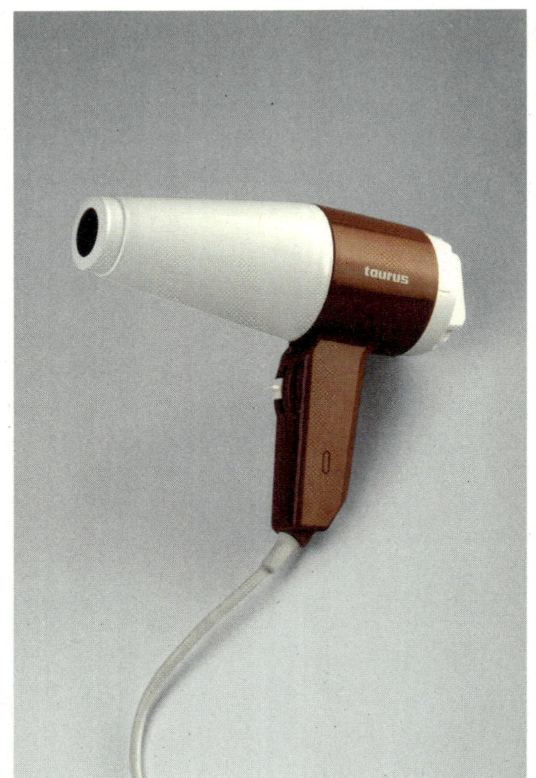

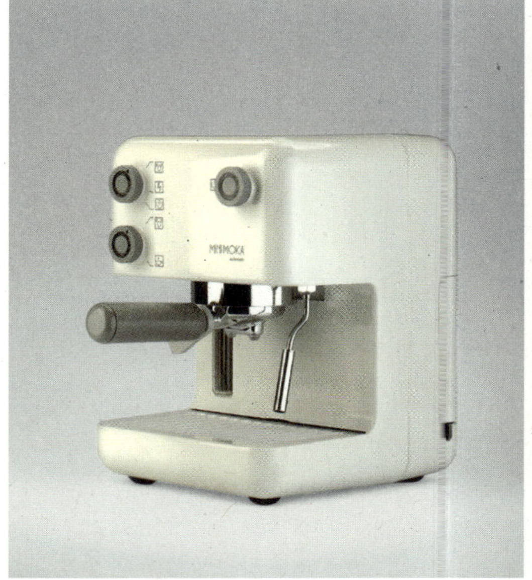

S3-MV hairdryer
Moulded polypropylene
Gabriel Lluelles i Rabadà, 1974
Manufactured by Taurus SA, Oliana
Donation, Quim Larrea Cruces, 1998 MADB 136.286

Juicer
Moulded ABS resin and polyacetylene
André Ricard Sala, 1988
Manufactured by Moulinex España, Barcelona
Donation, 1999 MADB 136.620

Dorothy heater
Steel, iron, brass and polyester
Technical equipment Fagor Electrodomésticos Sociedad Cooperativa, 1959
Manufactured by Fagor Electrodomésticos SCL, Arrasate / Mondragón
Donation, Maria Dolors Muntané Coca, 1999 MADB 136.5[illegible]2

M-600 Mini Moka Automatic Coffee Maker
ABS resin, stainless steel, copper and brass
André Ricard Sala, 1976
Manufactured by Moka Exprés SA, L'Hospitalet de Llobregat
Donation, Moka Exprés SA, 1994 MADB 135.708

Wall Phone T-1
Moulded ABS resin (Ravikral Anic) and electric wire
Ramon Benedito Graells, 1975
Manufactured by Fermax Electrónica SAE, Sant Cugat del Vallès
Donation, Benedito Design, 2017 MDB 1.762

CIRCULAR ARCHITECTURE: CONTEMPORARY RESOURCE REUSE PRACTICES IN CONSTRUCTION

BLANCA GARDELEGUI*

History of resuse: from *spolia* to self-building

Adaptive reuse of materials was a common practice in the history of architecture until the Technological Revolution, from the late 19th into the early 20th century. With the emergence of planned obsolescence, materials and products, as well as buildings, were given expiration dates. Additionally, labour costs increased, making disassembly more complex than demolition. The new machines that mechanized work streamlined this, but they cannot mitigate the labour-intensive effort involved in dismantling and reinstalling materials.

Prior to the Industrial Revolution, spoliation was already common in the Roman period. *Spolia* was the practice of reusing architectural elements from ancient structures to erect new buildings. This approach not only made use of available resources but granted prestige to new edifices through the inclusion of historic fragments. Throughout the centuries, the practice evolved, adapting to the needs and contexts of each era.

Today, adaptive reuse of materials in architecture is an exception, found mainly in informal self-building, where there is more workforce than resources, or in highly unique pilot projects. As a result, construction is now the sector with the largest global environmental impact, responsible for 39% of carbon emissions, 50% of the consumption of natural resources, and 40% of energy consumption. Moreover, given that most building materials do not come from Europe, their extraction entails exploitative practices and dependence, resulting in a form of contemporary colonization.

Reuse as a response to a decarbonized and decolonized future

Why reuse materials? Extending the life of materials through adaptive reuse reduces resource extraction, energy consumption, carbon emissions and the generation of waste. Also, reuse functions as a social activator at the local level, creating new jobs specific to the recovery of materials, the repair of components and the promotion of circularity. In this way, resource extraction ceases to be a colonizing activity and becomes a form of responsible waste management.

Despite all the benefits of reusing materials, lengthening the useful life of the entire building must always be the priority, as it offers the most advantages. Similarly, adaptive reuse of materials should also take precedence over recycling, which returns elements to their raw material state. While recycling reduces waste, in many cases the energy consumption and carbon emissions involved are comparable to the levels generated in the production of new materials.

In Europe, we are witnessing an increase in pilot practices and projects which embrace reusing materials as a key strategy in advancing towards a decarbonized future. A noteworthy initiative along these lines is Opalis. Established by Rotor in 2005 and implemented by various cooperatives, among them Bellastock and Atelier 45, with the backing of different European programmes and funds, including Interreg NEW, this project focuses on facilitating the use of reused materials in building and renovation endeavours in Europe. Opalis offers a wide range of resources, including a European reuse projects library, material supplier mapping in countries such as Belgium, Germany, Holland and France, and research initiatives categorized by material type. These research projects list the best practices, challenges and examples of resource recovery, as well as consolidating knowledge to promote the circular economy throughout Europe.

Zirkular, Switzerland

Zirkular is a consulting firm in Basel and Zurich, devoted to promoting the circular economy and professionalization of the adaptive reuse of materials in the construction sector. Founded in 2021 as a sister company of the architectural firm baubüro in situ, which has been involved in repurposing buildings and materials for twenty years, Zirkular collaborates with different interested parties, including companies, academic and government institutions, and architects.

They offer consulting services for pilot projects and tenders, assess future demolitions, look for materials to recover, and create material passports, among other activities, all with the aim of raising awareness and adopting the circular economy.

In 2022, the city of Zurich approved, with the support of 90% of its citizens, a referendum to introduce circularity into its constitution. In this context, the cities of Basel and Zurich organized the first two architectural tenders for public buildings based on catalogues of recovered materials. Zirkular created the online catalogues, thanks to which participants received available components from different buildings scheduled for demolition in the city which could be reused. Each component is shown with photographs, images and carbon emissions saved through its reuse.

The first tender, which includes several new residential buildings for more than 650 people and an immigration centre in Basel, will be carried out using pieces of prefabricated concrete from an obsolete car park that needs to be demolished. These pieces will be reused as slabs and for the new building façade. The second tender, a new recycling plant in Zurich, proposes a building erected from the deconstruction of several dismantled and reinstalled metal industrial warehouses. In addition, as a concrete reuse pilot project, the proposal entails reusing an in situ concrete building, cutting its slabs and columns. These two prototypes are examples of the future of circular architecture.

Rotor, Belgium

Rotor is an interdisciplinary cooperative known for its pioneering work in the reuse of materials. Founded in 2005, Rotor began recovering materials from the theatre world, where set designs have short life cycles and break frequently, and budgets tend to be low. This adaptive reuse practice was then exported on a larger scale.

In 2012, Rotor DB, a cooperative which designs and researches the organization of building materials and their social and environmental impact, was created. They are involved in education and communication projects, hoping to make reuse a more accessible practice for everyone. In 2016, the spin-off Rotor DC, devoted to the direct sale of recovered materials, was launched. Often, these materials are redesigned, thereby increasing their value. For example, their lamps, used by architects throughout Europe, are recovered from office buildings. In addition to direct sales of materials, Rotor DC provides a range of different services, from pavement cleaning to furniture rental.

Concular, Germany

In 2012, Concular launched restado.de, Europe's largest online marketplace for reclaimed building materials. The purchasing process, like any online store, also shows carbon emissions saved compared to buying a new component. Also, unlike other online reclaimed materials stores, Concular offers a one-year warranty for components. They work in close collaboration with manufacturers that guarantee the good quality of the material and perform any necessary repairs. It is important to point out that the availability of these reused materials depends on the dismantling of buildings, as most are still in place when they are sold. To meet this challenge, Concular created Urban Mining Hub, in Berlin, in which materials with the most potential can be dismantled and warehoused before they are sold.

Recetas Urbanas, Spain

Recetas Urbanas, literally Urban Recipes, has implemented several self-building projects since 2003, focused on reusing materials. In 2007, following the dismantling of a temporary settlement consisting of forty-two publicly-owned prefabricated modules, an initiative emerged to repurpose this material and avoid its being scrapped. The project gave rise to the GRRR (Resource Reuse and Redistribution Management) platform. GRRR Tools manages the reuse and redistribution of resources through nodes, participatory spaces such as collaborative projects, municipal warehouses and cooperatives that provide materials. The platform facilitates the identification and connection of these nodes, promoting the exchange of reusable resources for different uses, thereby encouraging the circular economy and sustainability. However, unfortunately the platform currently does not generate much activity.

Later, in 2014, another opportunity arose to implement better practices. The City Council of Barcelona inaugurated BCN RE.SET to celebrate the Tercentenary with different installations designed by international architects. Recetas Urbanas, in collaboration with Fundació Enric Miralles, mobilized to manage the adaptive reuse of most of the materials used in these installations, moving them to school courtyards in the city. This initiative not only stands out for its contribution to urban sustainability but also demonstrated the potential of reuse in large events and architectural projects.

Reuse challenges: from the exception to the rule

Despite the steps made in recent years towards the circular economy in construction, these advances still are not enough. Today, a new structure manufactured in Asia and transported to Europe continues to be more economical than reusing the components of a building nearby. Until this changes, adaptive reuse will remain an experimental field. Moreover, reuse entails certain challenges which not everyone is willing to assume: fluctuations in times, dismantling projects that sometimes do not unfold as planned, the scarcity of spare parts, lack of warranties, and design conditioned by what is available, to name just a few.

Nevertheless, there is no other option for moving forward: the scarcity of resources, limited waste management capacity and the urgency of climate change demand a change, and circularity answers this challenge. Carbon initiatives, already implemented in many European countries, are gaining more and more relevance as an important economic regulatory tool for a circular future, and this is true in the building sector as well.

Transforming the reuse of construction materials from being an exception to the rule is not only an environmental imperative but a crucial step towards a future in which circular innovation and sustainability guide our projects, thereby building a more resilient and fairer world for future generations.

* Blanca Gardelegui is architect and researcher. Founder of Kosmos Architects and member of Zirkular.

EMOTIONAL HERITAGE

We identify and define ourselves starting from the spaces we have occupied over the years. Personal and collective memories are forged in these relational places, giving and receiving meaning. Flores i Prats architectural office transformed the building of the present Sala Beckett theater, preserving the original structure and recovering elements such as doors, windows, and friezes. The result is a theater and drama center that reflects the memory of the original social club, where locals can recognize the settings where they had celebrated weddings and other festivities. The architectural firm Un Parell d'Arquitectes, led by Eduard Callís and Guillem Moliner and based in Can Sau, Olot, used a porous structure of vaults and niches to ennoble a piece of land. Now suitable for community use, this space rewrites local history and saves the neighborhood from previous environmental degradation. These two examples show how, through historical references, architecture can move us, bringing the past to the present and hence preserving our emotional heritage.

Sala Beckett
Flores i Prats Arquitectes, Barcelona, 2017
Photographs by Adrià Goula

<
Can Sau. Emergency Scenography
Un Parell d'Arquitectes, Olot, 2024
Photograph by José Hevia

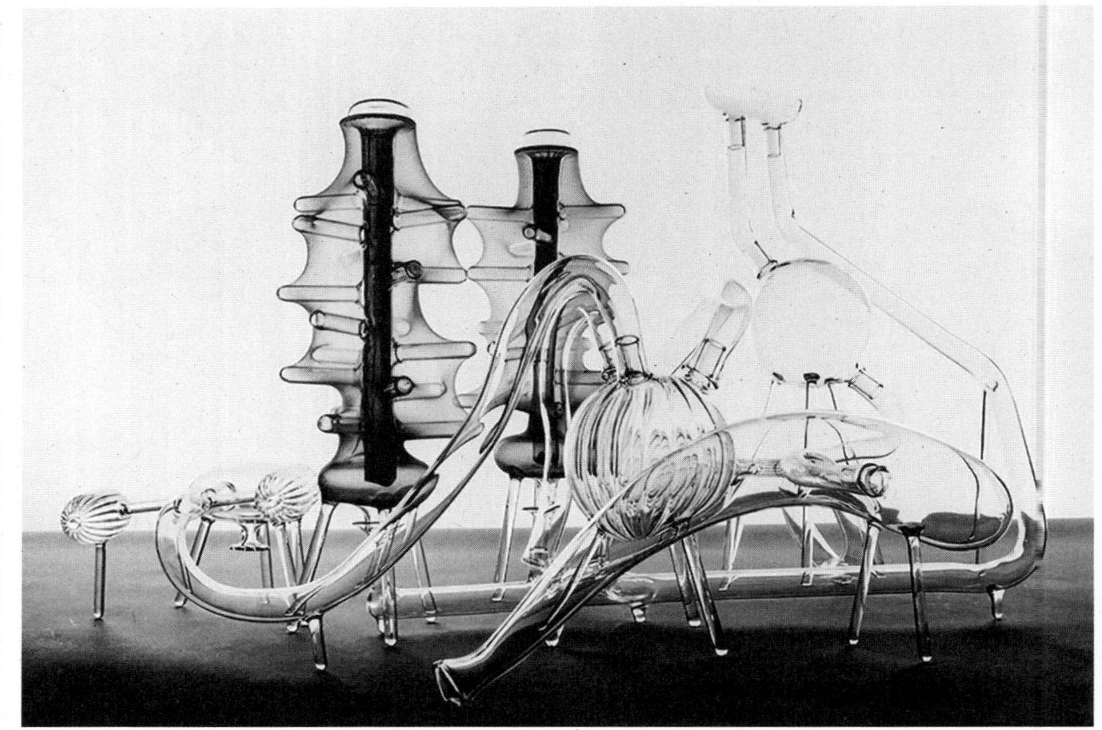

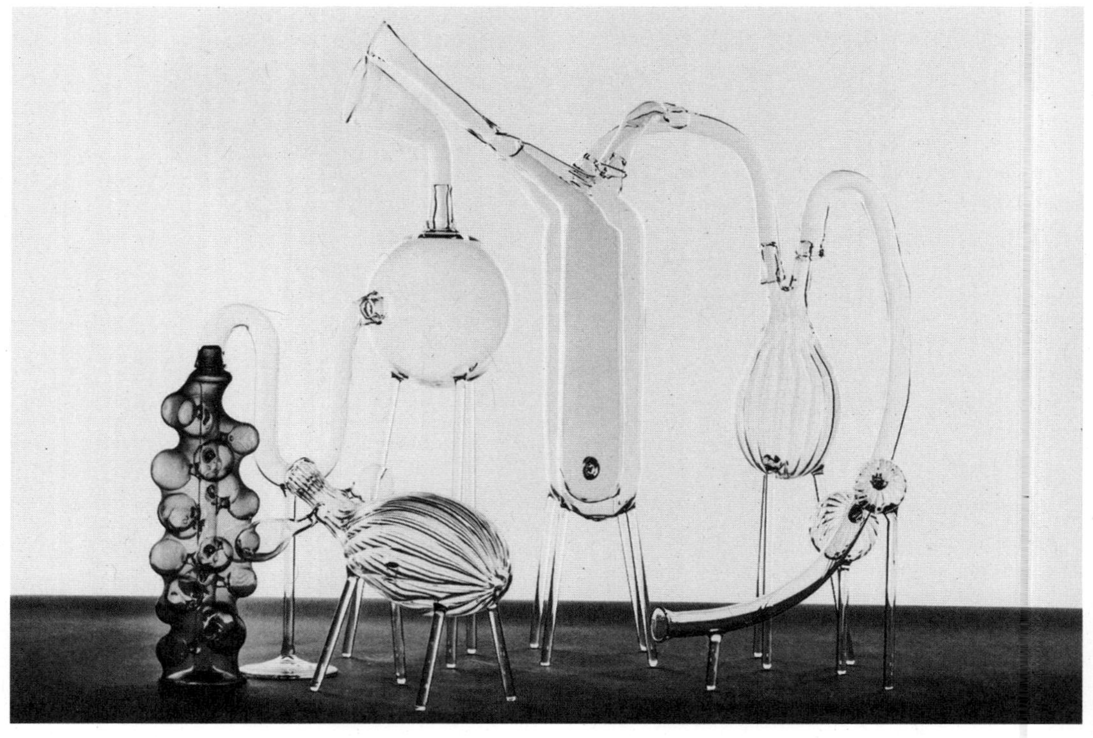

Body System I and *Body System II* installations (part of the *Re-materialisation of Systems, Bodies* project)
Borosilicate glass
El Último Grito, London, 2014
Loan, El Último Grito and Galería Elba Benítez

SPECULATIVE DESIGN

Critical thinking is fueled by curiosity, asking questions and reflecting, tools that can be used in the field of design. Brainstorming is a way of speculating on how things could be in order to imagine possible futures. *Rematerialisation of Systems_Bodies*, a project by El Último Grito collective, exemplifies this practice. The works contain ordinary elements found in familiar spaces that make us call into question what they stand for and why, inviting us to explore new realities through fictional creation. The group works on two levels, materially and conceptually, exploring ideas related to design, perception, and language. The choice of blown glass, an artisanal technique, is essential in this case to imagine worlds that summon up the image of a postindustrial future.

Porrón (wine pitcher)
Air-blown and pressed glass
Catalonia, 1800–1849
Depot, Acadèmia de Ciències i Arts MADB 38.309

Flask
Air-blown glass, with lacticinium threads and stretched
Catalonia, 1600–1649
Bequest of Emili Cabot i Rovira, 1924 MADB 23.373

BEYOND RADICAL DESIGN? SPECULATIVE EVERYTHING*

ANTHONY DUNNE / FIONA RABY‡

Dreams are powerful. They are repositories of our desire. They animate the entertainment industry and drive consumption. They can blind people to reality and provide cover for political horror. But they can also inspire us to imagine that things could be radically different than they are today, and then believe we can progress toward that imaginary world.[1]

It is hard to say what today's dreams are; it seems they have been downgraded to hopes – hope that we will not allow ourselves to become extinct, hope that we can feed the starving, hope that there will be room for us all on this tiny planet. There are no more visions. We don't know how to fix the planet and ensure our survival. We are just hopeful.

As Fredric Jameson famously remarked, it is now easier for us to imagine the end of the world than an alternative to capitalism. Yet alternatives are exactly what we need. We need to dream new dreams for the twenty-first century as those of the twentieth century rapidly fade. But what role can design play?

When people think of design, most believe it is about problem solving. Even the more expressive forms of design are about solving aesthetic problems. Faced with huge challenges such as overpopulation, water shortages, and climate change, designers feel an overpowering urge to work together to fix them, as though they can be broken down, quantified, and solved. Design's inherent optimism leaves no alternative but it is becoming clear that many of the challenges we face today are unfixable and that the only way to overcome them is by changing our values, beliefs, attitudes, and behaviour. Although essential most of the time, design's inbuilt optimism can greatly complicate things, first, as a form of denial that the problems we face are more serious than they appear, and second, by channelling energy and resources into fiddling with the world out there rather than the ideas and attitudes inside our heads that shape the world out there.

Rather than giving up altogether, though, there are other possibilities for design: one is to use design as a means of speculating how things could be – speculative design. This form of design thrives on imagination and aims to open up new perspectives on what are sometimes called wicked problems, to create spaces for discussion and debate about alternative ways of being, and to inspire and encourage people's imaginations to flow freely. Design speculations can act as a catalyst for collectively redefining our relationship to reality.

But assuming it is possible to create more socially constructive imaginary futures, could design help people participate more actively as citizen-consumers? And if so, how?

This is where we are. Not trying to predict the future but using design to open up all sorts of possibilities that can be discussed, debated, and used to collectively define a preferable future for a given group of people: from companies, to cities, to societies. Designers should not define futures for everyone else but working with experts, including ethicists, political scientists, economists, and so on, generate futures that act as catalysts for public debate and discussion about the kinds of futures people really want. Design can give experts permission to let their imaginations flow freely, give material expression to the insights generated, ground these imaginings in everyday situations, and provide platforms for further collaborative speculation.

We believe that by speculating more, at all levels of society, and exploring alternative scenarios, reality will become more malleable and, although the future cannot be predicted, we can help set in place today factors that will increase the probability of more desirable futures tomorrow. And equally, factors that may lead to undesirable futures can be spotted early on and addressed or at least limited.

We have long been inspired by radical architecture and fine art that use speculation for critical and provocative purposes, particularly projects from the 1960s and 1970s by studios such as Archigram, Archizoom, Superstudio, Ant Farm, Haus-Rucker-Co, and Walter Pichler.[2] But why is this so rare in design? During the Cold War Modern exhibition at the Victoria and Albert Museum in 2008 we were delighted to finally see so many projects from this period. The exuberant energy and visionary imagination of the projects in the final room of the exhibition were incredibly inspiring for us. We were left wondering how this spirit could be reintroduced to contemporary design and how design's boundaries could be extended beyond the strictly commercial to embrace the extreme, the imaginative, and the inspiring.

1 Stephen Duncombe, *Dream: Re-imaging Progressive Politics in the Age of Fantasy*, New York: The New Press, 2007, 182.

2 This history is very well documented; for example, see Neil Spiller, *Visionary Architecture: Blueprints of the Modern Imagination*, London: Thames & Hudson, 2006; Felicity D. Scott, *Architecture or Techno-utopia: Politics after Modernism*, Cambridge, MA: MIT Press, 2007; Robert Klanten et al., eds., *Beyond Architecture: Imaginative Buildings and Fictional Cities*, Berlin: Die Gestalten Verlag, 2009; and Geoff Manaugh, *The BLDG BLOG Book*, San Francisco: Chronicle Books, 2009; see also http://bldgblog.blogspot.co.uk. Accessed December 24, 2012.

We believe several key changes have happened since the high point of radical design in the 1970s that make imaginative, social, and political speculation today more difficult and less likely. First, during the 1980s design became hyper-commercialized to such an extent that alternative roles for design were lost. Socially oriented designers such as Victor Papanek, who were celebrated in the 1970s, were no longer regarded as interesting; they were seen as out of sync with design's potential to generate wealth and to provide a layer of designer gloss to every aspect of our daily lives. There was some good in this – design was embraced by big business and entered the mainstream but usually only in the most superficial way. Design became fully integrated into the neoliberal model of capitalism that emerged during the 1980s, and all other possibilities for design were soon viewed as economically unviable and therefore irrelevant.

Second, with the fall of the Berlin Wall in 1989 and the end of the Cold War the possibility of other ways of being and alternative models for society collapsed as well. Market-led capitalism had won and reality instantly shrank, becoming one dimensional. There were no longer other social or political possibilities beyond capitalism for design to align itself with. Anything that did not fit was dismissed as fantasy, as unreal. At that moment, the "real" expanded and swallowed up whole continents of social imagination marginalizing as fantasy whatever was left. As Margaret Thatcher famously said, "There is no alternative."

Third, society has become more atomized. As Zygmunt Bauman writes in *Liquid Modernity*,[3] we have become a society of individuals. People work where work is available, travel to study, move about more, and live away from their families. There has been a gradual shift in the United Kingdom from government that looks after the most vulnerable in society to a small government that places more responsibility on individuals to manage their own lives. On the one hand this undoubtedly creates freedom and liberation for those who wish to create new enterprises and projects but it also minimizes the safety net and encourages everyone to look out for him – or herself. At the same time, the advent of the Internet has allowed people to connect with similar-minded people all over the world. As we channel energy into making new friends around the world we no longer need to care about our immediate neighbours. On a more positive note, with this reduction in top-down governing, there has been a corresponding shift away from the top-down mega-utopias dreamt up by an elite; today, we can strive for one million tiny utopias each dreamt up by a single person.

Fourth is the downgrading of dreams to hopes once it became clear that the dreams of the twentieth century were unsustainable, as the world's population has more than doubled in the last forty-five years to seven billion. The great modernist social dreams of the post-war era probably reached a peak in the 1970s when it started to become clear that the planet had limited resources and we were using them up fast. As populations continued to grow at an exponential rate, we would have to reconsider the consumer world set in motion during the 1950s. This feeling has become even more acute with the financial crash and the emergence since the new millennium of scientific data suggesting that the climate is warming up due to human activity. Now, a younger generation doesn't dream, it hopes; it hopes that we will survive, that there will be water for all, that we will be able to feed everyone, that we will not destroy ourselves.

3 Zygmunt Bauman, *Liquid Modernity*, Cambridge, UK: Polity Press, 2000.

But we are optimistic. Triggered by the financial crash of 2008, there has been a new wave of interest in thinking about alternatives to the current system. And although no new forms of capitalism have emerged yet, there is a growing desire for other ways of managing our economic lives and the relationship among state, market, citizen, and consumer. This dissatisfaction with existing models coupled with new forms of bottom-up democracy enhanced by social media make this a perfect time to revisit our social dreams and ideals and design's role in facilitating alternative visions rather than defining them. Of being a catalyst rather than a source of visions. It is impossible to continue with the methodology employed by the visionary designers of the 1960s and 1970s. We live in a very different world now but we can reconnect with that spirit and develop new methods appropriate for today's world and once again begin to dream.

But to do this, we need more pluralism in design, not of style but of ideology and values.

A	B
Affirmative	Critical
Problem solving	Problem finding
Provides answers	Asks questions
Design for production	Design for debate
Design as solution	Design as medium
In the service of industry	In the service of society
Fictional functions	Functional fictions
For how the world is	For how the world could be
Change the world to suit us	Change us to suit the world
Science fiction	Social fiction
Futures	Parallel worlds
The "real" real	The "unreal" real
Narratives of production	Narratives of consumption
Applications	Implications
Fun	Humor
Innovation	Provocation
Concept design	Conceptual design
Consumer	Citizen
Makes us buy	Makes us think
Ergonomics	Rhetoric
User-friendliness	Ethics
Process	Authorship

A/B, Dunne & Raby.

vii PREFACE

"Speculative Everything started as a list we created list that we created a few years ago called A/B, a kind of manifesto. In it, we juxtapose d esign as it's usually understood with the kind of design we do. B was not intended to replace A but simply to add another dimension, something to compare it to and facilitate discussion. and facilitate discussion. Ideally, C, D, E and many others would follow."

—Dunne and Raby

A)
Affirmative
Problem Solving
Provides answers
Design for production
Design as a solution
Serving the industry
Fictitious functions
For what the world is like
We change the world to suit us
Science fiction
Futures
The "real" real
Narratives of production
Applications

B)
Critical
Problem finding
Raise questions
Design for debate
Design as a medium
At the service of society
Functional fictions
For how the world could be
Changing ourselves to adapt to the world
Social fiction
Parallel worlds
The "unreal" real
Narratives of consumption
Implications
Humor
Provocation
Conceptual design
Citizen
Makes us think
Rhetoric
Ethics
Authorship

* Text reproduced with permission from the authors and MIT Press.

* Anthony Dunne and Fiona Raby are architect and designer, respectively. Winners of the MIT Media Lab Award in 2015. Professors in Design and Emerging Technologies at Parsons, The New School, New York.

COSMOPOLITICAL PORTALS AND ECOLOGIES OF DESIRE

URIEL FOGUÉ*

A few years ago, Skeptical Science launched an online meter called *4Hiroshimas.info* which shows that earth's temperature is increasing at an amount equal to four Hiroshima atomic bombs every second, "due mainly to human activity".[1] Measurements began in 1998, and currently the count is above three million bombs. For Deborah Danowski and Eduardo Viveiros de Castro, these types of rhetorical artifacts indicate, more or less dramatically, that the time we live in is "off kilter."[2]

What can we do? While these data can lead to a certain paralysis, inaction is not an option. For a long time, architecture has been identified as one of the most prominent contributors to global warming and greenhouse house emissions,[3] that is, to one of the scenarios in which we seem to be racing towards a possible environmental collapse. Our field must act: it must *shift* from its usual *position*. What follows is what we believe are some of the *shifts* that could help architecture as a practice to *reposition* itself.

1. From metabolic machines to desiring ecologies

One of the common ways to address environmental problems in architecture is what we might call the "thermodynamic approach": one that describes nature as a balanced system of matter-energy exchange. From this perspective, architecture must contribute to the functioning of this ecosystemic "machine." Construction must alter as little as possible its fragile harmonious order.

This representation is nothing more than a modern projection of the "model-motor," insofar as it equates nature with an optimized metabolic machine and architecture with a "part" that must efficiently participate in the operation of this machine.

Yet this approach based on modern, functionalist reasoning is limited in scope, as it disregards other types of ecologic relationships that exceed any unified and standard image of nature. And while it shows a certain efficiency at the level of technological solutions, the metaphor of the metabolic machine falls short when trying to address socio-environmental problems in all their complexity.

According to Bruno Latour,[4] the narrative of a harmonious nature prevents us from understanding that what enables and encourages life on Earth is imbalance, not balance. Ecological dynamics, he argues, do not always operate based on functional relationships. Therefore, the challenge will be to reflect on how architecture can participate on those other disproportionate, excessive, redundant and "free" relational planes that shift away from a providential model, deploying other ecologies, other topologies, other philia, other intelligences, other natures...

Like desire.

Relationships and environmental intra-actions[5] are (also) articulated by desire. And not (just) reproductive desire but by other forms of desire beyond the economy of necessity. Accordingly, we cannot address ecological questions, or questions related to environmental justice, if we fail to acknowledge that we inhabit desiring ecologies.

Accepting desire as a vital ecologic force entails important consequences for our field. First, beyond being a set of techniques for balancing thermodynamic fluxes, building must be seen as a form of technical and spatial mediation that (also) channels fluxes of desire. If ecosystems are always penetrated by desire, the role of architecture cannot be one that suppresses desiring dynamics but one that embraces them: it must make desire inhabitable. Secondly, if architecture is a field in the service of desire, it then requires other genealogies, other histories that incorporate cases that have experimented with the spatialization of desire, such as "licentious" architecture[6] or queer ecology.[7] And, thirdly, we can only imagine and build a desirable ecologic future if we accept that desire is an architectural material, as much as a brick is.

2. From constructive detail to ecological contract

In the 1990s, philosopher Michel Serres published *The Natural Contract*,[8] an influential book in which he outlines some ecological approaches later developed by other authors, such as Latour.

1 https://skepticalscience.com/.

2 Deborah Danowski and Eduardo Viveiros de Castro: *¿Hay un mundo por venir? Ensayo sobre los fines del mundo*, Buenos Aires, Caja Negra, 2019.

3 United Nations Environment Program. *Emissions Gap Report 2023: Broken Record. Temperatures hit new highs, yet world fails to cut emissions (again)*, Nairobi, UNEP, 2023.

4 Bruno Latour: *Politiques de la nature*, Éditions la Découverte, 2004.

5 Karen Barad: *Cuestión de materia. Trans/Materia/Realidades y performatividad 'queer' de la naturaleza*, Madrid, Holobionte, 2023.

6 Uriel Fogué, Eva Gil and Carlos Palacios: *Super Petites Maisons*, Lausanne, EPFL, 2022.

7 Catriona Mortimer-Sandilands and Bruce Erickson (eds.): *Queer Ecologies. Sex, Nature, Politics, Desire*, Indiana University Press, Bloomington, 2020.

8 Michel Serres: *The Natural Contract*, The University of Michigan Press, 1995.

On the cover of the French edition is the painting *Fight with Cudgels* by Goya, where two individuals are battling each other with clubs. Both purposeful contenders, the philosopher explains, preserve a (violent) social contract without realizing that, the more they fight, the deeper they sink into the quicksand where the scene unfolds. The more they exercise their social contract, the more they condemn themselves to death. This is because they ignore the third party on the scene: the environment. The environment (for Serres) and Gaia (for Latour) were excluded from the modern project. This image encourages us to draft new ecological agreements that expand the cosmos of the political dimension of social contracts, incorporating the rest of what is human. Modern contracts must evolve into natural contracts, according to Serres, and into armistices, according to Latour, that will put an end to the ecological war we are languishing from. They will be instruments for managing ecological links, deploying other forms of coexistence, for experiencing a "complex we."[9]

This socio-ecological contract sets in motion a workspace that is decisive for architecture. Thinking about the ecological performativity of our projects implies understanding building processes as spaces where commitments are made, where, as in Goya's painting, bonds between humans, and between more than just humans, are defined. Confronting the ecological challenge entails understanding constructive details[10] such as inscription surfaces where different recognition rights are disputed. How do our architectures change when we accept that their details are natural contracts (if viewed from Serres' point of view) or battlefields, war zones or ecosystemic trenches (if seen from Latour's point of view), where moderns and earthlings battle for Earth in "Gaia's War"?

Before continuing, a few caveats. Firstly, here the word "contract" is not a metaphor. In ecological terms, constructive details are literally assembly blueprints where multiple temporal and spatial scales are compared and different agents co-determined. Secondly, socioecological contracts are not universal formulations but rather situated devices. The implementation and assessment of the performance of each clause must be carried out in a contextualized way. Thirdly, structural details are never neutral. Socioecological encounters occur usually under asymmetrical power conditions. The ecological effects of the construction sector are not homogenously distributed, nor is responsibility for these effects equal for all the planetary parts. Fourthly, their validity is temporary. They are the result of opportunist negotiations, and as with any contract, they need to be interpreted, assessed, revised and renewed. And finally, talking about contracts does not mean to exclusively limit ourselves to the legal realm. There is a long tradition connecting contracts with desire.[11] Architecture needs to find in these contracts opportunities to undertake ecologies of desire.

One could argue that "contract" is an anthropocentric legal term that favours humans. Or that "armistice" follows a warlike logic that prevents us from imagining a future beyond conflagration. Perhaps we need different terms. We venture to suggest a few: constructive details are "cosmopolitical portals," "multi-versal vicinity planes," "fields of interrelation and kinship with others," "cosmopolitical diplomacy interfaces," or sampling from Marisol de la Cadena's expression, "areas of pluri-versal contact."

9 Marisol de la Cadena: "An Invitation to Live Together: Making the "Complex We", *Environmental Humanities*, vol. 11, no. 2, 2019, pp. 477-484.

10 Together with budget allocation, technical specifications, reports and rest of plans.

11 Uriel Fogué: *Las arquitecturas del fin del mundo. Cosmotécnicas y cosmopolíticas para un mundo en suspenso*, Barcelona, Puente Editores, 2022.

Fight with Cudgels, F. Goya, 1823
The Natural Contract, M. Serres, 1990
Facing Gaia, B. Latour, 2015

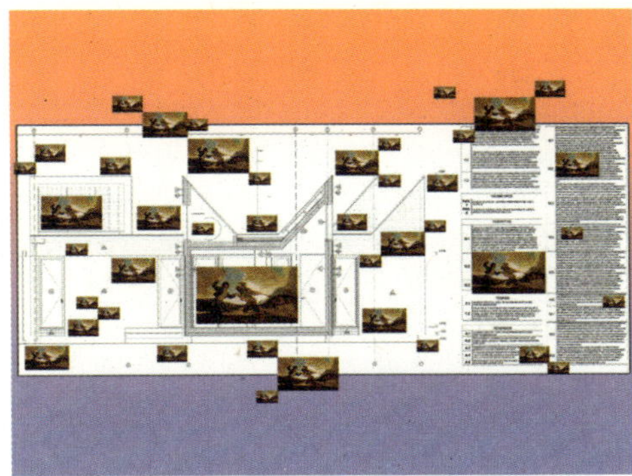

Ecological portals, elii, Neko, 2024

The consequences for our field are considerable. From the moment we outline our projects, we contribute to the composition of ecosystemic contracts that will be activated during construction. The details are ecological portals that connect more-than-human pasts, presents and futures.

3. Other *shifts*...

Other crucial shifts we cannot address here include: "From territorial to microbial scale," "From planning to ghost urbanism," "From a technological to a scenic black box," "From technological solutions to emotional space," "From urban metabolism to a cannibal carnival." Meanwhile, we will explore these "cosmopolitical portals and ecologies of desire," accepting that architectural processes unfold at multiple scales: that of the building and that of the ecological architecture of the planet.

* Uriel Fogué is Doctor in Architecture, researcher and professor at the Universidad Europea de Madrid.

TERRAFORMING*

BENJAMIN BRATTON#

Terraforming is the deliberate practical, political, and programmatic project to conceive and compose a viable planetarity. It is based on the secular disenchantment of Earth from 'world' to 'planet' through the ongoing artificialization of intelligence and the emergence of a general sapience that conjoins human and inhuman cognition. It names a potential futural condition realized by the rationalization of ecosystems toward diversification and order. More broadly, there is also a historical terraforming, which identifies the 105 year arc of hominization-induced and 103 year arc industrialization-induced ecosystem transformations respectively, as well as an *unconditional* terraforming, which identifies the momentum of planetary transformation that will continue in some form without homeostasis and which provides the context for the deliberate and normative project of composing viability.

The relation between terraforming and planetarity is therefore at least twofold. Terraforming is the effect of a *revealed* planetarity while it is also the cause of a *projective* planetarity.

First, a revealed 'planetarity' is the scientific and philosophical comprehension by specific sapient species of Earth and Earth life, including itself, as arising from a unique astronomic condition and not a 'Creation' given for an intuitive horizon. Over a span of billions of years Earth matter organized itself from chemical to biological complexity, from biology to societies of organisms, some of which became not only sentient but sapient. In time these came to organize epistemological technologies including telescopes and genome sequencing through which their own evolutionary material predicament came into view. For this, the phenomenological interiority of 'world,' the terrestrial bias of 'territory,' and the frozen abstraction of 'globe' can be understood as provisional approximations of what sapient self-location in physical space and time would and will become. This process, by which Earth produces creatures capable of comprehending and theorizing the planetarity of their own position, passes through sequences of 'Copernican trauma' through which culturally-determinant anthropocentric cosmologies give way to the revelation of a long-preceding reality from which those cultures emerged.

In turn, these recursions provide for a technically-mediated sapience by which subjects can calibrate their self-comprehension through artificial externalization and the abstracted simulation of their own positions and queries. At the aggregate scale, this is known as Earth Sciences. Earth Sciences are a foundational branch of *planetary scale computation* operating as a plural epistemological technology. As scientific planetarity is a function of the technological exteriorizations of astronomic imaging, the dynamic flux of planetary ecological process (i.e. 'climate change') is only comprehensible through the multivariate quantitative abstractions of planetary scale sensing and calculation of simulations of Earth's past, present, and future. This parallels the process by which sentient creatures became 'conscious' through an interiorization of their ability to model the intentionality of other external minds – predator, prey, friend, foe –recursively enabling the modeling of its own mental states (selfhood is self-othering).

The decisive paradox for general sapience is the dual recognition that its existence is extremely rare and extremely fragile, vulnerable to numerous threats of extinction in the near and long term, and also that the ecological consequences of its own historical emergence through historical terraforming has been a chief driver of the conditions that establish its very same precarity. That is, at the very moment its planetarity is known, it is understood to be in mortal crisis. For this, 'terraforming' is at once the process by which sapience is embedded in the planetary conditions of its own possibility and also clarified as the project of rectifying the violence of its own emergence.

Second, terraforming's relation to planetarity is not only that it is a revelation of its own preconditions, but also, that the *artificiality* of a planetarity-to-come is made explicit: a general sapience can no longer disown, evade, or abdicate its reality and its responsibilities. As extraplanetarity was becoming a reality during the 20th century via rocketry, satellites, lunar orbiters and landers, the imaging of other planets and moons in our solar system, and so on, the speculative premise of terraforming Mars or Luna to make them viable for Earth-like life was conceived by both science and science-fiction. In retrospect, this is understood as a kind of deferred appreciation of how Earth itself had been terraformed, first by biological life and eventually by modern industry: extraplanetarity framing and revealing planetarity. The terraforming project, however, is to make *Earth* continuously suitable for Earth-like life, long into the deep time of the future. Ostensibly, the number of humans (and other sentient creatures) who are now living is smaller than the total number that has ever lived in the past, but the total number who may live in the future is, one hopes, an order of magnitude or two greater than both combined. The viability that defines the terraforming as the normative project of a planetary general sapience (transindividual human, synthetic machine intelligence, etc.) is assigned on behalf of the continuance of that life and the emergence of a civilization with greater genetic and molecular heterogeneous order than that which preceded industrialization.

The critical apparatuses include automation, understood as an ecological principle of inter-entanglement more than a reductive autonomy; 'geoengineering' understood in terms of climate-scale effects more than a specific portfolio of techniques; a programmatic, de-anthropocentric

Feral Atlas, Acceleration
Anna L. Tsing, Jennifer Deger, Alder Keleman Saxena and Feifei Zhou

disindividuation of the attention of planetary-scale computation away from individual users and toward processes more relevant for long term viability; the anthropoforming of sapient species toward deliberate variation, including reproductive technologies, universal medical provision, synthetic gene therapies, etc.; a cultivation of synthetic mathematical, linguistic, and robotic intelligences with which general sapience deliberately evolves; an experimental programmatic competence with biotechnologies through which living matter composes living matter; an intensification of urban habitats and technologies as media for the general provision of universal and niche services; a projective and programmatic extraplanetarity through which the existing and potential planetarity comes into focus, including the creative and rational exploration of extraplanetary environments and perspectives; and an aggregation of prospective creative governing intelligences capable of the mobilization of resources toward regularizating and enforcing interventions.

Within the Humanities, terraforming represents an unorthodox position on the relations between political philosophy, philosophy of technology, and applied sciences. Just as historical shifts in scientific cosmology have informed corresponding shifts in geopolitical architectures, today the former and the latter are in radical disjunction. From the perspective of terraforming, this invites the misapprehension that the appropriate response to the founding violences of sapience and its ecological impacts is to withdraw from agential impact altogether, such as eliminating energy expenditures per se. This leads some to embrace a re-enchanted vitalism for which sentience and sapience are collapsed into a post-secular neo-animism based on an atavistic reification of cultural traditions and the pervasive anthropomorphization of objects and materials. The Terraforming draws a different even inverse implication from the challenges of planetarity. Instead of seeing matter and things, like rocks and tree frogs, as anthropomorphized 'persons,' it sees humans as a specific kind of material assemblage that has achieved a provisional but precious sapience through its deeply mutual evolution with forms of technical abstraction. For the terraforming, the *generalization* of sapience means the extension of the cognitive and technical capacity for both planetary self-modeling/ exterior modeling and self-composition/ exterior composition.

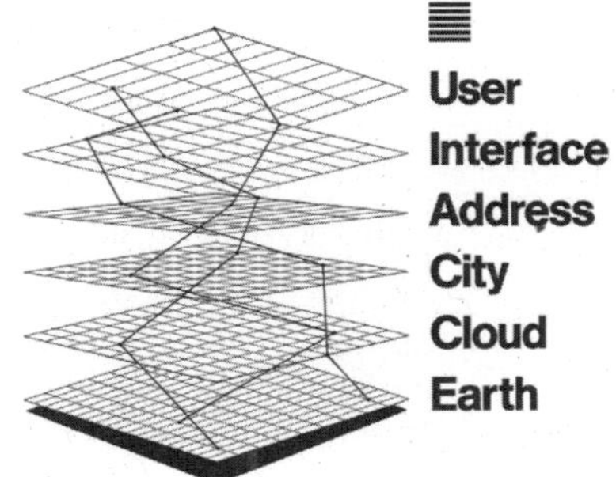

Stack diagram showing the 6 layers in which the planetary computational system is organized according to Benjamin Bratton, 2015, p. 66

* This article first appeared in the book *Words of Weather*, published by Onassis Foundation (2022) and is reproduced here with the permission of the author and publisher.

* Benjamin Bratton is sociologist. Professor of Philosophy of Technology at the University of California, San Diego.

RE-GROWTH: A NEW PARADIGM FOR THE FUTURE

EVA FRANCH I GILABERT*

In the last decade, a term to address the depletion of natural resources and ecological damage to the planet has emerged with force around the world: degrowth. Confronted with this word-thought, a sweet but dark generational fury rises to the surface, a resentment toward those who came before us. Degrowth invites us to reduce consumption, production and global economic activity to achieve environmental sustainability and social justice.

Undoing, disassembling, pulling back from the path of progress and growth that capitalism imposes on contemporary global societies demands that, with degrowth, we interact with those who have built their wealth on the unregulated exploitation of resources and labour, resulting in uncontrolled pollution and systemic inequalities. This reassessment invites us work alongside those responsible for growth and to rethink with them traditional economic markers such as GDP, interest rates and policies designed by governments, corporations and institutions across the world. In this context, the words of Audre Lorde resonate: “The master’s tools will never dismantle the master’s house.”

Considering this situation, we must ask ourselves if a different, lateral and independent strategy is possible, one not dialectically opposed to the initial problem. Understanding there is no zero-sum game in the growth-degrowth equation is essential. To achieve goals such as halting CO_2 emissions, reversing global climate change, and restoring and recovering biomass, ecosystems, languages, dialects, traditions and knowledge that have disappeared due to capitalism and the resulting global homogenization, we need more than just degrowth. We need a more profound, structural and optimistic reflection on the possible models of development to open the door to a richer and more complex alternative: regrowth.

The concept of regrowth asks us to see the world differently and to remake it. This new paradigm goes beyond the financialization of our environment in pursuit of the human capacity to create, contribute, innovate and transform. Regrowing is growing intellectually, emotionally and socially, ensuring that all disciplines and modes of action become part of the solution needed for present, past and future generations. Regrowing is taking charge of the past while building the future.

Post-capitalist collective imagination

Attributed to Fredric Jameson and Slavoj Zizek, the sentence "it's easier to imagine the end of the world than the end of capitalism" leads us to paralysis and expresses a crisis of the collective imagination in all areas. If we analyse contemporary works of fiction and art, as well as social works, we are confronted with apocalyptic visions that foresee inevitable degrowth because of climate and social collapse, visions opposed to a green capitalism built on extractive notions of traditional geo-engineering and tangentially positioned in ancestral or traditionalist collective imaginations that evoke, almost magically, the forces of nature.

Clearly, we must start to build collective imaginations that go beyond collapse and fossil fuel culture, ones able to suggest better futures. In this respect, schools, universities and cultural institutions must bear the heavy burden of helping us to unlearn, teaching us and inviting us to use our imagination comprehensively when exercising our citizenship.

Regrowth as criticism and an alternative

The concept of regrowth is a critique of our fossil culture and our inability to imagine economic, social and cultural spaces beyond extractivist capitalism. That we need to de-grow in many aspects is a fact, but we also need to grow in many others. Regrowing involves rethinking what are the values and driving forces of life, redefining relationships and restoring the social, economic, cultural and political balance.

This process means that some things may disappear so that others can thrive. We need degrowth in extractivist and destructive material matters and growth in terms of material reproductive issues, remediation, restoration and reconstruction.

This will not occur with an extractivist logic that depletes natural resources but by redefining what raw material is. And here is where imagination comes into play, the non-economic yet imaginative speculation of "what if." We must decrease the destruction of ecosystems, production and emission of CO_2 and creation of inequalities. We must ensure degrowth of cultural and ideological homogenization, but growth in matters concerning equality, biodiversity, generosity and multiculturalism.

Old and new ways of reimagining society

To regrow, we need new ways of imagining society, from rituals to the structures of government, to relational, legal, economic and material issues. Regrowth opts for the creation of a new value system.

Current questions surrounding the climate and inequality have been at the centre of many utopian visions of past futures. Utopia, a word widely used in architecture, political philosophy and literary circles since its creation at the beginning of the 16th century, has meant many things over time. Despite their differences, positive, negative, agrarian, feminist and industrial utopias share the desire to create an alternative to the current State and to existing ways of living. Essentially, a utopia challenges the dominant ideological framework, declares a new desirable condition, and develops a methodology for action. While since the 1980s, the expression "This is a utopia" has a pejorative, simplistic and naive connotation, today we see a new generation seeking through speculation – through "what if" strategies – the possibility of developing alternative scenarios to present realities.

Architecture, art and design as agents of change

Architecture, art and design contribute to building societies by providing possible collective notions about how to live together. Beyond shaping preexisting social, economic, energy, environmental, cultural and political agreements, these disciplines have the ability – and responsibility – to redefine the social contract in all its manifestations. Art, architecture and design schools, as well as advanced thinking labs, abound in transformative ideas capable of setting into motion alternative ways of reconstituting our societies and territories. What is missing is an interplay between the imagination and creative capital, political action and construction.

Today, utopias are at the service of a new socio-economic framework, with visions of the future and change that the West is incapable of encouraging. An important message for the economic and political elite around the world is the importance of cultivating and promoting talent, utopias and imagination, and of providing space and laboratories for action.

Regrowth: value and measure propositions

One of the major conceptual changes in the role of a creator (architect, artist, designer, etc.) is the design of strategic value production, systems of sharing and participation of the owners in the future value of what is built. This change in functions, responsibilities and benefits places in the hands of all participants the economic gains from property, understood always as a common good.

Permanent Temporary, Barcelona
Kosmos and Parabase, 2023

Mamífera: Collective breastfeeding space, Barcelona
Equal Saree, 2023

Free Air, Barcelona
Daryan Knobaluch, 2023

Model. Festival d'Arquitectures de Barcelona 2023
Artistic direction by Eva Franch i Gilabert
Organised by Ajuntament de Barcelona
and Fundació Mies van der Rohe
Photographs Ajuntament de Barcelona

Measuring and quantifying the physical and intangible dimensions of a place or an object is to articulate facts to create value. What can be measured can be monetized, historicized and sold. In the process of creating buildings, landscapes and spaces that accommodate social, emotional, energy and political relationships, architects bring to light the functions of society in operating and aspirational terms. From ideas to drawings to buildings and to cities, architecture and design are responsible first, for identifying the forces behind a project, for depicting them and finally translating them into a space able to perform the desired functions, effects and affects.

Towards a new measure of well-being

Art, architecture and design are constantly innovating in search of new ways to measure. In the specific case of architecture and design, these innovation processes require a planning effort that often proceeds from places of consensus, standards and guidelines that form part of praxis and the collective imagination, and which are often included in regulations or laws.

The quality of the air we breathe, noise pollution levels, the temperature in cities, the amount of vegetation, park and leisure areas, energy compaction, lighting, safety and the ability to walk to all the places we need to lead a full life are some of the values that allow us to measure the quality of life in the cities, towns and territories we inhabit. But they are not the only ones. Regrowth invites us to rethink the values we want to see reflected in the architectures that surround us every day, from our home in the city to natural habitats.

The concept of regrowth transcends the simple alternative of degrowth, offering a radically new, transforming vision of our collective future. It challenges us to rethink our priorities, values and developmental models to build a society that is more just, sustainable and rich in human and environmental values. This vision entails a profound transformation of how we understand growth and sustainability while suggesting an alternative that includes restoration, innovation and social justice as basic pillars. Now, more than ever, our active involvement in this regrowth process is essential, where we contribute ideas, talent and efforts to create a future that benefits both present and future generations.

* Eva Franch i Gilabert is architect and curator. Visiting professor at Princeton University School of Architecture. In May 2022, she was one of the three artistic directors of Model. Barcelona Architectures Festival.

TEKN

This book has been published for the exhibition *Matter Matters. Designing with the world* at the Museu del Disseny-DHub

Publisher
Barcelona City Council
Actar Publishers

Barcelona City Council Publishing and Publications Board
Xavier Marcé Carol, Gemma Arau Ceballos, Maria Buhigas San José, Ferran Burguillos Martinez, Núria Costa Galobart, Mireia Escobar Costa, Sonia Fuertes Ledesma, David Lizoaín Bennett, Oriol Martí Sambola, Lluís Mauri Roldán, Àlex Montes Flotats, Jaume Muñoz Jofre, Joan Ramon Riera Alemany, Pilar Roca i Viola, Miquel Rodríguez Planas, Edgar Rovira Sebastià, Montserrat Surroca Comas and Anna Giralt Brunet

Communications Director
Pilar Roca i Viola

Director of Publishing Services
Núria Costa Galobart

Publishing Services Management
Passeig de la Zona Franca, 66
08038 Barcelona
tel. 93 402 31 31
www.barcelona.cat/barcelonallibres

Actar Publishers
440 Park Avenue South, 17th floor
New York, NY 10016
United States of America

Roca i Batlle 2-4
08023 Barcelona
Spain

www.actar.com

EXHIBITION

Disseny Hub Barcelona Director
Mireia Escobar

Museu del Disseny Director
Jose Luis de Vicente

Curator
Olga Subirós

Curatorial support
Teresa Bastardes

Curatorial assistance
Olga Subirós Studio:
Leire Román and Sandra Prat

Coordination and registration
Anna Soler
Nordest Museum and Exhibit Services SL: Marina Aresté

Selection of pieces from the Museum's collections and documentation
Teresa Bastardes
Josep Capsir
Rossend Casanova
Isabel Cendoya
Isabel Fernández del Moral
Olga Subirós

Registration of the Museum's collection
Laia Callejà

Heritage acquisition coordination
Rossend Casanova
Nubilum: Claudia Martinez

Maintenance and restoration
Silvia Armentia and Veraicon:
Xisca Bernat, Cristina Navarro, Bea Urbano and Montserrat Xirau
Carolina Jorcano
Èlia López
Sandra Vilchez

Conceptualization, research and texts of the installation *Situated Matter*
Robert D. Thompson Casas, Iván Rodríguez Pérez - MaterFad. Centre de materials de Barcelona
Valérie Bergeron and Olga Subirós

Conceptualization of the *Still Life* installation
Isabel Fernández del Moral
Olga Subirós

Exhibition design
Olga Subirós Studio: Olga Subirós with Cristina Moreta, Sandra Prat and Leire Román

Graphic design
Todojunto.net

Production and setup
Croquis Dissenys Muntatges i realitzacions

Transportation
Feltrero División Arte

Translations and linguistic review
Twist Editors
Linguaserve

Selection of images from the Documentation Centre
Albert Díaz
María José Balcells

Accessibility resources
Carmina Borbonet
Audio descriptions: Adriana Bertran
Audio guide: Clara Grífol
Nubart

PUBLICATION

Editor
Olga Subirós

Micronarratives
Olga Subirós

Texts
300.000 km/s, Andreu Balius, Karen Barad, Ethel Baraona and Anna Puigjaner, Laura Benítez Valero, Jane Bennett, Francesca Bria and Malcolm Bain, Benjamin Bratton, Blanca Callén, Nerea Calvillo, Isabel Campi, Josep Capsir, Rossend Casanova, Maria Antònia Casanovas, María Íñigo Clavo, Antonio Cobo, Pilar Cortada - Eina, Kate Crawford and Vladan Joler, Jose Luis de Vicente, Anthony Dunne and Fiona Raby, Elvira Dyangani Ose and Raúl Muñoz de la Vega, Estampa, Pol Esteve, Isabel Fernández del Moral, Uriel Fogué, Blanca Garcia Gardelegui, Eva Franch i Gilabert, Raul Goñi, Clara Guasch, David Howe, Daniel Ibáñez, Tim Ingold, Institute for Postnatural Studies, Andrés Jaque / Office of Political Innovation, Zsofia Kollar, Joan Miquel Llodrà Nogueras, Marta Malé-Alemany and Tony Schoen, Valérie Bergeron, Timothy Morton, William Myers, Cris Noguer, Carles Oliver, Marina Otero, Javier Peña, Mónica Piera, Blanca Pujals, Philippe Rahm, Bika Rebek and Marlies Wirth, Iván Rodríguez, Olga Subirós, Robert Thompson, Laura Tripaldi, Ramón Úbeda, Alicia Valero

Design and layout
Alex Gifreu

Publishing coordinator
Anna Tetas
Actar Publishers: Ricardo Devesa

Publishing coordinator assistance
Olga Subirós Studio:
Leire Román and Sandra Prat

Linguistic review and translations
Kevin Krell
Twist Editors

Photo credits
Of the Museum's pieces:
CRBMC - Enric Gracia, CRBMC - Roser Casas, Estudio Rafael Vargas, Josep Maria Fabregat, Guillem Fernández-Huerta, La Fotogràfica, Quico Ortega, Xavi Padrós, Josep Vila Capdevila

Dust jacket image:
Red Smoke © El Último Grito
p. 1-5: Stills from the film *Slow Violence* by Joanie Lemercier
p. 388-389: Basurama
p. 392-396: Stills from the film *Strata Incognita* by Grandeza Studio / Locument

Image Retouching and Prepress
Xavi Parejo

Printing
Gràfiques Jou

Published in Barcelona:
February 2025

Disseny Hub Barcelona
Plaça de les Glòries Catalanes, 37-38
08018 Barcelona
T. 93 256 67 00
dhub@bcn.cat
dissenyhub.barcelona

Indexing
ISBN Ajuntament de Barcelona:
978-84-9156-611-3
DL: B-2474-2025
ISBN Actar: 978-1-63840-175-9
Library of the Congress Control Number (LCCN) 2024950730
This publication is available in Spanish (ISBN 978-1-63840-176-6) and Catalan (ISBN 978-1-63840-177-3)

The forest-based material in this product is recycled. The FSC® label on this book guarantees the responsible use of the world's forest resources. Interiors, cover, and dust jacket: Offset Cyclus 115 g/m², FSC® certified.
More information: www.fsc.org.
The Founders Grotesk and Timmons NY typefaces has been used.

Distribution
Actar D, Inc. New York, Barcelona

New York
440 Park Avenue South, 17th floor
New York, NY 10016
United States of America
T +1 2129662207
E salesnewyork@actar-d.com

Barcelona
Roca i Batlle 2-4
08023 Barcelona
Spain
T +34 933 282 183
E eurosales@actar-d.com

Promoter:

With the support of:

tvitec | CRICURSA

Andreu World

And the collaboration of:

ACKNOWLEDGEMENTS

Disseny Hub Barcelona would like to thank the following people for their contributions to the realization of the exhibition and the publication: 2Monos, 300.000 km/s, Samira Allaouat Benini, Frederic Amat, Guillem Amengual Garí - Cas Vila Franquer, Lourdes Andújar, Archigram-Vegap, Archivo Prada Poole, Arxiu Fotogràfic de Barcelona, Antoni Arola, Arrels Fundació, Suzie Attiwill, Marta Badia, Andreu Balius, Banzai Turba, Basurama, Elba Benítez - Galería Elba Benítez, Valérie Bergeron, Bicing - Ajuntament de Barcelona, Sílvia Brandi, Nerea Calvillo, Marc Campeny - Consorci del Museu Ciències Naturals de Barcelona, Leandro Cano, Jordi Carreras, Jorge Carrión, Matilde Cassani, Izaskun Chinchilla, Curro Claret, Antonio Cobo, Consorci de les Drassanes Reials i Museu Marítim de Barcelona, Cooperativa La Col, Albert Corbeto, Pilar Cortada - Eina, Pilar Cos, Kate Crawford, Toni Cumella, Domestic Data Streamers, ecoLogicStudio, Juan Emo-Comled, Eliurpi, Julia Esqué, Estampa, Teresa Estapé, Pol Esteve Castelló, Albert Ferré, Rosa Ferré, Ferran Figuerola - Tvitec-Cricursa, Flores & Prats Arquitectes, Fondazione Prada, Laura Freixas - Elisava, Noriko Fukushima - Spiber Inc., Ignacio Galán, Alex Gifreu, Laura González - Chiquita Room, Sara González de Ubieta, Grandeza Studio+Locument, Martí Guixé, Brad Haylock, Herobeat Studios, Cristian Herrera Dalmau - Galeria Il·lacions, Institute for Advanced Architecture of Catalonia (IAAC), Carlos Ipser, Andrés Jaque / Office for Political Innovation, Vladan Joler, Dolors Jurado, Youngmin Kang - Side Gallery, Eric Klarenbeek & Maartje Dros, Zsofia Kollar, Rem Koolhaas - Office for Metropolitan Architecture (OMA) - Tvitec-Cricursa, Legado Cajal-CSIC, Marc Longaron - Coop. La Capell, Joan Miquel Llodrà, Mary Maggic, Makeat, Materfad, Christien Meindertsma, Ana Mir, Txell Miras, Gerard Moliné, Joana Moll, Marc Morro, Iván Munera, Lucas Muñoz, Museu Etnològic i de Cultures del Món, Museu Nacional d'Art de Catalunya, Cris Noguer, Nomada Studio, Carles Oliver, Pep Paret, Javier Peña Andrés - Elisava, Rocío Peña Azpilicueta, Javier Peña Ibáñez - Concéntrico, Anastasia Pistofidou, Elisabeth Plantada - BAU, Miriam Ponsa, Josep Ponsatí, Maria Puig, Philippe Rahm, RCR (R. Aranda, C. Pigem, R. Vilalta Arquitectes) - Tvitec-Cricursa, Andrés Reisinger - Reisinger Studio, Joana Roda - Galeria Bombon Projects, Jaron Rowan - BAU, Iago Ruiz Subirós, Joan Ruiz Subirós, Enric Ruiz-Geli - Cloud9, Guillermo Santomá, Genís Senén, Eva Serrats - Coop. La Capell, Inés Sistiaga, SILA Studio, Spiber Inc., Squeeze The Orange, Fanni Stafford, Daniel Steegman, Studio Lemercier, Studio Jaia, Ricardo Suarez, Antonio Subirós, Suma arquitectura, TAKK (mireia luzárraga + alejandro muiño), Jordi Tamayo, The Glass Apprentrice, Top Manta, Tornen les Esquelles, Ramón Úbeda, Un Parell d'Arquitectes & Quim Domene, Joan Vellvé, Sílvia Ventosa, Maria Viñuales, Sanne Visser, Fleur Watson and all individuals, companies and institutions who loaned pieces for the exhibition, as well as donors of pieces for the Museum Collection.